Song and Significance

APPROACHES TO TRANSLATION STUDIES
Founded by James S. Holmes

Edited by   Henri Bloemen
               Dirk Delabastita
               Ton Naaijkens

Volume 25

Song and Significance
Virtues and Vices of Vocal Translation

Dinda L. Gorlée

Amsterdam - New York, NY 2005

Cover design: Studio Pollmann

The paper on which this book is printed meets the requirements of "ISO 9706:1994, Information and documentation - Paper for documents - Requirements for permanence".

ISBN: 90-420-1687-6
©Editions Rodopi B.V., Amsterdam – New York, NY 2005
Printed in The Netherlands

Table of Contents

Prelude and Acknowledgements

> It seems I could wrest my ideas from nature herself with my own hands, as I go walking in the woods. They come to me in the silence of the night or in the early morning, stirred into being by moods which the poet would translate into words, but which I put into sounds — and these go through my head swinging and singing and storming until I have them before me as notes.
>
> Ludwig van Beethoven (1770-1827)

Vocal translation is an old art, but the interpretive feeling, skill, and craft have now expanded into a relatively new area in translation studies. Vocal translation is the translation of the poetic discourse in the hybrid art of the musicopoetic (or poeticomusical) forms, shapes, and skills, harmonizing together the conflicting roles of both artistic media: music and language in face-to-face singing performances. In opera, folksong and art song, as well as in operetta, musical song and popular song we have a musical genre allied to a linguistic text (or rather subtext) which is a pre-existing work of art, but is subordinated to the musical text and rarely intended to lead an independent life. Vocal translation provides an interpretive model for the juxtaposition of different orders of sign-phenomena, extending the meaning and range of the musical and literary concepts and putting the mixed signs to a true-and-false test.

The topic of the book in hand, *Song and Significance: Virtues and Vices of Vocal Translation,* has engrossed me for a good many years and I tried to make some contributions (Gorlée 1996, 1997, 2002) to the scarce bibliography available in this area of translation studies. In my first publications, grounded on Honolka (1978) and Apter (1985, 1989 and other articles), and particularly in the later articles, where more bibliographical references were used, I made a deliberate attempt to put forward some theoretical approaches to the vocal examples from translating Richard Wagner's (1813-1883) German libretti and Edvard Grieg's (1843-1907) Danish and Norwegian song lyrics. When I worked at the University of Helsinki and taught my doctrine of semio-translation (1994, 2004), the semiotic approaches to translation concentrated on the semiotic works by Charles Sanders Peirce (1839-1914) and Roman Jakobson's (1896-1962) three kinds of translation: interlingual, intralingual, and intersemiotic translations. For this inter- and transdisciplinary reason, and because of my own interests in the semiotic approaches to the critical theory of translation focused on vocal translation, I led an international seminar, with technical help of my colleague Pirjo Kukkonen (1996), on the topic of this book in Imatra (Finland) in Summer 2003. The seminar was a part of the *International Summer Institute for Semiotic and Structural Studies*, a yearly semiotic sign-event directed by the musicologist Eero Tarasti, of the University of Helsinki. The international seminar was called *Song and Significance: Intralingual and Intersemiotic Vocal Translation* and had invited specialists on its program lecturing on the translation of scripts and scores. The editorial board members of Rodopi's Approaches to Translation liked the program and offered a volume of proceedings, under my editorship, in their series. They are presented here, under a changed subtitle. Let us hope that vocal translation in this Rodopi volume reaches the widest possible circle of readership rather than merely a specialized audience.

Vocal translation is an imaginative enterprise, yielding the temptation to bring out a translated symbiosis of poetic and musical texts. The enterprise is characterized as logocentrism and musicocentrism. What is seen here, both quantitively and qualitatively, is the relative artistic weight and importance given to either element of the double symbiotic construct. While logocentrism, a view defending the general dominance of the word in vocal music, may be called by the aphorism *prima le parole e poi la musica*, musicocentrism is expressed in its opposite, *prima la musica e poi le parole*. Musicocentrism is, for all practical purposes, a wordless approach. Not surprisingly, strict logocentrism is a rather weak position within the study of vocal music. A pronouncedly musicocentric view is advanced by Susanne K. Langer (1895-1985) in *Feeling and Form*, thus: "When words and music come together in song, music swallows words; not only mere words and literal sentences, but even literary word-structures, poetry. Song is not a compromise between poetry and music, though the text taken by itself may be a great poem: song is music" (1953: 152). In the close encounter of both media, Langer proposed, the verbal text is annihilated, and transmogrified into a musical text. This process is known, rather euphemistically, as the "principle of assimilation" (a term borrowed from Langer), but there should be no doubt about the fate of the underlying text, according to Langer, because as "mere plastic substance for another work" (Langer 1953: 154) it vanishes completely into the musical setting. Langer's argument is no doubt convincing in the case of many garden-variety libretti, which necessarily owe a great deal of their force to their musical setting. Yet such a musicocentricist standpoint seems to be a wild generalization in the case of truly great poetry. One could even invert Langer's argument and defend the position that the composer, in the process of taking total possession of a poetic text (regardless of its aesthetic quality) and of imprinting his own music on it, saves the verbal text from oblivion, but at a cost: the focus on music is always to the possible denigration of the particular character or quality which any original poem, however mediocre may have in and by itself.

Another, if more moderate, adherent to musicocentrism is the 1975 article written by the musicologist Francesco Orlando. Following ideas introduced by Jakobson and developed in semiological (ordinarily called structuralist) musicology (see particularly Ruwet 1972: 41-69), Orlando distinguishes between two separate but internally coherent sets of signs: the musical sign system and the verbal (literary) sign system. The verbal (poetic) material is, in Orlando's view, inserted into the musical material, where both sign systems coexist and interact meaningfully, while still preserving their own identity: the musical signifier has a musical signified, and the literary signifier a literary signified. According to Orlando, when the literary discourse is inserted into the music, the meaning of the words (and, in the case of opera, operetta, oratorio, and musical comedy, the meaning of the stage directions) influences the interpretation of the musical discourse, preceding, during and following the vocal parts of the musical score. And the meaning of the vocalized verbal language influences, and is influenced by, the elements of musical expression: pitch, duration, loudness, timbre, and dynamic, each governed by its own rules. This would mean that, despite the "general dominance of the musical factors op opera" (Hosokawa 1986: 649), the verbal poetry is still an essential and meaningful attribute of the musical performance. The power of words to produce musical effects can, however, scarcely be explained in dyadic terms alone, and is a multilayered web of meaning. Semiotically speaking, both Langer's "assimilation" and Orlando's "insertion" belong to the Saussurean tradition of signs (Ferdinand de Saussure 1857-1913). Assimilation and insertion imply an agent and a patient forced to interact from opposite points of derivation and with competing interests. This mutual interaction is directed toward replacing an element from one sign system with an element from a different sign system. To say that words, when brought into contact with music, become redundant and irrelevant, and must be broken down, demolished or reconverted to suit the new and lofty purpose is, however, an oversimplification, even a misconstrual of the real facts, because it fails to do justice to the challenge facing the composer and the poet-librettist alike: the creative fusion of two arts which, though different, complement each other through the virtues and vices of vocal translation, the title of the seminar and this volume.

Abstracted from the concrete phenomena of opera, art song, hymn, and other forms of word-music singing co-occurrence, spoken language and music, "[t]he two particularly elaborate systems of purely auditory and temporal signs," present a "strictly discontinuous, as physicists would say, granular structure"

(Jakobson 1971: 701). Jakobson added that music and language "are composed of ultimate discrete elements, a principle alien to spatial semiotic systems" (Jakobson 1971: 701), such as sculpture, painting, and photography. This description (clearly from a sign theory in the Saussurean tradition) makes musical "language" different from verbal language in such significant ways that both systems are only interchangeable to some degree. Therefore, as convincingly argued by Benveniste in his 1969 essay "The Semiology of Language," language and music make essentially uneven partners. Whereas language is a full-fledged semiotic system, with a finite repertory of (semantically meaningful) signs and well-defined rules for its (syntactic) combination, music lacks an unambiguous fragmentation into units. Besides, music lacks a clear representational dimension and is commonly not considered to mean, depict or communicate anything, to express anything beyond itself (an exception must be made for program music which represents musical images with a particular meaning and images to designate semiotic narrativity). Meyer argued in 1956 that music has a hypothetical meaning arising from the act of expectation (Meyer 1970: 37) in the musical performance of an inherited script with signifying lyrics. The evident meaning becomes revised in the determinate meanings "which arise out of the relationships existing between hypothetical meaning, evident meaning, and the later stages of the musical development. In other words, determinate meanings rise only after the experience of work is timeless in memory" (Meyer 1970: 38). Meaning in music obeys no objectified and informal rule, no instructions and prohibitions are allowed. The meaning (or "meaning") of music depends on the feeling and training of the listener (including the translator), activating his or her subjective "intuitive, precritical sense of the world … and non-sense (which is not nonsense)" of the world (Kramer 2003: 7, 8). In the new (also called postmodern) musicology, music possesses a relative autonomy from formalism and becomes "something readily intermixed with other media and with social occasions both public and private. On the one hand, music as aesthetic, disinterested, beyond good and evil; on the other, music — that is, the *same* music — as social, conditioned by human interests, a medium of ethical responsibility and recognition" (Kramer 2003: 8, Kramer's emphasis). Spitzer stated that "semiotics and aesthetics pull in opposite directions: semiotics towards determinate signification, aesthetics towards the critique, negation, … in order to point towards a musical experience that is expressly irreducible to *any* theory, 'semiotic' or otherwise" (202: 509, Spitzer's emphasis).

Already in his 1968 essay, "Language in Relation to Other Communication Methods," Jakobson wrote about the semiotic capabilities of the mixed medium, language:

> The exceptionally rich repetoire of definitely coded meaningful units (morphemes and words) is made possible through the diaphanous system of their merely differential components devoid of proper meaning (distinctive features, phonemes, and the rules of their combinability). These components are semiotic entities *sui generis*. The signification of such an entity is bare otherness, namely a presumable semantic difference between the meaningful units to which it pertains and those which *ceteris paribus* do not contain the same entity. A rigorous duality separates the lexical and idiomatic, totally coded units of natural language from its syntactic pattern which consists of coded matrices with a relatively free selection if lexical units to fill them up. A still greater freedom and still more elastic rules of organization characterize the combination of sentences into higher units of discourse. (1971: 707, Jakobson's emphasis)

This freedom and lack of freedom is discussed in the semiotic view of text, music, and particularly in the slippery text-and-music artifact which the translators manipulate in the translation. The "language" of music is discussed by Benveniste, who argued that its syntax

> … is organized from an ensemble constituted by a scale that is in itself formed of notes. The notes have no differential value except within the scale; and the scale itself is a recurrent whole at several (different) pitches, specified by the tone which indicates the key. The basic unit will therefore be the note, a discrete and contrasting unit of sound; but it only assumes this value within the scale, which fixes this paradigm of notes. Is it a semiotic unit? We can discern that it is in its own order, since it determines the oppositions. But then it has no relationships with the semiotics of the linguistic sign, and, in fact, it is not convertible into units of language, at whatever level this may occur. (1985: 236-237)

Benveniste's logocentric approach implies that these media, the verbal and the musical, are not directly comparable, and that a marriage between them seems destined to failure. Yet the language used in the hybrid arts of opera, folksong and art song, as well as in operetta, musical song and popular song, is of a special kind not addressed by Benveniste, whose concern is with everyday verbal language, but addressed by the authors of the articles in this book, who deal with verbal art with distinctive features and shapes which approach and distinguish the text to their music, thereby resolving the differences emphasized by Benveniste.

The essays in this volume give some down-to-earth practical advice on the constraints of vocal translation, but on top of the examples in these articles there is a theory in this controversial field affecting the actions of vocal translators. The theory is in many articles linked to a semiotic school or tradition (the Prague and Moscow-Tartu schools, Peircean scholarship, French structuralism, deconstructionism, etc.), dealing with the terminology used in the semiotic discovery. Some articles are written by genuine "practicians" of vocal translation, they unveal the secrets of their own speculative practice and are not grounded on a specific previous theory. Some are written by translation-oriented scholars, musicologists, or applied semioticians and are more open to the concrete applicability of the semiotic discovery. Semiotics is an all-encompassing and all-inclusive thinking method or knowledge strategy which studies how signs signify as vehicles of meaning — its construction and deconstruction. Semiotics is also concerned with sign users (senders and receivers, readers and listeners) and how signs composing messages are transmitted from one organism to another, how they are coded and interpreted, and the context in which such exchanges are carried out. The four principal points of current semiotic interest are the structure of signs (or signification), studying the way they are built; their function (or communication), studying what signs do; their origin (in evolution and history) analyzing collective and individual signs; and their development (over a lifetime or an era) including their birth and growth as well as their survival and death. Semiotics and the terminological thesaurus are in *Song and Significance: Virtues and Vices of Vocal Translation* applied to the process of the translation of verbal and non-verbal sign-phenomena. This applied discovery is concerned with the mental processes, including emotional and cognitive mediations, which take place in the comprehension and manipulation of complex sign structures and sign messages of vocal translation, reflecting and describing the practical minds and aesthetical experiences of the musically trained translators. Vocal translations carry a secondary cultural significance "aesthetical and ideationally connected to the society in which they are found," and as a cultural achievement the action of translating is dependent on the "way of being-in-the-world" of the primary document which the translated version needs to "promote and exemplify" (Turner 1976: 1478, 1476). Turner's semiotic analysis of "drummings, carvings, chants, and dances" (1976: 1476) is here applied to the singing of chants translated into what may be called a thousand tongues.

The articles written for this book have grown out of a selection from articles given during the Imatra seminar. Seven of the essays comprising this collection were written in response to the invitation. The papers have been re-read and altered with different shades of emphasis from the original seminar papers. This is also due to the semiotic discussions taking place during the seminar and the correspondences with the book editor. The eighth article, by Peter Low, of the University of New Zealand, was written especially for this volume. Following this Prelude to the argument, *Dinda L. Gorlée* (The Hague, The Netherlands and Bergen, Norway) tried in the introductory Preface to reveal a broad classification of semiotic classification of signs aspiring to semiosis as found in the singing of international(ized) church hymns in English language. The hymns were translated from Latin, Greek, and German into English, Dutch, and Norwegian — with varying success. This essay focuses in significant links in the vocal translation of this genre. The articles by *Marianne Tråven* (Stockholm, Sweden) and *Harai Golomb* (Tel Aviv, Israel) support their common project about the vocal translation of opera libretti with musical examples from Mozart's *Don Giovanni*, transposed in a different script. Tråven's article is relatively more theoretical and Golomb's essay seems to give more general insights. Tråven argues that the sign system of operas is a plural web of meaning, based on operatic convention but (re)model(ed) in the translated version. This is illustrated by the rhetoric of Mozart's time in which symbolic operatic figures and paralinguistic- or extralinguistic elements, make use of musically iconic signs. Golomb expanded Tråven's argument with his theoretical, textual, and practical perspectives relating to his "Music-Linked Translation" (referred to as MTL). Golomb explores new issues found in the Mozart/DaPonte corpus (*Figaro, Don Giovanni, Così fan tutte*) and analyzes the challenges posed by the subtleties and complexities of the interactions in the verbal text in the company of the dramatic action. These restraints are worded in the virtues and vices of the subtitle of this article, which is continued in the next article, written by *Ronnie Apter* (Mount Pleasant, MI, USA) and *Mark Herman* (Shepherd, MI, USA) with practical examples on the opera *Maria Stuarda* by Donizetti. The opera translators Apter and Herman studied and translated in their essay the details of the semiotic (or semioticized) clash between the Catholic belief and the upcoming later Protestant view, embodied in the dramatic figure of both protagonists in *Maria Stuarda*. In their English translation of this opera, Apter and Herman raised and solved this dual religious-textual conflict — with the music remained unchanged. *Peter Low* (Christchurch, New Zealand) continues the translation of the operatic tune and melody with other genres: folksong, French popular *chanson*, German *Lied*, and Maori song, all translated into English. Low uses his own paradigm, the "Pentathlon Principle," derived from the Olympic spirit of the Greek *athloi* performing in the five sports events (discus, long jump, javelin, wrestling and sprint-race) to ensure the desired wreath of olive leaves — now used by Low,

13

the "decathlon champion," to analyze the features of vocal translation as a balancing of his five criteria. The next article is written by the semiotician and anthropologist *Myrdene Anderson* (West Lafayette, IN, USA), a specialist in the area of Saami culture. She focuses on the signature of the yoik, an improvized Laplandish folksong with or without words. The singer's intellectual "property" of the yoik may be properly "translated," whether in word and deed when the souls of the singers are enflamed by proper Nordic fantasms. *Klaus Kaindl* (Vienna, Austria) continues with an analysis of the sociocultural impact of popular music. To keep the music alive in different countries, the intertextual imagery of the word-in-dialogue is described, analyzed and translated. As test cases, Kaindl uses different German versions (video clips and translations) of a French *chanson*. The Scandinavian (Norwegian, Swedish, Danish) translations of the English musical *My Fair Lady* receive a semiotic analysis in the article written by *Johan Franzon* (Kouvola/Helsinki, Finland). This article is based on their cultural practice and performances of this musical in the Scandinavia countries, and describes the theoretical and practical details encountered in the adaptation of the original context to new target cultures and languages.

I would like to express my gratitude to my son, Jorrit van Hertum, for his "cyborg" energy and technical time (Robinson 2003) to edit *Song and Significance: Virtues and Vices of Vocal Translation*.

Lastly, my thanks to the writers — my friends and colleagues — whose warmth of feeling shows on every page.

Dinda L. Gorlée
The Hague, 2005

Bibliography

Apter, Ronnie.   1985. 'A Peculiar Burden: Some Technical Problems of Translating Opera for Performance in English' in *Meta* 30—4: 309-319.

—— 1989. 'The Impossible Takes a Little Longer: Translating Opera Into English' in *Translation Review* 31: 27-37.

Benveniste, Émile.   1985. 'The Semiology of Language' in Innis, Robert E. (ed. and   intro.) *Semiotics: An Introductory Anthology* (Advances in Semiotics). Bloomington, IN: Indiana University Press. 228-246.

Honolka, Kurt. 1978. *Opernübersetzungen: Zur Geschichte der Verdeutschung musik-theatralischer Texte* (Taschenbücher zur Musikwissenschaft 20). Wilhelmshafen: Heinrichshofen.

Hosokawa, Shuhei.   1986. 'Opera' in Sebeok, Thomas A. (gen. ed.) *Encyclopedic Dictionary of Semiotics* (Approaches to Semiotics 73). 3 vols. Berlin: Mouton de Gruyter. 2: 649-651.

Gorlée, Dinda L.   1996. 'Opera Translation: Charles Peirce Translating Richard Wagner' in Tarasti, Eero (ed.) *Musical Semiotics in Growth* (Acta Semiotica Fennica 4). Bloomington, IN and Imatra: International Semiotics Institute. 407-425.

—— 1994. *Semiotics and the Problem of Translation: With Special Reference to the Semiotics of Charles S. Peirce* (Approaches to Translation Studies 12). Amsterdam and Atlanta, GA: Rodopi.

—— 2002. 'Grieg's Swan Songs' in *Semiotica* 142-1/4: 142-210.

—— 2004. *On Translating Signs: Exploring Text and Semio-Translation* (Approaches to Translation Studies 24). Amsterdam and New York, NY: Rodopi.

Kramer, Lawrence. 2003. 'Musicology and Meaning' in *The Musical Times* 144-1883: 6-12.

Kukkonen, Pirjo. 1996. *Tango Nostalgia : The Language of Love and Longing.* Helsinki: Helsinki University Press.

Langer, Susanne K. 1953. *Feeling and Form: A Theory of Art Developed From Philosophy in a New Key.* New York: Scribner's Sons.

Meyer, Leonard B.   1970. *Emotion and Music in Music.* 9th pr. Chicago : University of Chicago Press. (1st ed. 1956)

Orlando, Francesco.   1975. 'Propositions pour une sémantique du leitmotiv dans *L'Anneau des Nibelungen*' in *Musique en jeu* 17 : 73-86.

Robinson, Douglas. 2003. 'Cyborg Translation' in Petrilli, Susan (ed.) *Translation Translation* (Approaches to Translation Studies 21). Amsterdam and New York: Rodopi. 369-386.

Ruwet, Nicolas. 1972. *Langage, Musique, Poésie* (Collection Poétique). Paris : Seuil.

Spitzer, Michael. 2002. Review of *The Sense of Music: Semiotic Essays* by Raymond Moncllc (Princeton and Oxford: Princeton University Press, 2000) in *Music & Letters* 83-3 (August): 506-509.

Turner, Clifford.   1976. 'Art as a Cultural System' in *Modern Language Notes* 91-6 (December): 1473-1499.

Singing on the Breath of God: Preface to Life and Growth of Translated Hymnody

Dinda L. Gorlée

Religious hymns are verbomusical prayers, interwoven in the texture of the life of the people and the congregation. The performance practice is a speaking-and-singing meditation of praise of God. Church singing partakes of Peirce's threefold categories: feeling, willing, and knowing. The pure potentiality of feelings (firstness) would become a stream of events (secondness) to reach a continuous flow of messages (thirdness). The semiosis of hymns follows upwardly and downwardly the mobile categories in the unification of text and tunes (CP: 7.572) in any language. In translated hymns the melody and the native tongue must retain a rudimentary, abstracted notion of this application. The old hymns are muted, upheaved, refixed, edited, translated and retranslated without real signs of a primary sign and of the work of revisor and translator. The new hymns are, in turn, transitory vocal songs, and their text and tunes form the basis for further revisions, editions and translations. International hymns share the spiritualized feeling of a common fate, sharing the same pleasure, hardship, and misery worldwide. This semiotic study of English hymns is inspired by Peirce, Jakobson and Dewey, with further help from Cassirer, Pike and Maranda.

Genesis of Church Songs

The first beginnings of vocal music in the early Christian church arise from Saint Paul's *Letter to the Ephesians*, directed to the Christian community of Ephesus, a Greek city on the Aegean coast of Asia Minor. Paul's *Letter* suggests a date in the late 1ˢᵗ Century (80-100 A.D.). It takes the form and shape of a sermon offering practical moral advice on teaching and worship to the newly-formed Christian church. Paul writes, "Speaking to yourselves in psalms and hymns and spiritual songs, singing and making melody in your heart to the Lord" (*Ephesians* 5: 18-19 from the *The Authorized Holy Bible* in the *King James Version*). This semiotic sign means that singing in church offers a path cleared through the jungle of daily life, in order to reach God's spirit.

Saint Paul was the wild apostle with the ecstatic vision, the ever-travelling messenger of the Lord who during his lifelong missionary work "spoke with tongues more than ye all" (1 Corinthians 14: 18 ff.). Paul's deeds were a miracle, leaving deep puzzlement as a semiotic sign. Paul's sermons are equivalent to Jesus' parables, which are better called human encounters, meetings with Jews and Christians, natives and aliens. In these encounters, aimed at constructing the new Christian worship, Paul spoke to his brethren as a seer, announcing the advent of a new life and a new society based on Christian worship. As Paul was a semiotic prophet, he performed in word and in deed to manifest the spirit of God: "Wherefore tongues are for a sign, not to them that believe, but to them that believe not: prophesying serveth not for them that believe not, but for them which believe" (1 Corinthians 14: 22). Paul spoke in pseudolanguage and accompanied his acoustic cries with aggressive body thrusts and emotional gestures, offering indeed "an *effective sign*, like those signs in which the Old Testament had abounded, not only representing something else but at the same time causing what represented to come about" (Grant 2000: 121-122).[1]

The disturbance of the Pauline tongues are "a *semeion*: it combines both sense, perception and confirmation of an insight" (Rengsdorf 1971: 231, cited in Gay and Patte 1986: 797). This glossolalian insight, the speaking of foreign and unknown languages, is not only a verbal and nonverbal cue to factors of his prophetic personality but, especially on this day of Pentecost — the first day of this meeting in the congress *Song and Significance: Interlingual and Intersemiotic Vocal Translation* — this phenomenon is a heavenly vision, an exhortation to remedy the harms of "[w]rong living [and] impotent aspirations; 'What I would, that do I not; but what I hate, that do I,'" as Saint Paul said (James [1902]1977: 176). Thus, the telltale signs in Paul's words meant the signifying arrival of an adventure, that is, a bio-bodily and spiritual meeting with the virtues of singing, and maybe also the vices of singing. The prophetic encounters aroused in the community an active feeling, burden, and commitment of the speaking-and-singing art (discussed later) and its translations and paraphrases, which is today the semiotic theme of this congress on musicopoetic translation.

Paul stimulated the event of singing in church and, paradoxically, placed it in opposition to the ecstasy of drunkenness. See the following passages from the *Letter to the Ephesians*: "And be not drunk with wine, wherein is excess; but be filled with the Spirit; Speaking to yourselves in psalms and hymns and spiritual songs, singing and making melody in your heart to the Lord" (*Ephesians* 5: 18-19 from the *The Authorized Holy Bible* in *King James Version*). This historical Biblical passage is later revised and translated as modern poetry: "Do not besot yourselves with wine; that leads to ruin. Let your contentments be in the Holy Spirit; your tongues unloosened in psalms and hymns and spiritual songs, as you sing and give praise to the Lord in your hearts" (*Ephesians* 5: 18-19 from *The Holy Bible* in the *Knox Translation* of the *New Testament* 1945). In later Bible translations, Paul's moral advice is again rephrased: "Do not give way to drunkenness and the dissipation that goes with it, but let the Holy Spirit fill you: speak to one another in psalms, hymns, and songs; sing and make music in your hearts to the Lord; and in the name of our Lord Jesus Christ give thanks every day for everything to our God and Father" (*Ephesians* 5: 18-20 from *The New English Bible* 1970). And in the American Bible translations, see "Avoid getting drunk on wine; that leads to debauchery. Be filled with the Spirit, addressing one another in psalms and hymns and inspired songs. Sing praise to the Lord with all your hearts" (*Ephesians* 5: 18-19 from *The New American Bible* 1970); and "Do not get drunk with wine, for that is debauchery; but be filled with the Spirit, as you sing psalms and hymns and spiritual songs among yourselves, singing and making melody to the Lord in your hearts" (*Ephesians* 5: 18-19 from *The Holy Bible: New Revised Standard Version* 1995).[2]

All English versions arise from the same Greek source-text *(The Greek New Testament* 1985: 591). Abstracted from interlingual translations to other languages (from Greek to French, German, Spanish, Japanese as well as Mandarin, Swahili, Hindi, and other languages, even including the artificial language Klingon from the television series *Star Trek*), we are provided with a variety of revised versions to choose from. The English Bible translations can be an accurate translation from the original languages (the Greek language of the New Testament), or they can be a second-hand translation of the *Authorized Version* (published in 1611, and called *Authorized* for the Church of England). The *Authorized Version* was already archaic when it was made and is today less understood. More modern translations often can employ a contemporary idiom rather than use the traditional one. The translations can be the joint work of one or several committees, or they can use capricious, judicious, or wise suggestions from one Bible translator. New translations can characterize a certain denominational consideration and thereby exclude others. Discovery, leadership and guidance of the work of Bible translators belong to the three tasks of translatology (Gorlée 2004: 168-169).

In terms of contents, we see similarities and differences with Christian joyfulness – one avoids the lure of alcoholic delights. In the passage of the *Ephesians*, the pejorative rewards of alcoholism are stated using different cultural alternatives native to the taste and fashion of the enticements: dissipation, intoxication as well as debauchery. The vices of dissipation and intoxication turn with the term of debauchery into a sacred deconstructionism, going beyond the rigid and fixed discourse, beyond the surface of the sacred text and into the depth of it. The mood of the "word ασωτια is a negative formation from a root closely related to σωτηρια ("salvation"); it denotes the ruin of life in dissolute living of every kind. The thought is that drunkenness is the gateway to profligacy" (*The Interpreter's Bible* 1953: 714). The etymological escape from unconsciousness to consciousness creates hidden meanings provided with significant allusions to the Holy Spirit. From these allusions to the next deconstructionist allusion, to the excessive use of wine to singing divine songs is no verbal play in language but a voice from inside of Paul's text. On the positive side,

> ... when alcoholic delights are part of companioning, it produces sociability. The cocktail bar becomes a secular substitute for a church including the mystery of worship. A "spirit" is engendered in the followship of the wine bottle. It is not mere verbal accident that the words spirit and spirits join each other in the dictionary. All men are hungry for "spirit." They crave enthusiasm.The word enthusiasm and energy, like the word spirit, has religious overtones. It means, lit., "possessed by a god." When the first Christian fellowship at Pentecost broke out into enthusiasms by speaking in tongues, observers equated the effect with drunkenness, 'These men are full of new wine" (Act 2: 13). The Holy Spirit, too, ... has analogies with 'spirits' on the secular plane. (*The Interpreter's Bible* 1953: 714-715)

The key word of the relationship of solitary drinking wine to singing is spirituality, the spiritual community in the church with the purpose of approaching God. The *King James Version* speaks of singing individually, while the other translations argue the virtues of singing and making melody together in the community. From the original alcoholic hallucination of the individual person, the further experiences reach a higher purpose, called by the forefather of semiotics, Charles Sanders Peirce (1839-1914), the "immediate consciousness, as a melody does from one prolonged note"(CP: 1.381 = W: 6: 186, taken from *A Guess at the Riddle*). A personal feeling becomes a form of psychological togetherness (CP: 1.383). A togetherness (Peirce's term) which has, first, "an active and a passive kind, or Will and Sense and second, there are External Will and Sense, in opposition to Internal Will (self-control, inhibitory will) and Internal Sense (introspection)" (CP: 1.383 = W: 6: 186). Peircean classifications – feeling, willing, knowing – are the starting point of the threefold categorical paradigm used here to make a sign-oriented translatology of divine songs.[3]

Psalms and Hymns and Spiritual Songs

The *Letter to the Ephesians* discusses the introduction of the singing of psalms and hymns and spiritual songs without clarifying the similarities and differences between the three presented terms. Interesting is the double use of the "general purpose" linking word *and* between coordinating conjunctions, "psalms *and* hymns *and* spiritual songs" (Leech and Svartvik 1975: 160), creating a positive identification of the three words.[4] A *hymn* is historically a "term of unknown origin but first used in ancient Greece and Rome to designate a poem in honour of a god. In the early Christian period the word was often, though not always, used to refer to praises sung to God, as distinct from 'psalm'" (*The New Grove* 2001: 12: 17).[5] The word *psalm* comes from "an ancient Near Eastern or ancient Egyptian sacred poem exhibiting the following main characteristics: a theocentric subject, short bifurcated units of literary construction, and parallelism of clauses (*parallelism membrorum*, 'thought rhyme'); or a setting of such a poem to music" (*The New Grove* 2001: 20: 449, *The New Grove*'s emphasis). *Psalms* as sacred Hebrew poetry without music but provided with musical accompaniment continued from the Psalter attributed to David into the Greek tradition (Sarna 1993: 19-20). The psalmic genre is "used in the Septuagint for the book of Psalms, and in the new Testament" (*The New Grove* 2001: 20: 449). In the Psalms, "God reaches out to man [and] human beings reach out to God" (Sarna 1993: 3). Take the Biblical example of the young king David playing the harp (or lyre or another plucked string instrument existing in biblical days) to accompany his pastoral or, rather, heavenly songs in Hebrew, and the further story of the episode of Paul preaching at Ephesus on the subject of singing sacred songs. The *Septuagint* is the Greek version of the Jewish scriptures with which Hellenized Jews and Greek-speaking early Christians were familiar. The Father of the Church and Patron Saint of Translators, Saint Jerome (ca. 340-420), translated the Greek *Septuagint* in the Latin *Vulgate*, the most influential Bible from his day until Reformation times: the freely translated German Luther Bible.[6]

The Latin psalms in the *Vulgate* are the basis for the Roman Catholic psalms. The poetic text of the psalmody is a translation of a translation of a translation, which is again translated and re-translated into English, French, Dutch, French, Hungarian, etc., to suit the music. Semiotically, these sacrosanct products of multiple translation preserve little of the original texts. Christian liturgy, including the Protestant church hymnary, retained the use of the psalmodic texts, adding paraphrases and its translations of other Bible texts. All of these were poeticized and lyricized, rhymed and strophed in the mother tongue, to suit music and voice in all languages. In addition to the Psalms set to music, we have liturgical items such as "*Alleluia*" and "*Amen*," further "*Agnus Dei*," "*Kyrie eleison*" and "*Sanctus and benedictus qui venit*": "Thousands of composers have set [liturgical texts] to music and each setting consciously or unconsciously interprets the simple text," making them first "mysterious, the second is joyful, the third is deep and penitential" (Bell 2000: 30-31).

The original psalms were "borrowed" from the translation of the biblical Psalms, as opposed to the newly written hymns, old and modern. The old hymns, collected by hymn-makers, were rhymed and received a metrical tune to be sung in worship. As was the case with psalms, the text was subsequently translated and retranslated, first through the *Authorized King James Version* (a literary version, called a hymnical translation) and later through modern (or better, modernized) versified Bible translations set to singable melodies. They include such traditional hymns as "Hark! The Herald Angels Sing," "Be Thou My Vision," "Great is Thy Faithfulness," the hymn of Remembrance Service in praise of military veterans "Dear Lord and Father of Mankind," the popular "Jerusalem" on the melody "England's green and pleasant land" with words by William Blake (1757-1827), as well as the funeral hymn "Abide with Me" (all of them included as best-loved hymns in Barr 2002). Fur further examples see the old *The Church Hymnary* (1927: vii-viii) (first edition 1898), collected and recollected chapters on psalms and hymns on diverse subjects: God, the Holy Trinity, the Church, the Christian Life, Times and Seasons, Travellers and the Absent, National Hymns, Home and School, Mission Services, Doxologies and Ancient Hymns and Canticles, and the equally old-fashioned *The Psalms of David* (n. y.). And compare this to the new material: *The Church Hymnary, With Melody Line* (1996, first ed. from 1973) with old and new hymns. Today, modern English hymnaries include new children's songs, carols, songs from the Taizé community, Scottish folksongs, South African traditional songs, American or Gaelic melodies, and hymns made by the hymn-maker him- or herself. See, for example, "We Lay our Broken World in Sorrow at Your Feet," "Nada te Turbe," "Thuma Mina," and "Gabi Gabi" (*Songs of God's People* (1988) and *Common Ground* (1998).

Spiritual song is a general term that includes various hymnical forms in oratorio, anthem, and in operas (Foss 1946: 99, see Apel 1946: 346-347).

Examples are George Händel's (1685-1759) *The Messiah*, Johann Sebastian Bach's (1735-1782) *Saint Matthew Passion*, Ludwig van Beethoven's (1770-1827) *Hymn to Joy*, Hector Berlioz' (1803-1869) *Dies Irae* and opera melodies of Richard Wagner's (1813-1883) *Die Meistersinger von Nürnberg* and his *Parsifal*. Divine (or sacred) songs include all kinds of worshipful vocal church music. In the three kinds of congregational singing there is an upward degree of, *firstly*, the chronological order when original psalms produced a reaction in favor of the new man-made (and woman-made) hymns, which gave way to the free and almost secular performance not any longer in church but in concert halls; *secondly*, the relevant textual boundedness to the biblical sacred text and the emergent freedom allowed later to the poetic text and tune of vocal church singing; and, *thirdly*, the performance linked originally to church-music, sung by worshippers, and eventually played in dramatic concert, sung by professional singers. Even in the Bible book Ephesians (discussed above), the spiritual ecclesiastical factor demonstrated the universal and universalized power of divine songs, including popular and secular musical forms.

Prayer

Church-singing is a liberating event and Paul's words signify a free exhortation to share in performing this mixed art: poetic prayer in native tongue, set to music, destined to be sung in a religious ceremony (or, of course, sung in everyday activities like at home, at school, at a picknick) in order to, following the words of Saint Paul, "be filled with the Spirit." The mythico-religious significance of symbolic signs discussed in the semiotic works of Ernst Cassirer (1874-1945), which were *terra incognita* and now "discovered" as a "postmodern" philosophy of culture, is followed by Hutchinson's (1963: 229-236)[7] subdivision of the images of faith observance into seven meaningful linguistic forms:

- *confession or witness* is the "spontaneous cry of the heart" (1963: 229) embodied in statements of the personal nearness to God, and existing in all faiths and all languages: "The shema of Judaism 'Hear, O Israel, the Lord our God, the Lord is One,' the New Testament confession, 'Jesus is Lord'; the statement of the Buddhist monk, 'I take refuge in the Buddha, the Dharma, and the Sangha'; the Muslim confession 'There is one God Allah, and Mohammed is his prophet' — are but a few examples of this recurrent type of utterance" (Hutchinson 1993: 229);

- *prayer* is "closely related to confession" (1963: 229) and is a private and public "cry for security," a "cry of the heart for help and for fellowship ... Its language, like that if confession, is direct, expressive, and personal; and its contents are the needs and aspirations deepest in man's heart" (1963: 230);
- *ritual* is a formalization of confession and prayer, congealing from spontaneous and authentic signs "into fixed bodies of expressive words and nonverbal symbols" to create a rite or ritual that "consists of a configuration of expressive images in word, in act, and sometimes in other media, to be repeated at set times" (1963: 230) and by being repeated can become an empty melodrama;
- *myth, or sacred story* is "closely related to rite" (1963: 231) and illustrates the religious directions of a life or a community: "All three values — the sacredness, the narrative, and the function of expressing and justifying human values — are necessary to myth, and taken together" (1963: 231)[8];
- *commandment or moral imperative* consists of the religious laws and standards for human action, taken from rite and myth. The commandments govern the "thou shalt" or "thou shalt not" — or, from the human viewpoint, "I ought" (1963: 234) — and form the meaning of Christian ethics of a certain community;
- *homily and sermon* aims to communicate the exhortation of faith to the religious community. This type of "propaganda" language "uses expressive language for the purpose of propagating, stimulating, and sustaining" (1963: 235) of the community;
- *prayer scripture or sacred writing* consists of printed or written texts emerging "from the oral tradition and communication that precedes it through the practical motives of preserving these saying for posterity or making them available for a wider community" (1963: 235).

Althoug this division is not linked to a theory of semiotic signs, the last type (*prayer scripture or sacred writings*) signifies the applied action and product of translation studies. Hutchinson discussed the declamation of faith language but did not mention faith music, nor their dynamic interaction in hymnology. In liturgical moments, sung hymns and psalms (verbomusical songs) add musical melodies to worded songs. The synchronization of musical code with the verbal code work together with a scenical code, namely, the standing up during singing in worship, with arms raised toward heaven or the clapping of hands in the course of congregational hymn singing. It is not surprising to see people kneeling down in prayer, or, in the Muslim custom, falling to one's knees and pressing the forehead to the ground. All these kinetic acts produce a multimedial ceremony in which some of Hutchinson's types occur together: musical code, verbal code, and kinetic code, to create one single symbiotic event.[9]

Continuing Hutchinson's classifications, combined types can be made: within sung psalmody and hymnology, the private utterances (1 and 2: witness and personal prayers) flow together inside the group events (3 and 4: mass, liturgy, sacraments) in order to create events for 5: the teaching of moral lessons. In recitation with music, the public messages (6 and 7: sermon and sacred writings) are used for poetic content of what God says to man[10] and what man says to God. An example: the Christian authoritative formula "To Father, Son, and Holy Ghost" is a witness, a testimony of faith, the force of which becomes intensified in personal prayer on events in one's personal life. If pronounced in the framework of a holy service, the request and need for prayer give new life to the reciter, who can feel himself or herself fortified (particularly when worshippers submit themselves to the spirit of sacraments: baptism, marriage, which are personal events). The texts of biblical scriptures are the ethical *milieu* surrounding the prayers, lifting the man, woman or child up from his or her darkness or depression. We perceive here the force of personal messages that reach through ritual performance to seem adapted to public messages in worship. With musical arrangements the declamation of faith language is transformed into the ritual of divine song. Musical "language" impinges music-specific structures upon the song, in which the song needs to express what is a non-musical entity. Peirce's semiotics adds interrelations of expression, qualities and participants for sacred lyric used in worship.

Within the ministry of music in songs of praise, devotion and thanksgiving are highlighted during different moments in worship, offering various kinds of singing, with and without music. Psalmody (using the psalm text), hymnody (free poetic-religious songs) and other forms of vocal church music like the chorale, the anthem, and the oratorio are sacred lyrics for meditative use. Divine songs are verbomusical prayers, interwoven in the texture of the life of the people and the congregation. The word *prayer*, following Hutchinson's term, is meant here as both a private confession as well as a cry for help and fellowship. Prayer is textualized in divine songs set to musical melody. Psalm and hymn singing is a individual and group experience of uplifting spiritualized ideas, with the purpose of reaching up, to the spirit of God.

Imitation: Paraphrases and Translations

Even though the chronicle of events concerning the hymn is traditionally said to have been "divinely revealed ... as the authentic text of the hymn sung by the angels in heaven" (Dix 1949: 451) in order to be able to praise God "who sits between the cherubim" (Washburn 1938: 19), hymns do not grow wings and fly around, but are in our human experience constantly worked on as an instrument of a general human message. Hymns are constantly paraphrased and translated into different languages in order to serve worship in all parts of the world. Hymn books are both provincial and global, both private and general, both denominational and universal. The Roman Catholic tradition has long maintained the Latin-sung songs in which the role of the priests is highlighted and the lays sing short replying answers. The Latin music continues in the Gregorian chant tradition; the texts are unintelligible for most of the lays, but the hymns function for the regular churchgoers in "known" ecclesiastical Latin, which works under normal circumstances as an alien and archaic language for a general audience, but during mass it appears familiar and warm to Catholic worshippers.[11] Congregational hymns and tunes in the vernacular language started in Christendom with the Second Vatican Council in the late 1960s.

Martin Luther (1438-1546) as leader of the Protestant Reformation, wrote about the influence of religious song that "[t]ext and note, accent, melody, and method of enunciation should be dictated by mother tongue and voice, or else all is mere imitation" (quoted in Wibberley 1934: 111). Rejecting the conventional Catholic tradition, which was linked to the exclusive elite use of Latin (or better: Latinized) language, Luther advocated not the original Latin lyrics but their modern translation in order to compose High German psalms and hymns that were obviously better understood by his Christian brotherhood. Instead of recognizing doctrines like papal authority and supremacy of priesthood, Luther and his followers enunciated in his new doctrine the piety of all believers, understood not only by religious leaders but by all lay brothers and sisters, who act as professional and non-professional linguists-and-singers. The whole music of the church was also "democratized" (Wibberley 1934: 111). The hymn writers and hymn translators pursue this new folklike and liberal tradition with simple and accessible songs for all singers in the audience: high voices as well as low voices, including children's voices. The hymn writers are, indeed, no angels but devoted earthly believers. As translators they are flesh-and-blood individuals dealing with the poetic and rhythmic paraphrases and translations of the divine song in their man-made (or woman-made) "human" ways.

In the Protestant tradition, particularly, the divine songs have been created as a congregational art meant for all lays. Hymns in mother language are the rule, they are understandable for everyone. The songs are simple and clear in text and tune as well as easily readable in the hymn books. Singable melodies for average voices, accessible text with references to church festivities: Christmas, Easter, sacraments, holy communion, etc., as well as weddings, funeral services, and other events in the personal life of the average congregation. The performance practice has become, in Protestant churches, a speaking-and-singing meditation. This musical art of a liturgical nature with an evangelical spirit echoes with many voices in the interior of the barren church building. The songs are intoned or chanted by religious soloists, from the choir and/or lays. The songs are simple and have a lyrical-emotional expression possessing a moralistic nature for "everyone" in the community. This means that the church hymns are indicative, declarative and hortatory songs. Singing hymns is a vocal experience with the character of dialogue expressing the acts of Peirce's trinity of feeling, knowing, and willing expressing his firstness, secondness and thirdness.[12]

New interpretation and translation is a common presence in psalmody and hymnology. Interpretation and translation refer to changes in the music, in the text, or in both music and text. The metrical psalms were the first lyrics to be used for congregational singing and they survived in Protestant liturgical worship. The Hebrew psalter had a strong influence on text and music. But gradually, after a series of "hymnal revolutions," the singing of congregational hymns became a general practice, accepted and created everywhere. The influence of paraphrases and translations became a universal routine experience. Observing the beginnings of English hymnary, we see in the hymnal chronology the first traces of guiding paraphrases and translations. In a letter (ca. 1550) sent from English archbishop Thomas Cranmer (1489-1556) to King Edward VI (1470-1483) on the liturgies and prayer books of the Church of England, Cranmer wrote on the first changes of translation from Latin to English:

> I have translated into the English Tongue, so well as I could in so short a
> time, certain processions to be used upon festival days ... But in mine

> opinion the song, that shall be made thereunto, would not be full of
> notes, but, as near as may be, for every syllable a note, so that it may be
> sung distinctly and devoutly: as be in the Mattins and Evensong –
> *Venite*, the hymns, *Te Deum, Benedictus, Magnificat, Nunc Dimittis*, and
> all the psalms and versicles: and in the Mass – *Gloria in excelsis, Gloria
> Patris*, the *Credo*, the Preface, the *Pater noster*. And some of the
> *Sanctus* and *Agnus* ... Wherefore I have travailed to make the verses in
> English and have put the Latin note unto the same. Nevertheless they
> that be cunning in singing can make a much solemn note hereto: I made
> them only a proof to see how English would do in song. (quoted from
> Procter 1961: 42)

While Cramner wrote his words, the English exiles were returning from Protestant Geneva with modernized forms of prayers: new reprints added to translated hymns, religious ballads and songs. Some provoked a storm of local protests, others had suitable and worthy materials and were accepted at home. The same phenomenon occurred also to psalms, lyricized into rhymed and metrical tunes, some of which were "so freely paraphrased that a metrical psalm ... cannot be demarcated from a hymn" (*The New Grove* 2001: 20: 483). According to the distinguished *Dictionary of Hymnology* of 1892, the augmentation-and-addition of the ever-wider collection of new hymnology "seems to have been by various hands" (1892: 1021). This happened through a collective but separate effort at various times by music editors and coeditors, poets, composers and parochial advisors, but afterwards collected and approved by committees of the Anglican Church and other church denominations.[13]

In 1742, the Anglican Church Assembly appointed a special Committee to "make a collection of Translations into English verse or Metre, of passages of the Holy Scriptures, or receive in Performance of that kind from any that shall translate them" (1892: 1024). The long history of writing a new collection begun, after long delays, with reports by the Presbyteries on the growing hymns, making verbal alterations of all kinds according to the ecclesiastical and spiritual ideologies of the evangelical duties in those days. When the final report was presented, still callled a Draft, the work done was described as follows: "All the Translations and Paraphrases which had appeared in the former Collection are here, in substance preserved. But they have been revised with care. Many alterations, and, it is hoped, improvements, are made upon them. A considerable number of new Paraphrases, furnished either by members of the Committee, or Ministers with whom they corresponded, are added" (quoted from the *Dictionary of Hymnology* 1892: 1024). The definitive *Paraphrases* is dated to 1781. Here, the Assembly approved "these Translations and Paraphrases to be transmitted to the several Presbyteries of this Church, in order that they may report their opinion concerning them to the ensuing General Assembly; and, in the meantime, allows this Collection of sacred Poems to be used in public worship in congregations, where the Minister finds it for edification" (*Dictionary of Hymnology* 1892: 1024).

Here is an example to illustrate the somewhat later history of hymns of the English (Anglican) Church. Braley stated on the gradual growth of hymns that the 592 Church Hymns of 1871 can be broken down into the following:

Translated from the Latin of the first five centuries	17
Translated from the Greek	12
Translated from the Latin of the 6th to 16th century	30
Translated from the Latin (chiefly Gallican texts of the 17th and 18th centuries)	22
Translated from the German	30
Translated from other foreign languages	3
By American writers	6
English hymns of the 16th century	3
English hymns of the 17th century	11
English hymns of the 18th century	81
English hymns of the first half of the 19th century	95
English hymns by recent and living authors, previously published	239
English hymns appearing for the first time	43
	592

(Braley 1991: 118)

This classification meant that before the writing of the numerous Victorian hymns, English hymns had become the majority in liturgy, followed by translated hymns: some translated from Latin and Greek, yet most of the rest is again from paraphrases and translations, particularly from German hymns. Germany was the home country of Protestant hymnology, and English hymns had joined forces with German church songs since Luther's time (*Dictionary of Hymnology* 1892: 412 ff). The Victorian type of hymn tune, richly harmonious and sentimental, became very popular later on. They offer a narrative melodrama, provided with rhetorical figures such as a repetition and climax. Later, in the 20th Century, compiling a new hymn book changed again. Paraphrased and translated in the post-colonial world, Bible and liturgy concepts have come to accept the Other next to us here and in foreign countries, in which our understanding of the purpose of addressing God has changed, exchanging cultural identies. *Différences* between otherness and selfness struggle between race, class, and gender alternatives (see Grossberg

1996). The diaspora of hymnody changed a lot since colonial, that is, political times.

Modern hymns are still called *creative* hymns, that is, songs abstracted from the conventional psalms and paraphrases of Scriptural passages, liturgical texts and prayer chants. In the 20th Century many poor hymns which had found favor in the past were courageously dropped from new and revised hymnals. Creative hymns renew the "lost art" (Washburn 1938: 5). Liturgically, hymns are in this period

> … used as "fillers"; as "rest periods" in otherwise well-built programs;
> far too often with no thought of the logical and artistic unity of
> "services," so-called. Too seldom is attention given to the place of the
> hymn in the complete mosaic of a unified program, to the infinite loss of
> the value of the hymn, itself, and to the picture or program, as a whole.
> (Washburn 1938: 5)

Troubadour-style protest songs were common in the 1960s alongside with folk songs and jazz elements, then in vogue. Albrecht (1973: 72-76) discusses the *Schlager*-like production of new German hymns, where the pathos and sentimentality of older hymns is replaced by a contemporary, and maybe tougher, vision of the world and of the church as a new spiritual center, including the arrival of pop music: "*die Musik der schwarzen Kultur, Drama im Gottesdienst, electronische Musik*" as well as the performance of "*ein Multi-Media-Gottesdienst-Ereignis*" (Anders 1974: 188). Other German hymn-writers return to the softer vision of finding mystic and poetic verses in Goethe's (1749-1832) poetry[14] in order to modernize its special mood into vital hymns. In the Church of Scotland, the "creative" hymn-books *Songs of God's People* (1998) and *Common Ground* (1998), both publications from the Iona Community, were set to music and text by minister, hymn-poet and choral song leader John L. Bell in the company of Graham Maule. These modern hymn-books reach a creative modern hymnology of a subjective character with a special stress on the idea of social service. Non-Western (Ghanian, Gaelic, South African, Welsh, Fijian, Malawian, etc.) congregations and groups have arrangements and rearrangements united with their own interpretive spirit of the hymn singing. As examples, see from the modern materials *Common Ground,* firstly, "To Christ the Seed" (number 135), an arrangement based on an Irish Gaelic text in two different English translations and, secondly, "Come, Let Us Seek our God's Protection" (number 22), an English adaptation of a Malawian folk tune, a mantra-like tune accompanied by a drum, and the South African melody "Mayenziwe" (number 84) sung in Xhosa (the original language), a paraphrased but untranslated text to give the unfamiliar otherness (or Otherness) for English singers in the familiar native tongue (for the similar tradition in American congregational song, see *The New Grove* 2001: 12: 35).

The *Dictionary of Hymnology* has a special section on "The Translation and Paraphrases" (1892: 1024-1025, see also *Dictionary of Scottish Church History & Theology* 1993: 421-422) in order to formulate the efforts made in the 18th Century and beyond to provide a wider range of subjects. A "translation" provided reworked but pseudoliteral contributions from other countries and other languages, particularly of the "sacred poetry" of the Psalms by David (*The New Grove* 2001: 449). A "paraphrase" means the integration of alternative ways of singing outside the lyrical convention of the emotional range of the poetry of the Psalms. The access to free arrangements in form and shape, rather than literal scriptural renditions, was in the beginning a polemic principle. The liberty of expression was at first resisted since it lapsed into a kind of paraphrase or even a liturgical parody. Later, the verbal and melodic alterations received the formal sanction of the church, and the paraphrases provide a wider range of subjects in the hymnary, which gained popularity. A paraphrase is also called a "variation" which firstly echoes the parallelisms of Hebrew poetry in their musical constriction, but subsequently gave different – that is, "varying" and "varied" – details in terms of rhyming conditions, reiteration of alternate verses and half-verses, verses with repeatable refrain, modern allocations of syllables, and other stylistic and musical devices.[15]

A paraphrase changes both form and content of melody and words of the original texts. A paraphrase gives new variations of equivalence of material, and is called in semiotic translation theory a "metaversion" (also called metatext or metaliterature). A metaversion is defined as a "[s]econdary, derivative literary creation, the impetus for which has come from another literary work. It is preceded by metalinguistic (analytical) activity. Metacreation in translation is a synthesis of the translator's absorption in the text-generating process" (Popovič ca. 1975: 12). A metaversion is a paraphrastic translation, which embodies a "confrontational-creative context" of the source text and, despite an "invariant core," offers to the new audience a "reproduction and modificational nature" (Popovič ca. 1975: 12-13). This reproduction can be an explanation, a violation or a new reconstruction, and can be a serious or a mock imitation painfully dramatizing the difference between experienced and inexperienced hymn-writers. In relying on our knowledge of native insiders, the performance of the singers qualify or disqualify the nature of a hymn. The true subtleties of a hymn come not from studying but from the experience of singing a favorite paraphrastic hymn together.

Take the following two examples of visions and revisions of hymnal phrase and paraphrase. The Latin hymn on Pentecost, *"Beata nobis gaudia"* (4th Century, ascribed to Saint Hilary of Poitiers),[16] with the first germs of Latin rhyme, was in pseudo-modern days translated twice from Acts 2: 1-4 derived from the *Vulgate*, the Latin translation from Hebrew (Aramaic) and Greek. This hymn was increased into various stanzas and in the new, English language: 'O joy! Because the Circling Year" and "Rejoice! The Year upon its Way" by Percy Carter Buck (1871-1947). The tune was altered as well, first by Johan Ellerton (1826-1893), then by Richard Ellis Roberts (1879-1953) (*The Church Hymnary* 1996: 290-291). The text of "Dear Lord and Father of Mankind" was derived from two sources: Psalm 18 for the old melody, included in the 1561 English Psalter (*The Church Hymnary* 1996: 68), written in turn on a different melody of Frederick Hubert Hastings Parry (1848-1918) set in turn on a different text created by Quaker John G. Whittier (1807-1892) derived from "When ye pray, say, Our Father which art in heaven … And forgave us our sins" (Luke 11: 2-4). The entirely different melody is revised again by Frederick C. Maker (1844-1927) (*The Hymnal for Worship & Celebration* 1986: nr. 427). Whittier's hymn begins with

> Dear Lord and Father of mankind,
> Forgive our foolish ways;
> Reclothe us in our rightful mind;
> In purer lives thy service find,
> In deeper reverence, praise.

The prayer actualizes the original biblical psalm and the prophet's words by stating that we should today "Take from our souls the strain and stress" and in the end that in earthquake, wind and fire we must be compelled to recognize the "still small voice of calm!" The ethics of the old-fashioned society still lives today to find strength in new calamities surrounding us. The metaversion of "Dear Lord and Father of Mankind" is, according to a *Songs of Praise* interview, a "superhymn" and the interviewee adds that "It's a hymn about praise as a good hymn should be. It's a hymn about duty and a hymn about service too" (1984: 43).

In history and their private and collective meanings, the hymn books in present and past times reflect the universal(ized) but unsettled state of text and tune of religious psalms and hymns and spiritual songs. Both music and text are constantly rearranged and retranslated in order to make hymns popularly accessible singing music for average singers in the communal church, according to the ideological relevance of the church or denomination itself. The old hymns are muted in time and space, upheaved, refixed, translated and retranslated without real signs of a primary sign and of the work of revisor and translator. The new hymns are again transitory vocal songs, and their text and tunes form the basis for further revisions and translations. Some of the paraphrases and translation are literal versions, some omit and modify many passages from the psalm or hymn that were thought inappropiate for Christian use, some hymns have become ornamental and forgotten, some have been added. Some of the tunes have become utterly unrecognizable under the added rhymes and metrical structures. Hymns have tied their fate to the changing models of musicoverbal translation.

Rewording, Translation Proper, and Transmutation

The "permissible degrees" (Nida 1964: 176) of Nida's dynamic equivalence translating in composing translations (as opposed to formal equivalence translating) closely restrict and constrain the Bible translator, who is also meant to stay bound to certain theological and evangelical limitations.[17] The vocal or verbomusical translator (of the lyrics, the music stays the same) is governed by a different but even stricter policy. The translation of a poetic song, as we shall see in this article, reveals the freedom and constraints of Nida's dynamic equivalence as opposed to formal equivalence.[18] Nida stated that

> The translator of poetry without musical accompaniment is relatively free in comparison with one who must translate a song — poetry set to music. Under such circumstances the translator must concern himself with a number of severe restrictions: (1) a fixed length for each phrase, with precisely the right number of syllables, (2) the observation of syllabic prominence (the accented vowels or long syllables must match correspondingly emphasized notes in the music, (3) rhyme, where required, and (4) vowels with appropriate quality for certain emphatic or greatly lengthened notes. (1964: 177)

Though Nida's bibliographic references on song translating (with reference to the ideological-evangelical genius of hymn translation) are today out of date and in need of revision, his basic description of the problems of translating phrase and paraphrase is still accurate and useful.[19]

The present stream of textological and musical metaversions in the persuasive influx of old-made-new translations and paraphrases embody in their shapes and forms Roman Jakobson's (1896-1982) three types of translation (1959: 232-239), discussed by Gorlée (1994: 147-168) and Eco (2001: 65 ff.). Jakobson proposed his classification thus:

- Intralingual translation or *rewording* is an interpretation of verbal signs by means of other signs of the same language;
- Interlingual translation or *translation proper* is an interpretation of verbal signs by means of signs of some other language;
- Intersemiotic translation or *transmutation* is an interpretation of verbal signs by means of signs of nonverbal sign systems. (from Jakobson 1959: 233; Jakobson's emphasis)

Apparent in these types occurring between the future (desire) and the present (fulfillment), between the past (remembrance) and the present (perpetration), between the capacity and the act, is a semiotic series of temporal and spatial analogies as well as their differences. The analogies refer to the phenomenon of translation in a broad sense. The differences are time/space differences without any central presence or internal habitat, abstracted from the perception or intuition of the translator, but no objective "reality" (Gorlée 2004: 224-225) is available. The translation is performed in any present in changeable time, a locational time of which past and future would be modifications. In Jakobson's types of translation we speak of possible (ex)changes in time, tenses, and temporal-spatial differences, and their consequences on the act of translating text-signs. This situation generates imitations of all kinds, with direct and true mimetic and non-mimetic (that is, indirectly insinuating) insights, which propose a sense of perspective and, together with hymn, suggests its effects.

Interlingual translation or rewording consists of the translation of (in)variants as the creation of new equivalents according to new (ex)changes in time and place. The activity happens according to new habit(s) adopted by translators. It shows that in order to serve as an actual flexible instrument for communication, an instrument (here a hymn consisting of text and tune) must have a strong element of negentropy; it must have the tendency to adopt habits based on social consensus; therefore choices must be made, and rules and strategies established by the community. But it shows that the hymn as a linguistic and musical code is a multi-purpose tool, and that habit-forming (negentropy) in language needs to alternate with entropy — that is, habit-breaking geared towards the creation of new and ideally better habits of life.

That the new habits generated by the intralingual translation improve the old ones, and are meant to be considered at least as strong as them, is manifested by the high truth value which is claimed not only for the original sign but, *a fortiori*, for the "reworded" (in Jakobson's sense) sign. It is true that the of two signs, the new sign is supposed to better equipped — Peirce would say "more developed" (CP: 2.228) — than the primary sign to fit today's speaking-and-singing world.

As instrumental in logical reasoning, and hence in translation, the new argument is a "statement expressly designed to lead to a given belief"(MS 599: 43). The new sign advances a new conclusive meaning to give the objective truth, a sign of law (semiotic, not real, law). Transposed to intralingual translation, this growth is on the lexical, sentential, and textual level, whenever an archaic word, interjection, or phraseology is justified to match more naturally modern ears, and hence rephrased and rewritten to fit the mood and tastes of a new audience. In Toury's words on general translation theory, intralingual translating is "the replaced and replacing entities being functions of two variants within one and the same natural language, whether free (e.g., in a definition) or bound (i.e. belonging in two complementary systems of that language, such as two registers, two historical layers, or two stylistic types)" (1986: 1113). It is exemplified by al kinds of paraphrases, including restyling, rephrasing, summarizing, and rewording (e.g., encyclopedia items, biological journal articles in ordinary language for a new audience, such as school children, explaining political propaganda of the past to a modern readership).

Hymns are the liturgy of the laity. The singing of hymns warms the hearts of all individual and collective singers as well as satisfying them. Therefore, a modernization of the written note and word are in hymns "natural" facts. The rewording goes against the conventional stream, but rescues the melodies and re-awakens the popularity of the hymn, which is meant for "everyone." The intralingual intricacies in the hymnal narrative are in many ways purely economical. They involve the invisible mending of old, traditional hymns, see the examples given before. Take also: "Lo! he comes, with clouds descending, Once for favoured sinners slain" and particularly Felix Mendelssohn's (1809-1847) melody (altered in turn by William H. Cummings) "Hark! The herald angels sing" (*The Church Hymnary* 1996: 277, 149, *The Hymnal for Worship & Celebration* 1986: nr. 241, 133), written by famous hymn writer Charles Wesley (1707-1788) at the end of 18th Century. These old hymns have in present time ridiculous first lines for young as well as old singers and should be linguistically "mended" to adequately serve modern singers. Do young singers today understand ancient words such as "lo," "hark," "majesty," "redeemer," "naught," "manna," "magi," and "cherubim"? In old hymns, Georg Frederick Händel's "Thine be the glory" (from 1747) (*The Church Hymnary* 1996: 243) is in the United States "Thine is the glory" (*The Hymnbook* 1955: nr. 209, *The Hymnal for Worship & Celebration* 1986: nr. 227; the former one includes archaic forms such as "liveth" and "thou." In many other hymns, we should change the obsolete and ecclesiastical words "thine" and "thy" to the modern "your" and "thee" to the more familiar "you." These problems are necessary to solve, but the real problem in this translation is a different strategy inclusion (and exclusion) of new vocals and replacing sounds in the well-known lines of the music. Consider the favorite St. Patrick's hymn "Be though my vision" (*The Church Hymnary* 1996: 78, *The Hymnal for Worship & Celebration* 1986: nr. 382), which is a translation of an ancient Irish musical folk poem from Gaelic into English prose by Mary Byrne (1880-1931). The music was arranged by David Allen. The translated prose was turned into poetry by Eleanor Hull (1860-1935), thereby creating a sung praise to God with often irregular English syllables, hard to sing: "battleshield" pronounced as two syllables, "heaven's" and "power" pronounced as one syllable, and other mending problems in the process of vocal translating and retranslating (criticized in Gorlée 1996, 1997, 2002).

Mending can also become more dramatic, and can even clash with laity ideology or church doctrines (as discussed before in paraphrases and translations). Discourse referentiality (that is, meanings in discourse) having, for Jakobson, become an affair of twofold contextuality. Intralingual translation thus becomes the variety of "interpreting a verbal sign" where no cross-systemic transfer takes place, but only intrasystemic substitution. Since one contextual pole remains untouched, and hence unchanged, this should enhance the vocal performance of the interpreter and translator. I call intralingual translation *monadic* translation, because of its single-language-oriented semiotic equivalences and the direct link with verbal signs. Intralingual translation is then *dyadic* translation, since it involves two-language-orientedness: a kind of struggle or contradiction between Saussurean *language* and *parole*, a (re)encounter between textual and verbal human "reality." Jakobson's "intralingual translation, or translation proper"(1959: 233) is about two or more languages in close linguistic-cultural contact. It involves "two equivalent messages in two different codes" (1959: 233); and as verbal facts are transcoded across language boundaries, to match the musical melody. The two linguistic codes involved are made to meet, interact, and (eventually and ideally) interconnect with each other, creating a new habit which produces a new meaningful hymn for new native singers. This interlingual procedure is how different languages demonstrate their similarities and, especially, how they aim to overcome their differences.

This exercise in "equivalence in difference" (Jakobson 1959: 233) is inspired by the wish or need to increase communicational efficiency by deliberately modifying a sign in order to make a new sign in an alternative linguistic code, suited for a new audience. Now it is, after the Sapir-Whorf hypothesis, well-known that different languages verbalize and arrange things (i.e., semiotic objects, meaning here linguistic and musical objects) in different ways. Interlingual translation revolves around finding a contextual form in the target language, which refers in more or less the same way to an object as does the sign in the source language. The new hymn refreshes the worship in a different language, in a different culture for a new listener. Therefore interlingual translation is concerned with breaking up and dislocating familiar sign-structures and relationships between signs, and rearranging them meaningfully in the light of the new system. This makes interlingual translation into a semiotic verbocultural encounter between two *Weltanschauungen*, an exercise in getting to terms, in a practical problem-solving way, with alterity or mixed (that is, linguistic, religious, and cultural) genres of Otherness.

The original sign is informed by the object, which in turn informs the interpretant, which is the new hymn. The latter is, however, determined by the sign only to a point. The new hymn is not equivalent to the old hymn, but it leaves a certain margin of liberty of a religious, cultural, moral, linguistic, subjective and objective nature. The discovery of new material is textually and musically semiotic(ized). The text is translated and thus becomes a new proposition, while the tune often (but not always) remains the same as in the old hymn. Tuned in more ambitious key than the outcome of intralingual translation, interlingual translation certainly has a limited truth-value, depending on the time and place. A chosen proposition is, in Peirce's semiotics, a practical solution, one which works more or less happily in a given situation, but which is at constant risk of being superseded by a better or more workable solution. Language is uncontrolled and constantly changing: words and phraseology become old-fashioned, new expressions refresh our memories and create new signs (that is, translated hymns) with better enjoyment, explanations, and instructions. This explains why the new translations and retranslations created are no luxury, but a constant requirement to keep the ongoing worship of a universal church and native liturgy fresh for contemporary and future singers.[20]

Jakobson's third kind of translation, intersemiotic translation, is sequentially *triadic*, since it involves the union of intermedial translations into an embedded one.[21] The decentering of verbal language in intersemiotic translation was a novel project which showed Jakobson's acute awareness of the implications, both theoretical and practical, of general semiotics for humanistic studies. Intersemiotic translation was understood by Jakobson to refer to the one-way metalingual operation in which linguistic signs are recodified into nonlinguistic codes, producing two or more multimedia scores. Typical examples of this type of recoding are the free (on the part of the receptor) translations from verbal language into visual language (e.g., plastic arts, painting, sculpture, architecture, and photography) and kinesic languages (e.g., ballet and pantomime), into auditive language (e.g., music and song) and intermedial languages (e.g., cinema and opera):

> We can refer to the possibility of transposing *Wuthering Heights* into a motion picture, medieval legends into frescoes and miniatures. Or *L'après-midi d'un faune* into music, ballet, and graphic art. However ludicrous may appear the idea of the *Iliad* and *Odyssey* in comics, certain structural features of their plot are preserved despite the disappearance of their verbal shape. The question whether Blake's illustrations to the *Divina Commedia* are or are not adequate is a proof that different arts are comparable. The problems of baroque art or any other historical style transgress the frame of a single art. When handling the surrealist metaphor, we could hardly pass by Max Ernst's pictures or Luis Buñuel's film *The Andalusian Dog* and *The Golden Age*. (Jakobson 1960: 350-351)

These remarks, from Jakobson's article in 1960, reflected the then new techniques, but today these artistic efforts reflect postmodern technology and face social reality using traditional and innovative techniques to distinguish them from revivalist or traditionalist creators and spectators. This is a point worth stressing since it creates a hybrid language, the style of postmodern artists and writers. Consider the popular religious films such as *Last Temptation of Christ* and *The Omega Code*. Today (2004) we discuss the religious-political controversies around *The Passion of the Christ* (by director Mel Gibson), a new film giving violent visual images, actions, and sequences, pictorially rooted in the written texts of Christ's evangelical life. *The Passion of the Christ* is spoken in today unspoken languages, Latin by Romans and Aramaic by Jews — the latter the language of the Gospel writers. What these modes of intercode and intersemiotic transmutations have in common is that their source code is the written signs of a verbal language, while the target code is a language only in a mixed, metaphorical manner of speaking. By the same token, if music, painting and dance movements may be reconsidered, they are essentially private sensations, expressed publicly to the environment. Such signs are cognitively interpretable, thus presupposing codes of communication and hence general signs. This procedure must somehow consist of meaningful sounds and sound sequences corresponding to morphemes, words, word combinations, sentences, paragraphs, and other endocentric and exocentric elements of verbal language, thus enabling their mutual transcodification into the metaphorical similarity of iconic engineering.

Yet hymns are not a metaphorical art which cannot be subsumed under any of its components arts, but a mixed art of text and tune sung together. It is a mistake to think of poetry and music as two unrelated (or even unrelatable) entities within the hymn. Music and poetry are not foreign to one other, nor are they in conflict. If they act in unison and create new artistic life in this transmutation of shared codes, this is because both "languages" share important elements and/or qualities which actively determine the hymn singing. In poetry the emotional sense and style register is primarily addressed and dealt with, not the medium, materials and instruments — as is the case in genres of music, the tone of the individual voice and the chorus of voices together. The purpose of the hymn singing is not to declaim a printed text-sign, it is the experience of collective singing as conduit for higher praise to God.

The wholeness of singers appears to employ, naturally and artificially, a variety of processes and techniques to sing together, in order to produce the spiritual nature of text and melody as a mode of total participation. The congregational singing is (usually) accompanied by a musical instrument, the organ (piano, guitar, or other instrument) which has (as said) no leading role, nor does the direction of the (possible) leader of the chorus have such role. Those functions are to guide the singing experience as togetherness, but no more than that. The musical accompaniment has in itself no lyrical function, which belongs entirely to the role of the singing experience. The organic synthesis of synchronism and progression produces harmonizing in music, melody, harmony. This is called the actual polyphony in language, music, and other arts. Highlighted are the codes of feelings and passions brought in the collective act of singing by individual singers as well as the chorus; de-emphasized are secondary mediators used in the church ceremony to create congregational singability, and to avoid the congregational slowness of singing: the use of the hymn book (most singers know the tune and text of hymns by heart), the accompanying instrument (which sets the rhythm of the singers and chorus) and even the function of the conductor (the director of singability). To explain the fusion of intersemiotic translation, both functions (the primary objects and the transitional objects) should be studied in a holistic framework. This is found in transdisciplinary (that is, semiotic) doctrine and its terminology, which is characterized by communal, that is verbal as well as nonverbal, generalities applied to phenomena in hymnology.

The next common characteristic of Jakobson's reference is that all nonverbal codes are varieties of artistic codes (plastic, musical, and so forth). The translation of natural language into artificial languages covering the acoustic, optical, and tactile fields (such as computer languages, Morse code and the Braille system) is an extended speech procedure involving units with only one fixed articulation. Such units must, in the strict sense, be considered non-signs, because they are typically based on one-to-one fixed equivalence. Lacking interpretive freedom on the part of the receiver, they fall outside the scope of intersemiotic translation as it is approached here: that is, as generating Peircean interpretants (interpreted signs) which, somewhat paraphrasing Peirce's definition, are equivalent to the primary, verbal signs, or possibly more developed secondary signs. Here they become translated signs giving a creative liberty to the spectators and the audiences. Hymn singing is a free activity bound by stylistic and musicological church conventions but still producing free singing for individual voices, an untrained chorus linked to the text of the collective hymn book.

The partnership between the verbal and the musical arts, as heralded by the early Prague School, hinges upon Jakobson's concept of "poeticalness" (1960: 359) in language: the pre-eminence of the poetic function (emphasizing the message as such, for its own sake) over the referential (focusing on the cognitive, informational aspect of language). While the poetic function finds in poetry its purest manifestation, but without being confined to it, poetry is, for Jakobson, primarily (but not exclusively) a "figure of sound" (1960: 367): it contains musical elements which are unresistant to finding a further expansion outside music. These elements include: sound structure, metrical pattern, rhyme structure, alliteration, assonance, euphony, phrasing, repetition, stanza and versification. The effects in prosody and sound effects in poetic language — as opposed to everyday referential language — called the "internal nexus between sound and meaning," (Jakobson 1960: 373):

> In referential language the connection between *signans* and *signatum* is
> overwhelmingly based on their codified contiguity, which is often

> confusingly labeled "arbitrariness of the verbal sign" … Sound
> symbolism is … founded on a phenomenal connection between different
> sensory modes, in particular between the visual and auditory experience.
> (Jakobson 1960: 372, Jakobson's emphasis)

The semiotic notion of expansion makes the creative fusion of words and music into a musical setting and its words form a symbiosis, that is, an intermedial collaboration between tune and text of the hymn. Peirce spoke on the philosophy of the incomplete and the notion of development and growth. In the action of hymn singing a variety of intersemiotic interpretation (or intersemiotic translation) by which the sound elements and sound effects in the simple text become susceptible to being translated ("transmuted," borrowing Jakobson's sign) by a variety of simple musical forms which, in Peirce's terminology, are chains of repeatable interpretant-signs in tone and tune.

Donington writes: "Outwardly there are the objective acoustics and tangible instruments of music. Inwardly, there are the subjective emotions and tangible experiences of music. Across this polarity there is relationship. Symbols can build up," and adds, "And so it is that music, which inevitably somewhat obscures the words in opera, far more importantly enhances them by means of that singular directness of feeling and of intuition which it can both induce and inflect" (1992: 10). This observation goes for an operatic performance (Donington's meaning of symbols, which is different to Peirce's), but does it also work for the singing of hymns in a church ritual? Since music is ideally equipped to express the beauty of feelings, the connotative aspect of the meaning of words, word patterns and sentences (that is, the emotionally charged associations surrounding their performance) can effectively expand meaningfully into a musical tone, intonation, a melodic line or harmony, expressing an equivalent emotion. This implies that although verbal language, as a logical system disconnected from its referent in reality, corresponds to Peirce's category of thirdness, the connotations surrounding verbal language, the aspects of firstness incorporated into it, may be separately translated into music, thereby appearing twice, in two different codes.[22] While the dramatic power of the words thus receives a musical intensification in secondness, what necessarily remains untranslated (simply because the musical target code lacks the capacities to convey it) is the emotional, or connotative, meaning aspect of the verbal text: its firstness. It enters into vocal music as an aesthetic component in its own right.

This allows the intralingual, interlingual and intersemiotic hymn translator to replace words, word patterns, verses, and refrains with other words, word patterns, verses, and refrains, if the music so requires, with hopefully no harm done to the total musico-poetic effect. Rhyme, rhythm, stress, as well as tempo marks, meter and stanza forms and melodic phrasing through key words, climaxes, caesuras, pauses, enjambment and again rhyme, clearly conveys meaning through stress, intonation and silence, as well as through tone and modulation of the voice. In the translation of hymn tunes they must be recognized, respected and reproduced with new linguistic material in order to fit the music and reproduce the desired musical effect. In my articles on vocal translation (Gorlée 1996, 1997, 2002) we see that interlingual translation of whatever kind never refers unambiguously to the primary sign, but manipulates it clearly and creates a new metasemiotic sign responding to a translation of the denotative semiotics, borrowing items from the dictionary, the textbook on phonetics, and other regular and useful scientific tools, and also attempting to "translate" the marginal or deviant connotative semiotics, including religious, historical, social, sacral, regional, and psychological contents. The connotative varieties are countless and indefinable entities, and they are irregularly interwoven inside a lyrical text. They must be discovered, then paraphrased and translated in reference to the target culture.[23]

Dyadism and Triadism

Peirce's semiotics and his categorical overtones thus govern the continuing history of Jakobson's types of translation. Jakobson's qualitative and quantitative dualities, discussed above, have been characterized in dually opposed terms such as *text and tune, words and music, individual and collective, skilled and unskilled, free and bounded, simple and complex, inward and outward, fixed and changed.* Jakobson's oppositions form a perceptual judgment of good and evil, of vice and virtue, or other dualisms of all sorts: oppositions, antinomies, and dichotomies. This semiotic tradition of *différences* follows Saussure's semiology, to which Jakobson primarily belonged. These polarities follow the dual oppositions conventional in translation theory: not only free vs. faithful translation, word for word vs. sense for sense, prescriptive vs. descriptive norms but also source vs. target, translatability vs. untranslatibility, philological vs. artistic translation and other fragmentations. These double fragmentations are in turn repeated in early linguistic and semioticized translation-scholars: not only Catford's formal and/or textual equivalence (1965) but the opposition between the illusionistic and the anti-illusionistic work method by Levý (1963, translated to German language 1969) and Nida's 1964 formal and/or dynamic equivalence method (discussed in Gorlée 1994).

However, the Peircean tradition is a non-doctrinary judgment, which cuts through any oppositions and creates a triadic rather than a dual paradigm. On the whole, Peirce's integrated approach seems to indicate that the meaning of the text-sign must be holistically as well as logically conceived as relatively independent from the reader/interpreter and transpires wholly in what is an endless series of individual semiosic events of the signs themselves. As will be argued and documented in the following, this proposition provides a new and fruitful perspective on the phenomenon of psalms, hymns, and divine songs; one which undercuts subjective signification and elevates semiotic analysis to the plane of intersubjective and objective inquiry, thereby enhancing, not restraining, its creative component.

The mathematically dual oppositions of semiology (also called structuralism) are, following Greimas and Courtès' semiotic encyclopedia,

> … an epistemological postulate according to which the binary articulation or grasp of phenomena is one of the human mind. [The oppositions form a] set of historical and pragmatic factors has given binary structures a privileged place in linguistic methodology. This may be due to the binary coupling of phonological oppositions established by the Prague School, or due to the importance gained by binary arithmetical systems (0/1) in automatic calculus, or to the operative simplicity of binary analysis in comparison with more complex structures, since every complex structure can be formally represented in the guise of hierarchy of binary structures, etc. (Greimas and Courtès 1982: 25).

In short, "the elementary structure of signification" rests upon a "distinction of opposition," while the semiotic square is "the visual representation of [this] logical articulation" (Greimas and Courtès 1982: 308). Just how much this diagrammatical procedure implicitly owes to the neglection of the entire question of meaning (structuralism does not asks what words mean but how they mean) and the intuitive ramifications of firstness (such as icon, abduction, hypothesis, musement and instinct) is here, it would seem, shrewdly camouflaged. And why this "epistemological postulate" is indeed so powerful that it makes binarity the most basic logical paradigm, eclipsing other possible, and equally meaningful, divisions, is largely and uncritically ignored.

The alternative, as proposed by Peirce and developed here, would consist of a triadic paradigm. Peirce forcefully stated in *A Guess at the Riddle,* on going from dyad to the motion of triad:

> First and Second, Agent and Patient, Yes and No, are categories which enable us roughly to describe the facts of experience, and they satisfy the mind for a very long time. But at last they are found inadequate, and the third is the conception which is then called for. The Third is that which bridges over the chasm between the absolute first and last, and brings them into relationship" (CP: 1.359 = W: 6: 172).

Since triads include both dyads and monads, and thirds build upon seconds and firsts (discussed in this article), Peirce's thinking model does not reject the binary principle but, rather, places it within a broader conceptual framework – his conception of semiosis, where the sign has a burden of reference. The internalization of form and shape into the interactive sign-object-interpretant relationship proposes a variety of critical but non-judgmental meanings of the sign. As Peirce pointed out:

> Now triads have at all times recommended themselves to all minds. There are psychological attractions for other numbers than three. Two is the number of hard common sense, of the stern moralist, of the practical man. "Yes or no? Answer me categorically," says such a man. Heaven and hell, right and wrong, truth and fiction, gain and loss, agent and patient, living or dead, - on such distinctions our practical life turns. The philosophy of two comes within my scheme. (MS 907: 2)

Since triads include both dyads and monads, and thirds build upon seconds and firsts (discussed in this article), Peirce's thinking model does not reject the binary principle but, rather, places it within a broader conceptual framework – his conception of semiosis, where the sign has a burden of reference. The internalization of form and shape into the interactive sign-object-interpretant relationship proposes a variety of critical but non-judgmental meanings of the sign.

To be sure, the binary paradigm was, of course, no invention of Greimas', and no discovery after his passing. Before him and his colleagues (Claude Lévi-Strauss, Julia Kristeva, Tzvetan Todorov, among others), it had been a leading feature of classical European structuralism, building upon Saussurean and Jakobsonian linguistics, among others:

> Saussure's basic definition of differential units as "negative, relative and oppositive" has been seminal. The idea of opposition as the primary logical operation universally arising in humans from the first glimmerings of consciousness in infants and from youngsters' initial steps in the buildup of language was viewed as the natural key to the inquiry into verbal structure from its highest to its lowest levels. The inalienable property of opposition which separates it from all other, contingent differences is, when we are dealing with one opposite, the obligatory copresence of the other one in our minds, or in other words, the impossibility of evoking long without a simultaneous, latent idea of short, or expensive without cheap, "voiced" without "voiceless," and vice versa. (Jakobson and Waugh 1979: 20)

Saussure's original binary concepts (signifier and signified, *langue* and *parole*, paradigm and syntagm, matter and form, sound and meaning, synchrony and diachrony) are echoed in Jakobson's binarism (code and message, selection and combination, metaphor and metonymy, etc.) and in Louis Hjelmslev's dichotomies (expression and content, form and substance). Traditional structuralism has thus generated "this pervasive habit of the linguist of bifurcating his cosmos [which] continues to permeate semiotic method" (Rauch 1986: 917). Outside of French semiotic theory it is found in, for example, Thomas A. Sebeok's mutually opposed categories (inner and outer, vocal and nonvocal, verbal and nonverbal, witting and unwitting, etc.) (Sebeok 1985) and, last but not least, in Yuri Lotman's distinction between primary and secondary modeling systems, internal and external communication, closed and open cultures, primary and secondary encoding, primary and secondary value of texts etc. (see also Lotman's essays in Lucid 1988). Yet Lotman, in his chapter "The Text as a Meaning-Generating Mechanism" (1990) on poetic creation approaches to information in a natural language, moved toward the "threefold semantic value of the text; the primary general linguistic value; the secondary semantic value, which arises from the syntagmatic organization of the text and from yuxtaposition with the primary values; and thirdly, values that arise from the introduction into the message of extra-textual associations, ranging from the most general to the extremely personal" (Lotman 1990: 29). Lotman's system of textual rules is not based on Peirce (but, apparently on Charles Morris and Jakobson). The primary value is a formal (or formalized) code and this syntactic value becomes semantic with the secondary value. The categorical tension grows with the inclusion of pragmatic interpreting, including translating into a different verbal language or nonverbal code. This focus draws on the three types of translation (intralingual, interlingual, and intersemiotic) coming from the semiotic "patriarch" of translation studies, Jakobson himself.[24]

It was not Jakobson's intention to universalize and perpetuate the Saussurean model, demonstrated by his later and pioneering interest in the thought of Peirce, the forefather of American semiotics. As an alternative to the Saussurean division into dichotomies, Peirce's radically triadic thought was "discovered" by Jakobson as a new thinking model to be introduced into all language-oriented fields of research.[25] This happened at a time (the early 1950s) when Peirce was virtually unknown in the field of Jakobsonian "linguistics and poetics." Just how momentous Jakobson's insight really was, and still is, will not be fully appreciated until linguistics and poetics are studied within a thoroughly Peircean framework.

The Saussurean semiotic tradition has tried very hard to weld linguistics and poetics into one unified field of research, the subject of which is written texts, especially narrative texts. So far, however, Jakobson's prophetic vision has remained a mirage — alas for Jakobson, alas for the whole of humanistic scholarship. In spite of appearances to the contrary, this does not mean that the project itself was a utopian construct, a figment of Jakobson's visionary mind, best abandoned and forgotten. As I choose to interpret it, the misconception did not lie in the project but in the paradigms of structuralist methodology. Dyadic thought was not destined to become the master code suitable for bringing about the desired unification of all disciplines dealing with verbal messages. Following Jakobson's still embryonic focus on Peirce, a full-fledged Peircean semiotics not only unifies all language-based disciplines but, beyond that, provides one comprehensive theoretical framework which is applicable to all sign-based disciplines, verbal and nonverbal alike.

Mind, Matter, God

The mixed and intermediate art of divine songs can be described in Peirce's terms of the sign and its three semiotic relations. A sign signifies, because it possesses some quality or distinctive property or general attribute which turns it into a semiotic sign for someone. The interest for the sign implies that this sign must be somehow interesting, intriguing, or otherwise require someone's special attention, suggesting that it means something other than itself, or something more than itself, thereby inviting, even requiring some ulterior explanation or new information in the form of the interpretation or translation of the primary sign. The sign is oriented towards this higher goal, to be interpreted in the future and become, as Peirce said, a "growing tree" (MS 283: 98, 1906), a horticultural metaphor also employed by Peirce's friend, William James (1842-1910) in his *Principles of Psychology* (1910: 222) (discussed in Gorlée 2004: 123, 2004a: 167f, 176ff). A sign that is never interpreted ceases to be a sign; it becomes meaningless, a so-called non-sign, and dies. The evolution or growth comes through the influence of the law of love or *agapè* (CP: 6.287 ff.) (in the *King James Version, agapè* is misleadingly translated as "charity") functioning through faith and grace; that is, third comes through the forceful love of first and second.

These definitions are governed by Peirce's three categories, which we is already evident in Peirce's general concept of love as loving feeling — enumerated as, firstly, the "love of self," secondly, the "love of a limited class having common interest and feelings with one's self," and thirdly, the "love of mankind" (CP: 6.291). Love from hymn singing by a single singer, congregational singing toward the supernatural, is the great evolutionary agent of the universe. It is a growth from the incomplete towards definite purpose and recognizable in all objects we see, experience and analyze. In hymns we see a threefold act, involving Saint Paul's psalms, hymns and spiritual songs), it is the exhortation to seek admission to the spirit of God, at odds with the pursuits of narcissistic love and even with the love for mostly altruistic neighbors. Even the Pauline spirit in Christian experience is threefold: "... of the spirit of man, of the divine person (Holy Ghost), of the spirit which God supernaturally infuses in man?" or rephrased as a loving "contact with God, ... , under the influence of the Holy Spirit, ...; and the created spirit itself which is the human locus and 'subject' of the visitation" (Menasce 1968: 325). Spirit is also called in three terms: theology, christology and missiology (Bell 2000: 58-65) in order to show the icons of belief, adherence, assurance with the belief in the supernatural. This triadic paradigm follows the deeds and words of the prophets and the mission of the human church.[26]

The threefold aspects of music parallel the relations of "man as body, soul and spirit" (Wibberley 1934: 240), offering a Peirce-like analogy of the spirit of church text-and-music, and a vital force leading from mind to matter and towards God, and back again:

> The "body" of music is represented in the physical phenomenon of
> vibration that is the basis of it all, and which possesses one of the most

> remarkable of all qualities which dominate matter, inasmuch as there is no form of matter ... [to] give forth responsive rhythmic pulses. The "soul" of the music is found in the sensations which these vibrations awaken in the sensitive organism of the mind, and which so exactly and exquisitely correspond to the stimulus, that the cultivated ear can now detect vibrational differences which may be represented by the sixty-fourth part of a semi-tone. The "spirit" of music is its spiritual quickening, revealing power, which finds us in the deepest seat of our complex nature (Wibberley 1934: 240)

In hymn-singing we refer to the vibrations in the bodily vocal constraints, where the exercise of breathing is the central element. The breath consists of a taking a breath of air (forced inhalation) and letting it out (relaxed exhalation). Singing is expression during exhalation.The mechanical rate of breathing is controlled by a respiratory center in the brain stem that responds to changes like stress and activities. Air flows down through the windpipe, past the voice box or vocal cords to the lungs. The transported air is passed to the bloodstream and exchanged for waste products, like CO_2 (carbondioxide). CO_2 comes back through the mouth in the form of tone or vibrating breath reflected through the head in the form of speech, noise, and singing. Speech has indefinite and varying details, noise is irregular or erratic sound, while singing is speech with absolute pitch and a precise value in length. This is why we have upward and downward inflection and rising and falling sounds in the final quality of singing. The hymns express a vocalized "heavenly" variation upwards. The details between speech, noise and singing are measured by its regular-irregular and desired-undesired intensity, power and spectrum. Peirce states that respiration is "better carried on as [it] is, without any meddling by Reason; and the countless little inferences we are continually making, — be they ever so defective, — are, at any rate, less ill performed unconsciously than they would be under the regimen of a captious and hypochondriac logic" (CP: 7.448). Singing is a spontaneous and uncritical activity of the body.

The distinctions can be described in terms of chaos and order (Scheffcyzyk 1986: 607-609); yet, to give a sound a human content, a listener is needed to vitalize the created sonic form, although is it essentially composed of a chemical mixture which leads to the meaningful product: speech together with melody. The breath of God is described in Genesis 2: 7, where God breathed into man's nostrils the breath of life, so that Adam became a living person. God's life-inspiring breath serves as the nerve energy of life. This purpose of hymn singing is a belief in a miracle affecting body-and-soul. Breathing during singing changes the attitude of the singer, coming from direct oneness to indirect togetherness, with significant moments in the song such as beginning, end and refrain, as well as "a lengthened note, an absolute silence, or a momentary change of time, [which] could be used with telling effect to the listener" (White 1938: 140).

Peirce spoke of I, It, Thou, with reference to his nomination of the three categories.[27] The instinct, experience, and form (in the terms of thought or habits of life) correspond to the three possible interpreters, namely I, It and Thou (W: 1: 174) in the early Peirce. They speak of the truthful adequacy of the sacred (and hymnical) message, rooted in the individual essence, outward objectual essence, and communal thought. Peirce's words on the three references of these personal pronouns (as utterers in three universes) are that the verbal message:

> ... has three relations. The first is its relation to the pure Idea or Logos and this (from the analogy of the grammatical terms for the pronouns I, IT, THOU) I call this relation of the first person, since it is its relation to its own essence. The second is its relation to the Consciousness as being thinkable, or to any language as being translatable, which I call its relation to the second person, since it refers to the power of appealing to a mind. The third is its relation to its object, which I call its relation to the third person or IT. (W: 1: 174).

At an early date (1867), after "three years of almost insanely concentrated thought, hardly interrupted by sleep" (see "Introduction" by Max H. Fisch in W: 1: xxvi), Peirce presented to the American Academy of Arts his *On a New List of Modes of Categories* (CP: 1.545-1.559 = W: 2: 49-59). Peirce had "discovered" his ontological categories: firstness, secondness, and thirdness. According to Peirce's private *Logic Notebook*, the categoriology was " (if anything is) the gift I make to the world. That is my child. In it I shall live when oblivion has me – my body" (see *Introduction* by Fisch in W: 1: xxvi). The three categories constitute the foundation of Peirce's work and thought. The categories were identified thus to be the innate idea of the activity of the human mind, but also that of nature and the world at large: "Unlike an idea that enters into an of-relation with its object, and thereby concerns truth or falsity, an innate element is not predicated of anything beyond awareness. And so it either has no truth or falsity, or else is universally predicated of represented objects" (Esposito 1980: 42-43). Peirce dramatically crisscrosses the postulates of the dual oppositions, found in semiology and Saussurean tradition, and revised them with a non-doctrinaire conciliation of objects in reality, yet "without altering the fact" (MS 920: 46). The three categories interpret (and translate, or better "translate") the data with humans perceive and experience, with the function of guiding and stimulating further inquiry through the discovered qualities. The human mind transforms the formless data into emotions, objects and events as a structured dynamic organ. To give a categorical shape and form to the psalms, hymns, and religious songs we require a brief overview of Peirce's categoriology:[28]

Of the three ways of perceiving facts, firstness is, according to Peirce, qualitative immediacy, that claims to represent the real thing but gives no guarantee of the existence of the reality. Firstness is the hardest to understand, in spite of the fact that it represents "pristine simplicity"(CP: 7.551) and qualitative *"naïvité"* (CP: 8.329, Peirce's emphasis). Firstness means unanalyzed, instantaneous, immediate feeling. It offers direct "suchness" dependent on nothing else beyond itself for its comprehension. Peirce's suchness is the in-itselfness of the object-sign offering to the audience a maybe (or maybe not). Firstness is often fictive or hypothetical. For example, firstness is experienced in (Peirce's examples) the sensation of redness or blackness, the feeling of acute pain, an electric shock, a thrill of physical delight, the piercing sound of a train whistle, a penetrating odor; we could continue with non-Peircean examples such as listening to the choral portion of the *Ninth Symphony* and the tonal mood of *Goldberg Variations*; or any other impression which is forced upon the mind and compels its total sensory attention in order to give it an emotional meaning. Peirce himself also included in his list of firsts "the quality of the emotion upon contemplating a fine mathematical demonstration, the quality of falling in love" (CP: 1.304). Firstness is thus the idea of the timeless present instant experienced as "pure emotion of the *tout ensemble*"(CP: 1.311, Peirce's emphasis), an emotion prior to any thought on the object-sign. One cannot "think" a real first.

Whereas firstness means undivided and undividable oneness, secondness involves the dynamic time and space of Otherness and its two-sided consciousness, the experience of action and reaction, stimulus and response, change and resistance to change. The idea of hitting and getting hit is a true second, since it contains the elements of polarity, interaction, comparison, and struggle. While a first is a potentiality, a possibility, "merely something that *might* be realized," a second is a hard fact, "an occurrence … something that *actually* takes place" (CP: 7.538, Peirce's emphasis). According to Peirce, "the real is that which insists upon forcing its way to recognition as something *other* than the mind's creation"(CP: 1.325, Peirce's emphasis). Therefore, it is through the over-againstness of secondness that we face and deal with reality around us, and in this process of life acquire experience.

Secondness offers against hard forces brute opposition or weak resistance (muscular or intellectual opposition). All knowledge of the factual world and the more practical aspects of human life (such as opening a door, making a phone call, and kicking a football) are seconds. Secondness is involved whenever we make an effort, a decision, or a discovery; when we orientate ourselves in time and space; or when we find a surprise (CP: 5.52-5.58). Secondness differs from firstness in that secondness occurs *hic et nunc*; yet it must also be based upon the past and the lessons we draw from it. Peirce states that "we may say that the bulk of what is actually done consists of secondness — or better, secondness is the predominant character of what *has been done*"(CP: 1.343, Peirce's emphasis).

Beyond the vague generality of firstness, "a mere idea unrealized," and the definite nature of "real" secondness, "the cases to which it applies" (CP: 1.343), thirdness embodies continuity, also called in-betweenness. The mediating rule of feeling and action by general principles provide logical explanations, all intellectual activity is primarily a third. Logical thought, Peirce's thirdness, creates orderliness, law, and regularity as opposed to (and out of) chaos, randomness, and chance: "The thread of life is a third" (CP: 1.337). Since the assurance given by this mediation is concerned with continuity, thirdness is future-oriented and permits us to predict what is to be, and to adapt our attitude accordingly. Peirce argued that thirdness is an eternal value, discussed and rediscussed in the long run of history:

> This is not the kind of consciousness which cannot be immediate, because it covers a time, and that not merely because it continues through every instant of that time, but because it cannot be contracted into an instant. It differs from immediate consciousness as a melody does from one prolonged note. Neither can the consciousness of the two sides of an instant, of a sudden occurrence, in its individual reality, posibly embrace the consciousness of a process. This is the consciousness that binds our life together. It is the consciousness of synthesis. (CP: 1.381)

All "finer" feelings and "deeper" emotions such as love, hope, and religious fervor, which because of their sophistication are popularly considered to be peculiar to the human species (as opposed to animal and plant instincts) are thirds. The same is true of cognition, intelligence, and mental growth arising out of unconsciousness to consciousness. This is man's (and woman's) burden.

Peirce's three categories are not separate entities but act in togetherness through the adopted or chosen habit, grown in the types of regularities and irregularities we discover in the study of the sign and its object, which we embody in the given interpretation. The discovery process arises from an intellectual curiosity in order to eventually find the truth, which is opposed to the self-serving feeling of greed (CP: 6.291). Semiotically, the hymnical meditation is a semiosic representation fully aware of the intimate, close and thinking relationship of three elements signifying the friendship between sign, the object it stands for, and the interpreted or translated interpretant. In Esposito's view, Peirce had discovered that our "concepts, then, literally 'participate' in the reality is what is conceived … It is the nature of an idea to be a *representation* of something beyond our direct awareness of it …" (1980: 42). Musicoverbal songs possess a moralistic purpose, but the songs have a indicative, declarative and hortatory nature[29] in direct reference to Peirce's firstness, secondness, and thirdness.

This phenomenon can be interpreted in the sign-qualities of the songs themselves. The primary element in the spiritual songs, dominating the other categories, is firstness, an intensive and impersonal emotion, making a private message impossible to communicate to others. This unexplained message becomes in the hymnical sign-combination a personal, intimate and in-communicable message. In the influxual dependency of secondness and thirdness, the first impression in the form of self-enclosed and self-limited feelings becomes beliefs (secondness) and convictions (thirdness), meaning eventually public messages. This interdependency happens also to the body-oriented sensationism of the Peirce's conscious mind with its content physical appearances: sensations, ideas, volitions.

Thirds are the logical signs including the use of language. Language has the obligation to function with thoughtful signs, to stand for something else and be meaningful. Language must be interpreted according to some previously agreed general rule. In the absence of the object, thirds can deceive, lie or manipulate. It remains an open guess, unless a particular meaning is agreed upon by common (or communal) consensus. Since the association between thirds and the object is in language an arbitrary one, the interpretation may be changed at will and overruled by a new agreement. Language can be transformed into poetic verse lines, and thereby exchange the logical element for various elements of firstness. Many types of desire and fantasy are expressed in the verse form, expressing not only affected civilized prose but at the same time a private *mindset*, where personal feelings are the absolute priority. The verse form includes seldom-used rhymes and "literary forms like 'thou' and 'e'ver' …, but also departures from ordinary word order and sentence structure for the sake of rhythm, rhyme, emphasis, silence, and other aesthetic effects. The division into verse is often but not always expressed in speech, as on the stage, by slight pauses or inflections of tone" (Munro 1969: 482). The verse form is relaxing "so as to release the flow of fantasy from partly unconscious levels"(Munro 1969: 483). This habit is visible in hymns and hymn singing, where the force of Peirce's "musement" is at work, "a dreamy, hypnotic effect on conscious reasoning" (Munro 1969: 48), which is upgraded in the actuality of the church community to a still intimate and spiritualistic, but evidently public, experience. Thereby, musement is transformed into a more social functional intercourse, which possesses a more intentional and rationalistic argument.

Musement

Peirce's new term "musement" was creatively derived from "to muse," to think deeply and dreamily, and its derivatives "musing"and "museful" as well as the meaning of the semantically unrelated "muse"and "to demuse," as well as a word play on the term "amusement" as recreation. The term "musement" was coined by Peirce towards the end of his life, in 1908, as title for the introductory essay (CP: 6.452-6.465) of *A Neglected Argument for the Reality of God* (CP: 6.452-6.493). Peirce contended that the theologians had concentrated upon supplying rational support for the belief in God, thereby ignoring that the process of reasoning which will spontaneously generate such a belief is characterized as religious meditation, based on the mode of abductive reasoning, that is Peirce's "Pure Play" of musement (CP: 6.458). Abduction is the first and primary mode of reasoning, corresponding to Peirce's firstness. Here, a puzzling phenomenon is observed and a hypothesis is unthinkingly but intuitively formed and spontaneously selected in order to supply a plausible explanation for the sign. Musement greatly accentuates the playful aspect of abduction, where the human mind is in ludic intercommunion with the law of mind, Nature, thirdness, and the intercourse with the spirit of God by prayer.[30]

In order to enter this argumentation, the sign-inquirer or sign-investigator (in our case, a singer placed within a church ritual) must thereby enter a particular state of passive open readiness in which reasoning is disengaged from the personal mind. The mind is itself considered a self-reflexive and unconscious sign — a dreamy sign. Musement is self-returning into itself, without time and place habits, opposed to returning and self-controlled acts like listening, reading and planning. Musement is a daydream which stimulates indifference to the methodological imperatives and hardships that we are concerned with in our daily lives. Jourdain in his *Music, the Brain, and Ecstasy* speaks on the ecstasy when we "free-associate while our frontal lobes slumber" adding that "when we work, the frontal lobes constantly rein in parts of our minds to stop them from wandering from task at hand" (1997: 309). Musement generates the form of free and unbound playfulness and gives emotional and expressive feeling, pushing forward towards the autonomous unknown signs in the whole universe. In Peirce's attitude characterized by musement, semiotic discussions start with a drifting and fluctuating feeling, always vague, unseen, incoherent such as a paradox. Always a sign of uncontrolled firstness, which Merrell calls "autosemiopoetic activity" (1995: 215-216), presupposing a dreamy act leading to overdetermination and underdetermination of the integration of the sign into the wholeness of the universe of discourse.

Musement is a certain "reverie with some qualifications" (CP: 6.458) which presuppose the sounds of music with its remedy against boredom. Musement expects future anticipations and promises, pleasure and pain, as well as chromatism and dischromatism, all of them idealized in the harmony and disharmony of melodic contour and rhythmic phrases (Jourdain 1977: 319 ff.). Pike has analyzed the individual and collective behavior of the participants in a church service, signalling "either the alert focusing of attention to listen for encouragement, and inspiration, or else the setting of the mind in neutral so it can idly dream of things while the ear registrates word by word, but with no connected thought while the eye stares vacantly in space" (1967: 81-82). The dreaminess of musement, its "Pure Play"(CP: 6.458), is no recreation or perhaps a pastime: the play itself is a powerful creative skill or readiness, where the emotions of music presuppose the rules of first priority in order to become a perfect sign of the winding plans of our emotional lives.

The sign-inquirer, here embodied by the case of the hymn-singer, is "convinced of the truth of religion [which] is plainly not inquiring in scientific singleness of heart. But let religious meditation be allowed to grow up spontaneously out of Pure Play" (CP: 6.458). The hymnical sign "begins passively enough with drinking in the atmosphere of some nook in one of the three Universes" (CP: 6.459). After this primary beginning, the following "impression soon passes into attentive observation, observation into musing,

musing into a lively give and take of communion between self and self" (CP: 6.459). In the end, if "one's observations and reflections are allowed to specialize themselves too much, the Play will be converted into scientific study; and that cannot be pursued in odd half hours" (CP: 6.459). Musement is the firstness of thirdness: it is beautiful, inwardized and simple feeling, but (as said) a meditation with some Peircean qualifications: musement is a feeling-sign skill, with a capacity to be thrown into overdrive. Our brain is "endowed with an automatic control, as man's indirectly is" and is "so naturally and rightly interested in [promiting] his faculties that some psychological and semi-psychological questions would undoubtedly get touched" (CP: 6.462). This faculty leads up from the original pleasure and pain of musement towards "wide aggregates of unformulated but partly experienced phenomena" (CP: 6.463), like the growth of truth outside accepted time and space.

The attitude of musement is increased in the experience of singing as an individual and congregational musical form, which is not only aesthetic and pleasant but, as American philosopher, educator as well as social and political critic, John Dewey (1859-1952)[31] argued in his *Art as Experience*, song has "the psychological function of providing the artist with an outlet for his pent-up psychic energies — a means by which he can achieve outward, symbolic expression for his emotional conflicts and unsatisfied desires" (1934: 241). The singer is "pushed from behind, as it were, to translate his own personal drama, conscious and unconscious, into symbolic visual, musical, or verbal form; a personal drama which is never purely individual, but influenced by the psychic tensions of the cultural group and of the human race" (Dewey 1934: 241). According to Peirce's categoriology, music as indicative of personal enjoyment is primarily a first, with germs and roots creating emotions and feelings, but the firstness, which is in itself meaningless, maybe provided with a possible meaning or meanings.[32] The meaning of the song "is pushed from behind" and becomes a Peircean maybe, or maybe not. Such music possesses no logical force in terms of thirdness, but its artistic and aesthetic qualities can be enjoyed and manipulated to make the song more and more meaningful (significant). Musement is, as said, the firstness of eventual thirdness.

Music accompanied by words is integrated into genres, styles, fashions and even moods and becomes upgraded from firstness to secondness and towards thirdness. The persuasive semiotics surrounding musical performances leads the singers and audiences to their own beauty and their "values as profane and spiritual, as material and ideal" (Dewey 1934: 20). The hymns are called in "etherial things" (1934: 20, 32-34) in Dewey.[33] Their "heavenly" reasonings result from the spontaneous, imaginative human mind on its fallible way toward its goal and its "complete grasp and self-contained assurance" (Dewey 1934: 33). According to *Art as Experience*, the ultimate purpose of the hymns is the "contrast between the inertia of habit and the imaginative" (1934: 270), the eventual divine revelation. The quick expansion of human experience can easily fall back to the level of the "wild creature" (Dewey 1934: 33). This signifies that the religious ritual characterized by its "primitivity" arrives in turn at the pious wish of eternal glory and bliss; if not, it must start all over again. This is a sign of the repeatable nature of the so-called laboratory investigation, which is Peirce's workmanlike inquiry. The experience of hymn singing needs to be constantly resung and recited in order to work actively.

In *A Common Faith*, Dewey repeats that we have to leave the "most savage and degraded beliefs and practices" in order to reach a total "universality of religion" ([1934]1955: 7). The universe of religion heightens the ordinary and "primitive" self beyond itself to achieve the level of a "whole self" ([1934]1955: 19). A whole self is more than a vague term, since it embodies the intimate connection of human imagination with ideal elements, where "the idea of the integration of the shifting scenes of the world [changes] into that imaginative totality we call the Universe" ([1934]1955: 19). This ideality is the "anticipatory vision" we cherish ([1934]1955: 20) and such experience takes place in religious faith and belief tied up with approaching the face of God. Unconsciousness becomes thereby consciousness. Dewey states in his last book *Experience and Nature* that

> It is this double relationship of continuation, promotion, carrying forward, and of arrest, deviation, need of supplementation, which defines that focalization of meanings which is consciousness, awareness, perception. Every case of consciousness is dramatic; drama is an enhancement of the conditions of consciousness. It is impossible to tell what immediate consciousness is – not because there is some mystery in or behind it, but for the same reason that we cannot tell just what sweet or red immediately is: it is something had, not communicated and known. ([1925]1958: 306-307)

In the dramatic performance of hymn singing, the beautiful combination of verse with melody creates a "story, some whole, an integrated series of episodes" (Dewey [1925]1958: 307) with any meaning, so that the "'practice' from insight, of imagination from executive doing, of significant purpose [arises] from work, of emotion from thought and doing" (Dewey 1934: 21). The practice can be grouped into three evolutionary levels: firstness proceeds in the here and now to reach the surprise of secondness towards its purpose, the consummation (Dewey's term) of dramatic thirdness.

In spiritual songs, there exists a rhythmic co-presence of upward and downward confusion, in which Peirce's categories are mixed together. The three types are never mutually exclusive layers; there is a symbiosis of the values of categories. The same sign can, and often will function to the perceiver (the singer or the listener), at the same time as a first, a second, and a third. In Peirce's words, "That footprint that Robinson Crusoe found in the sand, … was a [Second] to him that some creature was on his island, an at the same time, as a [third], called up the idea of a man"(CP: 4.531). For the sake of completeness, Peirce should have added here that, shapewise, the creative footprint was first of all a first of some human foot. Thirds might involve seconds and first, and second might include firsts. This idea is stressed by Peirce (NEM: 4: 256, CP: 2.293, 2.248). The reverse — namely that seconds may also involve thirds, as seems to be suggested by Peirce — is a new proposition.[34] The key to this problem may be found by starting from the following passage, where it appears to be affirmed or denied: "The category of first can be prescinded from second and third, and second can be prescinded from third. But second cannot be prescinded from first, nor third from second"(CP: 1.353). Peirce posited pointedly: "Everything must have have some non-relative element; and this is firstness. So likewise it is possible to prescind secondness from thirdness. But thirdness without secondness would be absurd" (MS 487: 37-38). Peirce stated that though "it is easy to distinguish the three categories from one another, it is extremely difficult accurately and sharply to distinguish each from other conceptions so as to hold it in its purity and yet in its full meaning" (CP: 1.353).

Psalms, hymns and spiritual songs can be described according to the discovered qualities in this symbiosis of Peirce's three categories. In the reading and singing of the Psalms, God reaches out to man. In the human psalms, hymns, and spiritual songs, man reaches in turn out to God. In a religious environment, "we all share in the human-divine substance, that we are all God's children" (Fromm [1957]1965: 17). Church singing partakes of the threefold categories in the pure potentiality of feelings, which is the primary sign in music-verbal hymns. Through ecstasy, the act of singing becomes a stream of events to reach a continuous flow of messages, whereas the continuous flow becomes particularized in a stream of collective events towards an individual emotion. See Peirce's sensibility and motion leading to growth (CP: 1.393), where the developing movement of hymns is realized in an unfolding system of upwardly and downwardly changeable categories which follow not only the sign-activity of the singer's mind, his or her sensibility, motion, and growth of the petitional prayer from dream, desire, and purpose; but also the triadic unification of text and tunes in the enchantment of the singing heart.

This synergetic situation is expressed in the ecstatic quality, relation and representation of the act of hymn singing. The individual singing flows into the singing together in group identity toward the communal reality of God, as a direct effect of the beauty, skill and intelligence of the human singing abilities. Peirce stated that from "speculations on the homogeneities of each Universe, the Muser will naturally pass to the consideration of homogeneities and connections between two different Universes, or all three" (CP: 6.465). This growth from and toward human musement is firstly embodied in pervasive subjectivism, then embodied in group identity and eventually in general praise of God, the supreme purpose of hymn singing. Holy songs combine both sense, perception and confirmation of this divine insight.

Diflection of Text and Tune

From the mature Peirce and his musement, we go back to the young Peirce, who wrote the essay *Analysis of Creation* in Fall-Winter 1861 (MS 1105 in several drafts followed by MS 71 = W: 1: 85-90) as forerunner of the article *On a New List of Categories* (CP: 1.545-1.567 = W = 2: 49-59, written in 1967) to relate plurality to analytic unity. He described in *Analysis of Creation* how the abstract world becomes particularized in his key of the three categories to match the unity of meanings in human "reality" (discussed in Murphey 1961: 48ff., 66ff. and Esposito 1980: 56 ff.). Peirce wrote on the synergic qualities of the categories:

> The distinction between imaging and conceiving is part of the very alphabet of philosophy. To imagine is [to] reproduce in the mind elementary sensible intuitions and to take them up in some order so as to make an image. To conceive is to collect under a supposition, to make a hypothesis, and therefore cannot dispense with the use of words. (quoted from second draft of the *New List of Categories* cited from Murphey 1961: 67-68)

His path of inquiry means the road from intuition through imagination to concepts, from terms, propositions to arguments – the process from chaotic unconsciousness to conscious awareness. In *Analysis of Creation*, Peirce wrote on the efficacy of prayer, its thought and its doing, as follows:

> A prayer is not a prayer as long as the prayerfulness is wanting; neither is it one before prayerfulness regulates some rite, or at least some inward movement" (MS 1105: 10 = W: 1: 86).

According to Peirce's statement, a prayer is pronounced or declaimed in verbal language, but language is, in the company of music in hymns, downgraded to match the musical level of firstness. Hutchinson (1963, discussed above) implied that the prayer is an intimate "cry for security" which remains personal and dispirited unless it becomes integrated in a formal "ritual of expressive words and nonverbal symbols" (1963: 230). By being repeated and repeated, the prayerfulness, the hymnal narrative and the spiritedness are taken together to form a real myth.

Peirce's outline of creation in MS 1105 follows the order of the emerging categories. Creativity starts in the beginning with "sensation-things" (MS 1105: 2) which offer a pure expression — later called by Peirce an unconscious sign of musement. Musement concentrates on a common character or general mental quality, familiar to our intuitive consciousness. Using Peirce, Savan urges us to "think of words like 'Napoleonic,' 'Spartan,' 'Ghandian,'" adding that "the most disparate and haphazard collection of entities willl have some abstractable quality, even if it be only its own peculiar flavour of oddity or strangeness" (1987-1988: 7), say Hymnical, a pseudo-Peircean term. To arrive at the real meaning or even at a mixed "manifold of sense" (MS 1105: 11, W: 1: 88) of the term Hymnical presupposes a contrastive and personal activity of imagining, including consciousness of habitual logic, "belonging to a special time, to a special person, to a special subject to thought" (MS 1105: 8). This awareness includes the use of the human capabilities of language to highlight resemblances and differences in our "mode of expression between man and man" (MS 1105: 10 = W: 1: 86). According to Peirce, the use of language means the use of semiotic "gestures or speech or music or what" (MS 1105: 10 = W: 1: 86). These "regulative" signs (MS 1105: 10) are taken from all kinds of expressive languages, including "[g]eometrical figures, letters, conversation, music" (MS 1105: 4). Peirce's architectonic theory states that the "animal Kingdom is a language" is regulated by intersemiotic language, and similarly "human life is a language" regulated by our meanings (MS 1105: 10 = W: 1: 86-87). This amounts to Peirce's truism that the "minds & hearts of two people is a language capable of expressing a meaning which regulates them by value of their ratio" (MS 1105: 10 = W: 1: 87). Language is bound to Peirce's regulative signs, but still is a free intersemiosic exchange of verbal and nonverbal signs. The freedom of the critical discourse presents a close analogy with music.

Peirce meant the term "prayer" embodied in the emotional extremes involved in religious hymns, as showing expressive language in an extended or metaphorical way. This event meant more than pure musical expression in firstness, but refers to real (or realizable) meaning, including changeable elements in time and space across our emotional, daily and religious lives. This symbiosis of inward and outward paradoxes determines the source and force of Peirce's habituality in the interlingual translation embodied in the wholeness of hymnal poetry. All languages include breath and depth of human meaning, according to "the mode of expression between man and man" (MS 1105: 10 = W: 1: 86). Peirce stated that language means the simultaneously use of all expressive languages, verbal and nonverbal language: "with a variable character, at one moment appearing before the mind's eye," while "this Language consists of gestures or speech or music or what" (MS 1105: 10 = W: 1: 86). Peirce wrote on this subject in the same manuscript that "Language is an abstraction not only capable of realization, but combined (in a way of which we shall think directly) with other abstractions [to give them] realizability" and he enumerated the accompanying "languages," meaning (the mentioned) "[g]eometrical figures, letters, conversation, music are such languages" (MS 1105: 4). In this mixed sense, a spiritual song is a musically extended prayer and becomes in itself an intersemiotic translation, as discussed above, with its free and improvized translations from one "language" into another.

If the paraphrases and translations work as self-contained dreams, ecstasies, and other signs of firstness, Peirce's prayer becomes in the beginning an "inexpressive silence of soul" (MS 1105: 11). Hymns govern pure unthought meaning (firstness) of the particular prayerful utterance both in tune and in lyrics, but to work properly and functionally and have a noticeable meaning beyond the *"null* form" (W: 1: 85, Peirce's emphasis) of pure firstness, they need to function upward in the social and psychological reality of seconds and thirds "with all forms of service, speech, or thought" (W: 1: 87). Hereby Peirce meant the outward expression of an intertextual or extratextual context — realized in Peircean ego, ratio, ritual (W: 1: 85, 87). This force from inward firstness to outward secondness and thirdness affects the opinion on the authenticity of interpreting and singing hymns as an individual singer, as singing hymns in chorus, as participating in the worship, and as the organist accompanying hymn singing: all with the purpose to remedy the ordinary "human character with all constitutional frailties, thus becoming a mere mechanism" (W: 1: 87) of individual mastery and unmastery of the human act of singing. Through taking part in actual religious fellowship, the singer and interpreter becomes an acting spiritual sign, that is a semiotic sign, capable of semiosis or dynamic sign-action.

Firstness lacks real expression, it is a potential sign coming up from a lonely dream and giving an unreal (but still aesthetic) sense (see Meyer 1956: 266 ff). Firstness offers inwardized signs which are represented in feelings. See the receptive feeling shown in musement to give "body" to the dreams we "hear" during listening and hearing musical melodies. Music gives this enchantment of the listener's heart, but the emotion is personal firstness and can not be publicized. We sing and listen dedicating the melodies to our dreams, emotional images and mental representations, considering them beautiful, ugly or intermediate. Jourdain in his *Music, the Brain, and Ecstasy* (1997) stated that

> … most compositions lack a specific, agreed-upon reference to the contents of the world. But when we bring our own life situations to music, we can make what we will. Music idealizes emotions negative and positive alike. By so doing, it momentarily prefects our individual emotional lives. The "meaning" we feel is not the music as such, but in our own responses to the world, responses that we carry about with us always. Music serves to prefect those responses, to make them beautiful. By so doing, music imparts dignity to experience that often is far from dignified. And by imparting pleasure even to negative emotions, music serves to justify sufferings large and small, assuring us that it has not all been for nothing. (1997: 322)

"Meaning" of poetry of hymns starts not with "ego," but starts with "ratio" and "ritual" (W: 1: 85, 87), being together in a conscious and voluntary relation building on firstness toward secondness and thirdness. The music of hymns can therefore be melodious or flat, slow or quick, intense or weak, smooth or disjunct, continous or interrupted, baroque or rocky, etc. and their intermediate or mixed values can be otherwise. This is firstness with an element of secondness and thirdness. The motion of hymn music exists not only in the motion of the melodies, but gets its actual fulfillment with the poetically inspired text, working from secondness and thirdness "back" to the original firstness. The pleasure and pain of human existence and the praises to God are reflected in declaiming/singing the accessible poetry of hymns which depict the emotional and social backgrounds: from the personal story we reach the history of the fellowship: from an ill child to the advent of

Christmas, from a summer holiday to a baptism, from a personal welcome to the harvest-time. In the signs of secondness (and on the way to thirdness), the generality of textual motion is placed, including the positive and negative miseries of ordinary life. Secondness and firstness are a symbiosis of coordination and incoordination. In Peirce's semiotics a devoted normality (firstness) becomes through (in)coordination and particularization a collective focus of conformity (secondness and thirdness) (W: 1: 90) (see Esposito 1980: 239).

Tune and text are therefore a "fading process" (MS 1105: 5), a rudimentary and abstracted conformity or friendship with a "Manifold of Sense" (MS 1105: 11, W. 1: 88). The tune blends in the text, offering the opportunity of personal and collective meanings, generated up and down: from singer to chorus and from chorus to singer, as well as from individual to congregation and from congregation to individual, and hopefully from the singers to God. The "fading process" happens concretely in the downgraded firstness function of second and third language, which usually follows the normative rules of the grammatical structures, but now is not guided by its own instinctual rules of association. As Peirce stated on firstness and secondness:

> The mention of dreams suggests another argument. A dream, as far as its own content goes, is exactly like an actual experience. It is mistaken for one. And yet all the world believes that dreams are determined, according to the laws of associations of ideas, etc., by previous cognitions. If it be said that the faculty of intuitively recognizing intuitions is asleep, I reply that this is a mere supposition, without other support. Besides, even when we wake up, we do not find that the dream differed from reality, except by certain marks, darkness and fragmentariness. Not unfrequently, a dream is so vivid that the memory of it is mistaken for the memory of an actual occurrence. (CP: 5.218)

Language becomes in its use and abuse (as a sign of firstness, some secondness and thirdness) easily oversystematized and manipulated, in order to force the similarities and differences in the combination of language and music. Eco's "blowing up" and "narcotizing" of verbal and musical qualities co-occurs: "Semantic disclosures have a double role: they *blow up* certain properties (making them textually relevant or pertinent) and *narcotize* some others" (1979: 23, Eco's emphasis).[35] This means that not all verbal words or musical concepts are relevant to the particular influence of a text, they could be unfeatured and unmarked, be no actual part of the verbomusical text and only be virtually present for later interpretation and singing; some properties are marked and crucial, they are the actual qualities relevant for interpretation and performance. Within Peirce's "fading process," the focus of sacred lyrics adapts to the firstness of music without details on time and place. Here, language gives only musical emotion, moving away from rules for "regulation" (W: 1: 86), that is Peirce's secondness and thirdness. In the paraphrases and translations of hymns, we grasp a paradoxical situation of language: a translation of hymns occurs basically on the primary level of meaningless firstness, while the meaningful necessities of secondness and thirdness are considered as "unthinkable" fragments, downgraded to their own emotional moods to match everyone's musical dreams in firstness. In hymn-singing, there is no need for "regulation," no habits peculiar to time and place, all kinds of anachronisms are accepted, foreign languages are admitted, speculative and non- normative grammar is even accepted. To escape the influence of vague incompleteness of the religious feeling of subjectivism, hymns are sung by the voices of the congregation going from private devotion to public worship. The translators of hymn poetry focus on the concentration on prayerful language for the membership for all believers, regardless of their genes and social backgrounds. What is repeated — and repeated and repeated — in the singing of the hymns is the pure demonstrative application of the musical and textual religious clichés of the musicoverbal signs in our own, bodily native and familiar mother-tongue (CP: 5.219), speaking to us as the emotive meaning of a mother: beautiful, inwardized and simple.[36]

Heart-to-heart communication in the act of outward singing is intertwined by the melody. Their living combination goes upward and downward. Now the combination is reduced from meaningful mechanism to meaningless mediation, developing from quality and relation towards mediation. Consider the upgraded and at the same time downgraded qualifications in Peirce's categoriology: dream, desire, purpose (CP: 7.369, 5.175) — as well as sensibility, motion, growth (MS 920), flavor, reaction, mediation (MS L75 and NEM: 4: 18). In the experience from regulation to unfolding of regulation, we encounter two streams of cognition "one emerging out of the particularity of experience (feeling) under the governance of the categories, and the other subjecting previous experience to iconic and rhematic analyses (generality)" (Esposito 1980: 161). This degenerative and regenerative mediation happens (as always in Peirce's semiotics) without the emphasis of an "active" mediator, here the hymn writer or vocal translator, who "dynamically," meaning impersonally and intensively, seeks and discovers — Peirce said "suffers and resists" (CP: 1.358) — the vitality of secondness in an attempt to reach a degenerative insight of thirdness: "Only through this 'living' meditation … could the categories have metaphysical application" (Esposito 1980: 162). Peirce wrote that the interpretation process (and thus the singing and translation process) "consists, psychologically, in catching one of the transient elements of thought upon the wing and converting it into one of the resting places of the mind" (CP: 3.424). Expressive musical language performed by the congregation is body-oriented firstness, pushing upward to the final stage of the generality of thirdness.

In paraphrased and translated hymns the melody and the native tongue must retain a rudimentary, abstracted notion of the categorial application, and follow the degrees of actual degeneracy. The sign-structure of taking a degenerate and regenerative forms in any language to express the notions of mind, matter and God between the acceptable extremes of simplicity (the incomplex) and complexity. Translating the lyrics is semiotically an aesthetic experience (firstness) which includes cumulative attention (secondness) and consummatory exploration (thirdness). The expression of the thirdness of translating verbal thought-signs according to memory, intelligence, inference, formality, etc. is exchanged with the degenerate paraphrasing of verbal and musical images. To avoid sacrifices in categorial form, content and understanding, some relations are considered real (predicates of firstness and some in secondness), other are also considered rational (predicates of thirdness). We see this is in the unanalyzable, the inexplicable, and the unintellectual mediations together, sharing the feeling of the common fate accompanied by mutuality, sharing the same pleasure, hardship and misery in life.

The "regulation" of unaffected elements — such as sylllables in language as well as scales and rhythms in music (W: 1: 87) — turns the mind to the direction of "the absolute ... [and] to the factitious" (W: 1: 87), generalized elements which are "under physical and physiological control" (W: 1: 88), instead of turning away to the real force where the "inarticulate result" (W: 1: 88) lies, which is primarily represented in undeveloped "logic" (Peirce's firstness). This deviation from purely logical assertions to degenerate logic of a weaker truth is what Peirce called the "diflection" (MS 1105: 87, W: 1: 87-88). Applying this to the paraphrases and translation of hymns, this categorial degeneracy gives the translation of hymns an emotional focus, away from the possibility of rational thought: "On account of the machinery of language we must be content to express ourselves with what terseness and strength the language. ... Scales and times limit us as to melodies" (W: 1: 88-89). Firstness concentrates on the emotional qualities of tonal material, such as chromatism and keys, characteristic of harmonic temperament, not in scales and techniques of *solfeggio*; on cadence, rhythm, enjambment and tempo, not on irregular verbs and phonetic errors; on breathing, vibration, sonority, not on vocal disenfranchisement (Bell 2000: 95 ff.).

The interpretants of hymnal interpretants — including (re)paraphrases and (re)translations — offer not only an emotional interpretant, but also degrees of energetic and logical interpretants, all of them (wo)man-made, fallible, and fugitive interpreted signs. For the experience of the singers, the revelation creates emotional interpretants and degenerate energetic and logical interpretants, dealing in absolutes. Esposito states that, semiotically, "The reference to object can be found in *attention*; reference to ground, in *feeling*; and reference to interpretant, in some future experience which recounts in some fashion an experience of the past, in *thought*" (1980: 102, Esposito's emphasis), extending his argument from (Jakobson's) twofold to (Peircean) threefold turning of the object:

> Man, then, is an evolving semiotic system with a twofold complementarity as both symbolizing and symbolized. Thus it is more correct to say that persons are in symbols as their species than that symbols are in them. We are not "shut up in a box of flesh and blood," but instead have an "outreaching spirituality" (CP: 7.591), which we experience in communication with others. When someone else reflects upon what I think and express to him, he does not only take what is mine into himself; my soul itself becomes extended into his as well. Each soul is a combination of novelty and convention, just as in the earlier writings expression was seen as meaning. Something utterly novel could not be expressed, while something utterly conventional requires no expression. (CP: 7.592). (Esposito 1980: 102)

But do man and woman have a personal soul, a symbol in Peirce's sense — a raising to God (CP: 7.572)? A melody, a song without words is basically an expression of feeling and emotion; a hymns with words adds rational thought which is downgraded for the singer and vocal translator whose "specific and individual soul is but a shadow" (CP: 7.594). A translated hymn explores our nervous impressionability as vocal translators with rhythms, sounds, words, resonances and vocalizations. The invisible and impersonal translations of hymns follow Peirce's deflection: flexing away through a bend or turn from the word with its own agreed-on meaning, through a deviation (Latin *deflexio*) upside down and downside up. This deflected analogy happens in translations into all human tongues and give an equivalent experience. The translation brings the languages together in a complementation: "normality + formality → diflection" (Esposito 1980: 58). A diflection in a word/tune plurality is a plural act to "transflect" (Esposito 1980: 239), that is to transfigure a fugitive sensation into a stable new medium. A "faded" hymn "regulating a language" into melody (Esposito 1980: 60) becomes in itself a revelation in the invisible world. This happens in three ways:

1. in the world of time: *arbitrariness*
2. in the world of space: *dependence*
3. in the celestial world: *absoluteness* (Esposito 1980: 62, his emphasis)

When singers (and other listeners, such as hymn translators) get rid of our habits — the time and space continuum that carry out our visible life and thoughts. Sensation must contain the second form of invisible revelation, when we get rid of our temporal-spatial customs and neglect the dependence and spatiality determining our *"this-here"* and we relate to the *"what"* (Esposito 1980: 62, Esposito's emphasis). This oblivion of memories and freeing of rules create the possibility of a creative activity: a semiotic hymn which takes our breath away.

Iconic Imagery In Examples

Let us consider some practical examples (in chronological order) in order to inspect some details of the discussed changes in the process of the "singing of a hymn, the hymn a stanza, the stanza a line (or phrase), the line a word, the word a sound, and the sound is sung by a composite of articulatory movements" (Pike 1967: 78) as crucial elements in a church service (for methodology of examples in vocal translation, see Gorlée 2002). Starting with the Protestant Reformation, 37 German religious hymns were written by Martin Luther himself, all of them new "human" hymns and *Umdichtungen* (Albrecht 1973: 14 ff.), that means paraphrases and translations in the High German language. Luther's *"Ein feste Burg ist unser Gott"* is not new, it has been interlingually (grammar) and intersemiotically (visual imagery) borrowed. Luther's own translated text comes originally from Psalm 46, freely mixed with other biblical texts such as Ephesians 6: 10-19 and Revelation 12: 9-12. Luther first translated the Psalms as part of his new German Bible, using different manuscript versions and changed drafts with corrections, deletions, and additions, written in red and black ink. The "official" rendering of this first-draft and second-draft of Luther's interlingual translation was transmogrified by Luther into a singable hymn, set to a church tune.

The later English translation of the scholars of King James Authorized Bible (1611) were aided in their efforts by Luther's German Bible translation, his fragment of the Psalms, as well as the musical hymn. *"Ein feste Burg ist unser Gott"* has been literally and freely paraphrased into different versions in many languages. In the English language we have: "A Safe Stronghold our God is Still" translated by Thomas Carlyle (1795-1881), "A Mighty Fortress Is Our God" translated by Frederick H. Hedge (1805-1890) (*The Hymnal* nr. 26) and "A Fortress Sure is God Our King" translated in turn by Godfrey Thring (1823-1903) (*The Church Hymnary* 1996: 366-367). *"Ein feste Burg ist unser Gott,"* once called by Heinrich Heine (1797-1856) the "Marseillaise" hymn (Washburn 1938: 19) and now no longer in fashion, had an adventure in interpretation and translation (Spitta 1905 and Brecht 1979).

In his day, Luther, the Bible translator, studied his own translated Latin Psalm 46, creatively based on the first, Greek (Hellenic) *Septuagint* Bible (ca. 250-175) and its translation into Saint Jerome's Latin *Vulgate* (ca. 400), which were already (re)translations, now in turn freely interpreted in the "vulgar" tongue, extending the cultural and theological boundaries of the early High German language (see Schmidt 1926 for a detailed source-oriented approach). For a target-oriented approach, which was Luther's purpose, he structured to build his artistic hymn *"Ein feste Burg ist unser Gott,"* new German grammatical and phonological elements with suitable rhyme and harmony in order to make the hymn singable. He aimed to create an easily understandable tune and text with "movements of the tongue, lips, jaw, etc. (which lead to the vocal noises, organized into movements producing syllables, stress groups, etc.; the accompanying movements of the organist and song leader" and considered it not an "abstract" but a "concrete" variant for the physical action and behavior of the hymn-singing activity (Pike 1967: 89). Luther, as an language and vocal analist of his day, was supposed to "ask his informants for the emaning of the words, and utilized this evidence," yet "he must do so with caution because speakers of the language may be misinformed on technical vocabulary outside their experience ... ; or they may merely be unable to express in words the meanings and purposes to which they react; or they may be deliberately deceptive" (Pike 1967: 90). Luther was steeped in Gregorian and medieval chants, old German folksongs, morality stories, children's religious pageants and the mystery plays. He used part of this verbomusical "direct material" in his popularized church modes, sung in church by the congregation, independently from the musically trained clerics.

The testimony of the Scripture was freely interpreted by Luther (according to Nida's dynamical equivalence). *"Ein feste Burg ist unser Gott"* (composed in the period 1527-1528 and included in the German Psalter of 1529) guarantees his own creative abilities as poet and hymnist (Brecht 1979: 106). Luther's hymn is to a prominent degree a fictive poetics created into text-and-music, and does not vouch for the fidelity of the biblical text of Psalm 46 *"Deus noster refugium et virtus"* from the *Vulgate* into the Lutherian tuned version:

1. Ein feste Burg ist unser Gott.
ein gute Wehr und Waffen.
Er hilft uns frei aus aller Not,
die uns jeßt hat betraffen.
Der alt böse Feind
mit Ernst ers jeßt meint,
groß Macht und viel List
sein graußam Rüstung ist,
Auf Erd ist nicht seins Gleichen.

2. Mit unsrer Macht ist nichts getan,
wie sind gar bald verloren.
Es streit für uns der rechte Mann,
den Gott hat selbst erkoren.
Fragst du, wer der ist?
Er heißt Jesus Christ,
der Herr Zebaoth
und ist kein andrer Gott.
Das Feld muß er behalten.

3. Und wenn die Welt voll Teufel wär
und wollt uns gar verschlingen,
so fürchten wir uns nicht zu sehr,
es soll uns doch gelingen.
Der Fürst dieser Welt,
wie saur er sich stellt,
tut er uns doch nicht,
das macht, er ist gericht.
Ein Wörtlein kann ihn fällen.

4. Das Wort sie sollen lassen stan
und kein Dank dazu haben.
Er ist bei uns wohl auf dem Plan
mit seinem Geist und Gaben.
Nehmen sie den Leib,
Gut, Ehr, Kind und Weib,
laß fahren dahin,
sie habens kein Gewinn.
Das Reich muß uns doch bleiben. (Luther n.d.: 40, spelling after Spitta 1905: 88-89)

As a translator, Luther was both a poetic creator and a critic (see chapter "Martin Luther: Artisan of the German Language" in Delisle and Woodsworth 1995: 45-50). Bluhm (1965) called Luther a "creative translator," a verbomusical adapter to previous religious tunes and texts, opening up new horizons with the activity of singing and praying Psalms as inter-faith dialogue, and preparing the way for the "mighty music of the myriad-minded J.S. Bach, who not only reflected the growth of Christian music for almost a thousand years, but represented in many aspects its climax" (Wibberley 1934: 115). In the interlingual translations, we focus not on the development of the unchanged musicality of the tune but on the changes in the texts of the hymn.

In Luther's view, the Bible provides reliance on reason through faith. The singing of the hymns is an early product of mass media, where hymns belong according to Luther's force of communal belief. As discussed above, the singing of hyms is a regenerative mediation, serving unregenerate faith (Peirce called it degenerate) on its way towards logical ungenerate reason (Gerrish 1967: 5: 110-111). In Luther's view, man acts voluntarily to rise from him- or herself towards the level of godliness. The ecstasy of the song, as explained by Luther, is Peirce's musement in order to achieve salvation. The formal structure is the material images of faith, included in sermons, epistolary form, confessions, caricatures, fables, monolog and dialog, claim and reclaim in order to be born anew. Luther's spiritual revival is made visible through the employed poetic images in the pseudo-biblical songs, borrowed by from classical and medieval concepts (Brecht 1990: 36). The moralizing and apocalyptic image-symbols à la Hieronymus Bosch (ca. 1450-1516) were allegories on symbolic animals, concepts of nature, images of the devil and angels, hagiographies, and other symbolisms applied by Luther and his associates (Brecht 1990: *passim*). By the late Middle Ages, at the dawn of the Renaissance, the widespread fear of evil spirits is transformed into a painful searching of conscience, not only in the devout but even in more critically-minded doubters. This introspection, "touching on the heart of medieval piety, the sacramental system" (Gerrish 1967: 5: 109), we find in Luther's radical view of the "mass" publics, the communion of the laity as a continuous flux and reflux of messages of self-salvation through the Bible. In Luther's day, the singing of hymns is a transient flow of words and images to reach Heaven from Earth, and to elevate nature to a supernatural level.

In Psalm 46 the imagery sees God as an eternal rock against the stormy waves of crises of world history and troubles in human events. The artistic vision in the original Psalm, concentrates on the catastrophes survived in Israel: "The psalmist sees the peoples and circumstances round Israel in foaming foment, bringing change and decay, and in the midst of this turmoil he beholds Israel in secure, serene peace, exalted high above all these upheavals. Both the turmoil round about and Israel's peaceful calm are the work of God" (Hirsch 1997: 330). The stormy floods of events guides one quiet stream, led and guided by God. The word "rock" has in Hebrew and Latin many words and slightly different meanings (Sechrist 1981: 263). In the text of the Bible, numerous variants of "rock" include metaphors such as "fortress," "tower," "citadel," "refuge," "stronghold," "strength," "protection," "trust," "might" (Sechrist 1981: 112, 326, 54, 250-251, 307-308, 241, 330, 193). The lexicon is used poetically in the sung versions, giving different kinds of vocalic stress, vocalic-consonantal change, exchanges in quantity, stress, and pitch of the singing lines. The melodic variants provide, in different ways expressed in the action of singing (not reading) the text, a different "common meaning" of a defence or power against falsities and troubles. These meanings are derived from the literal sense of the Bible, memory-knowledge and from personal belief adapted from Peirce's thirdness, secondness and firstness, as explained. In different languages, this literal and dynamic sense (in Nida's terminology) happens according to the restraints of language and culture with the aim of governing Luther's moral and situational revival according to the interactive levels of Peirce's categories. The creative interpretation clearly shows "how important the *herz* (heart) was for Luther … [T]houghts, feelings and words were inseparable, and were all located in the heart, which was also the seat of faith" (Delisle and Woordworth 1995: 49, their emphasis). Although the common knowledge was the terror of being caught in the snare and the help given by God as Most High, Luther transposed the dangers of the forces of nature into a Christian struggle between evil and false in a military sense. We sing the warlike terms to show that we are warriors strong in personal faith. The images in the hymnical versions give different meanings; the singing from the heart (firstness) is not only a stylistic and singing experience (secondness) but also a theological experiment (thirdness).

This martial imagery is repeated in Luther's "*Ein feste Burg ist unser Gott.*" The experiment differs from the psalmic and other biblical texts in that Luther's poetic interpretation portrays visual images belonging to a Christ-centered salvation-history: the lost man (*der rechte Mann*) escapes the devil (*der alt böse Feind*) and is saved through the good works of God. The Emanuel motif is important in the well-known title and the first stanza (and perhaps in the fourth stanza) (Brecht 1979: 109-110). "God is with us" is embodied in the predominant metaphor of the "safe rock" (*feste Burg*) and its military parasynonyms (*Wehr und Waffen, Macht, grausam Rüstung*), as mentioned before. The second stanza is on Christ's interpretation of divine and human *(er heißt Jesus Christus)* (Brecht 1979: 110-114). God made man in order to save the world; yet man is lost through troubles. The third stanza is on Satan, the evil king of the world (*Fürst dieser Welt*) (Brecht 1979: 114-117). The remedy is obeying the word of God (or Christ) (*Wörtlein*). The last stanza repeats the divine word *(Wort)* and paves Christ's merciful way (*Geist und Gaben*) without the spirit of evil , who destroys our whole spiritual body (*Leib, Gut, Ehr, Kind und Weib*) for a better future (Brecht 1979: 118-120, Spitta 1905: 117-123).

A Safe Stronghold Our God is Still
(Translator: Thomas Carlyle 1795-1881)

A safe stronghold our God is still,
A trusty shield and weapon;
He'll help us clear from all the ill
That hath us now o'vertaken.
The ancient prince of hell
Hath risen with purpose fell;
Strong mail of craft and power
He weareth in this hour;
On earth is not his fellow.

With force of arms we nothing can,
Full soon were we down-ridden;
But for us fights the proper Man,
Whom God himself hath bidden.
Ask ye who is this same?
Christ Jesus is his Name,
The Lord Sabaoth's Son;
He, and no other one,
Shall conquer in the battle.

And were this world all devils o'ver,
And watching to devour us,
We lay it not to heart so sore;
Not they can overpower us.
And let the prince of ill
Look grim as e'ver he will,
He harms us not a whit;
For why his doom is writ;
A word shall quickly slay him.

God's word, for all their craft and force,
One moment will not linger,
But, spite of hell, shall have its course;
'T is written by his finger.
And, though they take our life,
Goods, honour, children, wife,
Yet is their profit small;

These things shall vanish all:
The city of God remaineth. (*The Church Hymnary* 1996: 366)

A Mighty Fortress Is Our God
(Translator: Frederick H. Hedge 1805-1890)

A mighty fortress us our God,
A bulwark never failing;
Our helper He amid the flood
Of mortal ills prevailing.
For still our ancient foe
Doth seek to work us woe
His craft and pow'r are great,
And, armed with cruel hate,
On earth is not his equal.

Did we in our strength confide,
Our striving would be losing,
Were not the right man on our side,
The man of God's choosing.
Dost ask who that may be?
Christ Jesus, it is He.
Lord Sabaoth His name,
From age to age the same,
And he must win the battle.

And though this world, with devils filled,
Should treaten to undo us,
We will not fear, for God hath willed
His truth to triumph through us.
The prince of darkness,
We tremble not for him;
His rage we can endure,
For lo! His doom is sure;
One little world shall fall him.

That world above all earthly powers,
No thanks to them, abideth;
The Spirit and the gifts are ours
Through Him who with us sideth;
Let goods and kindred go,
This mortal life also;
The body they may kill:
God's truth abideth still;
His Kingdom is forever. AMEN. (*The Hymnal* 1955: nr. 91)

A Fortress Sure is God Our King
(Translator: Godfrey Thring 1823-1903)

A Fortress sure is God our King
A shield that ne'ver shall fail us;
His sword alone shall succour bring,
When evil doth assail us.
With craft and cruel hate
Doth Satan lie in wait,
And, armed with deadly power,
Seeks whom he may devour;
On earth where is his equal?

O who shall then our champion be,
Lest we be lost for ever?
One sent by God – from sin 'tis he
The sinner shall deliver;
And dost thou ask his Name?
'Tis Jesus Christ – the same
Of Sabaoth the Lord,
The Everlasting Word;
 'Tis he must win the battle.

God's word remaineth ever sure,
To us his goodness showing;
The Spirit's gifts, of sin the cure,
Each day he is bestowing.
Though naught we love be left,
Of all, e'en life, bereft,
Yet what shall Satan gain?
God's kingdom doth remain,
And shall be ours for ever. (*The Church Hymnary* 1996: 367)

The three interlingual translations are made more or less during the same period (ca. 1840-1860), yet they differ greatly. The verse and stress marks are more or less equal, the rhyme is more or less the same (Gorlée 2002), but what differs is the stance forms (four in Luther and the Carlyle and Hedge translations, but diminished to three stanzas in the later Thring translation) and the modulation and harmony of the voice in the sharing of symbols, in the shape of Peirce's iconic images.

A symbolic icon is, in Peirce's semiotics, called an icon — such as a portrait, a map, a photograph or a caricature. An icon is a image-sign that refers to its object through a resemblance or likeness between the sign and its object. A sculpture resembles the model to a certain degree, a photograph has some similarity to the subject, a map resembles a territory, yet in a different shape and material. An icon provides a direct feeling or immediate meaning of a certain parallellism in form, shape, color, material, or another physical connection. It requires no thought or interpretation in order to work; the likeness is "just there" and the inquirer (reader, listener, etc.) sees the resemblance. Semiotically, the iconic image refers to the level of firstness, a certain mood of feeling between sensory aspects of the sign and what it refers to: "A pure icon can convey no positive or factual information; it affords no assurance that there is any such thing in nature" (CP: 4.447). The iconic feeling is the immediate image felt by the reader or listener to mark some (but not all) characters of the "outward object which excites in consciousness the image itself" (CP: 4.447). The icon looks like a picture-image or replica of the object signified in the appearance of the sign: we use it in logic as a hypothetical state of affairs, but also in everyday "exercises," where we see verbal and non-verbal images in dreams, desires, literature, and publicity (Johansen 1993: 100).

The tempting icons of publicity images tends to provide a traditional, yet tempting and seductive, signhood. Peirce called this iconic sympathy forms of "attractive observation" (CP: 2.227) where we experience a feeling of a recoding of the mythological icons where we, the inquirers now transformed into "Cinderellas, salesgirls, devoted housewives, Jack (of the beanstalk), newspapers boys, tired executives … all feel, at the back of their minds, the nagging dream of the great adventure that culminates in long-lasting and private blissfulness" (Maranda 1972: 17). Maranda adds that our myths are universal emotions governing our "Western" cultures, where "[o]ur myths are made of depilatories, royalty, pets, antiques, political ideologies, religion, hair tonics, cinemactors [sic], scientific theories, cars, etc. — enticing avenues to the Paradise of which, ultimately we refuse to acknowledge the loss;" Maranda adds the history of iconicity: "Long ago, many strong components of our semantic systems were expressed as well as consolidated in the book of Genesis. God and the snake still thrive among us" (1972: 17).

The iconic imagination is seen in all kinds of signs; the hymn singer (including the translator of hymns) "searches his heart, and in doing so makes what I term an abstractive observation. He makes in his imagination a sort of skeleton diagram, or outline sketch, of himself, considers what modification the hypothetical state of things would require to be made in that picture, and then examines it, that is, observes what he has imagined, to see whether the same ardent desire is there to be discerned" (CP: 2.227). In the original and, also remaining, in the English translations of *"Ein feste Burg ist unser Gott,"* there is an iconic mediation in the tone and melodic phrasing of tune and text.

Firstly, the tune sung in *tempo giusto*, which was a proper and solid speed for an early German religious song, and not changed in the fashion of the later translations. The only adornment in Luther's hymn is the regular use of harmonic triads placed on the key words (*Burg, Waffen*, etc. in the first stanza). Yet the timbre jumps from the upward first four rhymed lines downwards eight tones, a whole octave used for the following four rhymed lines, with an area of meaning that the words of God are turned down toward the Devil. The last line rhymes or half-rhymes with a previous rhyme, presenting in turn this double tonality up-down signifying the repetition of this "magic of analogy" (Cassirer 1946: 92). The last line suggests in its implied harmony that God is a being thought as being up in heaven while the devil sunks down into the earth. The respective icons are spatialized in different sections of the first stanza in order to show within these musical metaphors the different phases and stages of human life (Johansen 1993: 101ff.).

Secondly, the iconic lyrics of *"Ein feste Burg ist unser Gott"* speak of a metaphorical link between language and myth. God as "rock," the "root metaphor" (Cassirer 1946: 85) breaks away in the translations. In the first stanza, see the "radical metaphors" (Cassirer 1946: 87) of Carlyle's first translation "A safe stronghold our god is still, A trusty shield and weapon," "Hedge's second translation "A mighty fortress us our God, A bulwark never failing" and Thring's third translation "A Fortress sure is God our King, A shield that ne'ver shall fail us." The poetic metaphors serve not only as phonetic homonyms with different stress and rhyme, but they also enforce a dramatic impact of the military icons used in their translations. The same force of transforming the root metaphor, we see in Luther's description of *"der alte böse Feind"* characterized literally by Carlyle as "the ancient prince of hell" and by Hedge as "our ancient foe" yet explicitly named by Thring as the evil opponent of God, Satan, in the company of his devilish insignia. The homonymity was not only a metaphor "before"or "after" Luther and the previous translations, but is supposed to direct the way for an "intensification" of the mythic fantasy of the formulations (Cassirer 1946: 88-89) toward interpretations (and translations) in the future. The growth of God and the devil "begins with some individual, single perception, which we expand, and carry beyond its original bounds, by viewing it in more and more relationships. The intellectual process here is involved is one of *synthetic supplementation*, the combination of the single instance with the totality" (Cassirer 1946: 89, his emphasis). Cassirer continued: "Here one is reminded forcefully of the principle which might be called the basic principle of verbal as well as mythic metaphor – the principle of the *pars pro toto*. Whoever has brought any part of the whole into his power has thereby acquired power, in the magical sense, over the whole himself. (Cassirer 1946: 92, Cassirer's emphasis). The same mythic animation is also "accorded to *images*, to every kind of artistic representation. Especially in the magical realm, world magic is everywhere accompanied by picture magic" (Cassirer 1946: 98, his emphasis). The translators formulate their own variety of the images (Peirce's icons) in a different mythico-magical form.

The myth-making union of the "heart and the tongue" (Cassirer 1946: 46) of the translators has created different English translations of the paraphrased and translated *Ur*-hymn, "*Ein feste Burg ist unser Gott.*" The spatialized iconic imagination has hardly changed in time, unless Thring's efforts to reduce the hymn and make it terminologically more dense or compact. The wear and tear of this hymn has become a fossilized sign, almost a non-sign; except the first stanza which today is still vital. "When a translation loses vitality, when it becomes obscure, impenetrable, we replace it with a newer one; that is, whereas the original text is treated as valuable, translations are a disposable item" (Stavans 1995: 33). This is particularly true in mass culture, where religious hymns have a strong standing based on Luther's force of communal belief.

The next example is "As the deer longs" (*Common Ground* nr. 10) on the fervor of the desire to be next to God, away from displeasure and towards the divine pleasure. "As the deer longs" has a built-in iconic metaphor of the hunted deer, once an allegorical image (Jung 1964: 29) but transposed into a sung prayer, in a completely modern poetic hymn sung in many languages. This hymn arises first and foremost from a translated re-arrangement of the original text of *Psalm* 42: 1-5 and 8-11; see the lyrics in the *Authorized Version* (1611) starting as follows:

> As the hart pantheth after the water brooks:
>   so pantheth my soul after thee, O God.
> My soul thirsteth for God, for the living God:
>   when shall I come and appear before God?
> My tears have been my meat day and night:
>   while they continually say unto me where is thy God?

This biblical text is still used unchanged in *The Church Hymnary* (1973: 204) and for a singable lyrics the terminology looks antiquated and curious. The word "hart" (see also the related word "hartebeest") means a male deer looking for a stream. In later Bible translations the first verse is more understandable, saying "As a hind longs for the running streams, so I long for thee, O God" (*The New English Bible* 1970: 420). The use of "deer" gives instead a more familiar expression, later used in the versions of the hymn. Other old-fashioned verbal terms such as "panteth," coming from the old verb "to pant," have later disappeared to make way for more intelligible words for a less instructed native speaker of English, such as makes up the general audience of the singers. Archaic forms take into account images of psalm-versions to read and to recite, not to sing: "Like as the hart desireth the water-brooks; so longeth my soul after thee. My soul is athirst for God, yea, even for the living God: When shall I come to appear before the presence of God," composed by Miles Coverdale in the first half of the 16th Century (Davie 1996: 7). Later paraphrases have changed the tune (from an Appalachian folk melody to various alternative arrangements in different tunes) as well as changing the text, so that the whole hymn has eventually become a completely different song — only understood because of the constant metaphor of the hunted deer.

The American *Hymnbook* (1955: 275) has mentioned the previous arrangement of the tune by Louis Spohr in 1835 and gave a "New Version"of the Elizabethan "Old Version," made by Nahum Tate and Nicholas Brady in 1698 with the following first verses:

> As pants the hart for cooling streams
> When heated in the chase,
> So longs my soul, O God, for Thee,
> And Thy refreshing grace.

This version is drastically abbreviated, leaving out the sentimental images in the *Methodist Hymn-Book* (Davie, ed. 1996: 179). After a couple of modern paraphrases and rearrangements by Bob Hurd (who changed text and tune) and Craig S. Kingsbury (who changed tune), we possess today a modernized English hymn, contrasted with a conventional responsorial setting of the psalmody, where a cantor or a choir sings the repeated refrain of the antiphon:

> As the deer longs for running streams,
> So I long, so I long, so I long for you.

and the congregation "reflectively" (*Common Ground* nr. 10) sings the rest of the song of thirsting for the living image of God in this modernized (and even actualized) paraphrase:

Athirst my soul for you, the God who is my life!
When shall I see, when shall I see,
See the face of God?

Echoes meet as deep is calling unto deep,
over my head, all your mighty waters,
sweeping over me.

Continually the foe delights in taunting me:
'Where is God, where is your God?'
Where, O where are you?

Defend me God, send forth your light and your truth,
They will lead me to your holy mountain,
To your dwelling place.

Then I shall go unto the altar of my God,
Praising you, O my joy and gladness:
I shall praise your name. (*Common Ground* 1998: nr. 10)

Apart from the polarities of the old and new versions — historization and modernization, exotism and naturalization — the translational implications — the attention given to the target-texts and the distancing and oblivion of the source-texts (Gorlée 1997a) have been discussed. We cling to the melodies and phrases of our iconic past, but have inserted new texts and uplifting refrains which feature modern words and a changing rhythm and flow of singing for the singers today.

In the reformed translations into the Dutch language by Louis Bourgeois (1510-1572), the musical leader of the old Genevan hymns, we find the same phenomenon of linguistic changes within different music, yet more drastic modifications concerning the change in languages: "*'t Hijgend hert, der jagt ontkomen, Schreeuwt niet sterker naar het genot Van de frissche waterstroomen Dan mijn ziel verlangt naar God. Ja, mijn ziel dorst naar den Heer: God des levens, ach! Wanneer Zal ik naad'ren voor uw oogen; In uw huis uw' naam verhoogen?*" (1773) (*Het Boek der Psalmen* 1867: 46-47). This old-style Dutch hymn, embellished with 18th Century grammar, orthography and style is later replaced by "*Evenals een moede hinde naar het klare water smacht, schreeuwt mijn ziel om God te vinden, die ik ademloos verwacht. Ja, ik zoek zijn aangezicht, God van leven, God van licht. Wanneer zal ik Hem weer loven, juichend staan in zijn voorhoven*" (*Liedboek voor de kerken* 1973: 71). The new hymn provided a metaphrase of the old hymn, but by consulting the first hymn to draw a comparison, still maintains an ancient tone and old-fashioned style. In terms of details, the second hymn has transmogrified the deer into a female animal; in the first hymn the deer was crying yet in the second one is merely exhausted and weak. At the same time, the last rhyme of the second hymn states an unknown plural *voorhoven* ("courtyards [of God's abode]"), a displacement of place adding new and unnecessary material to fill the verse. We have a new hymn which looks like an old traducement. Interesting is the beginning of the modern Norwegian translation: *"Slik som ein hjort som sprang seg vill, lengtar til frisk og kjølig vatn, tørstar eg støtt til deg, min Gud, treng eg å vita du er nær"* (original Iona text by John L. Bell and Graham Maule 1989, translated into Norwegian by Heidi Strand Harboe 1999) (*Sanger fra Vest* 2000: 28-29). This new Norwegian hymn has turned the deer into a stray or lost animal, turning away from the herd and actually not crying for a lack of water (as Hirsch explicitly mentions in his analysis of this Psalm on the alarm cries of animals in general: the roar of the lion and the braying of the donkey to keep them alive: *The Psalms* 1997: 306). In short, this new interlingual paraphrases of the lyrics in English, as well as the extralingual translations into Dutch and Norwegian, have freed themselves from equivalence with the old Psalms — except for the beautiful metaphor of the deer and his thirst for water.

Despite the adaptations and changes, this metaphor of the hunted deer kept expectations alive and well. The deer imagery is highlighted in all versions, old and new versions of the icon and stays in our heart and mind, haunting our spiritual consciousness. The imaginative meditation — which is Peirce's musement — wrestles on a memory of the self, in search of the inner center of the total psyche — God, the super-soul. In Carl G. Jung's (1875-1961) archetypal theory, the image is helped in his endeavors by the symbolic personification of a helpful animal with support from the trio of Jakobson's translations. The dream of the deer in spiritual thirst, a mythological image was used in Walt Disney's cartoon film (released in 1942) — based on the story of the Hungarian-Viennese writer Felix Santen's (1869-1945) novel translated as *Bambi : A Life in the Woods* ([1928]1982) — and comes unavoidably back to the inner of our hearts. The memories of the animated images of the baby-deer Bambi, growing up in the forest, seem to be revived in "As the deer longs," where the natural cry of the deer, faint with thirst, looking for a solution in the desert, alarms not only the children, but also the adults. The deer metaphor is deeply meaningful, as icon it can give a guidance to the man or woman needing to find his or her way through the wilderness of both his inner and his outer life and our surroundings. The metaphor is — according to a Jungian hypothesis — a meaningful coincidence of saving the soul, penetrating into the inter-relation of psyche and matter. In the hymn "As the deer longs," the original "darkness before the dawn, the final pains of exile before redemption, are here cryptically conveyed, but not so enigmatically as to prevent our perceiving the slow, repetitive build-up to an eschatological conclusion" (Goldstein 1987: 78). A iconic sign of hope.

Continuing on the hymn "Still the Night, is also called "Silent the Night" and "Silent Night! Holy Night!," is an evergreen with a long and popular hymnal tradition. This Christmas song with many revisions, returnings, and retranslation in many languages is no longer based on the Psalms, but is in itself an original "human" song, yet adorned with mythological icons. "*Stille Nacht! Heilige Nacht!*" was written and performed on Christmas Day in 1818 in the Tyrolean village of Obersdorf near Salzburg by the young Catholic priest Joseph Mohr (1792-1848) with music written by the organist of the Obersdorf church, Franz Xaver Gruber (1787-1863). The six stanzas sound as follow:

> *Stille Nacht! Heilige Nacht!*
> *Alles schläft; einsam wacht*
> *Nur das traute heilige Paar.*
> *Holder Knabe' im lockingen Haar,*
> *Schlafe in himmlicher Ruh!*
> *Schlafe in himmlicher Ruh!*
>
> *Stille Nacht! Heilige Nacht!*
> *Gottes Sohn, o wie lacht*
> *Lieb' aus deinem göttlichen Mund,*
> *Da uns schlägt die rettende Stund.'*
> *Jesus, in deiner Geburt!*
> *Jesus, in deiner Geburt!*
>
> *Stille Nacht! Heilige Nacht!*
> *Die der Welt Heil gebracht,*
> *Aus der Himmels goldenen Höhn,*
> *Uns der Gnaden Fülle läßt sehn,*
> *Jesum in Menschengestalt!*
> *Jesum in Menschengestalt!*
>
> *Stille Nacht! Heilige Nacht!*
> *Wo sich heut alle Macht*
> *Väterlicher Liebe ergoß,*
> *Und als Bruder huldvoll imschloß*
> *Jesus die Völker der Welt,*
> *Jesus die Völker der Welt!*
>
> *Stille Nacht! Heilige Nacht!*
> *Lange schon uns bedacht,*
> *Als der Herr von Grimme befreit*
> *In der Väter urgrauer Zeit*

> *Aller Welt Schonung verhieß,*
> *Aller Welt Schonung verhieß!*
>
> *Stille Nacht! Heilige Nacht!*
> *Hirten erst kundgemacht*
> *Durch der Engel Alleluja*
> *Tönt es laut bei ferne und nah:*
> *Jesus der Retter ist da!*
> *Jesus der Retter ist da! (*Thuswaldner 2002: 52-53, *Gotteslob* 1975: 219)

"Stille Nacht! Heilige Nacht!" is a *tyrolienne*, a German folksong on the familiar Christmas text-and-tune changed into the scenery of the Alpine valleys in Austria. The traditional Christmas icon picturing the Virgin Mary from which Christ was born is strangely alternated with pictures of the independence struggle of the Tyrolian peasants against the predominance by Bavaria and its allies, the French. The patriotic rebellion brought fire and fury to the Tyrolian population, a struggle mentioned poetically in a few stanzas of the song. Thanks to the gaining popularity of this Christmas song, the contents moved beyond Austria and became universal — such as is the fate of all hymns. Yet the intimate and pastoral melody treasures the Tyrol-like song, characterized by the quick passing of the singing voice from a low chest voice to a high head voice (*falsetto*), and back again. The traditional yodel singing of the mountainous shepherds with its special jumping rhythm, melody and tempo (accompanied by a primitive *alphorn,* as used by the herdsmen in the Alps used for signalling over long slopes), is in the melody of *"Stille Nacht! Heilige Nacht!"* diminished in a low-key assimilation offering a more "general" song structure (in the original 1815 version accompanied by guitar, and today by the traditional organ).

Yodel is originally a voice alternation while singing meaningless syllables, a regional practice to communicate over great distances from one mountainside to another. The "nonsensical" yodel syllables and sounds are meaningfully embodied in the "new" sounds in *"Alleluja"* further echoed in *"Nacht"* and other rhymes. *"Stille Nacht! Heilige Nacht!"* constitutes therefore a crossroad message with the help of meaningful musical and textual echoes — going from monophonic to polyphonic singing of yodel. The Christmas song mirrors the later dubious transpositions in time and space characterized by conflict and independence, regarding both fiction and fact. At the same time the song safely echoes the formulaic recitation of the original texts: the icon of the manger, the wise men and the animals in the birth of the Little Child in Betlehem. The developments of this German Christmas song are in a romantic vein described in the historical biography *"Stille Nacht! Heilige Nacht! Die Geschichte eines Liedes"* (Thuswaldner 2002), in which the poet

Mohr is described as a Robin Hood hero and the Napoleonic war in the Austrian winter scenery is presented as a special *mise-en-scène* for this popular song.

The crescendos on the intralingual, interlingual and intersemiotic translations of *"Stille Nacht! Heilige Nacht!"* come from the kitschy translations into German and other languages, adhering to rules of historical, sociological and political rules and feelings (Peirce's dynamical habits).[37] The *"Paradebeispiele für Kitsch"* (Thuswaldner 2002: 123-124) composed in Germany and elsewhere, give the familiar object, our Christmas song, transposed with a shift in scale, color, or here the language or spirit into an incongruous new use — but with just enough modifications to keep the resemblance intact. The retexted hymns claim artistic value but are pretentious and tasteless. Pike stated that songs like *"Jingle Bells"* are no real hymn, since they "react consciously and unconsciously to other characteristics" in a church service; and reversely, when the church participants "were to hear *My Hope is Built* used as a theme song of a beer advertisement, [they] would consider both activities sacrilegious" (1967: 83, Pike's emphasis). If we see the parodical translations made in Germany, they eloquently speak not on Christmas, but are, in a manner of speaking, old publicity slogans with a new politics and poetics.

The intralingual translations create a new text, following only the light of power and brotherly love of the stanzas on the independence struggle of Tyrol. The Christmas theme is absent in the new song, which is political and speaks on the rival ideologies they stand for (texts are borrowed from Thuswaldner 2002: 133-143). In 1892, the first stanza of a new proletarian song for a German working-class movement is as follows:

> *Stille Nacht, traurige Nacht,*
> *ringsumher herrscht Geldesmacht,*
> *und man zahlt der Mühe zum Lohn*
> *nach wie vor nur Hungerlohn,*

The translation proper (Jakobson's interlingual translations) into many languages was of course a treasure for the "progressive" devotion as well as a good business for *"Stille Nacht! Heilige Nacht!"* It was easily placed in the American churches:

Silent Night! Holy Night!
(Translator: John F. Young 1820-1895)

Silent night, holy night,
All is calm, all is bright
Round yon Virgin Mother and Child.
Holy Infant so tender and mild,
Sleep in heavenly peace,
Sleep in heavenly peace.

Silent night, holy night,
Shepherds quake at the sight.
Glories stream from heavenly afar,
Heavenly hosts sing alleluia;
Christ the Savior is born!
Christ the Savior is born!

Silent night, holy night,
Son of God, love's pure light.
Radiant beams from Thy holy face,
With the dawn of redeeming grace,
Jesus, Lord, at Thy birth,
Jesus, Lord, at Thy birth. (The Hymnal 1955: nr. 147)

Somewhat later, the continental English translation of "*Stille Nacht! Heilige Nacht!*" was integrated in the vast collection and publication of the traditional carols in England (*Dictionary of Hymnology* 1892: 205 ff.). The English *carolling* with a dancing procession integrates musical and verbal codes with a scenical code in terms of dance, instead of the Methodist hymns where the singers stood to sing. Dancing or "the poetry of motion" was in those days a "wholly secular" activity and "unfit for employment in the ordinary solemnities of Christian worship"(*Dictionary of Hymnology* 1892: 205-206):

Still the Night
(Translator: Stopford Augustus Brooke 1832-1916)

Still the night, holy the night!
Sleeps the world; hid from sight,
Mary and Joseph in stable bare
Watch o'er the Child beloved and fair,
Sleeping in heavenly rest,
Sleeping in heavenly rest.

Still the night, holy the night!
Shepherds first saw the light,
Heard resounding clear and long,
Far and near, the angel-song,

> 'Christ the Redeemer is here!'
> 'Christ the Redeemer is here!'
>
> Still the night, holy the night!
> Son of God, O how bright
> Love is smiling from thy face!
> Strikes for us now the hour of grace,
> Savious, since thou art born!
> Saviour, since thou art born! (*The Church Hymnary* 1973: 155).

The tune is hardly a modernization; it is basically the old melody, singable by the "common people" and their "unsteady holding of notes than to their facility in florid singing"(*Dictionary of Hymnology* 1892: 207). The tune today is characterized as "irregular" and the text is a revision of a revision of a revision (*The Church Hymnary* 1973: 155).

Both "*Silent Night! Holy Night!*"and the later translation "*Still the Night*" are grounded in the traditional Christmas features, with only poetics and no politics involved. Both texts concentrate on the first, sixth, and a mixture of the second and third stanzas of the original Austrian song. The same (sub)division signified that Brooke had Young's translation at his side when he changed and revised it for his own translation. In the first stanza, Mohr's original words highlight the sleeping Child sporting the famous curly hair watched over by the Holy Couple. Young, the American translator, increases the devotion of Mary nursing the Child (yet without his curls), while Brooke is a more literal translator, introducing at Mary's side the child's foster-father by his name, Joseph. In the singing process of the translations, Mary outshone Jesus. In the second stanza, corresponding to the last stanza in Mohr, we have the role of the shepherds hearing the mythological alleluia of a single angel, echoed in the American hymn in a host of singing angels under the glorious star. This plurality is brought back in the later, English translation, again a more literal paraphrase, where we hear only one singing angel, and no alleluia is mentioned. God the Father and the birth of his Son radiate in the last stanza of Young's translation. Brooke repeats a different refrain to end the hymn on the birth of the Saviour, Christ.

The American and the English translations will show how the growth in intensity from one Christmas feature to many is equally multiplied in the proportion of the stress contours. The yodel tune is naturally divided in stressed sentences, with final exclamation points for emphatical singing. The words are up-and-down fragments receiving constant stress in the first component in the singing voice, weakened to a second stress. Young's

English translation has initial [s] rhymes as first stress, weakened into [o] as second stress,the downward stresses integrated into upward final rhymes: [i] and [a] as third and fourth final stresss: [s] in "silent," "sleep," "shepherds," "stream," "Savior," [o] in "holy," "Mother," "hosts," "son of God," "love," "born" and the rhyming final: [i] in "night," "bright," "Child," "sight," "with," "birth," [a] "peace," " heavenly," "alleluia," "face," "grace." The predominance of the stressed compounds of vocals [o], [i], [a] in the company of stressed consonant [s] echoes Mohr's Austrian-German source-text. Brooke's English translation follows the same principle, but seems more reflective. Brooke repeats several times simple words like "sleeps" and "sleeping," and "beloved" and "love" where Young used "tender and mild" and "love is smiling;" he uses "rest" instead of Young's "peace" and "light" instead of "sight," "angel-song" substituting "alleluia."

For an example of a "newer" English hymn, take "Be still my soul," which also has an expanded and enigmatic international history:

> Be still, my soul: the Lord is on thy side;
> Bear patiently the cross of grief or pain;
> Leave to thy God to order and provide;
> In every change he faithful will remain.
> Be still, my soul: thy best, thy heavenly Friend
> Through thorny ways leads to a joyful end.

And so it continues for three more stanzas (*The Church Hymnary* 1973: 592-593). The music is a simple version of a melodic, almost a choral, fragment at the closing scene of Jean Sibelius (1865-1957) symphonic poem *Finlandia* (Op. 26, 1899). After this devout beginning of the first stanza, the funeral hymn "Be still my soul" becomes prudently "political" in the next stanzas on Sibelius's melody:

> Be still, my soul: thy God doth undertake
> To guide the future as he has the past.
> Thy hope, thy confidence let nothing shake;
> All now mysterious hall be bright at last.
> Be still, my soul: the waves and winds still know
> His voice who ruled them while he dwelt below.

Finlandia was actually composed in order to celebrate the Finnish efforts to protest against the oppression and censorship by the Russians. The text is not borrowed from Sibelius' *Tondichtung* (or *Sinfonische Dichtung),* since this means a poem without words; nor, it seems, was the hymn derived from *Finlandia Hymns* (Op. 113 No. 12) elaborated in 1938 by Sibelius himself on the original *Finlandia* set on three textual versions: the religious *"Oi Herra armias, soit päivän koittaa"* revised as *"Oi Herra, annoit uuden päivän koittaa"* written by Wäinö Sola (1883-1961), as well as the patriotic song from 1940 *"Oi Suomi, katso sinun päiväs koittaa,"* the *Finlandia Anthem* written by V[eikko] A[ntero] Koskenniemi (1885-1962) (Op. 26 No. 7) (Dahlström 1987: 72-73). For the genesis of the English hymnal text, it came unexpectedly as an old German text written by Katharina von Schlegel (1697-?): *"Stille, mein Wille; dein Jesus hilft siegen,"* translated into English by Jane Laurie Borthwick (1813-1897). The vocal translation was in turn borrowed or adapted from the psalmodic text "Be still, and know that I am God" (Psalms 46: 10) (*The Hymnbook* 1955: nr. 374, *The Hymnal for Worship & Celebration* 1986: nr. 347). The hymn "Be Still My Soul" is evidently a musicoverbal translationese of Sibelius's tune, composed after Borthwick's death, with different words to match.

Patterns and Signs in Hymn Translation

The change and growth of intralingually interpreted and interlingually translated hymns responds to my concept of semio-translation (or semiotranslation, coined in Gorlée 1994: 226 and further developed in 2004, particularly 99-143):

> Semiotranslation is a unidirectional, future-oriented, cumulative, and irreversible process, a growing network which should not be pictured as a single line emanating from a source text toward a designated target text. Rather, we must conceive of any number of such translational lines radiating in all directions from a starting state to end-states of variable value. Semiotranslation advances, in and by successive instances, toward higher rationality, complexity, coherence, clarity, and deter-mination, while progressively harmonizing chaotic, unorganized, and problematic translations (and elements and/or aspects of translations), as well as neutralizing dubious, misleading, and false ones. By steadily integrating new pieces of information about the object, translations of it make the real meaning of the original ever more complete, detailed, and continuous. Yet informational lacunae will always remain. By this token, a translation is never finished and can always, however mini-mally, be improved upon. The survival of text-signs lies in their being translated and retranslated. A standard translation or "authorized version" is in fact an oxymoron. (Gorlée 2004: 103-104)

Language and religion are no exceptions to this semiotranslational rule. Not only the Bible translations but also the church hymns emerge in expansions through transformations of all kinds — including the divine use of language becoming secular use. The hymnbook is only a written guide; the hymns (that is, its singable material, contents, the praise to God) "float around" in a meaningful act of communication (Schmidt on Luther as vocal translator uses the German verb "*vorschwebt,*" Schmidt 1926: 101). In a semiotic paradigm, equivalence in communication is thus not merely a linguistic affair; it is always connected (Peirce's diflection) with a religious function (public and private, even intimate, myths according to Peirce's three categories) and related to a cultural purpose, where emphasis is placed on the idea of growth through the praise to God. The doctrine of equivalence, a central topic in translation theory, was treated rather cursorily in Peirce's semiosis-directed view with only analogous and semioticized signs (Gorlée 1994, particularly 169 ff.). Peirce seems to have taken the view that sign relations, and all the elements which compose them as well as those "included" in them (such as the translator), are vulnerable to constant change and exchange. Everything is semioticized and nothing is fixed in sign translation: the translating text-sign, the translated text-sign, the linguistic and nonlinguistic codes, the translator, and the translational and general-cultural norms are all subject to continual interaction and change, even if to a minute degree. Outside the text, too, the human "reality" (where the dynamical or real object of language and music is to be found) is also evolving in time and space, as is everything in both lived and imagined reality. If both the world we experience and the world we create are both constantly expanding, then our knowledge of the world in all its manifestations is not only fallible but lags behind, and thus requires continuous criticism, improvement, and correction. This is certainly true for religious language, where the practical examples aim to demonstrate that a translation is always translatable to a certain degree.

Jakobson's trio of translation modes has cultivated in our manifold cultures and subcultures "an essential taste our intellectual life has gotten used to, the seasoning that keeps our cosmopolitan spirit afloat" (Stavans 1995: 33). A hymn is never standardized but arranged and modified to be a speculation on artistic symmetry in a relatively future sense (Peirce's habits). The translation of hymns is a future, target-oriented habituality. The source-text is "naturally" neglected in the singing activity, and remains restricted to a brief mention of names and dates in the margins of the hymnbook. The translator, editor and agent are equally invisible in the chorus. The hymn translator can be a reverend or a poet, man or woman, well-known or unknown, but led "by the same inward activity" (CP: 5.481). The hymn translator is guided by certain motives, such as devotion and readiness. A translated hymn "first arises when upon a strong, but more or less vague, sense of need is superinduced some involuntary experience of a suggestive nature; that being suggestive which has a certain occult relation to the build of the mind" (CP: 5.480). A vocal translator is a muser and his spiritual readiness is what Peirce meant with his doctrine of musement. The muser acts "in a certain way under given circumstances and when actuated by a given motive is a habit; and a deliberate, or self-controlled, habit is precisely a belief" (CP: 5.480). Hymn translators "imagine ourselves in various situations and animated by various motives; and [they] proceed to trace out alternative lines of conduct which the conjectures would leave open to us" (CP: 5.481).

The musement of hymn translators is a spiritual exercise expressed by the "heart and the tongue" (Cassirer 1946: 46), subdivided into three interactive stages: firstness, secondness, and thirdness and reversely thirdness, secondness, and firstness. These categories are followed by the singer(s) (including the translators) kept by Biblical "love and charity" to accompany the life of the force and craft of the congregation with the purpose of reaching Peirce's dialogical community. The categoriology of thirdness, secondness, and firstness comes back to the dark corners of our creative firstness, recycling on the firstness of thirdness. Thirdness is as yet unreachable. Secondness is the human "reality" which is the adventures experienced, in the singing ritual. The images of the muser steadily repeat the heart-felt icons arranged such as the hunted deer, the silent night, the fortress, the spirit of Satan, and other archetypal motifs imprinted as "dreamy" icons in our memory's deepest recesses (Jung 1954). The imagery of the icons consists in the deflected tonality of Peirce's indefinable moods — yet defined as the human role of signs of firstness.

Firstness in hymns diflects "in continuous connection" with the "diverse elements of nature, say by some curious symmetry, or by some union of a tender color with a refined odor" (CP: 6.158), reaching upward to the thirdness of the communication of man/woman with a personal God. Peirce asked himself: "Now, if that be the case, the question arises how it is possible that the existence of this being should ever have been doubted by anybody. The only answer that I can make is the facts that stand before our face and eyes and stare us in the face are far from being, the ones most easily discerned. That has been remarked from time immemorial" (CP: 6.159). Such facts are the imagery integrated in the pictorial and auditory icons. To signal these icons, the singer and the vocal translator "can stare stupidly at phenomena: but in the absence of imagination they will not connect themselves in any rational way" (CP: 1.45). Through attention, effort and love, these phenomena get arranged in some order to publicize the miracle — to become the act of worship. The act of worship works to rebind the pictorial icons to the singer's family and heritage, bringing light and shadow to the inner center of the self. This extended self concerns Peirce's belief in "individual, substance, organism, and mind" (Colapietro 1989: 80). An interpreted and translated hymn is both a relative and equivocal fracture and a pliable and meaningful fragment — for all its translators, singers and other practitioners, an eternal and incomplete process of revision of the real experiment.

Notes

[1] See further the biography of Saint Paul (Grant 2000).

[2] For secondary literature on Ephesians 5: 18-19, see Klein (1996: 164, 165, 168).

[3] The (German) works on semiotic approaches to Peircean theology are discussed in Vetter (2002). The subject of divine songs is not mentioned there.

[4] "Expressive identification of word" is defined by Popovič as an "[a]scertainment of the general value of a word by means of a stylistic and semantic interpretation within the framework of the expressive system. The stylistic value is ascertained empirically and theoretically at the same time" while in general , the expressive words psalms and hymns and spiritual songs "obtain its stylistic affiliation only on an intuitive basis" (Popovič c. 1975: 7). The intuitive basis is discussed later in this article on Peirce's "musement."

[5] For a modern survey of the historical development of hymnody and psalmody, see *The New Grove* (2001), especially Hymn vol. 12: 17- 36, Psalm vol. 20: 449-471, with an extensive bibliography.

[6] See further, Nida (1964) and Barnstone (1993). Nida stated on the divine spirit or inspiration of the translators that: "The inspirational vs. the philological points of view in Bible translation were well defined by the differences between Augustine and Jerome. Augustine, for example, fully accepted the tradition of Aristeas, together with later elaborations, concerning the alleged miraculous translation of the Septuagint by seventy-two men (six from each of the twelve tribes), who, in groups of two and in complete isolation from other translators, translated the entire Old Testament with such divine inspiration and control … St. Augustine recognized that the Greek text of the Septuagint does not always agree with the Hebrew. He explained the differences by saying that the Spirit 'with divine authority could say through the translators something different from what he had said through the original prophets – just as, through these prophets had two meanings in mind, both were inspired by the Spirit … We will conclude, in the case of something in the Hebrew which is missing in the LXX that the Spirit elected to say this by the lips of the original prophets and not by the lips of the translators" (1964: 26).

[7] Hutchinson (1963) is an "early" semioticized treatise on theological and religious language discussing church signals, signs, and symbols. Although no explicit semiotic method is adopted in Hutchinson, it builds implicitly on the semiotic works on mythology and religion discussed in Cassirer's symbolic forms (Hutchinson 1963: 28ff, 117f.). (For "semiotic" procedure, see Gorlée 1994: 16-17 and note 8 and 9.) Hutchinson is not mentioned in Nöth's general chapter on the early references on Christian theology (1990: 381-384); Nöth starts modern semiotic linguistic theology with Güttgemans' developments in German language, taken from the *Interdisziplinäre Zeitschrift für Theologie und Linguistik* (edited by him from 1970), the survey article Güttgemans (1982) and further works: see Güttgemans (1986) on liturgy.

[8] Hutchinson (1963) uses the terms rite and myth differently from later semiotic anthropologists like Claude Lévy-Strauss and Milton Singer. On differences between myth and rite, see Güttgemans (1986: 470-471).

[9] See the American-African body language shown during the group performance of "negro" spirituals as well as, during popular festivals and rock and popular songs. The soloist's and group's rocking and swaying motions sway back and forth with each phrase and the performance almost approaches an erotic dance (Montagu 1971: 137 ff.).

[10] For vocal music, the term man refers to man, woman, and child.

[11] The same circumstance is visible in the use of Hebrew language in songs sung in synagogues outside Israel.

[12] Peirce's and Jakobson's semiotic theories are followed here. Definitions of semiotic terms will follow in this article. For Dutch hymns analyzed from Saussurian assumptions by the principles of binarity polarity, see Speelman (1995, 1995a, 1996). Spitzer questioned the alleged fact that "semiotics and aesthetics pull in opposite directions: semiotics towards determinate signification, aesthetics towards the critique, negation, and overcoming of music's 'language character' ([Theodor] Adorno's phrase) in order to point towards a musical experience that is expressly irreducible to *any* theory, 'semiotic' or otherwise" (2002: 509, Spitzer's emphasis).

[13] See the Presbyterian Church of Scotland with its own hymnody of Scottish-Celtic origin, on which I as a member of that church intend to concentrate in this article. Scottish hymnology has its own history between the 1564 *Psalter* and the 1973 edition of *The Church Hymnary* (Andrews 1993: 421- 423). After a long tradition of singing psalmody, and particularly the old 14th Century sequence "*Dies Irae*" with text in Latin (*Dictionary of Hymnology* 1892: 295-301), the "human hymns" (Andrews 1993: 422 in *Dictionary of Scottish Church History & Theology*) were introduced from the late 18th Century. These hymns are ascribed by the novelist, balladist, and English translator of Goethe, Walter Scott (1771-1832) (Andrews 1993: 422 in *Dictionary of Scottish Church History & Theology*, see also *Dictionary of Hymnology* 1892: 1020) as well as other professional hymnwriters, often ministers themselves. The hymns represent a characteristically 19th Century Romantic fashion. Old Scottish church hymnals include translations of bardic Gaelic songs with evangelical appeal into the English language. Scottish hymnology took part in numerous translations from German and other languages into English (Andrews 1993: 422-425 in *Dictionary of Scottish Church History & Theology*).

[14] Johan Wolfgang von Goethe (1749-1832) was a literary and musical genius in his time. Apart from his supreme dramatic masterpiece *Faust*, he wrote poems that were set to vocal music (see *Der Erlkönig*, and others) and he was a translator. Goethe knew French, English, Italian, Latin, Greek, and Hebrew and translated works by Diderot, Voltaire, Byron, and others. As translation-theoretician Goethe wrote *West-Östlicher Divan* ([1819]1952), introducing Eastern spiritual, religious and nomadic passions into Western literature. To integrate unfamiliar/unknown into familiar/known literature in his days, Goethe introduced three types of literary translation: *informative-prosaic*, like Luther's German Bible; *adaptation*, called a target-oriented parody, far away from the images of the source text; and *reproduction*, a likeness of source and target texts in terms of dialect, rhythm, and figurative language. These three modern types are not semiotic entities, but they deserve semiotic discussion.

[15] Robinson stated this religious use as a "less technical use of the term 'paraphrase'" (1998: 167) which arises from classical rhetorical style and not from modern linguistics. The term paraphrase became popular in the tradition of Chomsky's generative approach as the transformation of syntactic rules from surface sentence as extended paraphrase of the deep sentence with the basic meaning (Harris), as well as in text linguistics (Petöfi, van Dijk). Outside grammar in applied translation studies, semantics includes the information conveyed by the sentence. See Nolan (1970) and Fuchs (1982). In translation studies after Catford, linguistic terms such as *Umkodierung* and *Neukodierung* were used (Willss, Kade and Koller). In Bible translation "paraphrase" was discussed differently, "in the sense of a reworking or translation

90

that proceeds sententially, taking as its criterial segments whole sentences rather than individual words" (Robinson 1998: 166). See Nida's early article "Translation or Paraphrase" (1950), meant to be used by missionary translators into aboriginal languages. Nida (1975: 65) connects the linguistic function of paraphrase to Peirce's interpretants.

[16] "*Beata nobis gaudia*" was written in "the first infancy of Latin hymnody, and before the metres of the old heathen Latin poets had been wholly banished from the Christian service of song, or the rhyming metres, which afterwards became so general and so effective, had been introduced into such compositions, they can scarcely be expected to take very high rank" (*Dictionary of Hymnology* 1892: 522). Before the modern translations, the hymn "*Beata nobis gaudia*" was translated before into English and other languages. See the previous English translations and re-translations: "Again the Circling Seasons Tell" by W.J. Copeland (published in 1848), "Hail the Joyful Day's Return" by R. Campbell (1850), "Blest Joys from Mighty Wonders Wrought" by J.N. Neale (1852), "Round Roll the Weeks our Hearts to Greet" by W.J. Blew (c. 1850), "Joy! Because the Circling Year" by J. Ellerton and F.J.A. Hort (1871), and others (*Dictionary of Hymnology* 1892: 120).

[17] Nida wrote that dynamic equivalence translation is "the closest natural equivalent to the source-language message," while the formal equivalence translation is source-oriented and "is designed to reveal as much as possible of the form and content of the original message" into the translation (1964: 166, 165). Both principles do not exclude each other but are overlapping. See further the semiotic approaches to sacred writings: Nida (1964 and other volumes), Barnstone (1993) and Soukup and Hodgson (eds) (1997, 1999).

[18] On dynamic equivalence translation of poetic psalms into English, see Smalley 1974.

[19] It must be emphasized that *prima facie* appearance, interlinear translation (that is, word-for-word and/or syllable-for-syllable translational activities) is not adequate for the singing translation of musico-verbal songs, sung in actual performance. For singable text and their bibliography on opera and song translation, with examples from Richard Wagner (1813-1883) and Edvard Grieg (1843-1907), see my articles Gorlée 1996, 1997 and 2002.

[20] See Preface of Baughen's *Hymns for Today's Church: Music and Words Edition* (1982).

[21] The three kinds of translation were still rather narrowly defined by Jakobson, who appears unconcerned with the reverse operation, the translation of nonlinguistic into linguistic signs.

[22] Barnstone's statement that "literary translation is concerned with a message containing unrepeatable and indeterminate elements such as expression, connotation, aesthetics, and diction" (1994: 90) is only apparently contradictory to this statement.

[23] According to Short (1998: 99 and 119-120), Jakobson's translation theory was meant, initially, for the translation of denotative thought-signs, and later, also for connotative signs (the relevant years are not mentioned by Short). Short separated interpretation from translation, saying that interpretation can be used to "*describe* a sign's function, which is different from translation, wherein different words that roughly *perform* the same function are substituted for the given words" (1998: 120. Short's emphasis).

[24] Translation studies is almost entirely governed by a dual approach. See the twofold series in translation practice and translation studies, translation process and translation product, translatability and untranslatability, source-oriented and target-oriented translations, faithful and free translations, accuracy and receptibility of translations, presciptive and descriptive translations, linguistic and literary translations, philological and artistic translations, naturalizing and exoticing translations, adapting and alienizing translations; and in scholarship Nida's formal and dynamic equivalence, Levy's illusionism and anti-illusionism, Holmes' serial and structural level, Catford's textual and formal performance, and other theories.

[25] Jakobson began drawing on Peirce's work in the middle of his intellectual career, at a time when his semiotic insights were already largely formulated. Jakobson presented a version of Peirce's thought, availing himself of Peirce to strengthen the case of structuralism. This procedure was possibly in part of the heterogeneous and fragmentary nature of Peirce's collage-

like *Collected Papers* (CP). That Jakobson read Peirce rather selectively, and gave his own interpretation of it than a balanced view is demonstrated, for instance, by his attempts to transpose the binary oppositions to Peircean terms, transmogrifying the latter into "a genuine and bold forerunner of structural semiotics"(Jakobson 1971: 565). See further Shapiro (1998) and Short (1998).

[26] In the Old Testament, God's holy spirit is a principle of dynamic action. The Hebrew female word *ruach* serves to mean spirit, breath, current of air, wind as well as, generally, life, vital principle, mind, and intellect. In the New Testament, the Greek term is a neutral word, *pneuma*, a term translated as wind, air, breath and spirit (Smith 1983: 55). According to the tradition of the Hebrews, the blowing of wind (*ruach*) expresses the nature of divine, and "borrowed" from it, human spirituality. Breath links *ruach* and *pneuma* to the whirlwind of the act of singing. Singing is the vital force animating the human body, spirit to an abstract, disembodied, etherial force. For "etherial" see discussion of Dewey in this article and particularly note 31.

[27] Peirce's I, It and Thou are not coextensive with Freud's triad id, ego and superego

[28] See further Savan's account of the categories (1987-1988: 7-15).

[29] The term hortatory is called evangelical in Christendom.

[30] This is further discussed in Bateson's *A Sacred Unity* (1991) on the phenomena of hypnosis and trance.

[31] Dewey studied logic with Peirce at John Hopkins University. He saw a good deal of Peirce and became a member of the Peirce-directed *Metaphysical Club* in Hopkins (Menand 2001: 272-273, 274-275). Dewey's organic perspective in which the emotional and logical universe opposed the static and fixed dualisms in philosophy and other disciplines, has the nature of the dynamic experience in Peirce's semiosis. The holistic character of Dewey's theory of experience is infused with an evangelical spirit, as also happens in Peirce. Dewey stated that "music, painting, sculpture, architecture, drama and romance were handmaidens of religion, as much as were science and scholarship" (1934: 31). On the differences between Peirce and Dewey, see Menand (2001: 88, 363ff.).

[32] Real meaning (logical habituality) goes beyond the emotional structures of indications of tempo of a musical piece, according to the mood of the listener(s); see the Italian terms *allegretto, prestissimo, andante, accelerando, veloce* as well as "vague" indications such as *con brio, con moto, con passione* (Johansen and Larsen 2002: 136). As discussed in Gorlée (1997: 265), the elements of the music are not static marks, but music synthetizes three dynamic elements: (1) *melody* (subdivided into pitch relationship, upward and downward movement, harmonic patterning and polyphonic structures), (2) *intensity of impulse* (subdivided into getting louder and softer, loudness and softness, stress and emphasis, as well as attack and release), and the discussed (3) *rhythm* (subdivided into: tempo, repetiviness, speeding up and speeding down, and phrasing) (Ostwald 1973). The elements are changeable through the moods and fashions in time and space. The harmony, tempo, rhythm, timbre, and intensity of music is in turn influenced and diverged by the different elements of the meaning of vocalized verbal language: stress, rhyme, rhythm, as well as tempo marks, meter and stanza forms and melodic phrasing of the voice. These mixed phenomena occur in translations and paraphrases.

[33] Dewey's etherial things are borrowed from Romantic mystery poetry of John Keats (1795-1821): "The Sun, the Moon, the Earth and its contents, are material to form greater things, that is, etherial things – greater things than the Creator himself made" (Dewey 1934: 20 note). See note 27, where "etherial" means pneumatic wind of the Holy Spirit.

[34] See Gorlée (1994: 93) and Merrell (1995: Chapter 4).

[35] See also Hatten 1994: 263.

[36] To translate a text is to enjoy "the transcendence of difference, the process of internalizing the probabilities of non-communication, an acute doubt as to whether the thing can be done at all, [and] demands *Wahlverwandtschaft* (elective affinity). At close linguistic-cultural quarters, the translator often finds himself in a state of recognition. The hermeneutic and praxis of this

decipherment and subsequent restatement are those of mirrors and *déjà-vu*. He has been there before he came. He has chosen his source-text not arbitrarily but because he is kindred to it. The magnetism can be one of genre, tone, biographical fantasy, conceptual framework. Whatever the bonding, his sense of the text is a sense of homecoming or, as the sentimental tag precisely puts it, of a home from home" (Steiner 1977: 379, his emphasis). On translational *déjà-vu*, see Gorlée 2004: 225.

[37] Films featuring "*Stille Nacht! Heilige Nacht!*" are not discussed here, since the subject deals with the use of text and music.

Bibliography

Albrecht, Christoph. 1973. *Einführung in die Hymnologie*. Göttingen: Vandenhoeck & Ruprecht.

Anders, Charles R. 1974. 'Report 1973 Conference on Worship in Minneapolis, Minnesota' in Ameln, Konrad, Christhard Mahrenholz and Karl Ferdinand Müller (eds), *Jahrbuch für Liturgik und Hymnologie* 18 (1973-1974). Kassel: Johannes Stauda Verlag. 186-188.

Andrew, J. S. 1993. 'Scottish Hymnology & Gaelic Hymnology' in Cameron, Nigel M. de S. (gen. ed.), *Dictionary of Scottish Church History & Theology*. Edinburgh: T & T Clark Ltd. 421-425.

Apel, Willi. 1946. *Harvard Dictionary of Music*. Cambridge, MA: Harvard University Press.

Bambi. 1942. (Cartoon animated film, 70 min.) Dir. David Hans. Voice artists: Hardie Albright, Stan Alexander, Donnie Dunagan, Bobby Stewart, John Sutherland, Paula Winslowe, *et al*. Walt Disney Company.

Barnstone, Willis. 1993. *The Poetics of Translation: History, Theory, Practice*. New Haven and London: Yale University Press.

——— 1994. 'Translation Theory with a Semiotic Slant' in *Semiotica* 102-1/2: 89-100.

Barr, Andrew. 2002. *Songs of Praise: The Nation's Favourite Hymns*. Oxford: Lion.

Bateson, Gregory. 1991. *A Sacred Unity: Further Steps to an Ecology of Mind*, Donaldson, Rodney E. (ed.) (A Cornelia & Michael Bessie Book). New York: Harper Collins.

Baughen, Michael (ed.) 1982. *Hymns for Today's Church: Music and Words Edition*. London, etc.: Hodder and Stoughton.

Bell, John L. 2000. *The Singing Thing: A Case for Congregational Song* (Iona Community). Glasgow: Wild Goose Publications

——— and Maule, Graham 2000. *Sanger fra Vest* (Sponsored by Wild Goose of Iona Community) Oslo: Verbum (In-text references are to *Sanger fra vest*)

Bluhm, Heinz. 1965. *Martin Luther: Creative Translator*. St. Louis, MI: Concordia Publishing House.

Braley, Bernard. 1991. *Hymnwriters*. Vol. 1. London: Stainer & Bell.

Brecht, Martin. 1990. *Luther als Schriftsteller: Zeugnisse eines dichterisches Gestaltens* (Calwer Taschenbibliothek 18). Stuttgart: Calwer Verlag.

—— 1979. 'Zum Verständnis von Luthers Lied "Ein feste Burg"' in *Archiv für Reformationsgeschichte* 70: 106-121.

Cassirer, Ernst. 1946. *Language and Myth* (tr. Susanne K. Langer). New York: Dover Publications Inc.

Catford, J.C. 1965. *A Linguistic Theory of Translation: An Essay in Applied Linguistics*. Oxford: Oxford University Press.

Cameron, Nigel M. de S. (gen. ed.) 1993. *Dictionary of Scottish Church History & Theology*. Edinburgh: T & T Clark Ltd.

Colapietro, Vincent M. 1989. *Peirce's Approach to the Self: A Semiotic Perspective on Human Subjectivity* (SUNY Series in Philosophy), Albany: State University of New York Press.

Common Ground: A Song Book for All Churches. 1998. Full Music Edition. Preface: John L. Bell. Edinburgh: Saint Andrew Press.

Dahlström, Fabian. 1987. *The Works of Jean Sibelius* (Sibelius Society, Helsinki). Helsinki: Sibelius-Seura / Sibelius-Samfundet.

Davie, Donald (ed.) 1996. *The Psalms in English*. London: Penguin Classics

Delisle, Jean and Judith Woodworth. 1995. *Translators Through History* (Unesco Publishing) (Benjamins Translation Library 13) (Published under the auspices of the International Federation of Translators (FIT)). Amsterdam and Philadelphia, PA: John Benjamins Publishing.

Dewey, John. [1925]1958. *Experience and Nature*. New York: Dover Publications Inc.

—— [1934]1955. *A Common Faith*. 12th printing. New Haven: Yale University Press London and Oxford University Press.

—— 1943. *Art as Experience*. New York: Minton, Balch & Company.

Dix, Dom Gregory. 1949. *The Shape of the Liturgy*. 4 printing. Westminster: Dacre Press.

Donington, Robert. 1992. *Opera and Its Symbols:The Unity of Words, Music, and Staging*. New Haven and London: Yale University Press.

Dowley, Tom (ed.) 1984. *Songs of Praise: The Nation's Favourite Hymns* (by arrangement with the British Broadcasting Corporation BBC). Foreword by Archbishop of Cantebury. Hants: Marshall Morgan & Scott.

Eco, Umberto. 1979. *The Role of the Reader: Explorations in the Semiotics of Texts*. Bloomington, IN: Indiana University Press.

—— 2001. *Experiences in Translation* (Toronto Italian Studies) (tr. Alistair McEwen). Toronto, Buffalo and London: University of Toronto Press.

Esposito, Joseph L. 1980. *Evolutionary Metaphysics: The Development of Peirce's Theory of Categories*. Athens, OH: Ohio University Press.

Foss, Hubert. 1946. *The Concertgoer's Handbook*. London: Sylvan Press.

Fromm, Erich. [1957]1965. *The Art of Loving*. London: Unwin Books.

Fuchs, Catherine. 1982. *La paraphrase*. Paris: Presses Universitaires de France.

Gay, Volney and Daniel Patte. 1986. 'Religious studies' in Sebeok, Thomas A. (gen. ed.) *Encyclopedic Dictionary of Semiotics* (Approaches to Semiotics 73). 3 vols. Berlin and New York: Mouton de Gruyter. 2: 797-807.

Gerrish, B.A.. 1967. 'Luther, Martin' in *The Encyclopedia of Philosophy*, Paul Edwards (ed.). 4 vols. New York: Macmillan Publishing Co. & The Free Press and lLondon: Collier Macmillan Publishers. 5: 109-113.

Goethe, Johann Wolfgang. [1819]1952. 'West-Östlicher Divan' in Grumach, Ernst (ed.) *Werke Goethes* (=Deutschen Akademie der Wissenschaften zu Berlin). Berlin: Akademie-Verlag. 2: 186-189 and 3: 130-131.

Goldstein, David. 1987. 'On Translating God's Name' in Radice, William and Barbara Reynolds (eds) *The Translator's Art: Essays in Honour of Betty Radice*. Harmondsworth, Middlesex: Penguin Books. 72-80.

Gorlée, Dinda L. 1994. *Semiotics and the Problem of Translation: With Special Reference to the Semiotics of Charles S. Peirce* (Approaches to Translation Studies 12). Amsterdam and Atlanta, GA: Rodopi.

—— 1996. 'Opera Translation: Charles Peirce Translating Richard Wagner' in Tarasti, Eero (ed.) *Musical Semiotics in Growth* (Acta Semiotica Fennica 4). Bloomington, IN and Imatra: International Semiotics Institute. 407-425.

—— 1997. 'Intercode translation: Words and music in translation' in *Target* 9-2: 235-270.

—— 1997a. 'Bridging the Gap: A Semiotician's View on Translating the Greek Classics' in *Perspectives: Studies in Translatology* 5-2: 153-169.

—— 2002. 'Grieg's Swan Songs' in *Semiotica* 142-1/4: 142-210.

—— 2004. *On Translating Signs: Exploring Text and Semio-Translation* (Approaches to Translation Studies 24). Amsterdam and New York, NY: Rodopi.

—— 2004a. 'Horticultural Roots of Translational Semiosis' in Withalm, Gloria and Josef Wallmannsberger (eds) *Macht der Zeichen, Zeichen der Macht / Signs of Power, Power of Signs* (TRANS-Studien zur Veränderung der Welt 3). Vienna: INST Verlag. 164-187.

Gotteslob: Katholisches Gebet- und Gesangbuch Stammausgabe. 1975. Bischöfen Deutschlands und Österreichs und Bistümer Bozen-Brixen und Lüttich (eds). Stuttgart: Katholischen Bibelanstalt.

Grant, Michael. 2002. *Saint Paul*. London: Phoenix Press. (This biography was first published in 1976).

Greimas, A[lgirdas]-J[ulien] and J[oseph] Courtes. 1982. *Semiotics and Language: An Analytical Dictionary* (Advances in Semiotics). (tr. Larry Crist, Daniel Patte *et alii*). Bloomington, IN: Indiana University Press (The French original is *Semiotique: Dictionnaire raisonné de la théorie du language*. Paris: Hachette, 1979)

Grossberg, Lawrence. 1996. 'Identity and Cultural Studies: Is That All There Is?' In: Hall, Stuart and du Gay, Paul (eds) *Questions of Cultural Identity*. London, Thousand Oaks, and New Delhi: Sage Publications. 87-107.

Güttgemans, Erhardt. 1982. 'Semiotik und Theologie: Thesen zur Geschichte und Funktion der Semiotik in der Theologie' in *Zeitschrift für Semiotik* 4: 151-168.

—— 1986. 'Liturgy' in Sebeok, Thomas A. (gen. ed.) *Encyclopedic Dictionary of Semiotics* (Approaches to Semiotics 73). 3 Vols. Berlin, New York and Amsterdam. 1: 467-473.

Hatten, Richard S. 1994. *Musical Meaning in Beethoven: Markedness, Correlation, and Interpretation* (=Advances in Semiotics). Bloomington and Indianapolis, IN: Indiana University Press.

Het Boek der Psalmen nevens de Gezangen bij de Kerken van Nederland, Nederlandse Bijbel-Compagnie (eds) 1867. Amsterdam: J. Brandt and Haarlem: Johannes Enschedé.

Hirsch, Rabbi Samson Raphael (ed. and comm.) 1997. *The Psalms* (tr. Gertrude Hitschler). New, corr. ed. Jerusalem and New York, NY: Feldheim Publishers [Sponsored by The Samson Raphael Hirsch Publications Society] (First ed. 1960)

Hutchinson, John A. 1963. *Language and Faith: Studies in Sign, Symbol, and Meaning*. Philadelphia: The Westminster Press.

Jakobson, Roman. 1959. 'On Linguistic Aspects of Translation' in Brower, Reuben A. (ed.) *On Translation* (Harvard Studies in Comparative Literature 23). Cambridge, MA: Harvard University Press. 232-239.

—— 1960. 'Concluding Statement: Linguistics and Poetics' in Sebeok, Thomas A. (ed.) *Style in Language*. Cambridge, MA: The MIT Press. 350-377.

—— 1971. *Selected Writings Vol. II: Word and Language*. The Hague and Paris: Mouton.

Jakobson, Roman and Linda Waugh. 1979. *The Sound Shape of Language*. Brighton, Sussex: Harvester Press.

James, William. [1902]1977. *The Varieties of Religious Expression: A Study in Human Nature*. Introd. Arthur Darby Nock. New York: Fount Paperbacks.

—— 1910. *The Principles of Psychology: Vol. 1*. London: MacMillan and Co., Ltd. and St. Martin's Street.

Johansen, Jørgen Dines. 1993. *Dialogic Semiosis: An Essay on Signs and Meaning* (Advances in Semiotics). Bloomington, and Indianapolis, IN: Indiana University Press.

—— and Svend Erik Larsen. 2002. *Signs in Use: An Introduction to Semiotics* [transl. from Danish by Dinda L. Gorlée and John Irons]. London and New York: Routledge.

Jourdain, Robert. 1997. *Music, the Brain, and Ecstasy: How Music Captures Our Imagination*. New York: William Morrow and Company, Inc.

Julian, John (ed.) 1892. *Dictionary of Hymnology, Setting Forth the Origin and History of Christian Hymns of All Ages and Nations: With Special Reference to Those Contained in the New Books of English-Speaking Countries, and Now in Common Use; Together With Biographical and Critical Notices of Their Authors and Translators; and Historical Articles on National and Denominational Hymnody, Breviaries, Missals,*

Primers, Psalters, Sequences, &c. &c. &c. London: John Murray. (In-text references are to *Dictionary of Hymnology*, followed by page numbers)

Jung, Carl Gustav. 1954. *Man and his Symbols*. London: Aldus Books.

Klein, William W. 1996. *The Book of Ephesians: An Annotated Bibliography* (Books of the Bible 8). New York and London: Garland Publishing, Inc.

Leech, Geoffrey and Jan Svartvik. 1975. *A Communicative Grammar of English*. Burnt Mill, Esseex: Longman Group.

Liedboek voor de Kerken: Psalmen en Gezangen voor de Eredienst in Kerk en Huis. 1973. The Hague: Boekencentrum and Leeuwarden: Jongbloed-Zetka [Sponsored by the Interkerkelijke Stichting voor het Kerklied, The Hague]

Baughen, Michael (ed.) 1982. *Hymns for Today's Church: Music and Words Edition*. London, etc.: Hodder and Stoughton.

Levý, Jiři. 1969. *Die literarische Übersetzung: Theorie einer Kunstgattung* (tr. Walter Schamschula). Frankfurt am Main and Bonn: Athenäum.

Lotman, Yuri M. 1990. *Universe of the Mind: A Semiotic Theory of Culture*. (tr. Anne Shukman). Introd. Umberto Eco. London and New York: Tauris.

Lucid, Daniel L. (ed. and tr.) 1988. *Soviet Semiotics: An Anthology*. Foreword Thomas A. Sebeok. Baltimore and London: The John Hopkins University Press.

Luther, Martin (n.d.). *Geistliche Lieder*. Leipzig: Im Insel Verlag.

Maranda, Pierre (ed.) 1972. *Mythology: Selected Readings*. Harmondsworth, Middlesex: Penguin Books.

Menand, Louis. 2001. *The Metaphysical Club: A Story of Ideas in America*. New York: Farrar, Strauss and Giroux.

Menasce, Jean de. 1968. 'The Experience of the Spirit in Christian Mysticism' in *The Mystic Vision: Papers from the Eranos Yearbooks* (Bollingen Series 30). Princeton, NJ: Princeton University Press. 324-347.

Merrell, Floyd. 1995. *Semiosis in the Postmodern Age*. West Lafayette, IN: Purdue University Press.

Meyer, Leonard B. 1956. *Emotion and Meaning in Music*. Chicago and London: The University of Chicago Press.

Montagu, Ashley. 1971. *Touching: The Human Significance of the Skin*. New York and London: Columbia University Press.

Munro, Thomas. 1969. *The Arts and Their Interrelations*. Rev. and enlarged ed. Cleveland and London: The Press of Case Western Reserve University.

Murphey, Murray G. 1961. *The Development of Peirce's Philosophy*. Cambridge, MA: Harvard University Press.

Nida, Eugene A. 1950. 'Translation or Paraphrase' in *The Bible Translator* 1-3: 97-109.

—— 1964. *Toward a Science of Translating: With Special Reference to Principles and Procedures Involved in Bible Translating*. Leiden: Brill.

—— 1975. *Componential Analysis of Meaning: An Introduction to Semantic Structures* (Approaches to Semiotics 57). The Hague and Paris: Mouton.

Nolan, Rita. 1970. *Foundations for an Adequate Criterion of Paraphrase* (Janua Linguarum, Series Minor 84). The Hague and Paris: Mouton.

Nöth, Winfried. 1990. 'Theology' in his *Handbook of Semiotics* (Advances in Semiotics). Bloomington and Indianapolis, IN: Indiana University Press: 381-384.

Peirce, Charles Sanders. 1931-1966. *Collected Papers of Charles Sanders Peirce*, Charles Hartshorn, Paul Weiss, and Arthur W. Burks (eds). 8 vols. Cambridge, Massachusetts: Belknap Press, Harvard University Press. (In-text references are to CP, followed by volume and paragraph number)

—— 1979. *The New Elements of Mathematics by Charles S. Peirce*, Carolyn Eisele (ed.). 4 vols. The Hague and Paris: Mouton and Atlantic Highlands, NJ: Humanities Press. (In-text references are to NEM, followed by volume and page number)

—— 1982-2000. *Writings of Charles S. Peirce: A Chronological Edition*, Peirce Edition Project (eds). 6 vols. Bloomington, IN: Indiana University Press. (In-text references are to W, followed by volume numbers and page number)

—— *Unpublished Manuscripts*. Peirce Edition Project. Indiana University - Purdue University at Indianapolis. (In-text references are to MS, followed by manuscript number and page number)

Pike, Kenneth L. 1967. 'Glimpses of a Church Service' in his *Language in Relation to a Unified Theory of the Structure of Human Behavior* (Janua Linguarum, Series Maior 24). 2nd, revised ed. The Hague and Paris: Mouton. 73-97.

Popovič, Anton. c. 1975. *Dictionary for the Analysis of Literary Translation*. Edmonton, Alta: Department of Comparative Literature, University of Alberta.

Procter, Francis. 1961. *A New History of The Book of Common Prayer, With a Rationale of Its Offices*. Revised and rewritten by Walter Howard Frere. London: MacMillan & Co. Ltd. And New York: St. Martin's Press.

Rengsdorf, K. H. 1971. 'Semeion' in Kittel, G., G. Friedrich and G.W. Bromiley (eds). *Theological Dictionary of the New Testament*. Grand Rapids, MI: Eerdmans. 200-268.

Robinson, Douglas. 1998. 'Paraphrase' in Baker, Mona (ed.) *Routledge Encyclopedia of Translation Studies*. London and New York: Routledge. 166-167.

Sadie, Stanley and Tyrell, John (eds). 2001. *The New Grove: Dictionary of Music and Musicians*. 20 vols. London: Macmillan Publishers Limited. (In-text references are to The New Grove, followed by volume and paragraph numbers)

Salten, Felix. [1928]1982. *Bambi: A Life in the Woods* (tr. Whittaker Chambers). Foreword John Galsworthy. Illustr. Barvara Cooney. New York: Archway Paperback.

Sarna, Nahum M. 1993. *On the Book of Psalms: Exploring the Prayers of Ancient Israel*. New York: Shocken Books.

Savan, David 1987-1988. *An Introduction to C. S. Peirce's Full System of Semeiotic* (Monograph Series of the Toronto Semiotic Circle 1). Toronto: Victoria College of the University of Toronto.

Scheffcyzyk, A. 1986. 'Noise' in Sebeok, Thomas A. (ed.) *Encyclopedic Dictionary of Semiotics* (Approaches to Semiotics 73). 3 vols. Berlin and New York: Mouton de Gruyter. 2: 607-609.

Schmidt, Hans. 1926. 'Luthers Übersetzung des 46. Psalms' in *Jahrbuch der Luther-Gesellschaft* 8: 98-119.

Sebeok, Thomas A. 1985. 'Zoosemiotic Components of Human Communication' in Innis, Robert I. (ed.) *Semiotics: An Introductory Anthology* (Advances in Semiotics). Bloomington, IN: Indiana University Press. 292-324.

Sechrist, Alice Spiers (ed.) 1981. A Dictionary of Bible Imagery: A Guide for Bible Readers. 2nd pr. New York, NY: Swedenborg Foundation, Inc.

Shapiro, Michael. 1998. 'A Few Remarks on Jakobson as a Student of Peirce' in his (ed.) *The Peirce Seminar Papers Vol. 3 Essays in Semiotic Analysis* (Critic of Institutions 12). New York, etc.: Peter Lang. 1-10.

Short, T. L. 1998. 'Jakobson's Problematic Appropiation' in Shapiro, Michael (ed.) *The Peirce Seminar Papers Vol. 3 Essays in Semiotic Analysis* (Critic of Institutions 12). New York, etc.: Peter Lang. 89-123.

Smalley, William A. 1974. 'Restructuring Translations of the Psalms as Poetry' in Black, Matthew and William A. Smalley (eds) *On Language, Culture, and Religion: In Honor of Eugene A. Nida.* The Hague and Paris: Mouton. 337-371.

Smith, Robert E. 1983. 'On the Translation of "Spirit" ' in *Notes on Translation* 94: 53-56.

Songs of God's People: The Church of Scotland Supplement to the Church Hymnary Third Edition. 1988. Published on Behalf of The Panel on Worship The Church of Scotland. Oxford etc.: Oxford University Press.

Soukup, Paul A. and Robert Hodgsin (eds) 1997. *From One Medium to Another: Basic Issues for Communicating the Scriptures in New Media.* New York: American Bible Society.

—— (eds). 1999. *Fidelity and Translation: Communicating the Bible in New Media.* Franklin, WI: Sheed & Ward and New York, NY: American Bible Society.

Speelman, Willem Marie. 1995. *The Generation of Meaning in Liturgical Song* (Liturgica Condenda 4) Kampen: Kok Pharos Publishing House.

—— 1995a. 'The Analysis of a Song as a Syncretic Object: A Generative Approach' in Monelle, Raymond and Catherine T. Gray (eds) *Song and Significance: Studies in Music Semiotics.* Edinburgh: University of Edinburgh. 18-27.

—— 1996. 'The Analysis of a Holy Song' in Tarasti, Eero (ed.) *Musical Semiotics in Growth* (Acta Semiotica Fennica 4). Bloomington, IN and Imatra: International Semiotics Institute. 389-406.

Spitzer, Michael.. 2002. Review of Raymond Monelle, *The Sense of Music: Semiotic Essays*. (Princeton and Oxford: Princeton University Press, 2000). *Music & Letters* 83-3: 506-509.

Spitta, Friedrich.. 1905. *"Ein feste Burg ist unser Gott". Die Lieder Luthers in ihrer Bedeutung für das evangelische Kirchenlied*. Göttingen: Vandenhoeck und Ruprecht.

Stavans, Ilan. 1995. 'The Original Language' in *Translation Review* 48/49: 33-37.

Steiner, George. 1977. *After Babel: Aspects of Language and Translation*. Oxford: Oxford University Press. (Reprint from 1975)

The Church Hymnary Authorized for Use in Public Worship by the Church of Scotland, the United Free Church of Scotland, the Presbyterian Church in Ireland, the Presbyterian Church in England, the Presbyterian Church of Wales, the Presbyterian Church of Australia, the Presbyterian Church of New Zealand, the Presbyterian Church of South Africa. 1927. Revised ed. Oxford etc.: Oxford University Press.

The Church Hymnary, With Melody Line. 1996. Third ed. Oxford etc.: Oxford University Press. (First ed. from 1973)

The Holy Bible: A Translation from the Latin Vulgate in the Light of the Hebrew and Greek Originals. 1956. 2nd ed. London: Burns & Oates (The Knox Translation of the New Testament first published in 1945).

The Holy Bible Containing the Old and New Testaments: Authorized King James Version (n.d.). Oxford: Oxford University Press.

The Holy Bible: New Revised Standard Version. 1995. (Containing the Old and New Testaments with the Apocryphal / Deuterocanonical Books) Anglicized ed. Oxford: Oxford University Press.

The Hymnal for Worship & Celebration. 1986. Nashville, TE: Word Music.

The Hymnbook: Presbyterian Church, the United Presbyterian Church in the U.S.A., Reformed Church in America, John Ribble (ed.) 1955. Philadelphia and New York: Richmond.

The Interpreter's Bible: The Holy Scriptures in the King James and Revised Standard Versions With General Articles and Introduction, Exegesis, Exposition for Each Book of the Bible. 1953. Vol. 10 of vol. 13. New York and Nashville: Abingdon Cokesbury Press.

The New Testament According to the Majority Text, Hodges, Zane C. and Arthur L. Farstad (eds). 1985. 2nd Greek ed. Nashville, Cambden and New York: Thomas Nelson Publishers.

The New American Bible: Translated from the Original Languages with Critical Use of All the Ancient Sources by Members of the Catholic Biblical Association of America. 1970. Sponsored by the Bishops' Committee of the Confraternity of Christian Doctrine. Paterson, New Jersey: St. Anthony Guild Press.

The New English Bible: The New Testament. 1970. 2nd ed. Oxford: Oxford University Press and Cambridge: Cambridge University Press.

The Psalms of David in Metre, According to the Version Approved by the Church of Scotland and Appointed to be Used in Worship (n. d.). London, Glasgow and Melbourne: Oxford University Press.

Thuswaldner, Werner. 2002. *Stille Nacht! Heilige Nacht! Die Geschichte eines Liedes.* Salzburg, Vienna and Frankfurt: Residenz Verlag.

Vetter, Martin. 2002. 'Theologie und Semiotik: Zum Stand des Gesprächs am Beispiel der Peirce-Rezeption in jüngeren Arbeiten evangelischer Theologie' in *Zeitschrift für Semiotik* 24-1: 111-129.

Washburn, Charles C. 1938. *Hymn Interpretations.* New York and Nashville: Abingdon-Cokesbury Press.

White, Ernest G. 1938. *Science and Singing: A Consideration of the Capabilities of the Vocal Cords and Their Work in the Art of Tone Production.* Revised and reset 5th ed. London: J. M. Dent and Sons Ltd.

Wibberley, Brian. 1934. *Music and Religion: A Historical and Philosophical Survey.* London: The Epworth Press.

Wittenberg, Andreas. 1974. 'Militär-Gesangbuch und Militär-Seelsorge in Vergangenheit und Gegenwart' in Ameln, Konrad, Christhard Mahrenholz and Karl Ferdinand Müller (eds) *Jahrbuch für Liturgik und Hymnologie* 18 1973-1974 Kassel: Johannes Stauda Verlag. 97-162.

Musical Rhetoric – the Translator's Dilemma: A Case for *Don Giovanni*

Marianne Tråvén

This article deals with some of the initial problems facing a translator of Da Ponte's libretto to Mozart's opera *Don Giovanni* (1787) (Wolfgang Amadeus Mozart 1756-1791, Lorenzo Da Ponte 1749-1838). The attention is focused on the musical rhetoric of the baroque period and the set of conventions that Mozart emulated in his musical language, creating a complex interrelationship with the verbal text. Since musical rhetoric was a semiotic system capable of communicating with the audience with or without the aid of verbal text, the music can enhance the verbal text, add information to or contradict the verbal text. My intention with this article is to show a few examples of operatic situations where the translator's knowledge of the musical semiotic system as it was used during the baroque period is essential to his or her success in finding adequate material in a TL text. This article is linked to the following article by Prof. Dr. Harai Golomb that describes theoretical, methodological issues related to music-linked translation. I am indebted to Prof. Golomb for his views and observations on many topics related to this article.

Musical Rhetoric and Mozart's Personal Musical Style

Libretto translation usually means restrictions depending on form and content, but translating libretti to a certain kind of music, governed by the laws of musical rhetoric, can be even more complicated than usual. Musical rhetoric was a sign system developed during the baroque period to communicate emotions. This compositional technique was used all over Europe but formalised mostly by German music theorists like Johann Mattheson (1681-1764), Johann Phillip Kirnberger (1721-1783) and Joachim Burmeister (1564-1629). During the baroque period vocal music held precedence over instrumental music, something that becomes clear when reading for instance Johann Georg Sulzer's encyclopaedia *Allgemeine Theorie der schönen Künste*, published between 1771 and 1774. Instrumental music could, according to Sulzer, never be as clear, because without words the meaning was open to interpretation and thus could not communicate the intended message or emotion as exactly as music supported by words. Since the main aim of music was to move the feelings through the display of different emotions, transmitted by means of the "doctrine of affections," this was of course a source of insecurity. The "Doctrine of Affections" was first introduced at the end of the Renaissance when a group of Florentine academics attempted to restore what they perceived to be the pure word-to-music relationship advocated by classical Greek philosophers such as Plato. The doctrine was manifest in the seventeenth and eighteenth centuries as a presupposition that the motivic germ of a composition, its *inventio*, was more than mere representation, but also formed a tangible embodiment of *Affekt[1]*: an emotional state of being. It was believed, for example, that a *lamento* bass (see below) was the palpable expression of sadness, while a rapidly rising sequence of thirds was the opposite – euphoria. This doctrine is clearly spelled out in numerous theoretical works of the eighteenth century, among others by Mattheson (see Buelow 1980).

In short, musical rhetoric lacked the precise quality or communicative skill of the spoken language, and since vocal music was considered to affect both the mind and the heart, as opposed to instrumental music that "spoke" more to the heart, it consequently had a higher standing than purely instrumental music.[2] Music as a means of communication was therefore often viewed as a mirror of linguistic elements and meaning. After 1750 the "doctrine of affections" and the figures of musical rhetoric gradually lost their objective content in favour of a more personal aspect, visible for instance in Mozart's music. But, a set of figures, like the *lamento* or the *tirata,* remained as compositional conventions and were used and their rhetorical meaning recognised by most composers. The *lamento* figure is in fact a variation of the *passus duriusculus* (meaning a hard or cumbersome walk) and was used to portray feelings of suffering, anguish and sorrow. It is an intervallic figure consisting of a chromatically stepwise falling fourth. The force of the figure depends on the harmonic implications, the greater they are the more powerful the figure appears. A very effective use of the *lamento* is in Mozart's c minor mass KV 427 at the words *"Qui tollis peccata mundi."* Here the figure is combined with vigorous dotted figures in the instrumental parts, a technique that can also be seen in *Don Giovanni, introduzione*, mm 90-92. See figure no. 7 in this article. The *tirata* (comes from the Italian word *tirare* and means to pull something) is a figure defined by Michael Praetorius (1571-1572) in his theoretical work *Syntagma musicum* as *"lange geschwinde Läufflin, so gradatim gemacht werden, und durchs Clavier hinauff oder hinunter lauffen"* (1967: 263). The *tirata* consists of a rapid succession of stepwise notes up or down the scale and were used to portray actions like striking or running, things falling or flashes of lightning. It could also be used for designating feelings of inner turmoil or anger. One example of the first kind is found in the duelling scene in *Don Giovanni, introduzione,* mm. 167-175. See figure no. 11 at the end of this article.

The musical rhetorical figures used by Mozart's contemporaries were either transmissions of linguistic figures or creations based on purely musical content. Those that lacked linguistic mediation, were usually based on some sort of likeness to the object or act that they signified, that is, they signified by portraying or painting it, being iconic signs (Unger 1941: 62 ff.). For instance, the concept of flight or running was depicted using a succession of fast notes in an upward direction, in other words a form of transmission of the event. It is on such transferred features that Mozart builds part of his musical "language" (Born 1985: 25). Mozart transferred, not the word, but the event or the object, a technique that can truly be called intersemiotic. This gives Mozart's opera scores a visual quality that is often overlooked. Unique for Mozart was however that such intersemiotically transferred features were given access to all musical parameters in his operas creating a complex structure.

Apart from musical rhetoric in the traditional sense of the word, Mozart's music contains compositional features inspired by paralinguistic and extralinguistic content. Mozart combined paralinguistic features to represent the speech situation, and extralinguistic features like for instance musical gesture to paint dramaturgical components such as actions. These features are also transmitted through a form of translation and create yet another level of the "text" with dramaturgical significance (Kaindl 1995: 39). A visual representation of the components could look something like the figure below if we take the libretto to be the source of inspiration:

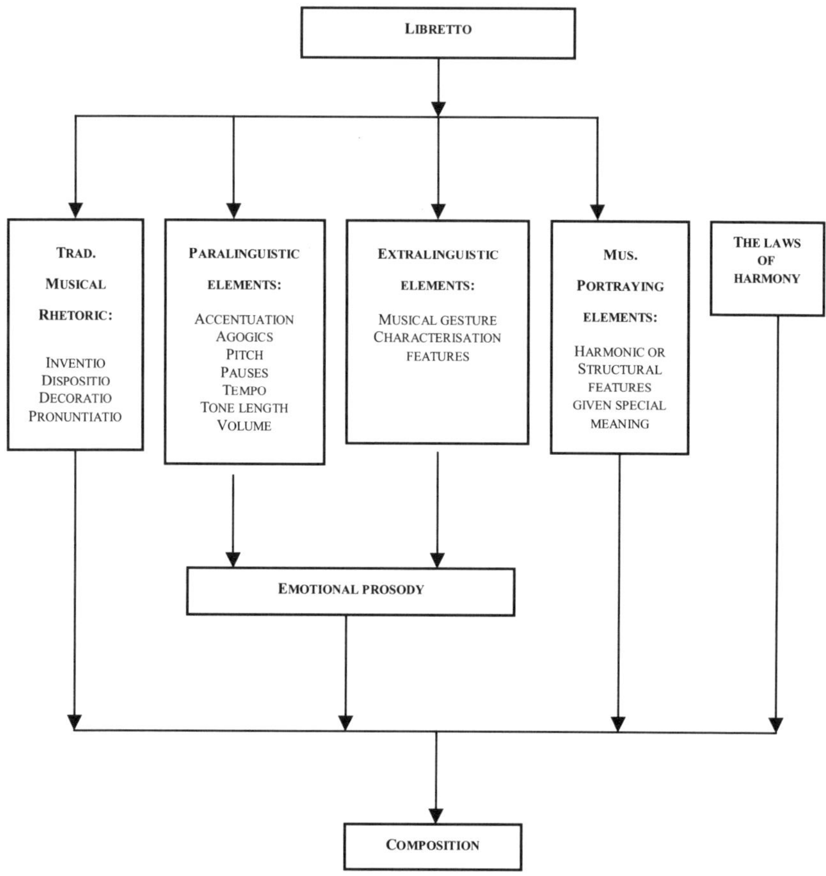

For the translator, translating what is in fact the basis of another form of translation where both components are bound together by semantic and dramaturgical content is a challenge and calls for very specific strategies, based on critical awareness and profound knowledge of the musical and rhetorical meaning.

The rhetorical figures of Mozart's personal "language" tend to operate on different levels. The musical equivalent of the text is not always a 1:1 relationship and a translator may have to analyse the musical surrounding for additional meaning, if he wants to render the initial interrelationship between the verbal text and the musical text. There are definite differences concerning the arrangement of words in relation to their musical counterparts, some words and phrases having a direct musical equivalent, others depending on the dialogue between music and verbal text for their interpretation. Musical rhetorical figures often add information to, or underline the verbal text, sometimes opposing it, a fact that the translator must take into consideration if he wants to avoid contradictions.

The Direct and Indirect Interrelationships Between Verbal Text and Music

First we have the direct relationship between a specific word and its musical rhetorical equivalent. A word portrayed in this way will nearly always have to remain in the same position as it occupied in the original, and the translator will have to find as good an equivalent as he can. For instance in the last scene of the second act finale we have the words *"è sempre ugual"* (is always the same), the whole text reading: *"Questo è il fin di chi fa mal; E de' perfidi la morte / Alla vita è sempre ugual."* The important word for Mozart was *"ugual"*, equal or the same, and he portrayed it with a mirror effect using the same figure going up and down the scale, but not at the first occurrence of the word (in mm. 808)! It is not until it carries conviction in mm. 843-844 that Mozart presented his idea, later varied with shorter or longer figures, finding its optimal effect in the figure presented in mm. 851-855. To translate this passage with *"die letzte Stunde naht. / Voller Lohn wird jeder Tat"* as Franz Grandauer does (Mozart s.a.: 655) is depriving the listener of a significant dimension of the full text. Some translators will undoubtedly argue that such considerations are unimportant, since the effect of the figure will be lost on all listeners but the initiated analysts. Even if I think that this is to underestimate one's public, I can understand the exasperation of the translator who ponders on how to meet the problem of having to choose equivalent material for every little rhetorically enhanced word in Mozart's score. My point however is that to make the right choices one has to know what one chooses and what one loses in the process. Since all forms of musically linked translation means losing some information, and most translational strategies work with hierarchic scales of what sort of information to communicate and what can be regarded as optional, the translator has to be familiar with the musically added values to the verbal text.

Figure 1, *Scena ultima, "Questo è il fin di chi fa mal,"* mm. 843-844.

A word of caution though; this kind of word-painting is not limited to single words but can also apply to a whole phrase, like in the following example, taken from Leporello's aria *"Madamina, il catalogo è questo"* in the first act. At the words *"V'han frà queste contadine, cameriere, cittadine, v'han contesse, baronesse, marchesane, principesse"* Mozart divides the material into a continuously rising sequence.

Figure 2, *"Madamina, il catalogo è questo"*, mm. 38-45.

This figure is called *gradatio* (Latin term meaning staircase or ladder) and belongs to the group of traditional musical rhetorical figures that had, at Mozart's time, become conventions of the musical "language." It can appear as a repetitive phrase, each repetition on a somewhat higher level, or as a stepwise rising movement. This figure was used to designate feelings as well as objects rising. Here it mimics the rising social significance of *Don Giovanni*'s ladies. The second form can be seen in mm. 110-115 in the same aria. *Gradatio* is the Latin word for climax and it was used in rhetoric for an arrangement of words, phrases, or clauses in an order of increasing importance, often in parallel structure.[3] More specifically, climax was the repetition of the last word of one clause or sentence at the beginning of the next, through three or more clauses or sentences.[4]

Hierarchic relationships like these, where the word order is given such musical prominence, can seem like a straitjacket to the translator. But, since it is the position of the words in a hierarchic structure, rather than their individual semantic value that Mozart chose to underline, the translator can, within reason, change the semantic meaning as long as the hierarchy is retained. But, to disarray the list of women for want of similar sound, like Grandauer does -- *"Mädchen sind's von jedem Stande, / hier aus Städten, dort vom Lande, / Bauernmädchen, Baronessen, / Kammerzofen und Prinzessen"* (Mozart s.a.: 100-101) -- would mean a loss of quality in the translation.

Another category of figures that appear in the orchestra alone relates indirectly to the text, and are therefore often overlooked by translators. A telling example of this, and somewhat tricky for the translator, is when Donna Anna is telling Don Ottavio of the assault by Don Giovanni in no. 10, *"Or sai chi l'onore"* in the first act. In measures 48-52 we have the words *"a forza di svincolarmi"* (by freeing myself), *"torcermi"* (wrenching), *"e piegarmi"* (crouch down), *"da lui mi sciolsi"* (I escaped from him). Donna Anna is describing how she wriggled to get loose from Don Giovanni's grasp. The music of the violins and the bass shows how she wriggles to get free. At the third try, in the last measure, she succeeds as the music enters a new key. Both the wriggling and the regained freedom have been rendered in music and leave the translator no choice but to try to find similar words in the target language.

Figure 3, "*Or sai chi l'onore*", mm. 48-52.

Just before these measures, at measures 37-40 in the same recitative, Donna Anna describes her cries for help "*grido: non viene alcun*" (I called out, but no one came), trying to escape from Don Giovanni. The vocal line is dropping a quarter in a matter of fact statement. In Donna Anna's part Mozart has chosen to depict the paralinguistic elements, she is calmly restating what happened. Here the melody of the vocal line does not force the translator to retain the original position of the word "*grido.*" Instead it is the delayed reaction of the orchestra in measures 38-39 that portrays the cry. This is often the case in Mozart's music: the orchestra, and not the vocal line mimics the story told by the singer, thereby showing her actions or how she felt at the time of the assault. If we compare this example with the cry of Zerlina in the first act Finale where Mozart has rendered a cry in the "present time," the difference becomes clear. Here the cry for help is placed within the vocal line itself over one chord giving all the prominence to the vocal line. It is instead followed by a commotion in the orchestra that concentrates on depicting the upset feelings and confusion caused by Zerlina's cry for help. The outcome for the translator is the same as before, no changes in position is possible if we want to retain the interrelationship between words and music.

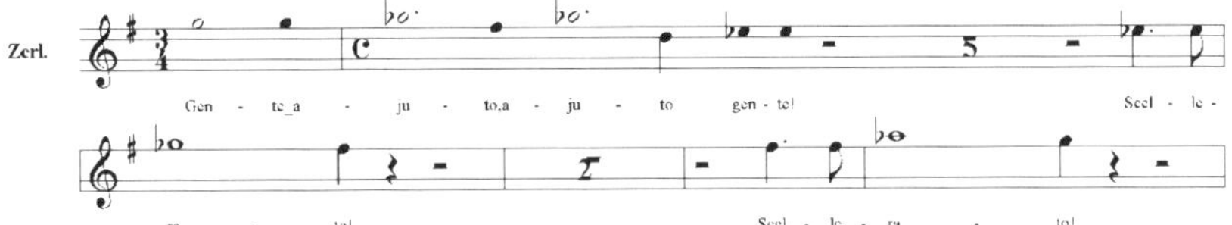

Figure 4, *"Or sai chi l'onore"*, mm. 36-40.

Figure 5, First act finale, mm. 467-483.

Musical Additions

A third group of figures consists of words commented on by musical means, thereby adding information, for instance linking them to earlier events, or giving them an extra dimension. This is however not to be confused with Richard Wagner's (1813-1883) *"Erinnerungsmotiv"*, since Mozart's figures are never taken "out of the blue" but relate either to traditional rhetorical conventions, paralinguistic- or extralinguistic elements or make use of musically portraying elements. One example of this is his use of the traditional *lamento* figure, a chromatically sinking fourth that designates mourning and sorrow. The first time we encounter this figure in *Don Giovanni* is in the introduction when the Commendatore is fighting Don Giovanni in mm.167-172, and later when he is dying in mm. 190-194.[5]

Figure 6a-b, *"Introduzione"*, mm. 167-172 and mm. 190-194.

As in the example from Donna Anna's narration it is not the character that is given the figure, but the orchestra, and it appears accordingly to prepare the audience of the horrors to come and later, after his last breath, as a confirmation. This is a traditional way of using the *lamento* figure that most of Mozart's contemporaries would have understood. The simple statement and restatement of the *lamento* figure after the word *"partir"* (disappear) simply tells us that the soul has left the body and that the Commendatore is dead. In the opera Mozart also uses the *lamento* figure to tell us more of what is going on in the mind of Donna Anna. An incomplete version of the figure, lacking two notes, turns up in her part during the encounter with Don Giovanni in the introduction, mm. 90-92 at the words *"Gente! Servi! Al traditore!"* (Family! Servants! After the traitor!). At first Mozart's use of the *lamento* in this passage seems inconsistent, after all the *lamento* signify sorrow and mourning, possibly pain, but not as we would expect a cry for help. So what is she mourning, the fact that Don Giovanni will escape unknown, or her lost virginity? Or is this a premonition of her father's death?

Figure 7, "*Introduzione*", mm. 90-92.

Next time the *lamento* figure appears is in the quartet "*Non ti fidar, o misera*" in mm. 40-44, at the words "*che mi dice per quell' infelice cento cose che intender non sà*" (that he tells me of this unhappy person a hundred things I can't understand).

Figure 8, "*Non ti fidar, o misera*", mm. 40-44.

Here Donna Anna is actually continuing a line that Don Giovanni has already started in mm. 19-20 as he tells them that Donna Elvira is crazy.

Figure 9, "*Non ti fidar, o misera*", mm. 19-20.

So in a way Donna Anna is responding to his statement, which is a mock version of the *lamento,* enlarging the meaning by two notes to a full *lamento,* showing her sincere concern. This is of course a simple explanation, but there is also a more complex relationship; in that case Don Giovanni's melodic line is exactly the same as the one that Donna Anna voiced in the introduction. So, is her utterance in the quartet just a sign for compassion, or a simple acceptance of Don Giovanni's statement? No, I think it is a reminiscence of her own encounter with Don Giovanni. She is in fact beginning to realise that her own fate is similar to that of Donna Elvira. If it should be judged as a *lamento* figure or a variant of the *passus duriusculus* is open to debate, but I think it is important to realise that Mozart's use of the conventional rhetorical structures was relative. The *lamento* was one of the most widely known and effective figures of the time and playing with its significance must have appealed to him.

The last time the *lamento* figure appears is in the second act, *Scena ultima,* in mm. 701-711. The text reads "*certo, ceto è l'ombra che l'incontrò!*" (sure, sure that was the shadow that encountered her!). It is an enlarged, doubled version of the figure showing true mourning. This figure does not accompany the text at first, and is performed by both Donna Anna and Donna Elvira. So why doesn't Mozart use the figure the first time the text appears? I think that at the beginning of this scene there is still some doubt about the identity of the shadow, and the melodic line shows this by slowly taking on more and more characteristics of the *lamento.* If we compare the first two renderings of the text in music we will see that Donna Anna's melody consists at first of three notes g-b and c on which she recites the text. The next time the melodic line is richer, comprising nearly a full *lamento* – g, f, e flat, d, c sharp d. The vocal line is broken by rests, a traditional rhetorical figure called *tmesis* that denotes hesitation.[6] The missing notes: f sharp and e, are then added as the full implication of the ghost of her father dawns upon Donna Anna in the third repetition of the text. She is now truly mourning for him and perhaps also for Don Giovanni, as is Donna Elvira.

Figure 10, *Finale*, mm. 701-711.

Such hypertexts are not uncommon in Mozart's operas, and require of the translator a special sensibility to musical connotations. In this case the translator of the vocal text has to be very careful if he wants to vary the repetitions of the original text.

Dramaturgical Relations

There is also a large group of figures that have mainly dramaturgical significance, presented by the orchestra without accompanying words. I use the term dramaturgical to denote musical phenomena that seem to mimic actions taking place on the stage. This group contains many references to how Mozart understood the characters of the opera, their desires, sorrows and, above all, their interrelationships. One example of this can be seen and heard in the introduction of the first act when the Commendatore is fighting Don Giovanni. The actual blows are painted in music showing the thrusting swords in successive order starting with Don Giovanni in the violins followed by the Commendatore in the bass. If we look carefully at the music we can see (and hear) the somewhat lame parry by the Commendatore whereas Don Giovanni's blows are forceful using two octave leaps at the end. When the final octave of every blow is left out in the bass, we know that the

Commendatore has lost the fight. Don Giovanni strikes three times and the Commendatore has been mortally wounded. The horror of the moment is portrayed through a diminished chord, a symbol of pain, suffering and sorrow. This was a conventional symbol of death and destruction in Mozart's time and one that he used in a conventional way here. This diminished chord will appear again as the stone guest appears in scene XV, carrying the same breath of death and destruction but this time for Don Giovanni.[7]

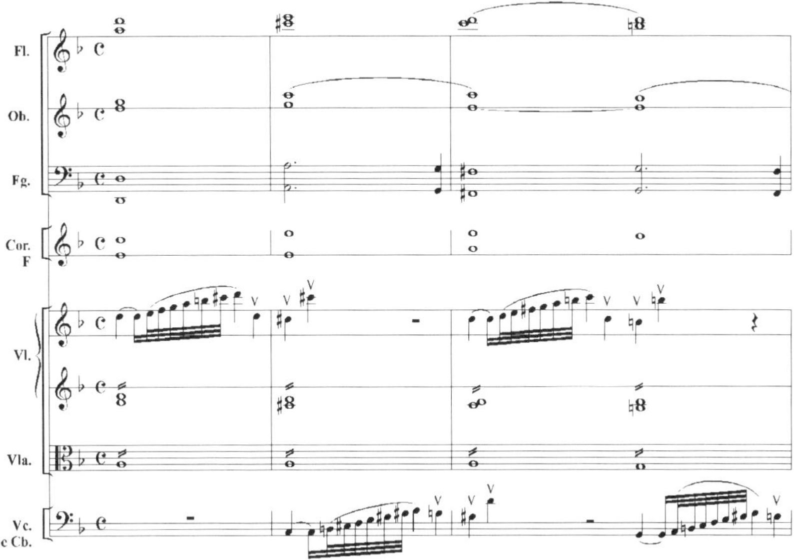

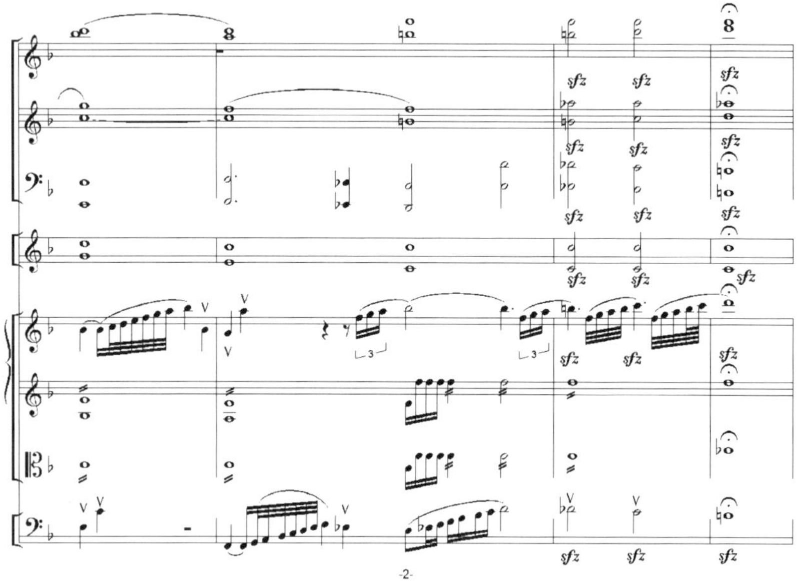

Figure 11, Introduzione, mm. 167-175.

Conclusions

In many respects Mozart used music as a painter, giving the music a visual quality, a rare phenomenon among his contemporaries. Rhetorical and pictorial elements are to be found at most levels of the text, rendering paralinguistic and extralinguistic features, portraying objects and movement. Some of them were used for characterisation, some for dramaturgical reasons, and some highlight the emotional status of the characters. I earlier mentioned that working with translations of Mozart's operas was like working in a straitjacket, and this is not far from the truth since close interrelationships between libretto and music leaves little space for movement. Most translation strategies aim at reducing information to gain communication of those features that are considered vital. I think we must remain open to the fact that a lot of these rhetorical figures are, like Sulzer

118

(1771-1774: 783-784) said, flexible, and sometimes open to interpretation. The flexibility does however not mean that the figures can be ignored by the translator. It is my firm belief that no translator should take up his pen until he has thoroughly studied the score of this opera leaving no page unturned. Only then can he or she make adequate choices.

Notes

[1] I have chosen to retain the German spelling here since the word *affec*t in English does not quite match the original semantic meaning.

[2] This does, however, not mean that instrumental music was in any way inferior to vocal music from a technical point of view. See Bond 1991.

[3] The last word(s) of a clause become the first of the next through three or more clauses, like in the following lines by the English poet T. S. Eliot (1888-1965): "All our knowledge brings us nearer to our ignorance, / All our ignorance brings us nearer to death, / But nearness to death no nearer to God" (Choruses from *The Rock*. 1934).

[4] This is in fact a form of repeated *anadiplosis*, a rhetoric figure where the last word of a phrase is repeated as the first word in the next phrase. See Unger 1941, p. 68.

[5] I do not count the occurrence of this figure in the overture since it was actually written after the completion of the opera. See Tyson 1990: 12.

[6] *Tmesis* (Greek word meaning "cutting") has also been used in later linguistic theory for the breaking up of a preposition separating it from its verb, and in poetry to separate two elements of a compound word for the sake of emphasis. In music *tmesis* is a "general pause or silence within a musical texture where silence is not expected" (Buelow 1980: 800).

[7] I do not think that one should attach too much importance to the interrelationship between these chords but they should be considered as conventional rhetorical means of portraying death and destruction.

Bibliography

Allanbrook, Wye. J. 1981. 'Metric Gesture as a Topic in Le Nozze di Figaro and Don Giovanni' in *Musical Quarterly* 67-1: 94-112.

—— 1983. *Rhythmic gesture in Mozart: Le Nozze di Figaro and Don Giovanni*. Chicago and London: University of Chicago Press.

Bond, Mark Evan. 1991. *Wordless Rhetoric: Musical Form and the Metaphor of the Oration*. Cambridge: Harvard University Press.

Born, Gunthard. 1985. *Mozarts Musiksprache: Schlüssel zu Leben und Werk*. München: Kindler Verlag GmbH.

Buelow, George J. 1980. 'Rhetoric and Music' in *The New Grove Dictionary of Music and Musicians*, Stanley Sadie (ed.). London: Macmillan Publishers Ltd. Vol. 15. 793-800.

Eliot, Thomas S. 1934. *The Rock: A Pageant Play Written for Performance at Sadler's Wells Theatre 28 May-9 June 1934*. London : Faber.

Kaindl, Klaus. 1995. *Die Oper als Textgestalt: Perspektiven einer interdisziplinären Übersetzungswissenschaft*. (Studien zur Translation 2). Tübingen: Stauffenburg Verlag.

Mozart, Wolfgang Amadeus. (*s.a.*) *Don Giovanni* (tr. Franz Grandauer). London and Mainz: Ernst Eulenburg Ltd.

Praetorius, Michael. 1967. *Syntagma musicum III. Wolfenbüttel 1619.* (Facsimile) 2nd ed. Kassel: Bärenreiter.

Sulzer, Johann G. 1771-1774. *Allgemeine Theorie der Schönen Künste.* Leipzig: Weidmanns Erben und Reich.

Tyson, Alan. 1990. 'Some features of the Autograph Score of *Don Giovanni*' in: *Musicology* [Special issue: Israel Studies: Beth Shamgar (ed.)] vol. 5. 7-26.

Unger, Hans-Heinrich. 1941. *Die Beziehung zwischen Musik und Rhetorik im 16.-18. Jahrhundert.* Würzburg: Konrad Triltsch Verlag.

Music-Linked Translation [MLT] and Mozart's Operas: Theoretical, Textual, and Practical Perspectives[1]

Harai Golomb

The present article is concerned with several issues related to Music-Linked Translation [MLT]. In its first part, it surveys theoretical and methodological matters, formulating specific conditions for the operation of this specialised kind of translation, notably the characteristic hierarchies between its components. In its second part, it explores practical aspects of the subject, addressing its very *raison d'être*: how, when and why the need to engage in, or benefit from, MLT arises. Finally, in its third part, the article examines a small number of verbal/musical instances from the Mozart/Da Ponte corpus, observing them both in the original and *vis-à-vis* corresponding English MLT-specimens. This section, then, analyses the enormous translational challenges posed by the subtleties and complexities of Mozart's musical and dramatic genius, as manifest in the intricate interactions between his music on the one hand and specific moments in the verbal text and the dramatic action on the other hand, and shows the attempts of specific practitioners to meet these challenges. This article is closely linked with the article by Marianne Tråvén in this volume, both articles sharing a number of observations and a Mozart/Da Ponte focus. I am gratefully indebted to Dr. Tråvén for her cooperation in earlier stages of preparing this article and for her musicological erudition and sophisticated insights, which contributed greatly to my article.

1. Theoretical Remarks: Some Distinctive Features of MLT

1.0. "What's in a Name?" — Notes on Terms and Terminology

The particular type of translation to which the present book is devoted has been called by different names. However, like William Shakespeare's famous rose (*Romeo and Juliet*, II, ii, 43-44), this phenomenon retains its qualities when called "by any (other) name", i.e., whether the adjective preceding the noun "translation" is "equirhythmic(al)", "singable", "singing", "vocal" (the latter is prevalent in this book), "synchronised", "music-linked" (which I slightly prefer, and will use in this article), or any other, as long as it is clear what the term refers to. Basically, MLT is not **standard** translation, since it is not a predominantly semantically-oriented preservation of signifieds while replacing the signifiers of one language (SL=Source Language) with those of another (TL=Target Language); nor is it what Roman Jakobson (1896-1982) termed "inter-semiotic translation" (1987: 429).[2] In what follows I will raise some issues related to the nature of MLT, starting with a terminological note.

In this article the term "music" (and its derivatives) applies only to Western, tonal and metred music, and the term "verbal text" (and its derivatives) applies only to texts in languages in which stress is phonologically significant and potentially variable in its intra-lexical location (such languages tend to develop accentual-syllabic versification in their poetries);[3] in fact, all my MLT examples will be drawn from English, but the points of principle relating to the rhythmical level of texts almost invariably apply to any similarly characterisable language. The term **music-linked verbal text** (MLV), then, refers **here** to an instance of verbal text "set to", or linked, aligned, or synchronised with, an instance of music, whether this setting/linking/aligning is made *a priori*, by original design (i.e., when new music is composed deliberately to be aligned with an existing verbal text, or vice versa) or *a posteriori* (i.e., in the rare cases when a potential possibility to match two pre-existing components, verbal and musical, is discovered and activated at a later stage). As will be seen below, the phrase "setting a text to music" (or "linking", or "aligning" the two, or making one "conform" to the other), will apply here at first to the **rhythmical** aspect of musico-verbal interrelationships, manifest mainly in the agreement between **stresses** in the two. This stress on stress is the main reason for restricting the terms "music" and "verbal text" in the manner just specified. This restriction is not whimsical; as we shall see, stress agreement is, or has become, a minimal binding requirement, or basic norm, of MLV/music interrelationships in the verbal-musical cultures dominated by "music" and "verbal text" as delimited above.

1.1. Preliminary Considerations: Hierarchies and Interactions

Any translation can be viewed as a process of making sacrifices: it starts with the very act of "sacrificing" the original, i.e., giving it up through replacing it by a substitute from another language. Then, of course, within the translation process, one has to sacrifice sound for sense, accuracy for elegance, fidelity to a source text for communication with a target audience etc. etc. (and after each such pair of terms one can add, "or vice versa"). In what follows, Music-Linked Translation [MLT] will be characterised first and foremost in terms of the peculiar nature of the sacrifices it makes, demands, or tolerates.

Setting a verbal text to music rarely, if ever, results in a simple combination of the two. Rather than an arithmetical addition yielding the formula "verbal text + music = musico-literary text (opera, Lied etc.)", it is a complex process, potentially involving a myriad of heterogeneous qualities inherent in both constituent texts, the verbal and the musical, creating an **interactive relationships** between them, each affecting the makeup and perception of the other.

What can music and verbal text do to each other? A translation-oriented attempt to answer this eternal question yields two types of reply, both admittedly partial and simplistic, just scratching the surface (which is unavoidable in an article of the present scope).

1. Ideally, each of the two should contribute to their "marriage" what it can do best; this means that the music lends the combined work its emotive intensity, textural complexity, and structural unity,[4] in ways inimitable verbally, whereas the verbal text "gives to airy nothing [of the music] a local habitation and a name", to use Shakespeare's formulation of what poetry does to its subject-matter (*A Midsummer Night's Dream*, V, i, 14-17);[5] in other words, the verbal text gives the combined work an anchor of time, place, and other concrete coordinates of reality. This, in turn, ideally adds to the combined musico-verbal text's emotive intensity.

2. By being synchronised and merged into one integrated medium-heterogeneous (musico-verbal) utterance, music and verbal text **can** (and often do) change each other's previously- or otherwise-autonomous internal relationships and hierarchies, creating fresh, cross-medium hierarchies, operating only within the joint utterance. Thus, constituent elements of each of the two synchronised components are foregrounded inasmuch as they enter into meaningful interactions with constituent elements of the other component; there is of course a complementary resulting tendency, whereby elements **not** entering into such interactions can be backgrounded, becoming less prominent than they would be within a separate existence of text-free music or music-free verbal text. This can also be described as **selective interaction**: each component "makes a selection" of constituent-elements within the other component, activating as it were a magnet which draws to the fore elements sensed as relevant to the cross-medium interaction, and rejects or repels elements sensed as irrelevant to that interaction, figuratively using the other magnetic pole (to carry this analogy a step further). This mechanism applies not only to sound, but also to meaning: semantic content of the verbal text can be foregrounded or

backgrounded according to its relative closeness to emotive and structural components of the music; analogous processes can work in the opposite direction.[6] This is also describable as **mutual elimination of 'irrelevancies'**.

Potentially and ideally, MLT strives to re-create those musico-verbal interrelationships, interactions and hierarchies in the target-language. It seems to follow, then, that for MLT music is a constant, to be preserved almost at all costs, whereas the verbal text is placed in the subordinate position of a variable, barring rare, special cases and circumstances.[7] However, as we shall see, the situation is far more complex.

The interactive relationship just mentioned is created, then, between two fundamentally different types of sign-systems. This genuinely semiotic dimension of MLT is the potential object of dissertations and book-length studies, aiming to explore the entire range of its theoretical and methodological ramifications, by studying (e.g.) the nature and role of repetition, the interaction between semantic and non-semantic components of verbal and musical texts, the "vertical" — i.e., harmonic/simultaneous — dimension of music and its effect on the perception of sung texts, the creation and manipulation of hierarchies in each component, through its interaction with the other, etc. It involves a more thorough survey of similarities and differences between music, language, and literature with all its genres, each considered separately before being juxtaposed with others. No such ambitious project will be attempted in this short study.

If we adopt the norm, or ideal, of "adequate" (or, to use admittedly intuitive and less-scientific, but still communicative, terms like "faithful", "normative", "satisfactory", or even simply "good") translation, differences in definition notwithstanding,[8] MLT is truly "adequate" if it manages to render the meaning (the semantic component) of the source text as closely as possible, while making it sound as 'naturally' as possible (in terms of stress pattern, rhythmical structure, and even sound) when synchronised with the music to which the source text had been set. More precise and focused aspects of this ideal adequacy will be discussed below. However, before taking this ideal apart — largely in the name of the attainable and realisable — stating it, in its ideal form just proposed, is called for.

MLT is **any** type of music-linked translation — regardless of its purpose, its 'clients' or users (singers, listeners, composers, conductors, directors, spectators, etc.), the size of its performing bodies (soloists, consorts and ensembles, choirs, companies etc.), its genres (e.g., canonised ones like opera, Lied, madrigal; popular ones like operetta, musical, pop and rock music; folk music of all parts of the world), etc. The present study, though, is concerned with one genre only: canonised opera, and one single corpus — the Mozart/Da Ponte (Wolfgang Amadeus Mozart 1756-1791, Lorenzo Da Ponte 1749-1838) trilogy (*Le Nozze di Figaro*, 1786; *Don Giovanni*, 1787; and *Così fan tutte* 1789).

1.2. *Masters and Servants in the Operatic Medium: A Brief Historical Note*

The history of opera — by now, a 400-years-old art-form — can be told, *inter alia*, as a story of rivalry, or at least competition, between its musical and verbally-encoded[9] components, vying with each other for prominence and centre-stage attention. Histories, encyclopaedias and textbooks tell us that the Founding Fathers of opera in Florence around 1600 had in mind the revival and re-creation of the ancient art of Greek Tragedy, which for them meant "*dramma per musica*". In other words, opera was conceived first and foremost as **drama,** and music's role was to serve and enhance the dramatic elements. Taking this metaphor of "serving" more literally, music was supposed to become drama's **obedient servant.** Yet, being a servant's master implies a built-in dilemma, faced even by a selfish master: a timid and over-obedient servant cannot render a good service to his master if he is even figuratively weak or crippled; a strong and wilful servant, however, may have "funny ideas" of replacing his master and becoming one himself (as Leporello puts it, in his famous aria which opens *Don Giovanni*: "*non voglio più servir*" ["I no longer want to serve"]). Apparently unaware of the implications of this inherent dilemma, the makers of the very first operas took care to emasculate and incapacitate the music, by limiting it to non-polyphonic, monodic textures, devoid of repetitive patterns vital for musical structure and its perception, and subordinating it to the rhythms of standard, 'music-free' speech. Non-musical music of this kind could not survive the test of time. And, indeed, the first great creator of operas, Claudio Monteverdi (1567-1643), disregarded the 'no-no's of his immediate predecessors, and in his first opera, *L'Orfeo* (as early as 1607), allowed his music to be autonomous, and obey its own most elementary rules (e.g., certain types of repetition, melismatic sounds, and even harmony and polyphony, were re-introduced; this was done with even greater verve and conviction in later operas, by him and by others). By doing that, Monteverdi unleashed the powers of music in opera forever, and laid the foundations for the major feature of the art of opera ever since, namely, that though the competition between its musical and non-musical components is never-ending, the outcome of that competition is predetermined: willy-nilly, opera has become first and foremost a music-based art, part and parcel of the musical scene, much more than it can ever be part of the literary, dramatic, and even theatrical scene. True, specific opera **productions** can give greater prominence to non-musical elements and components; yet, at least as far as the first three and even four centuries of its existence are concerned, opera's ontological status, its mode of existence, resides in written pages, on which hardly anything exists other than musical notation and the (usually sung) words of verbal texts. And once the visual-theatrical elements are eliminated from the "work" and relegated to the performing-interpreting artists, the opera "itself", consisting of words and music, is inevitably first and foremost a work of music.

1.3. *Hierarchies in MLT Makeup: Constants and Variables*

1.3.1. *Music's Predominance.*

For this reason alone, as if there were no other, it is understandable that music is almost invariably treated with greater reverence than the verbal text in MLT. However, there are also other reasons — perceptual, cognitive, cultural, etc. — which usually make music more prominent than verbal texts whenever the two are synchronised. Suffice it to say that this is usually the case, at least simply because music is perceived as added to a verbal text **for a reason**, and its interference with the 'normal' flow of verbal communication can be tolerated only if sensed as significant. Thus attention is naturally focused on music. But besides, and even more significantly, music is more prominent in auditory cognition; as we shall see, it dominates the scene of acoustic perception in almost all its facets. In the context of the present study, focused on Mozart's operas — a corpus unsurpassable in terms of cultural reverence and canonisation — the dominance of music over text is even more pronounced than in most other cases.

The production of music-linked **translation**, then, can be described as **translating an MLV in SL into an MLV in TL, keeping the music (to which the source MLV was originally set) intact.** This seems to mean first

and foremost, as suggested in 1.1 above, that in MLT music is the constant
and MLV is the variable. Yet, there is no neat symmetry here. If we regard
MLT as a 'direct' activity, there is no mirror-image 'inverse' activity to
complement it: granted, it is possible to compose new music designed to be
set to a pre-existing verbal text, in which case indeed the music is a variable,
and the verbal text is a constant; however, this is not the mirror-image
opposite of MLT, simply because one instance of music cannot be the
translation of another, in the way that verbal texts in different languages
can.[10] Composing new music to an existing verbal text, then, is a fresh
original act of artistic creativity, in which the previous music linked with the
same text cannot function as a source for translation (though, of course, the
new music can allude to the old one, imitate it, quote from it, etc.). **In this
specific sense** producing MLT is more complex than composing new music,
since the former has to address itself both to the music and to a source text.
This fundamental asymmetry between music and verbal text lies at the very
core of the MLT phenomenon.

The supremacy of music over verbal text in most vocal works is generally
recognised in studies of MLT as well. Thus, in a seminal, richly documented
article on translations of Edvard Grieg's (1843-1907) "Swan Song", Dinda
Gorlée (1997: 237) writes: "Vocal music of all sorts is generally regarded by
scholars as a primarily musical genre, and the preoccupations of its criticism are
inevitable musical, not literary. The text … though often a pre-existing work of
verbal art, is usually subordinated to the musical text. … There are, of course,
many notable exceptions, as when a famous poem forms the basis of a musical
composition". Can we really conclude, then, as stated and implied here so far,
that in MLT the verbal component is a variable, whereas the musical one is a
constant? Not quite: as in any other translation, only the actual verbal
signifiers of the source MLV supplied by SL are variables, to be replaced by
signifiers of the target MLV supplied by TL, whereas the **signifieds**, ideally,
are as much as possible preserved as constants, alongside the music.
Moreover, it is a common practice in MLT to strive towards maximum
preservation of the segmental phonemes (vowels and consonants) of the
source MLV, in order to retain at least some of the original **sound,** especially
in rhymes and other telling positions.[11] Of course, this is often impossible
(and can never be a binding norm), since differences between the sounds of
signifiers are the very essence of the separateness of languages. However, out
of the phonetic and rhythmical source material, the **suprasegmental**
components,[12] especially those relating to intralexical stress, are often
selected for mandatory preservation in MLT, most specifically when such
stress is corroborated by musical stress patterns (through metre,[13] agogic or

pitch-governed accents, *sforzandi,* articulation peculiarities, syncopation etc.).[14]

1.3.2. *Music and Suprasegmentals: Absolute Tyranny.*

I would like to focus on the metrical/rhythmical aspect, which in the types of music and languages I am discussing is the mandatory requirement, or binding norm, for elementary "Chomskyan grammaticality" of MLVs. This is the modern binding, minimal norm, which at least in 20th century practice governs both the composition and the translation of MLVs. It can be stated simply: one must avoid "at all costs" a situation in which the musical stress patterns would impose a principal (single strongest) stress in a polysyllabic word on any syllable other than its phonologically stressed one (i.e., the one marked as stressed in the word's dictionary entry).[15] Thus, for instance, a verbal text cannot be said to "conform" to an instance of music that would make the noun "dEsert" [=wilderness; capitalisation represents phonological stress] sound like the verb "desErt" [=to abandon], or like "dessErt" [=pudding]). In fact, in composing and translating MLV one is not in a position to allow or to forbid the music to distort the phonological stress pattern of the words; to the contrary, the words are selected and combined to conform to the constant, unchangeable music, so that no stress discrepancy of the kind and magnitude just described can arise in the first place. **Music is the absolute ruler of suprasegmentals, dominating the actual outcome of any conflict.**

Thus, for instance, it would be unacceptable — i.e., considered "ungrammatical" — that the music should impose the normative, phonological stress on the first syllable of the Italian word "*signor*"; and indeed, Mozart almost invariably makes his music stress the last syllable when this word is used (and it is indeed used, and correctly stressed, countless times in *Le Nozze di Figaro* and his other Italian operas); yet, in the first aria of Figaro in Act I, "*se vuol ballare, signor contino*", the very same word is forced by no other than Mozart himself to be stressed incorrectly, on the first syllable, time and again in this aria, from measure 1 on,

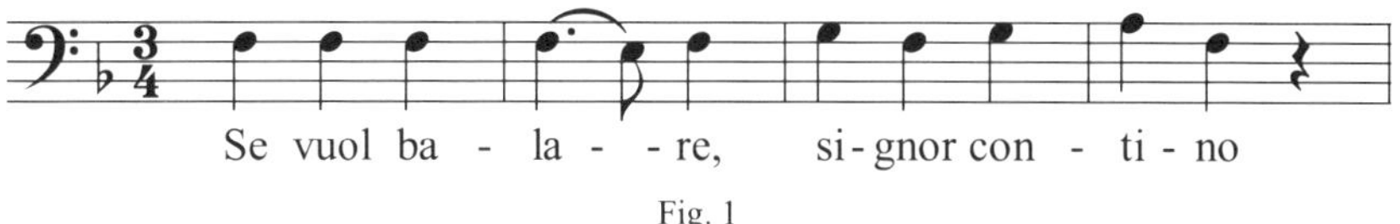

Fig. 1

but subsequently it reappears again and again, **correctly** stressed by the
music, throughout the opera.

Likewise, Monteverdi repeats the Italian interjection *"Ohimé"* twice, in the
same line (from his 9th book of madrigals): *"Ohimé che cado, ohimé"*. The
first *Ohimé* is tressed by the music on the first syllable (wrong!), and the
second one, sung within a few seconds after the first, is stressed by the music
on the second syllable (right!).[16]

Fig. 2

Modern sensibility, though, tends to insist in stress-timed languages on the
correct placement of stress, structuring MLVs accordingly; however, it does
tolerate other rhythmical inconsistencies, such as the optional use of elisions,
oscillating between counting and disregarding certain unstressed syllables,[17]
the manipulation of syntax, repetition and word- and phrase-order,[18] and
other textual and rhythmical liberties and licences. Such 'liberated' practices
can make the hard life of authors and translators of MLVs somewhat easier
and free them from the constraints of rhythmical straitjackets. One has to re-
emphasise, that all these constraints and licences are activated within the
relation of target-MLV to the **music**, rather than to the source-MLV (see
notes 13 and 14). Thus, for instance, one can produce a target MLV (through
MLT), which is substantially longer than its source, if one absolutely has to,
taking advantage of verbal-musical repetition in the source. In such a case,

then, a long single phrase in the target can be allowed to spread over the musical space used for two repetitions of the same shorter phrase in the source, replacing its second appearance in the source by a fresh text, not used before, in the target. Such tricks should be used with caution and discretion (see below), and the translator must ascertain that the repetition in the source is not crucial in significance or structure; yet translators do resort to this device, thus sometimes saving the target text from missing vital points, or from being clumsy, over-cryptic, or incomprehensible.

In short, regardless of whether in SL the text preceded the music, chronologically (which is the usual case), or vice versa, in MLT the music invariably predates the text. And this is not merely a matter of chronology, but of substance.

Music, once again, absolutely dominates the scene of verbal suprasegmentals: the psycho-acoustic parameters of pitch, duration, and loudness (and hence stress and metre) are not just affected by the music, but determined by it in MLV, and the verbal text 'has no say' in these matters once set to music. Young Roman Jakobson, in his early Russian Formalist days, said that metre and poetic versification perform "organised violence" on the rhythms of language. Compared to music, though, poetic metre is a docile lamb: the non-metrical rhythmic structure of the verbal text can, and very often does, resist the metrical pulse vying with it for prominence; yet no such leniency to the rhythms of language is shown by music, which in this sense is a rampant tyrannical force. Thus, for instance, Papageno's text in Act II, scene 29 from *The Magic Flute* is *"Nun wohlan, es bleibt dabei / weil mich nichts zurücke hält, / gute Nacht, du falsche Welt"*. The verse-text in German is structured to yield only one metre, which is purely binary (trocheic): nUn wohlAn es blEIbt dabEI, and so on [¯˘¯˘¯˘]. The music, however, "has a mind of its own"; it is scanned in ternary metre (here the quaver is the basic pulse-unit: 6/8 measure = two 3/4 measures)

Fig. 3

and the trochee of the text simply vanishes into thin air.[19] For the MLT translators this means, once again, that they have to worry only about what the music can do to their texts in terms of metre, stresses etc.; the texts can do absolutely nothing to the music **in that sense** (as long as its rhythms remain intact). Setting MLV to music incorrectly means, then, subjecting it to a musical-rhythmical structure, which subverts and distorts the phonological stress system. In such a case the ear hears a different placement of stress; yet this is not a matter of acoustic hearing, but of verbal cognition. The listener who knows the rules of the language identifies an error; those rules, unable to affect the acoustic outcome, can and do create in the listener a sense of discord, produced by the clash between linguistic awareness of the former and actual hearing of the latter (as in Figures 1 and 2). If new music composed for a pre-existing text creates such errors, it is made to abuse its powers. If the text comes later, it must take those powers into account.

A related matter, which I will not be able to discuss here, is the relation of verbal intonation and music. Of course, the absolute dominance of music over verbal pitch, loudness and duration squashes the autonomy of all products of these three parameters of sound, whether operating on the level of single words and lexemes or on the level of phrase, clause, sentence and beyond.[20] So, in short, the study of verbal intonation in MLV and MLT texts amounts to the study of what does not exist because of the music, or what would have existed if these texts were not aligned with music. Bearing in mind that without such alignment most of these texts would not have been created in the first place, the study of the hypothetically autonomous verbal intonation patterns **in such texts** is a futile endeavour indeed. Texts of literary repute set to music after their composition (see note 7) is another matter, of course; the study of their music-free intonation is not futile at all (see note 20), but it is irrelevant to the study of MLT as such.

1.3.3. Music and Segmentals: Competition and Tolerance.

As for segmental phonemes, music treats them with greater 'consideration': at least it does not obliterate them.[21] The sounds of vowels and consonants are still heard when set to music and sung. This topic is basically in the province of the singer-oriented approach (see next section), and I shall not dwell on it here. Suffice it to say that vowels and consonants can cooperate with music (e.g., in creating soft or harsh atmosphere in both) or compete with it, when features of the two work at cross-purposes. Such competition, though, is intrinsically unfair: in terms of sheer sound, music is potentially incomparably richer, more varied, and more striking than verbal segmentals. To allow the verbal sounds a role in a verbal/musical work, music should be restrained, as it was by the founders of opera (to avoid polyphony, 'attractive' melodic or structural patterns, etc.).[22]

1.3.4. MLT's Inverted Sound/Sense Hierarchy.

So far I have not addressed an issue, which is of crucial significance in any discussion of MLT, perhaps even the most important one: the practically-inverse hierarchy of importance of the various components of the text, compared to music-free translation. Certainly in almost all cases of prose translation, but even in most cases of poetic translation, the preservation of semantic content of the source text is of primary importance (as maintained, e.g., by Fónagy; see note 10). Usually, most formal and non-semantic elements (rhythm in all its facets, syntactic structure, sound properties of segmental and suprasegmental phonemes, etc.) are openly sacrificed in translation if this is indeed needed in order to achieve greater semantic adequacy. In MLT, by definition, this hierarchy cannot be allowed to work, because of the supremacy of rhythmical alignment with the music as specified above, which reflects the supremacy of music itself. Thus, if anything has to be sacrificed, it is never the rhythms dictated by the music.[23] Consequently, the semantic component of the text is no longer immune from deliberate deviations in the service of the all-important rhythmical component.

Be that as it may, common sense must of course prevail. The macro-semantic and thematic content — i.e., what the text is **about** — as well as verbal elements crucial for plot, characterisation etc., cannot be sacrificed without damaging the entire operatic whole; however, many local semantic elements can be modified, e.g., by changing word- or phrase-order (unless this order is crucial), by giving the general idea while ignoring semantic detail, etc. Semantic approximations and loose summaries, that would be hair-raising in music-free contexts and normally rejected as translational non-starters, can be accommodated on the micro-level in MLT, especially if sacrifices of this type earn the text such valued qualities as rhythmical elegance, witty and effective word-music alignment, immediate communicability, etc.

Indeed, there is no 'correct/incorrect' music for a verbal text (although considerations of emotive correspondence do apply), but MLT can be 'correct/ incorrect' for the basic semantic content of its MLV source.

1.4. Hierarchies in Views of MLT

Views of MLVs, whether original or translated, can vary, for those who create, analyse or use them. After discussing some of the inner hierarchies within MLT itself in previous sections, I would like to focus on hierarchies of considerations in analytical scholarship and evaluative criticism.

1.4.1. Micro-Level Considerations

In viewing MLT, prominence can be given to some components, at the inevitable expense of others. Thus, one can give prominence to the needs of vocal technique; according to such an approach, an evaluation of a translator's work should be focused on his/her choice of vowels and consonants, and their collocations or synchronisations with pitches, pauses, stresses, and articulation peculiarities of the music. According to the advocates of this approach, the value of the MLT translation is directly proportionate to the attentiveness it exhibits to the needs, potentialities, constraints, and even comfort and ease of voice production. This can be called a **singer-oriented** approach to MLT (which can be adopted by translators in their work, by scholars and critics, preferring it in their evaluation of that work, and of course by singers).

Prominence can equally legitimately be given (again, by translators and scholars/analysts alike) to the observation of rules: of syntax in language, and/or of harmony in music, and/or of metre in either/both, etc. Such preference can be called **analyst-oriented**. Similarly, other components of the MLT complex can be considered central; the two approaches presented here are just an illustration of a principle of preference.

1.4.2. Macro-Level Considerations

Likewise, practical and/or scholarly/critical preference can be given to sophisticated structural and thematic features of the artistic work as a whole. This applies, *inter alia*, to musico-literary rhetoric, manifest in semantics, syntactics and pragmatics within single works and entire corpuses of musico-literary or musico-dramatic art, especially in complex, canonised instances of such corpuses. Such 'macro' considerations are admirably discussed by Marianne Tråvén in her paper in this volume. Indeed, in that article the Mozartian operatic corpus (and, more specifically, *Don Giovanni*) is viewed primarily as a repository of challenges for potential MLT practitioners, and only marginally as a field where actual works of such practitioners can be found and analysed. Tråvén's examples demonstrate the intricate structures created by Mozart in his manipulations of rhetorical figures (e.g., *lamento*, *gradatio*), and other patterns of high sophistication. The magnitude of the challenge for the translator is indeed great, and meeting it is often impossible, or at least difficult in the extreme. Tråvén's article is convincing in arguing that very important features and components of the greatness of Mozart's operas (and, arguably, of any vocal work of comparable subtlety and complexity) suffer total loss, or at least reduction to relative insignificance, at the hands of translators unaware of these features, or unable/unwilling to do them translational justice. The article forcefully implies, then, that only conscientious, sensitive, highly erudite and gifted professionals are entitled to undertake MLT when works of the Mozart calibre are at stake. Such an approach I would term 'author-oriented', for obvious reasons.[24]

I would like to conclude this section by introducing another approach, to complement rather than replace the ones already identified. I would call it listener-oriented (or audience-oriented), as it focuses on the listener's needs, and views the entire process from his/her standpoint, guiding the working practitioner and the observing analyst to ask how the interests of the listener, as the end 'client'/'customer'/'user' of the product, would be best served. This approach may also be labelled as 'perception- (or 'cognition-) oriented'.[25] Its point of departure, in principle, is not the perfection of ideals, but the imperfection of practicality. That is why it is conceived in a spirit of relativity, compromise, and functional sacrifice: as we have seen, one can rarely attain one good quality in a translation without sacrificing another. It's all a matter of choosing which quality one places higher in one's hierarchy of preferences, and it does not have to be always the same quality: hierarchies can be flexible, changing not only with time, place and taste, but also, much more quickly, with the process of listening to a single work. It is virtually impossible in MLT to attain the goals of singer-, composer-, analyst-, and listener-oriented approaches at once. In fact, such simultaneous perfection is rarely attained even in the source MLV itself (see below). With a potential, inevitably imperfect listener in mind, this approach seeks to realise for that listener the maximum of the potentialities inherent in the source work, inasmuch as they can be perceived and interpreted intelligibly. In real life, the perfect is often the enemy of the very good, even the excellent.

Indeed, one can find some instances of imperfection and inconsistency even in the work of the greatest masters; some of these have direct bearing on the work of MLT translators. Micro-examples can serve as illustration for macro-principles.

An amusing example of inconsistency on the technical level of word/music alignment is the following: the famous first aria of Figaro (Act I, no. 3) begins with the words *"se vuol ballare, signor contino, il chitarrino le suonerò"* (mm 1-12). There is a graceful feminine (penultimately stressed) cadence in the music assigned to the word *contino*, and an assertive masculine one (ultimately stressed) on the word *suonerò*

Fig. 4

However, when Figaro quotes himself *verbatim*, the same words set to almost the same music, within a recitative in Act II, he sings the text of the first phrase, with its feminine ending, to the tune of the second, with its originally masculine ending. This 'transplant' requires repeating a note without any musical justification, only to accommodate an extra syllable, which sounds quite contrived and clumsy, as the work of someone who cannot scan (especially when contrasted with the accomplished Act I original, inevitably evoked here).

Fig. 5

Mozart could easily make Figaro quote himself more accurately, repeating the music of Act I as it was. He deliberately chooses not to do that, thereby **sacrificing** the perfect word-music match for a local comic effect, which serves him better at this moment in the action. The point is that Mozart, even in his original, does not treat his own music, and the word-music alignments that he so masterfully created, as an infallible and unchangeable holy script. A translator would have been severely chastised by critics had he dared to 'violate' a Mozartian text, adding a syllable to conform to an easily-avoidable discrepancy between original text and music. Yet, as a practising MLT-translator, I find relief and reassurance in that Mozart himself gives the likes of me the go-ahead to add or omit a syllable in cases of 'translational distress'. Of course, it's all a matter of local considerations, when and how to use such licence without abusing it.

Indeed, the hierarchical nature of all art, including of course all great operatic art, means that even the greatest of composers (e.g., Mozart) occasionally sacrifice some qualities for others, and that never in a work of art is everything equally significant, because if **all** is **equally** significant, then all is equally **insignificant**. Moreover, there are weak, or loose parts or moments in almost every work of art, however great; these are not always moments of deliberate repose or comic relief: sometimes — admittedly rarely in the greatest works — they are simply moments of carelessness, of being off one's guard.[26] If the great masters are not infallible, no ordinary mortal — which all MLT practitioners are, at least compared to a Mozart — should be vain enough to aim higher. This does not mean, of course, a licence to be sloppy, not to try one's very best; it only means that a certain amount of imperfection is inevitable, and one must exercise damage control and try to choose the components one sacrifices advisedly, locally and individually.

The entire discussion up to this point has been conducted as a talk within a closed community of professionals: it features the personae of composers/librettist, scholars, critics, and performers; and even though listeners and audiences were finally brought into the picture, they were conceived as constructs arising from the texts, as **implied** audiences. In the next part of the article, questions regarding real-life audiences, made out of lay listeners and spectators, will be addressed.

2. Practical Questions: MLT for Whom? For What?

> "Reason not the
> need!"
> (*King Lear*, II, iv, 260)

2.1. "Reasoning the Need", Socially

In an article by Peter Low (2003) distinctions are drawn between various types of texts used to mediate between a given MLV and audiences unfamiliar with its SL.[27] Thus, he places MLT in a wider perspective of his user-oriented approach, implicitly asking the question of its *raison d'être* in practical terms: who needs it, for what purpose, under what circumstances, etc. It seems to me that Low's article implies (though never states) that in this day and age the social need for MLT is not as clear as the need for other types of mediating texts.

This type of question is rarely addressed in academic/scholarly text-analysing discourse.[28] As scholars we hardly ever ask what our object of study is needed for, the underlying assumption being that its very existence is also its *raison d'être*; our main role is to analyse it, to investigate how it is structured, how it functions, etc., rather than to justify or account for its existence. And, indeed, in its first part the present article attempted this kind of investigation, as if the "need" is obvious and needs not addressing. Yet, I think it can and even should be addressed, as a meta-question, both in social and in inner-structural terms.

If we adopt an end-user-oriented approach, it is not self-evident that the very existence of operatic MLT is its *raison d'être*. Reasons can be given for viewing it as a superfluous preoccupation, even a harmful one, at least at the beginning of the 21st century. In a way, it is comparable to dubbing (voice-over) translation in films. In both cases the loss can be greater than the gain: destroying the original fusion of heterogeneous components is hardly justifiable when viable alternatives (in film, subtitles; in opera nowadays, film/TV's subtitles and live stage performances' "surtitles" [or "supertitles"]) are available.

In short, MLT — to be sure, a highly specialised and professional activity — may be a waste of time, energy, and even money; arguably, a lot of flair, skills and expertise, and versatile talents and knowledge, are invested in vain, to produce an unnecessary product. It may at best be a legitimate subject for research and academic deliberation (as demonstrated, e.g., in the present article, indeed in the entire present volume) rather than a pursuit fulfilling a need in "the real world". Who needs it, then?

Professional singers? Nowadays, they strive towards mastering as many languages as possible; they regard the ability to sing in the original language as a proof of their professionalism, a challenge they demand from themselves to face, even if they are totally ignorant of SL and need strenuous coaching in it.

Real-life audiences of lay operagoers? They have today the benefit of simultaneous surtitles in live performances and subtitles in video, DVD and television broadcasts. Arguably, such texts function and communicate more effectively with their audiences if they are prosaic, matter-of-fact and concise rather than ornate and sophisticated, as MLT texts often tend to be, with their often inevitably convoluted syntax, reversed word-order, etc. Such electronic captions require minimal reading time (to avoid distraction and allow the audience's eyes to return to the action on stage or screen as promptly as possible). Moreover, such audiences are equipped with programme notes, which usually include detailed synopses, and sometimes even entire bi- or even multi-lingual libretti; and anyway, audiences are often led to believe that (a) opera libretti are usually silly and simplistic, *ergo* unimportant (see refutation of this claim in the next sections, especially 2.2), and (b) verbal texts sung in operatic performances are anyway hardly audible.[29]

Whose text is MLT anyway, then? Perhaps only the translator's own, toying
with him/herself? Maybe the production of MLT texts is largely prompted by
such motivations as the arguably narcissistic need of translators (present
company included...) to show off their unique and unneeded expertise, to
experience the pleasures of flexing their mental muscles, overcoming
challenges to the mind, and even to earn part of their keep in the process? In
short, do we, MLT translators, initiate a vicious circle — first try to convince
consumers that they need our merchandise, and only then satisfy those
alleged needs, created by us? And is it really necessary, rather than obsolete
in this day and age, to maintain such opera houses as the *English National
Opera* in London, or the *Volksoper* in Vienna, whose very *raison d'être* (i.e.,
their very existence alongside the more prestigious opera houses in those
cities, which perform in the original languages) is singing in the local
vernacular? Is there a genuine **need** for such singing?

Well, let us "reason the need", King Lear notwithstanding... The very fact
that MLTs are being done is evidence enough that there is a need, not as a
philosophical or theoretical argument, but as a practical observation:
unneeded things that have a price tag simply do not survive that long. The
question is, then, what is the nature of the need and who is, or are, the
'needy'.

One type of need, even in today's society, can be found among 'peripheral'
audiences and other lay, non-professional consumers of opera. In outlying
areas, away from the metropolitan centres, where performers can be semi-
professional unable to acquire training to sing in foreign languages, where
surtitles are technically and financially unattainable, there can be groups of
monolingual people capable of enjoying and appreciating opera as audiences,
or even as amateur performers. They can well make use of good MLT
products. The same applies, with greater force, to audiences consisting of
children and teenagers, who can be initiated into the world and experience of
opera only through MLT.

Another type of audience, which as it seems no one ever thinks about, is the
home spectators-singers, or what one can call the 'operatic shower-singers',
whether they live in metropolitan centres or in provincial and rural areas.
Obviously lay amateurs, even dilettantes, and audiences ignorant of SL,
would (thank God) never dare to sing from their seat in the opera house
during performance, but can enjoy singing operatic excerpts during domestic
listening to a professional recording or, in the privacy of their homes, even in

the kitchen or the shower. For the artistic enjoyment of such people MLT is essential and irreplaceable. Moreover, the existence of such people, self- or school-trained to need and enjoy the instantaneous micro-level synchronisation of word and music (whose importance is illustrated below, in the last part of this article), justifies the use of MLT in surtitles and subtitles as well, when the actual professional singing is performed in the original language. Such members of the audience in the opera house can match the music they hear with the text they read **and understand** here-and-now, enjoying their immediate interaction as if the text — though sung in SL — is sung in MLT. Such 'matching' is a complex cognitive process, and may distract the audience from moving their eyes back to the stage action in a flash; yet, speaking again about sacrifices, there is a profit to be gained for that loss. I suppose this works differently for different people, but I know for a fact that some people do derive a lot of profound pleasure from watching opera performed while MLT surtitles are shown. This happens even more frequently with subtitles to televised and videotaped performances, the latter enabling spectators to return to the same material as often and as many times as they please, to recapture those fleeting moments and absorb the subtleties and complexities of word/music interaction as fully as one can — hearing, albeit without understanding, the verbal sounds of the original as actually sung, while singing the understandable MLT version in their mind's ears, or even aloud at home, and watching the dramatic/theatrical action on screen. One can perform this complex process again and again, focusing on different part(s) of it every time, cumulating sensual and cognitive experience to produce a lasting highly complex overall memory of the piece.

Anyway, this at least partly answers the question of "who the hell needs it?"

2.2. *"Reasoning the Need", Structurally*

One can say that using SL in opera performances, where the local vernacular is different from that SL, indicates **preferring musical communication with the composer to theatrical communication with the audience**, whereas resorting to MLT in such circumstances indicates the reverse. As we have just seen, the argument that immediate theatrical communication is attainable through synchronised captions is only partially true: for a live audience no silent reading of a text, trying to absorb and process it intelligibly while processing a complex multi-channel production, can replace the experience of hearing intelligible words coming out of a singer's mouth, here and now.

Thus, there is room for MLT, and there is a role only it can play in terms of cultivating structural listening in linguistically uninitiated (or partially-initiated) audiences, regardless of, and in addition to, the social needs spelled out in the previous section. Almost paradoxically, MLT's vital role, and its true *raison d'être*, reside precisely where it is most problematic: in the supreme semiotic significance of word/music interaction which takes place in the source text and language, particularly in the highest and most complex forms of opera. In other words, the most powerful reasons establishing the indispensability of MLT stem from the near-impossibility of producing it adequately, let alone satisfactorily.

I am talking about the popular yet basically nonsensical rhetoric, according to which all verbal components of opera are nonsensical and insignificant. Indeed, actual libretti are often mediocre, occasionally inferior, sometimes even silly verbal texts; moreover, one can even generalise that no libretto originally written for the sole purpose of being sung in an opera has been designed or realised as a great work of literary/dramatic art, that could be read, appreciated, and performed theatrically, without the music. Yet, within the framework of opera, especially (but not exclusively) in great operatic art, knowing the libretti, even their subtlest details, is often indispensable for appreciating the music itself.

Most of the complex signification process in such operas is the result of interactions between the music and the verbal, dramatic, and other extra-musical components of the operatic whole. Indeed, much of it can work intuitively, without formal knowledge, for any sensitive and sensible spectator/listener; but without informed awareness of what the heterogeneous elements are, and how they converge, diverge and interact, one very often fails to respond correctly and intelligently to the music. Of course, such awareness cannot be attained without thorough knowledge of semiotic, communicative and rhetorical processes and conventions in the music and in SL alike. The only chance that a person not proficient in SL can experience a substantial part of these rich and complex processes of signification and structuration (see Mozart examples in Tråvén's article and below in the next sections) is through MLT. In other words, for such a person MLT is indispensable for a fuller experience of great opera.

True, even high proficiency in SL cannot guarantee cognitive understanding and intuitive experience of these processes; such proficiency is a necessary yet insufficient condition for such understanding. Thus, a musically, rhetorically, and operatically uninformed listener is **likely** to miss fine points and crucial elements of the opera, manifest in text **and music** alike, even if s/he is a native speaker of SL; but a listener ignorant of SL is **doomed** to miss them. There is no hope for such a listener to retrieve some of those losses through reading silent synchronised captions. MLT is the only procedure that can possibly simulate the effect of synchronised verbal/musical/rhetorical fusion, as it functions in the original, transmitted from a singer's mouth to a listener's ears as an interaction **realised in sound, sense and gesture.**

This is why the complex operatic interaction, which seems to make adequate MLT almost unattainable, is precisely its major source of strength. The need as reasoned here, in internal-structural terms, is admittedly a refined and sophisticated one, rarely sensed or shared by large audiences; rather, it is a matter for the highbrow, for the initiated, for those who can genuinely savour and celebrate the micro details of opera, not only its macro grandeur. But high art — be it visual, verbal, or musical — has always been the concern of the few: **those who genuinely need it; those whose need for it is genuine.**

And the need is indeed genuine not only because some people can honestly vouch for it. Its genuine nature can be demonstrated (as shown above) textually, in structural and semiotic terms. **The core of operatic art, with its intricate interrelationships and interactions between heterogeneous components, can supply the evidence for the genuine need to experience it without compromising its complexity.**

3. More Mozartian Challenges: Micro Illustrations of Macro Problems

To conclude this paper I would like to add a few Mozart examples to the ones already given above (and in the article by Tråvén); each example is a world of its own, but they all demonstrate the complexity and heterogeneity of operatic art under the hand of one of its greatest masters of all time, if not **the** greatest. The purpose of some examples is merely to demonstrate the vital importance of understanding the verbal text at a precise moment, in order to experience the totality of the operatic whole, and the music within it, as a challenge to MLT practitioners; in other examples, actual English translations will be discussed.

3.1. Anachronisms and 'Infidelities': Da Ponte's "Victorian Lovers"

In *Così fan tutte,* in a *recitativo secco* in the beginning of Act II, Don Alfonso advises the two bridegrooms, who are too shy to his taste, to stop behaving like people from "*secolo passato*" [literally, "the past century", meaning of course "old timers"]. This is variously rendered in MLT translations: in the Kalmus Vocal Score (tr. 5, p. 219) the nameless translator writes: "Such ceremonious fashions are utterly exploded"; Browne/Cox's text (tr. 6, p. 97) is "such ceremonious fashions belong to days gone by",[30] whereas Jeremy Sams (tr. 7, p. 28) says: "This old-fashioned nonsense is getting us nowhere".

In the version used by "The Opera Factory" (a company founded in Sydney, Australia, which later moved to London),[31] the phrase is "don't behave like Victorian lovers". This is an example of a special type of translational adequacy, achieved paradoxically through blatant anachronism and brazen 'infidelity'. Precisely because Mozart/Da Ponte in 18th century Vienna could not have possibly spoken about "Victorian lovers" in 19th century England, this text can be exonerated from one of any translation's "mortal sins", namely, attributing the translator's own invention to the original author: "invented by the translator" is written all over this text, and it indeed communicates to its target audience, consisting of late 1980s Londoners, what is **to them** "*secolo passato*", which is indeed Victorian England, with its reputation for prudishness and timid attitude in addressing the opposite sex. Watching this production performed in London's Queen Elizabeth Hall in the late 1980s, I joined the local audience in bursts of laughter at this point. The creators of the production, translator included, could have said to themselves with relief, "mission accomplished". Of course, such a practice is not a matter of general consensus, and must be adopted with great caution and discretion. In this instance, to my mind, it worked.

3.2. Fun Puns and Fine Pinnings

A powerful yet astoundingly subtle counterpoint is offered in "The Letter Duet" (the *duettino* no. 20, Act III, *Le nozze di Figaro*) between three elements:[32] the actual words sung, the music, and the dramatic moment (plot, intrigue). Let us start with the latter: it is a moment of cunning and conniving (with good reason and for a good cause, with which the audience is prompted to identify, but still cunning and conniving), when the two singing ladies —

the Countess and Susanna — scheme to lure the lecherous treacherous Count into the trap of a phoney meeting for illicit lovemaking. Only an audience totally ignorant of the most basic elements of the plotline can fail to notice that. Yet the actual words, if taken literally and naïvely, are full of hot air, to put it bluntly: empty platitudes and quasi-poetic clichés, devoid of sound and fury, but signifying nothing. They speak about a song sung *sull'aria* ["to (or over) the air"],[33] mention light zephyr blowing under the pine-trees in the orchard, and precious little more than that. Thus, there is no hint of the deception, or of the seduction, in the words proper. The music, however, is almost painfully beautiful, soft and gentle throughout, full of seductive longing addressed **to the audience**. Rounded, caressing melodic lines and the most soothing consonant intervals (lots of parallel thirds) make it a pinnacle of sweetness. The two components, then, each in its own individual way, have absolutely nothing to do with the intrigue. Yet there is one micro-linguistic element, which as it were winks at the audience with a shrewd smile: the text keeps repeating, without any apparent reason, the word *"pini"* [literally, "pine-trees"], whose phonetic resemblance to the word *pene* [penis] is evoked more than once in this opera.[34] A subtler insinuation, though, occurs the end of this duet, when the two ladies sing *"ei già il resto capirà"* and later *"certo, certo il capirà"* ["and he will understand the rest", "certainly, certainly he will understand"], with an obvious wink at each other and at the audience. Literally, there is no hidden hint that the Count has to "understand" if we take the words at face value, conveying just the bland platitudes signified by their dictionary sense. Specifically, that is, there is no mystery to unravel about gentle zephyrs, fragrant gardens and pine trees; only the 'dirty' pun can explain the last line of the duet text. If the sheer beauty of the music were not so overpowering, it would have had an almost sanctimonious effect when combined with the dramatic moment and the camouflaged lewd phonetic association.

No English MLT known to me of these texts has faced the challenges; it is even likely that the translators were not aware of its existence. Thus, Edward J. Dent's version (tr. 1, p. 103/4) is "How delightful 'tis to wander / By the breath of evening fanned / Where the scented pines are closest / And the rest he'll understand". Jeremy Sams's text (tr. 2, p. 43) says: "Would you feel the gentle breezes / Blowing through the trees tonight. / You can feel them in the pinewood / This is all you need to write."[35]

Mozart plays an analogous trick in *Don Giovanni*, in the seduction duet *"Là ci darem la mano"* (I, 7). There, the word *pene* itself is used just as shrewdly: placed in the telling position of enjambmental rhyme, it discharges its homonymic function — meaning both the singular of the Italian for "penis" and the plural of *pena*, the Italian for "pain", extendable to "pang", "pining", etc. Thus, it activates the same playing-the-innocent wink, as if only the latter, 'respectable' sense is actually there.[36] The authorial irony is made even more poignant in the next line, where the words "**innocent** love" are brazenly sung.

Here, too, it seems that translators were unaware of the Mozart/Da Ponte pun, or too cautious to handle it. In Dent's version (tr. 3, p. 71) the lines under discussion are "Where youth and love invite us / With pleasure to delight us, / Of joy we'll take our fill!" whereas Norman Platt and Laura Sarti's (tr. 4, p. 62) version is "We go, we go, my treasure / To share the lasting pleasure / That innocent love can give."[37]

3.3. Major Order for Minor Disorder: Challenges for MLT

This subsection will oscillate between analyses of two arias in *Don Giovanni:* Leporello's "Catalogue Aria" (Act I, no. 4) and Don Giovanni's own aria beginning with the words *"Fin ch' han dal vino"* (I, 12),[38] focusing on word/music interaction as potential challenge to MLT translators. Out of the myriad of relevant devices, I shall confine myself to three, prominent in both arias: transitions to the minor key; chromaticism (within a context of constantly-shining major-key melody and harmony, chromaticism has a definite minor-key effect, so the two are interrelated); and prominent repetitive patterns.

No. 12 is one of the most important arias sung by Don Giovanni.[39] This aria poses special challenges both to its performers and to its would-be MLT translators.

The minor key is prominent where Don Giovanni is planning his seductive strategy: to use the confusion amidst a busy crowd, engaged in simultaneous dances, in order to make love to as many women as he possibly can. This phrase is culminating with the word *"amoreggiar"* [literally, "to flirt"; in context, "to make love"] repeated three times in the minor key, when Giovanni is apparently savouring this virtual lovemaking repeatedly in his imagination, as it were.

Fig. 6

The coincidence of the minor key with *amoreggiar* is very significant, and most translators have not noticed the precision of this synchronisation (see *Appendix*). It makes no sense at all to interpret the minor key here as conveying sadness-related emotions; rather, it is an instance of a specific type local digression to the minor key, momentarily departing from within a solid major-key environment and then returning to it, which definitely appealed to Mozart in more cases than one. I prefer to call this device "the insinuating (or "the mysterious) minor". It conveys a gesture of mentally winking at the audience, characterised by an air of sharing a dark secret of sorts. A similar use of the insinuating minor digression can be found in aria no. 4, when Leporello, as it were, confides in Donna Elvira and makes her privy to the 'classified information' that Don Giovanni's rule of indiscriminate attitude to all women has one exception: his preference for young beginners, i.e., virgins. This special preference is singled out musically in this consistently-major-key aria by its sole digression to the minor (mm 130-135; the harmonic reduction in the lower stave represents the orchestra):

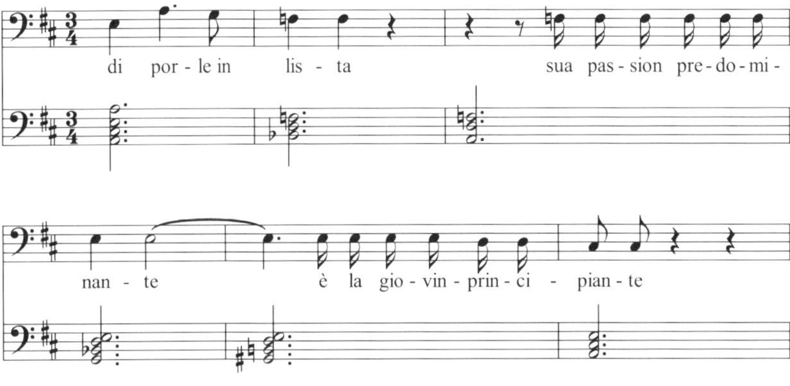

Fig. 7

Similar in terms of comic-erotic function is a case of 'insinuating chromaticism' in aria no. 12: in its beginning, when Giovanni speaks of luring the girls from the village square to attend his banquet, the descending chromatic tetrachord (mm 20-24) is shrewdly used as a mock-*lamento* device, mimicking and ridiculing the time-honoured **genuine** *lamento* motif[40] (discussed in this volume in Tråvén's article). This is a significant, though much too brief moment.[41] Giovanni is mentally winking here, producing an effect of a dramatic-theatrical "aside", as if sharing with the audience another dark secret: how, and for what purpose, he is scheming to lure the village girls to his palace.

Fig. 8

It is significant that in this aria (no. 12) the most brazenly sexual musical gestures do not coincide with the relatively explicit image evoked by *"amoreggiar"* (set, as we have just seen, to the 'insinuating minor'), but with the verbal references to the indirect, **implicitly** sexual catalogue of dances, which Don Giovanni plans to activate simultaneously (as he actually does, through Mozart's synchronised multi-metred feat, at the banquet scene in the Finale of Act I). In the absence of any musical or structural justification, it seems that the likely interpretation of what sounds like a series of many **arbitrary** repeats of the same thrusting figures and gestures, pounding again and again, is an imitation (or rather, in the context, an imagined premonition) of a sexual act. In terms of temporal sequence it is analogous to foreplay, preceding not only the actual event (which is doomed never to occur) but even the verbal reference to it; musically, however, it is the event itself, occurring in Don Giovanni's mind, out of joint with the (non) action in reality. A remarkable feature of this aria is that the final, least motivated, and longest repetitive series of this pounding gestural motif (mm 105-120) consists of ten identical thrusts (each coextensive with one measure, each articulated with a *sforzando — **fp*** in the score). After these ten identical measures (or, more precisely, five identical pairs of measures, each odd-numbered measure tonic-oriented and each even-numbered one dominant-oriented) there is an additional, more ornate thrust, crowned by a jubilant liberating coda in mm 117-120.

Fig. 9

This coda anticipates the triumphant ending of the entire aria, where
Giovanni, in Da Ponte's text, explicitly plans to celebrate the addition of ten
names ("*una decina*") to his catalogue in the next morning, documenting ten
fresh nocturnal conquests.[42]

It is also remarkable that in the beginning of this aria (no. 12) Don Giovanni
is scheming to seduce his ladies by offering them a **variety** of dances, each
according to her taste and rank, in order to reduce them all at the end of the
day to **identical** sex objects. As we have seen, the ten identical thrusts
represent — and, to Giovanni, anticipate — totally identical (feverishly
imagined) sex acts with ten individual women, whose individuality is
nullified through the process.

This interpretation is corroborated by Giovanni's individuality-negating
attitude to women in the entire opera. Thus, in no. 4 once again, the rhetorical
figure of *gradatio* is used to introduce the "conquered" women according to
class and rank, as demonstrated convincingly in Tråvén's article. Graded,
indeed, is Leporello's class-conscious view of the women **before** being
subjected to Don Giovanni's 'egalitarian treatment'. However, the same
words referring to the classes of women, after their *gradatio* setting, are now
re-introduced to parade them all, as it were, up and down Giovanni's scale-
ladder, regardless of their previously held ranks (mm 70-75).

Harai Golomb

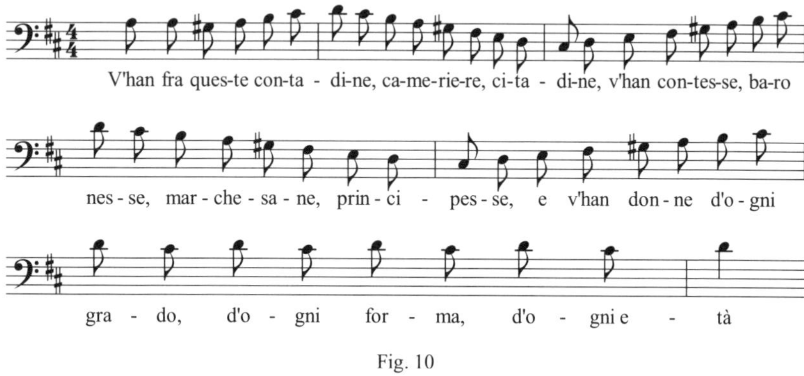

Fig. 10

Mozart's music, then, shows how country wenches who had been on the lower part of the ladder in the *gradatio* setting, are now starting to climb to its top, whereas princesses who had been on top are now descending to its bottom. This is the musical reflection of an idea repeated in so many words, describing Giovanni's wooing strategies, in the rest of the aria and elsewhere in the opera.

Indeed, chances that an amateur or even a professional listener, erudite in Italian and in Mozart's operatic language alike, would be aware of these patterns from just listening to them once or twice are close to nil. Yet they are there; and only carefully designed MLT of the piece can offer an attentive, erudite and analytically minded listener, who is nevertheless ignorant of Italian, a rare opportunity to experience this revelatory instance of Mozart's musical and theatrical genius.[43]

3.4. Diminished Harmony of Dominant Desires

Last but not least, an example from *Così fan tutte*. In the famous *terzettino* (I, 10) the text says: *"Soave sia il vento / Tranquilla sia l'onda / Ed ogni elemento / Benigno risponda / Ai nostri desir"* [literally, roughly: "May the wind blow gently / And the waves be calm; / May every element / Respond benignly / To our desires".] The music is one of the most typical examples of what Nikolaus Harnoncourt (1988:136) calls "Mozartian Bliss": the wavy, murmuring melodic lines of the strings imitate the tranquil breeze and calm

150

ripples, and every melodic and harmonic interval, every rhythmical and dynamic pattern and every detail of orchestration — indeed, "every element" [of the music], as the text itself says — contributes to the heavenly sweetness of the piece.

Now the most important word set to this music is the very last one, "*desir*". Potentially (like its English etymological twin, "desire"), it can signify an entire semantic field around the concept of **will**, covering the whole range between the extremes of the 'angelical' wishes and aspirations of the spirit and the 'bestial' drives and lusts of the flesh. Under the musical conditions just described, the balance is strongly tilted in favour of the former: the 'high', 'noble' meanings are foregrounded through the selective support of the music, whereas the 'low' ones are pushed aside and marginalised, as it were, being unrelated to the nature of the music.[44] And indeed, when the word "*desir*" appears for the first time, it is not singled out in any way, perfectly blending with the other words in producing that blissful effect. However, when the word appears for the second time, Mozart throws in a surprising flash of a totally unexpected and seemingly unmotivated tense chord, delaying the closural solution, musically expected at this point, with dissonant harmonies, which produce a dark and ominous effect. He is not satisfied until he repeats this ominous harmony twice within a couple of seconds, with the same solution-delaying harmony,[45] realised melodically with few insignificant changes; this effect is striking, totally unmissable, working as it does on all musical levels — of melody, harmony, rhythm, structure, articulation, and orchestration; yet its main significance resides of course in word/music interaction: the sinister chord, synchronised exactly with the second appearance of the word "*desir*", highlights its darker semantic components;[46] as if Mozart, through his music, is saying to us: Take heed, it's not only lofty, benevolent aspirations and well wishing that we have here — though (to be sure) these, too, are there, foregrounded by the general effect of the music — but also, even mainly, "Black and deep desires", as Shakespeare's Macbeth puts it (I, iv, 51). [47] The musical reference to these passions and lusts is ominous, particularly at this early stage in the unfolding plot, foreshadowing the crucial role of deep-seated passions both in propelling and in signifying the upcoming events, as well as the emotional upheavals of the major characters from this point on, to the end of the opera. The fascinating ways in which Mozart's music addresses a multi-layered and multi-faceted panorama of human desires give this opera a profound, passionate dimension, overlooked by quite a few musicians and critics for over two centuries. This dimension goes far above and beyond the erroneous reputation of this opera as a **mere** frivolous farce, which it has so wrongly acquired since its composition.

Fig. 11

It is essential for an MLT practitioner to identify and nurture these precious operatic moments, where the synchronisation of specific words, messages and significations with localised musical events is so vital and crucial for the understanding of an entire opera. It is remarkable, then, that all three English translators whose work I have checked have failed a test in translating this exquisite example, which in this particular case is a surprisingly, even intolerably easy and simple one. Personally, I envy the unearned luck of all translators of this text into English, since their language provides them with a ready word, "desire", which is etymologically and semantically identical with the Italian *"desir"*, and even phonetically close. It strangely looks as if Mozart and Da Ponte adopted an exceptionally considerate attitude towards future English translators, in preferring the heightened and truncated form *"desir"* to a variant like *"desire"* [in the penultimately-stressed Italian pronunciation], or to *"desio"* (which Mozart and Da Ponte use elsewhere, e.g., in Cherubino's aria in Act I of *Le Nozze di Figaro*), or to the synonym more prevalent in modern Italian, *"desiderio"* (the latter, of course, has more syllables and would require a change in the music). The chosen option, *"desir"*, like the English "desire", is disyllabic and stressed on the last syllable, and is released in this context from the bonds of rhyming. For an MLT translator it is a rare gift. It is just astounding, then, not to say infuriating, that the three translators did not opt for the only obvious and correct solution. The cornerstone of any English translation of this *terzettino* must be substituting "desire" for *"desir"*, and the rest of the text must follow from this mandatory matching.[48] So let us look at the three failures of English MLT translators.

In the Kalmus bi-lingual vocal score (tr. 3, p. 64-66) the MLT text is: "O wind gently flowing / O'er ocean be playing / O tide calmly flowing / The ship safe conveying / In peace to the shore. / O sun brightly shining / Shed happiness o'er them / Be nature combining / Ere long to restore them / To greet us once more". The temporary [?] 'operatic deafness', contracted at least at this point in the text by the 19th century translator Marmaduke E. Browne, was not cured by John Cox in his revision of this text (tr. 6, p. 70), leaving Browne's blunder intact.[49]

The company named "Opera Factory" of Sydney/London (see 3.1 above) performed their witty English version of *Così fan tutte*, televised for England's Channel 4 in 1989. It seems that David Freeman, the company's founder and director, is also responsible for the English text (no credit to a translator is given in the televised version, which is my only source[50]). Be that as it may, the English text of the *terzettino* as sung by members of this group sounds as follows: "Blow gently, you breezes, / Rest quietly, great ocean; / For heaven surely pleases / To grant them protection, / And guide them to shore." Once again, then, we encounter the same unbelievable error: the bland and lukewarm "shore" coincides with Mozart's striking ominous chord, and replaces the only legitimate word that must be used here, "desire".

Jeremy Sams, whose more recent version is witty and sparkling in many instances, at this particular point also turns a deaf ear to Mozart's music. His text is: "With winds gently blowing, / And seas softly flowing, / Let nature caress them, / Protect them and bless them, / And keep them from harm."[51] Mozart's startling harmonies sound quite inexplicable with all of these insensitive translations; and amazingly, the conductors, who should know better, seem to have held their peace.

All three versions, then, are in flagrant violation of translational adequacy. It is bad enough that "desire" is ignored as a word; but moreover, as a result, it is ignored as an idea as well, which is more inexcusable. All the quoted translations oversimplify Mozart's complexity, reducing his conceptual counterpoint to flat uniformity, aligning the dramatic potency of his music with lukewarm textual platitudes.

Once again, it can be claimed, not without cause, that under usual conditions of performance members of the audience are highly unlikely to be aware of the workings of that single word, "desire", whether in Italian or in any other language. The same though can be said with equal validity about many complex devices and messages in art. Great creative minds in all arts often communicate with their audiences by addressing subliminal levels of perception and activating cognitive processes, which take time, and repeated exposures to the same artistic texts, to develop, mature, and reach conscious awareness. And even if such awareness is a rare phenomenon, the creative energies invested by the artist (in our case, Mozart) to activate it are there, observable and analysable in the artistic texts (in our case, his operas). Mozart's creative investment should be addressed with respect, i.e., with a matching effort on our part to realise its potentialities as fully as we can, each of us in his or her capacity as performer, analyst, listener/spectator, translator, etc. At any rate, audiences willing and able to make such an effort, yet hindered because of language limitations, deserve a translator's effort to help them to the fullest operatic experience.

The fullness of such an experience depends to a decisive extent upon the subtle synchronisation of words and music in the most crucial points in the opera. As we have seen, audiences with no command of SL cannot experience this unique synchronisation of music, verbal sound and rhythm, referential sense of words, moments of plot action and characterisation, without MLT. They have legitimate cause for malpractice complaint if a translator deprives them of this experience by withholding vital artistic and semiotic information.

This, ultimately, is the constant need, the durable *raison d'être*, of MLT.

Appendix: Three English Versions of Don Giovanni's Aria no. 12

Now while the drinking
Stops them from thinking
Feasting and dancing
We will prepare.
More girls we'll pillage
Out of the village,
Search every street and
Search every square!
Down with formality!

Mix them together,
Some minuetting
Some the folia
Clod, cavalier
What do I care?

For in the meanwhile
I shan't be seen while
I'm cultivating
My special flair…
And in the morning
You'll be adorning
Your list with ten more
Ten more, I swear!
[N. Platt & L. Sarti]

For a carousal
Where all is madness,
Where all is gladness
Do thou prepare.
Maids that are pretty
Dames that are witty
All to my castle
Bid them repair.
I'll have no discipline

Folly shall rule it
Some minuetting,
Each one shall fool it,
Some a fandango,
So they are fair.

Then in the gloaming,
Pensively roaming,
Some pretty damsel
With me will stray…
Beauties in plenty
My list adorning
Will ere the morning
Not say me nay!
["Kalmus", unnamed]

Song, Wine and women
Who'd be without them?
I'll have my pleasure
Morn, noon and night.
These comely wenches
Fresh from the country
Fill me with rapture
Joy and delight.
Ask every girl you see

Make no distinction
Ask all the village
Ply them with liquor
Set them a-dancing
Till it be light,
Make no [etc.] /Ask all [etc.]
I'll all invite
Then while the menfolk
Drink and are merry
I'll play at love's game
Safe out of sight…
And in the morning,
Yes, in the morning
You'll have a dozen
More names to write!
[Edward J. Dent]

The Original Italian Text:

Fin ch'han del vino/ calda la testa/ una gran festa/ fa preparar/ Se trovi in piazza/ qualche ragazza/ teco ancor quella/ cerca menar./ Senz'alcun ordine,/ La danza sia,/ ch'il minuetto,/ che la follia,/ chi l'Alemana/ farai ballar;/ Ed io frattanto/ Dal'altro canto/ con questa e quella/ vo' amoreggiar./ Ah la mia lista/ Doman mattina/ d'una decina/ deve aumentar!

Notes

[1] I would like to express my general indebtedness to three articles: Dinda L. Gorlée (1997 and 2002) and Peter Low (2003). I am particularly indebted to Gorlée (2002) for its splendid scholarship and sophisticated analyses, and to Low 2003, for its functional, down-to-earth yet comprehensive conceptual framework. Parts of all these articles are at the core of the present study, to the extent that I refrained from giving specific credit with page references every time this was justified, to preclude repetitiveness and tedious reading of this article.

[2] In his words: "Intersemiotic translation, or **transmutation** [emphasis supplied], is an interpretation of verbal signs by means of signs of nonverbal sign systems" (Jakobson 1987: 429). MLT is basically verbal translation, variously conditioned, shaped, affected and constrained by a "nonverbal sign system", namely music, but not an interpretation of the verbal "by means of" that nonverbal system.

[3] This does not imply, of course, that I consider this to be the sole 'correct' use of these terms. The restrictions specified here are adopted only for the purpose of the present discussion.

[4] This triad — Unity, Intensity and Complexity — constitutes the three canons of artistic value according to Monroe C. Beardsley (1958: 462).

[5] "And as imagination bodies forth / The forms of things unknown, the poet's pen / Turns them to shapes, and gives to airy nothing / A local habitation and a name".

[6] As we shall see below, there is no perfect symmetry between the two components in this and in many other respects; this complex subject will be dealt with only briefly in this article.

[7] Notably when the verbal text is an autonomous, canonised work of literary, poetic or dramatic art, e.g., when Benjamin Britten (1913-1976) uses Shakespeare's text as libretto for his opera *A Midsummer Night's Dream*. Counter examples include Modest Musorgsky's (1835-1881) *Boris Godunov*, where the composer's own libretto is freely based on Alexander Pushkin's (1799-1837) play, or Giuseppe Verdi's (1813-1901) use of commissioned libretti, rather than Italian canonised translations, for his Shakespearean operas.

[8] I am aware of course of the differences between all these terms in general, and of controversies and differences relating to the term "adequate" in particular; however, for the purpose of the present discussion, these differences are marginalised, the idea being the existence of a basic norm of acceptability, however applied or defined.

[9] By this term I mean everything included in the written libretto — sheer language elements, as well as literary, poetic, dramatic and theatrical ones, notably stage directions. In opera the basic dichotomy juxtaposes music with all the rest, then the latter cluster is subdividable into various heterogeneous components.

[10] In the extreme formulation of Ivan Fónagy (2001: 430): "Translation consists of the transposition of verbal content from one language to another. This means, for the translator, concentrating on the meaning and entirely disregarding the form of expression." Subsequently Fónagy himself exempts the translation of poetry from his rule, and of course his formulation cannot (nor does it claim to) apply to MLT.

[11] Such preservation of sounds is often regarded as merit in verse translations; in MLT the sound component, as a rule, is of paramount importance, often even more than in verse translations, yet its preservation is usually difficult and frequently impossible. Rhymes tend to acquire special significance in MLVs, being their most viable sound pattern (one can usually hear rhymes in sung texts even when other verbal sound patterns are obliterated, or at least blurred, by the music). Therefore most MLT practitioners tend to preserve the rhyme system, and try their best even to reproduce the original sounds of rhymes when possible.

[12] Aspects of the musical treatment of paralinguistic and extra-linguistic features are discussed in Tråvén's article in this book; the present study is concerned with the musical and the linguistic only.

[13] Note, however, the correct observation by Arthur Graham (1989: 33) as quoted in Gorlée
(2002: 167): "The framework for translation [of vocal texts] must be the music, not the original
poem. Further, the translator should avoid thinking in terms of poetic metric feet; such scansion
does not always match musical notation."

[14] In the words of Eugene Nida (1964: 177), as quoted in Gorlée (1997: 245): "The translator of
poetry without musical accompaniment is relatively free in comparison with one who must
translate a song — poetry set to music. Under such circumstances the translator must concern
himself with a number of severe restrictions: (1) a fixed length for each phrase, with precisely
the right number of syllables, (2) the observation of syllabic prominence (the accented vowels or
long syllables must match correspondingly emphasized notes in the music, (3) rhyme, where
required, and (4) vowels with appropriate quality for certain emphatic or greatly lengthened
notes." Most of Nida's points are adopted here, with some modifications, and within a more
hierarchical perspective.

[15] This is very similar to the rule of correlation between poetic metre and linguistic phonology,
for which I am indebted to Harshav's studies (e.g., 1971). His many writings on prosody in
Hebrew and English further develop this concept. See also the many discussions of, and
arguments about, the concept of "stress-maximum in weak position", prevalent in the literature
on prosody and metrics in recent decades, e.g., Halle and Keyser (1971); Tsur (1997 and 1998);
and the works they cite. By the way, the internet link supplied for Tsur 1997 (see Bibliography
below) enables the reader to hear sound files demonstrating the issue through recorded readings
of English poetry.

[16] Another early-music example I can recall is an incorrect first-syllable stress in the French word
allons in a chanson by Guillaume Costeley (1531-1606), and there are many others. In Henry
Purcell's (1659-1695) *Dido and Aeneas* one can hear a music-imposed incorrect ultimate-
syllable stress in the word "hero" (see illustrations of this matter in Figures 1-3). Such practices
imply attributing lesser significance than in more recent periods to the placement of intra-lexical
stress. In Hebrew, a stress-dominated language, mediaeval poets rhymed and scanned their verse
disregarding stress, a practice unthinkable in modern Hebrew verse. See Harshav (1971).

[17] Thus, for instance, the very first word of the text of the catholic Mass, Kyrie, is sometimes set
to music by Giovanni Palestrina (ca. 1526-1594), but also by much later composers, as two
syllables, although the very same composers much more often treat the same word as three
syllables; other examples abound.

[18] Each of these is a wide and very important topic, which the scope of this paper does not permit
me to elaborate and illustrate sufficiently.

[19] I am indebted to Marianne Tråvén for pointing out to me that the final outcome is fluent and
natural in terms of the regular rhythms of German speech; but this, again, is so only because the
music allows it, freely choosing to maintain patterns of natural breathing and pausing. The
formal relationships, though, still exhibit a discrepancy between a binary metre in the verbal text
and a ternary one in the music. In this case, then, Mozart's music **chooses** to be attentive to the
rhythms of relaxed speech, while obliterating Schikaneder's formal trochaic metre in the libretto,
which in itself is much less attentive to those rhythms (Mozart's librettist, Emanuel Schikaneder
1751-1812). In the verbal text, in its music-free state, the trochee interacts with the speech
rhythms; this interaction cannot work with music, and is replaced by other interactions, typical to
word/music interrelationships.

[20] The subject of intonation, with and without relation to music, has been widely discussed in the
literature. See, for instance, a seminal collection of studies in Bolinger (1972); see also Fónagy
(2001:124-190), and Golomb (1979:269-300). Extensive bibliographies are included in each of
the latter two studies.

[21] This is so because segmental phonemes are determined by timbre, the only psycho-acoustic
parameter in linguistic phonetics that retains its autonomous existence when aligned with music.

[22] The subject can, of course, be elaborated much beyond the scope of this discussion. Benjamin Harshav (1980) develops a detailed, thought-provoking model, classifying sound/sense relationships in poetry and language, that can yield interesting results if applied to verbal/musical sound/sense interactions, which he does not discuss. I shall attempt such an application in a separate study.

[23] This categorical statement can be slightly modified in specific types of musical composition — notably, the recitative — in which music is designed to be more closely aligned with the rhythms of natural speech. However, these are exceptions that reinforce the rule; moreover, even in recitatives every case should be checked locally whether a viable musical (usually melodic) pattern has been created and is worth preserving intact through music-dominated translation.

[24] By the way, there is no contradiction between these approaches. A practitioner, and a scholar, can well adopt an author-oriented as well as a singer-oriented approach, or any other combination. In principle, in an ideal world, there is indeed no conflict between these approaches; but in imperfect reality, where 'sacrificial' choices must be made, one has to adopt an order of preferences. A practitioner can do that intuitively; a scholar, however, must do it advisedly and explicitly.

[25] By the same token, the composer-oriented approach can be called 'composition-oriented', the analyst-oriented one is 'structure-oriented', and the singer-oriented one is 'performance-oriented'.

[26] I am referring here, as a rare example, to the way in which Mozart transfers the theme sung by loving and contented Figaro and Susanna, in Act 4 of *Le Nozze di Figaro*, set to the words "*pace, pace mio dolce tesoro*", to the cunning and frustrated Count, whose entire being at this moment is sharply contrasted with the emotions of the couple as celebrated by this theme (of course, the Count sings the same tune with different words). This moment of exceptional musical beauty betrays an instance of dramatic carelessness, rare and untypical in Mozart. There is no need to excuse this moment with contrived explanations designed to establish Mozart's super-natural infallibility; after all, even a genius like Mozart was human, and could (and rarely did) err, failing to meet his own standards.

[27] He speaks about various types of texts used by performers, writers of programme notes for concerts and inserts/liner-notes for recordings, etc., summarising/paraphrasing the source text. Only the types of texts purporting to represent the MLV in full, claiming the status of translation, concern the present discussion; yet I do subscribe to the user-oriented nature of Low's approach.

[28] How a need is determined, and how criteria for determining it are established, and by whom — these are scholarly questions in their own right, addressed, if ever, in social sciences.

[29] This is unfortunately indeed the case in many instances: even some of the most famous opera singers blur their texts, especially the consonants; and indeed some opera houses adopt the use of surtitles even when the opera is sung in the language of the audience, i.e., the actual texts, while being sung, are also shown in captions, no translation involved. This practice is sometimes explained as assisting the hard of hearing, but it also helps the hearing audience overcome singers' enunciation problems.

[30] The resemblance between the texts may indicate that Browne is the anonymous Kalmus translator.

[31] This version is unpublished to the best of my knowledge; I took dictations from a home-made video recording of a television broadcast.

[32] Actually, this presentation of the matter is simplified, if not simplistic. The number of components is far larger than three, since each is subdividable into significant parts and sub-components, too many and too varied to enumerate here.

[33] The obviously coincidental association to the generic-operatic term "aria" does not make this text more comprehensible in context.

[34] Thus, in Act IV, right after Barbarina's celebrated F minor aria, the short *secco* dialogue between her and Figaro evolves around a too-repetitive mention of "*pini*", set in an insinuating

context; the other central word is *"spilla"*, which by total chance can translate into English as pin....

[35] For lack of space I discuss throughout this section only the quoted translations' (lack of) treatment of a specific local challenge. I cannot discuss their other faults and merits.

[36] In both cases it can be claimed (with different amount of conviction for different characters and situations) that the characters could be unaware of the insinuations their words are making, but no such dispensation can be made for Mozart or Da Ponte.

[37] Platt/Sarti's version, bringing together "pleasure" and "innocent love", may be said to hint at the original direction, but it is certainly not half as bawdy. Literally, there is even a contradiction between the "pains" or "pangs" of the original and the "pleasure" of the translation in the rhyming word; however, a careful reading of the text shows that there is no real contradiction.

[38] I provide three English versions of this aria as Appendix, without discussing them, for readers' consideration; the numerous details require a separate study.

[39] It is important not only because of its fame and popularity, but mainly because it is Don Giovanni's most frank and genuine aria, sung at a rare point when he has no reason for pretence or make-believe: at this point in the plot he is not seducing anybody, nor running/cunning for his life, nor having to impress anyone.

[40] As Nikolaus Harnoncourt (1991: 23) says: "Mozart uses none of the old forms in the traditional manner, but always adds something which brings it up to date."

[41] This poses a special challenge to the performers. All (more than a dozen) performances known to me, without exception, execute this aria very fast, at a speed that cannot maintain tangible effects of the digressions to minor and chromaticism. Thus the two digressions, which cannot be coincidental, are lost on listeners in performance. Conductors and singers, just as translators, are indeed often unaware of the significance of these rhetorical devices. Admittedly, Mozart did not make the choice of tempo easy, marking this aria *presto*, a tempo suitable for most of it, but less so for the minor and chromatic digressions. It seems that he was not aware of the fact that amazing effects of some of his creative energies, invested in producing astounding feats of composition, cannot be sensed because most ordinary humans need more time than his tempo supplies in order to notice and experience them.

[42] I am very cautious in suggesting that Mozart deliberately produced here a precise numerical match between the ten identical thrusts in the music and the ten projected conquests in the text: there is no way to prove or disprove such a claim. Rather, 10 is a (round) figure (of speech), to denote in this context merely "many", and this applies intuitively also to the music. The basic effect on the listener would have been quite the same if the number of thrusts were nine, eleven, or any similar number for that matter, as long as it would make an impact of excessive repetitiveness while not trying the listener's patience beyond endurance.

[43] Such subtleties are not obvious even to scholars and professionals; thus, it took me decades of intense acquaintance with the opera and years of work as an MLT translator to discover some of them, and I am sure there are many more to discover, unnoticed yet by anyone. Allanbrook (1983), for instance, gives a typically insightful and sensitive reading of this aria (see pp. 220-223), but the three matters on which the present discussion focuses — the use of chromaticism and the minor key, the repetitive pounding pattern, and the tempo problems in performance — seem to escape her notice. Such cases of oversight occur time and again in the best analyses of great works of art; more than anything else, they attest to the inexhaustibility of such works.

[44] This illustrates my theoretical point about "selective interaction" in Section 1.1 above: verbal and semantic elements become foregrounded through their interaction with the music, and backgrounded in the absence of such interaction.

[45] The precise definition of this chord (diminished-seventh-chord of the secondary dominant on a pedal of the [primary] dominant), is less significant here than its striking effect (this chord, by the way, was adopted more often at later stages in music history, e.g., in Mendelssohn's *A Midsummer Night's Dream* overture).

[46] In the words of Nikolaus Harnoncourt (1991:22): "Mozart is writing a totally dissonant, magical harmony on the word 'desires', which tells an entirely different story."

[47] Harnoncourt (1991:23) once again uses very apt words characterising this moment: "… there is this 'second text' like **a devil behind an angel, both speaking the same words but meaning something entirely different**" [my emphasis — H.G.].

[48] The case is so clear-cut, and the crucial importance of the word and its synchronisation with the music is so blatant and incontrovertible, that this is one of the rare cases where a scholar can relinquish his descriptive and analytical stance and adopt a shamelessly prescriptive posture.

[49] The entire translation is erroneous, **unnecessarily** inventing texts for two stanzas when the original has only one (repeated twice), and committing other translational 'sins'. Yet for reasons of space I confine my remarks to one keyword and its mistranslations, as I do in other sections of this article; here this word is *desir*.

[50] There seems to be no printed data about the company, the production, and the English version. My sole source is a home-taped video recording, from which I also tried to take dictations of textual excerpts.

[51] Sams's translation produces here an interesting effect, though a wrong and probably unintentional one: in his text the ominous chord is always synchronised with the word "harm"; at first, the blissful music supports the entire phrase, "and keep them from harm", but when the unique chord appears, it seems to connect to the word "harm" itself, isolated and decontextualised, foregrounding its autonomous sense (without "keep them from"). Needless to say, this has nothing to do with Mozart's or Da Ponte's meaning, nor do I believe that this twist was envisaged by Jeremy Sams himself.…

Bibliography

Allanbrook, Wye Jamison. 1983. *Rhythmic Gesture in Mozart:* Le Nozze di Figaro *and* Don Giovanni. Chicago and London: University of Chicago Press.

Beardsley, Monroe C. 1958. *Aesthetics: Problems in the Philosophy of Criticism.* New York and Burlingame: Harcourt, Brace and World.

Bolinger, Dwight (ed.). 1972. *Intonation: Selected Readings.* Harmondsworth, Middlesex, England: Penguin Books.

Fónagy, Ivan. 2001. *Languages within Language: An Evolutive Approach.* (Foundations of Semiotics 13). Amsterdam and Philadelphia: John Benjamins.

Golomb, Harai. 1979. *Enjambment in Poetry: Language and Verse in Interaction* (Meaning and Art Series, 3). Tel-Aviv: The Porter Institute for Poetics and Semiotics, Tel-Aviv University.

Gorlée, Dinda L. 1997. "Intercode Translation: Words and Music in Opera" in *Target* 9 (2): 235-270.

—— 2002. "Grieg's Swan Songs" in *Semiotica* 142 (1/4): 153-210.

Graham, Arthur. 1989. "A New Look at Recital Song Translation" in *Translation Review* 29: 31-37.

Halle, Morris and Samuel Jay Keyser. 1971. *English Stress: Its Growth and Its Role in Verse.* New York: Harper and Row.

Harnoncourt, Nikolaus. 1988. *Baroque Music Today – Music As Speech: Ways to a New Understanding of Music* (tr. Mary O'Neill). Portland, Oregon: Amadeus Press.

—— 1991. "The School of Love or the Confusion of Emotions" (interview with Anca-Monica Pandelea). Insert/Liner notes to a CD Recording of *Così fan tutte* [Teldec recording 9031-71381-2]

Harshav, Benjamin. 1971. "Prosody, Hebrew" in *Encyclopedia Judaica*, vol. 13. 1195-1240.

—— 1980. "The Meaning of Sound Patterns in Poetry: An Interaction Theory" in *Poetics Today* 2 (1a): 39-56.

Jakobson, Roman. 1987. "On Linguistic Aspects of Translation" in Pomorska, Krystyna and Stephen Rudy (eds.). *Language in Literature.* Cambridge, Massachusetts: The Belknap Press of Harvard University Press. 428-435 [1st ed. of this article is from 1959]

Low, Peter. 2003. "Translating Poetic Songs: An Attempt at a Functional Account of Strategies" in *Target* 15 (1): 91-110.

Nida, Eugene A. 1964. *Towards a Science of Translating: With Special Reference to Principles and Procedures Involved in Bible Translating.* Leiden: E.J. Brill.

Tsur, Reuven. 1997. "Poetic Rhythm: Performance Patterns and their Acoustic Correlates" in *Versification: An Electronic Journal Devoted to Literary Prosody*, 1. (http://staff.washington.edu/versif/backissues/vol1/essays/tsur.html)

—— 1998. *Poetic Rhythm: Structure and Performance: An Empirical Study in Cognitive Poetics.* Bern: Peter Lang.

List of sources for the Mozart/Da Ponte translation examples:

tr. 1: *The Marriage of Figaro (Le Nozze di Figaro)*, Vocal Score, English Version by Edward J. Dent. London: Boosey & Co., 1947.

tr. 2: *The Marriage of Figaro,* English translation by Jeremy Sams. London: ENO (English National Opera), 2001-2002.

tr. 3: *Don Giovanni*, Vocal Score, English Version by Edward J. Dent. London: Boosey & Co., 1946.

tr. 4: *Don Giovanni,* English translation by Norman Platt and Laura Sarti. Opera Guide 18, English National Opera. London: John Calder, 1983.

tr. 5: *Così fan tutte,* Kalmus Vocal Scores no. 6318, bi-lingual (Italian-English) edition, 1968. Name of translator withheld, most probably Marmaduke E. Browne (c. 1890).

tr. 6: *Così fan tutte,* English translation by Marmaduke E. Browne (c. 1890), revised by John Cox. Opera Guide 22, English National Opera. London: John Calder, 1983.

tr. 7: *Così fan tutte,* English translation by Jeremy Sams. London: ENO, 2001-2002.

A Semiotic Clash in *Maria Stuarda*: Music and Libretto versus the Protestant Version of British History[1]

Ronnie Apter and Mark Herman

Giuseppe Bardari's (1817-1861) Italian libretto for Gaetano Donizetti's (1797-1848) opera *Maria Stuarda,* based on Friedrich von Schiller's (1759-1805) German play *Maria Stuart,* expands Schiller's fictional invention of a competition between Elizabeth Tudor (1533-1603) and Mary Stuart (1542-1587) for the love of the Earl of Leicester, and makes an explicit love triangle the core of the plot. Translators of the opera into English face a semiotic clash arising from two choices made by the opera's creators. Bardari's libretto largely takes the Catholic view that Mary was a religious heroine and Elizabeth her murderer. The Protestant view, held by most English speakers, is that Elizabeth was a great ruler and Mary a potential usurper. Also, despite the opera's Elizabethan setting, Donizetti's music continually signifies 19th-century Italy. This article discusses the problems for a performable English translation stemming from the resultant semiotic clash, only some of which were solvable by the authors in their translation for Ricordi in Milan.

Introduction

According to Robert Donington (1990: 13), "The total symbolism which is opera will not add up unless the staging is basically compatible in style with the words and the music." He probably would not have approved of a 1997 Dutch production of the opera *Maria Stuarda* by Gaetano Donizetti, first performed in 1835. The opera depicts events leading up to the execution of Mary Stuart on 8 February 1587 at Fotheringhay Castle in England. Sung in the original Italian, the Dutch production made no effort to set the opera in 16th-century England, despite some period gestures in the costumes and set. Symbolism introduced by the stage director included bald-headed women strolling around Westminster Palace, what may have been a cocaine-sniffing scene, and a dancer, sometimes representing Mary Stuart and sometimes representing Elizabeth Tudor, worked like a marionette by George Talbot, the Earl of Shrewsbury.

None of this was "basically compatible in style with the words and the music" (Donington 1990: 13). And yet, the same director's interpretation of the characters of Elizabeth, Mary, and Robert Dudley, Earl of Leicester, was of considerable interest, and possibly *not* in spite of the above-mentioned oddities. Therefore, it is well to consider something that Donington does not: opera, like all art forms, plays with and against both the conventions existing at the time and place of its creation and those existing at the time and place of its performance. Furthermore, the symbols of an opera are not absolute; they depend on the conventional frame. What was perceived as a unified whole in Italy in 1835 may appear inconsistent in the United States a century and a half later; it may be totally incomprehensible to those used to other conventions, say those of Chinese opera.

Such semiotic clashes are present in *Maria Stuarda* for contemporary audiences, especially for those in areas where Protestant culture dominates. The director of that Netherlands production may have been deliberately drawing attention to them. The clashes arise both from the Italian libretto by Giuseppe Bardari and from Donizetti's music. The libretto deviates greatly from the Protestant version of the execution of Mary Stuart familiar to English speakers. The music signifies 19th-century Italy, not 16th-century England.

Probably, the original audience of the opera did not perceive any clashes. From its perspective, Mary was a Catholic martyr and Elizabeth her evil executioner. The music was what the 1835 audience expected to hear. It would not have accepted British Renaissance music, or music that alluded to it. However, the attitudes of the original audience are irrelevant to the problems of a contemporary director.

Equally irrelevant for a translator of the opera into English is the fact that a contemporary English-speaking audience may experience few or no semiotic clashes at a performance *in the original Italian*. When translated into English, the clashes reveal themselves full force, and translators must constantly choose whether to highlight them, let them stand, or blur them.

History and Myth

Before translators begin, they must understand which underlying assumptions they are choosing among. They must learn the inflammatory history of Mary Stuart, Queen of Scots, and the attitudes history and myth have fostered. It is no wonder that Mary struck composer Donizetti and librettist Bardari as a crowd-pleasing topic for an opera. Her tale includes accusations of conspiracy and adultery, passion and murder -- and equally passionate rebuttals. From her own lifetime on, Mary Stuart has been the stuff not only of history but of myth, romance, and poetry. Her unwilling nemesis, Elizabeth Tudor, Queen of England wrote a poem about her which presciently called her the Daughter of Debate:

THE DAUGHTER OF DEBATE

> The dread of future foes exiles my present joy,
> And wit me warns to shun such snares as threaten mine annoy.
> For falsehood now doth flow, and subject's faith doth ebb;
> Which would not be if Reason ruled, or Wisdom weaved the Web.
> . . . .
> The top of hope supposed the root of ruth will be,
> And fruitless all their graffed guiles, as shortly ye shall see.
> . . . .
> The Daughter of Debate, that eke discord doth sow,
> Shall reap no gain where former rule hath taught still peace to grow.
> . . . .
> (quoted in Cowan 1971: 198)

The undisputed historical facts underlying the debate are that in 1567 Mary's cousin and second husband, Henry Stuart, Lord Darnley, was murdered, and within a few months Mary was remarried to James Hepburn, Earl of Bothwell. Soon thereafter, Mary, who was Catholic, fled Scotland in fear of her life at the hands of parties supporting its Protestant Reformation. She sought refuge in England despite the fact that it, too, was Protestant, although there were a large number of openly and secretly Catholic English subjects. Because of Mary's claim to the English throne as the great grand-daughter of Henry VII, a claim Mary refused to repudiate, Queen Elizabeth put her under house arrest. Catholic antagonism towards Elizabeth became official when, in May 1570, Pope Pius V issued the papal bull *Regnans in Excelsis.* According to Plowden (1999: 171), this bull excommunicated Elizabeth, denounced her as "the servant of wickedness," stripped away her title of Queen of England, and absolved her Catholic subjects of any allegiance to her. Eventually, matters came to a head when Mary was tried, convicted, and sentenced to death for complicity in the so-called Babington plot of 1586 against Elizabeth. After a delay, Elizabeth finally signed the death warrant and Mary was beheaded in February 1587.

Throughout the years, the Catholic and Protestant interpretations of the above facts have been very different. The extreme version of Catholic opinion regards Mary as a Catholic martyr who was persecuted and murdered by Elizabeth. From this point of view, Mary was the rightful Queen of England, and Elizabeth merely a bastard daughter of Henry VIII with no legitimate claim to the throne. More moderate Catholic opinion maintains that Mary and Elizabeth both had claims to the throne of England, that at the least Elizabeth should have named Mary as her successor, and that Mary's incarceration and execution at Elizabeth's hands were criminal acts. In England itself, after Mary's death, "while the English Catholics could have welcomed the peaceful succession of Mary Stewart with clear consciences, . . .

when the dreaded Armada [of Catholic Spain] actually appeared in the English Channel the nation, Catholic and Protestant alike, could unite against a common enemy" (Plowden 1999: 221).

On the other hand, extreme Protestant opinion has deemed Mary an adulteress with Bothwell and a co-murderer with Bothwell of Darnley, a conspirator against the life of Queen Elizabeth, and a satanic woman whose execution was well warranted. More moderate Protestant opinion holds that Mary's personal guilt or innocence is irrelevant, that her very existence as a Catholic pretender to the English throne, especially after the Pope's excommunication of Elizabeth, made Mary a serious threat both to the life of Elizabeth and to the stability of the English realm, a threat that had to be eliminated.

The tenor of 19th-century Catholic opinion regarding Mary can be discerned from an anthology edited by Ian Cowan (1971). Here are three statements by Mary's advocates, written or published about the time of the creation of the opera:

> . . . there was not a conspiracy against the Queen of Scots, . . . in which Elizabeth was not concerned against Mary: Neither were there a murderer, a traitor, a rebel, who fled, from Scotland, to England, that Elizabeth did not protect. . . . [W]hen the wise Lord Burghley, sat down to write formal reasons, to justify the Scottish Queen's imprisonment, he found it too hard a task . . . . From all these facts, it is apparent, that Elizabeth, and her ministers, considered every thing convenient to themselves, to be consistent with law, and agreeable to morals, without regarding the wrongs of the Queen of Scots. (George Chalmers 1818: I.382, quoted in Cowan 1971: 196-97)

> Elizabeth was extremely anxious to implicate Mary . . . , and, for this purpose, sent commissioners to her to reproach her with her offences. Mary heard all they had to say with the utmost calmness; and when they called upon her for her answer, she replied, that, though she was a free Queen, and did not consider herself accountable, either to them or their mistress, she had, nevertheless, no hesitation to assure them of the injustice of their accusations. She protested that she had never imagined any detriment to Elizabeth . . . , but was, on the contrary, most ready to reveal any conspiracy against the Queen of England which might come to her ears . . . . Satisfied with this reply, the commissioners returned to London. (H. Glasford Bell 1831: II.198, quoted in Cowan 1971: 199)

> Certane serwantis of Boithwellis, guiltie of the heinous crime, wer executed to death, after they had beene extraordinarielie racked, to draw some one woorde, if they could be driwen therto throwe the paine of the torment, although not true in the selff, against ther Mistres [Mary], after ewerie blowe and stroake of the bitle or hammer, askinge whether ewer her Maistie had spoken to them of the facte, or commaunded the murder of her husband. . . . But notwithstandinge anie torment they could uise, to bringe foorth so much as one woorde against her Maiestie to her preiudice, they wold newer accuse her, saying often, fie upon such crueltie,

> they wold not speake against her to condemne themselwes to the devil, do what
> they wold against ther bodie, ther soules was Godis. (Adam Blackwood 1834 (re-
> published), original date unknown: 51-52, quoted in Cowan 1971: 118)

A largely Protestant audience would have been hearing from Mary's detractors. Samples of their allegations follow:

> The queen's [Mary's] supine inattention to the murder of her husband, after the
> promise of such rigorous vengeance, can neither be imputed to excess of grief,
> nor to the imbecility incident to a female reign. . . . But if accessory, or in the
> least privy to the murder of her husband, she must have acted precisely as she
> did. (Malcolm Laing 1819: I.53-55, quoted in Cowan 1971: 131-32)

> . . . the French king, as likewise the queen of England, had seriously dissuaded
> the queen [Mary] from the same [marrying Bothwell] by their letters; but she, led
> by the violence of passion, and abused by the treacherous counsels of some about
> her, who sought only their own ends, would hearken to no advice given her to the
> contrary. (John Spottiswoode 1847-51: II.54, quoted in Cowan 1971: 145)

> Even were we not furnished with the most unquestionable proofs of her
> complicity by the confessions contained in her letters, the authenticity of which
> we have established elsewhere, as well as by the declarations made in presence of
> their judges and upon the scaffold, by the subaltern actors in this tragic drama,
> her conduct both before and after the murder would suffice to convince us that
> she was a party to the crime. (François Mignet 1851: I.271-72; quoted in Cowan
> 1971: 116)

And what is the judgment of historians? Was Mary innocent or guilty? Schiller stated in his play *Maria Stuart* (1800: V.7, lines 3697, 3729-30), and historians at the time believed, that Mary was complicit in the murder of Darnley but innocent of conspiring against Elizabeth. Modern historians believe the opposite, that Mary was innocent of any foreknowledge of Darnley's murder (Fraser 1969: 331), but that she definitely did, under extreme provocation, write letters joining herself to the Babington plot against Elizabeth, a plot that was largely not a plot at all but an entrapment scheme designed to lead to Mary's execution (Fraser 1969: Chapter 24).

The opera *Maria Stuarda* was written in 1834 for a Catholic audience. The action begins after Mary has been condemned but before Elizabeth has signed the death warrant, and ends with Mary's execution. It is not surprising that the opera presents Mary in the best light and Elizabeth in the worst. More surprising is that, bowing to the view of some respected 19th-century historians, the opera intimates that Mary may have been complicit in the death of Darnley and plots against Elizabeth.

At least one modern historian, Jenny Wormald, complains that the entire question of Mary's guilt or innocence has been a distraction from more important historical matters (1988; revised 2001: 18). But it is just such speculation about crimes of passion, especially if absurd or lurid, rather than the dry facts of history, that attracts the most attention, that becomes the stuff of romance, opera, and Hollywood films. According to Cowan, "the dual legend of Mary, the innocent martyr or the adulterous murderess, . . . [is an] enigma which was given manifestation at that time [the sixteenth century] [and] will persist until histories of the Queen of Scots no longer command attention" (1971: 34). Cowan continues, "Historians will never agree to her character, and in these circumstances, it is perhaps inevitable that the picture of a romantic but ill-fated queen painted by Schiller and Swinburne, amongst others, is the one most likely to engage popular sympathy" (1971: 34).

Schiller's Alteration of History

The transformation of the history of Mary Stuart into the fictional opera *Maria Stuarda* begins with Friedrich von Schiller's German play *Maria Stuart*, the basis for Giuseppe Bardari's opera libretto. Schiller is neither the first nor the last writer to distort history for dramatic purposes. Consider the 1978 musical *Evita* or the 1994 film *Immortal Beloved*, supposedly about Beethoven. Now, while the distortion of history *can* improve a drama -- or make a political point -- it also results in a semiotic clash for people who know the true story, especially if, unlike *Evita,* the resulting work does not obviously proclaim itself as fiction.

Schiller's *Maria Stuart* does not so proclaim itself, despite the fact that its central event is a fictional meeting between Mary Stuart and Queen Elizabeth. Throughout her captivity in England, Mary did repeatedly beg for such a meeting, for she hoped that a face-to-face meeting would persuade Elizabeth to release her. However, Elizabeth always refused.

Also fictional is Schiller's depiction of Robert Dudley, the Earl of Leicester and a favorite of Elizabeth. Schiller makes Dudley into a lover and partisan of Mary who wants to free her and marry her. Historically, in 1563 and 1564, more than twenty years before the action of Schiller's play, Queen Elizabeth proposed Dudley as a husband for Mary, who was then reigning in Scotland. It is true that Elizabeth was jealous of any praise of Mary's beauty. However, no one in Scotland, including

Mary, took the proposal of Dudley seriously (Fraser 1969: 245-46). Furthermore, there is no historical basis for believing that Dudley and Mary were ever in love. In fact, it was probably Dudley, together with William Cecil, the Lord High Treasurer, who secured permission for Mary's cousin Henry Stuart, Lord Darnley, to travel to Scotland and meet Mary in February 1565 (Fraser 1969: 252). Darnley became Mary's ill-fated second husband, and Dudley had no further consequence in Mary's romantic affairs.

In Schiller's play, not only is Dudley in love with Mary, but, when Elizabeth discovers this, he denies it and betrays Mary to secure his own safety.

Another of Schiller's historical inaccuracies makes Elizabeth more villainous than she actually was. Historically, to salve her conscience over the execution of Mary, Elizabeth made her secretary Davison "the scapegoat[; he] underwent a token period of imprisonment and had a fine of £10,000 imposed on him" (Fraser 1969: 626). Schiller implies that Elizabeth had Davison executed. He has her order, *"Man führ ihn nach dem Tower, es ist mein Wille,/ Dass man auf Leib und Leben ihn verklage"* (Schiller 1965: V.15, lines 4011-12) [Let him be led to the tower, it is my will that he be prosecuted for a capital offense.][2]

Schiller also altered the ages of his protagonists: Mary is to be performed as if she were about 25, and Elizabeth as if she were about 30. At the time of Mary's execution in 1587, their actual ages were 44 and 54.

As mentioned above, not all of Schiller's inaccuracies were deliberate. He probably thought the implications of Mary's final confession to be factual, though, according to Fraser (1969: 617), the confession itself is fictional. Schiller has Mary say: *"Den König, meinen Gatten, ließ ich morden / . . . / Doch nie hab ich durch Vorsatz oder Tat / Das Leben meiner Feindin angetastet!* (Schiller 1965: V.7, lines 3697, 3729-30) [[I let my husband, the king, be murdered / ... / But never have I through intention or deed / attacked the life of my (female) enemy!]

Here Mary is confessing her complicity in the murder of Darnley but denying complicity in any murder plot against Elizabeth. As indicated above, modern historians believe the opposite.

In addition to outright historical inaccuracies, Schiller also slants characterizations and descriptions in ways contrary to the British Protestant version of the events. For example, one character's description of Protestantism virtually equates it with extreme Puritanism, while Catholicism is depicted as a far more humane religion. Elizabeth is seen as a person who has unnaturally and unsympathetically reined in all her feelings, though Schiller makes it clear that this was necessary to survive as a queen in a man's world. And Schiller reshapes Mary's final prayer, written down by Mary for posterity. The historical prayer asks that Elizabeth serve God in the years to come and that God avert his wrath from England in retaliation for Mary's execution (Fraser 1969: 621-22). Schiller's version forgives Elizabeth outright for Mary's death and pleads that God preserve Elizabeth and her reign for many happy years.

Bardari's Italian Libretto

If Schiller's play is a distortion of historical reality, Bardari's libretto is a complete subversion of history in the service of early 19th-century Italian opera conventions.

Dudley's love of Mary, a subplot in Schiller's play, is expanded by Bardari to a full-blown love triangle which becomes virtually the only motivating force for the actions of Elizabeth, Mary, and Dudley. The fact that Mary has been sentenced to death by a court for participation in a conspiracy against Elizabeth, carefully explained by Schiller, is omitted by Bardari. Therefore, to an opera-goer ignorant of history, it could very well appear that Elizabeth is not dithering over whether to sign Mary's death warrant and carry out the sentence of the court, or pardon Mary and overrule the court, but agonizing over whether or not, on her own, to execute or spare her rival for Dudley's love. Unlike Schiller's Dudley, Bardari's is true to Mary till the end -- although stage business in the above-mentioned Netherlands production had him self-interestedly return to Elizabeth. In Bardari's libretto, it is left to William Cecil to press for Mary's execution; he is the obvious villain of the opera, but as such he proclaims the true reason for Mary's execution: the threat Mary's very existence posed as a rallying point for Catholic forces plotting to end Elizabeth's reign and life.

Other historical inaccuracies in Bardari's libretto include the slight one of Cecil's addressing Elizabeth directly by name in public (P-V Score I.2: 24, 28) -- royalty was simply not so addressed except during private intimate moments -- and the greater inaccuracy of having Elizabeth's courtiers repeatedly beg for mercy for Mary (P-V Score I.2: 18-33). If anything, Elizabeth's courtiers urged Mary's execution.

Bardari, to a greater extent than Schiller, also slants events to generate sympathy for Mary and opprobrium for Elizabeth. For example, Bardari eliminates the final scene of the play, which Schiller had given to Elizabeth; thus, Bardari lets Mary have the last word -- literally. Bardari also increases the importance of Mary's being a Catholic martyr in the long final prayer sung by Mary and chorus (P-V Score II.8: 284-307).

Curiously, Bardari alters Mary's guilt and innocence. As indicated above, Mary's guilt in Darnley's murder, according to Schiller, was certain. But Bardari makes it ambiguous: "*Arrigo! Arrigo, ahi! misero, per me soggiacque a morte* (P-V Score, II.5: 247) [Harry! Harry, ah! wretched man, because of me you were put to death]. Likewise, Mary's innocence of any conspiracy to murder Elizabeth, certain according to Schiller, is questionable according to Bardari, who has Mary say: "*fu error fatale* (P-V Score, II.5: 252) [it was a fatal error].

Donizetti's Music

The semiotic discrepancy between the opera and the actual history, or at least the Protestant version of it, is, of course, largely to be found in Bardari's libretto. But Donizetti's music can and does reinforce the idea of Mary as the doomed Catholic martyr, the character most deserving of the audience's sympathy. A good example is the Prelude, the very first music the audience hears, before any words are sung at all. Donizetti goes beyond Bardari, who lets Mary have the last word. By means of the Prelude, Donizetti allows Mary to musically open the opera as well, even though the first actual scene is set at Elizabeth's Court in Westminster Palace. In the Prelude, measures that are *Allegro vivace,* representing the awesome power of the state as executioner, alternate with measures that are *Lento,* representing the serenity with which Mary, the heroine, awaits her fate. The beginning of the Prelude is shown in Figure 1.

Figure 1: Beginning of the Prelude

In the opera's final scenes, Donizetti uses all his compositional powers to fully support Bardari's sympathetic portrait of Mary, as critic William Ashbrook notes: "One of the most impressive numbers in *Maria Stuarda* is the eloquent prayer in the final scene... Mary's confession duet with Talbot and her aria-finale are among the most affecting moments in the opera -- indeed, in Donizetti's entire output" (Ashbrook 1992: 214).

Donizetti also directs attention to Mary by giving more music to her than to Elizabeth. While the amount of music devoted to a particular character varies from production to production depending on tempi, cuts, and repeats, it is clear that Mary has more to sing than does Elizabeth. For instance, on the 1976 Decca recording, excluding the long scene in which both Mary and Elizabeth appear, Elizabeth's scenes last about 29.5 minutes, while Mary's scenes last about twice as long: 59.5 minutes.

While the creation of sympathy for Mary may be a semiotic clash for some English speakers, it is not necessarily so for all. In the largely Catholic Republic of Ireland, Mary might be thought of as the heroine of history. However, even there the problem remains that the music largely denies the opera's setting, which is not merely England, but Westminster Palace in London.

Upon Elizabeth's first entrance in Act I she sings a short recitative stating that the King of France is seeking her hand in marriage. The music is very Italian, but the semiotic clash is not too jarring because it is recitative and not an aria. The beginning of this recitative is shown in Figure 2.

Figure 2: Beginning of Elizabeth's Opening Recitative

Elizabeth sings her first aria directly after this recitative. The words indicate that she fears marriage. The reason, ambiguously, is either that marriage will rob her of her liberty or that it will set up a barrier between her and her true love, Robert

Dudley. In the second measure of the orchestral introduction to the aria (P-V Score: 13, m. 131), the notes run up and down scales in parallel thirds, an Italian folk-song motif that firmly anchors the opera in Italy and not in England (see Figure 3).

Figure 3: Introduction to Elizabeth's Opening Aria

The scales in parallel thirds are a recurring motif, and not only for Elizabeth. In an Act I aria, Dudley tells Elizabeth how beautiful Mary is, and argues that Elizabeth should extend pity to her. The running parallel thirds (P-V Score: 67, mm. 82-83) occur just before Dudley begins singing (see Figure 4).

Figure 4: Introduction to Leicester's Act I Aria

Yet another example of the running parallel thirds comes in Act II, when Elizabeth is agonizing over whether or not to sign Mary's death warrant. They are first played in the orchestra (P-V Score: 198, mm. 76-80) in the interval between the first two parts of Elizabeth's aria (see Figure 5). These running thirds clash not only with the setting but also with Elizabeth's emotions, undercutting any sympathy the audience may feel for Elizabeth's plight. We cannot know whether Donizetti consciously wrote this music to mock Elizabeth, but the result is certainly disdain for a woman who is unwomanly by Italian standards.

Figure 5: Orchestral Interlude from Elizabeth's Act II Aria

As discussed earlier, the original Italian audience probably felt no semiotic clash. A contemporary Italian audience may still overlook any discrepancy between Italian sound and English setting as a matter of stage convention. For members of a Catholic audience, the depictions of Elizabeth and Mary may be close to their preconceptions. Even for an English-speaking, largely Protestant audience, some of the clashes may be muted if the opera is sung in Italian. But when the opera is sung in English, the semiotic clashes are fully perceived.

Translating Maria Stuarda *into English*

How, then, does one go about translating *Maria Stuarda* into English? Obviously, translators are faced with problems beyond the ordinary, great as the ordinary problems are.[3] One approach is simply to live with the semiotic clash. But there are other approaches.

One might write an adapted version which fits the existing music. Since the problems in part are inherent in the Italian Catholic view of the two main characters, this adaptation might have to be about two different characters entirely! However, we had no desire to rewrite the libretto, and Ricordi in Milan had specified a moderately close translation.

One might take the position that *Maria Stuarda* has nothing to do with history. We could have forgone studying British history and written a libretto about two 19th-century fictional Italian queens named Elisabetta and Maria. Clashes with our audience's view of history would no longer have been a problem. Even the problems arising from the Italianization of the names would have disappeared. Five-syllable "*Elisabetta*," for instance, could often have been set where Donizetti set it. We would not have been forever searching for a spot to set the 4-syllable "Elizabeth."

But we believe that Bardari and Donizetti intended to write a historical drama, and that we as translators should honor their intentions. We believe this because there are many elements in the opera that tie it to actual history. In addition to the central historical fact of Mary's execution in 1587, the opera makes numerous correct historical references to off-stage figures like Anne Boleyn and Mary's second husband Henry Stuart, Lord Darnley (1545-67); and to off-stage incidents like Darnley's death. Given the necessary paring down of Schiller's play, these references are not explained in detail. Therefore, in the opera these references make no sense unless the audience can supply more of the historical background than is explained onstage. It could be argued that the adaptation from play into opera was done ineptly. We prefer to take the position that Donizetti and Bardari knew, and expected their audience to know, English history, but that they disagreed with the Protestant view of it. Therefore, we decided to present their view of history as best we could; to lessen the degree of semiotic clash in the few cases where to do so would not violate their intentions; and for the most part to live with the semiotic clash. After all, many people would be going to the opera mainly to hear Donizetti's music.

In order to translate *Maria Stuarda* as a historical drama within these limitations, we did three things. First, we gave the characters their correct historical names, despite the resultant problems in setting those names to Donizetti's music. Second, we corrected minor historical inaccuracies which did not consequentially impinge on Bardari's libretto. Third, we slightly shifted the characterization of William Cecil. Bardari's Cecil, as he rants and raves against Mary, is the obvious villain of the piece. But, as discussed above, his rants and raves are arguments for Mary's execution. We took advantage of that to point up the material giving the actual reason Mary was executed: her very existence was a rallying point for those Catholics plotting to depose Elizabeth.

Let us look at these three attempts at minimizing semiotic clash.

Consider the problem of setting an English historical name on a musical underlay intended for an Italianized version. At the beginning of Act I, the chorus and the Earl of Shrewsbury ask Elizabeth to show Mary mercy. The original 17-syllable mostly iambic Italian line is *"Il bel cor d'Elisabetta segua i moti di pietà.* (P-V Score, I.2: 23-24) [Let the good heart of Elizabeth follow the promptings of pity]. It becomes in our singable translation: "Listen to the voice of pity! Good Queen Elizabeth, relent!"

Donizetti sets the line on four musical measures, with each half-line taking up two 4-beat measures. The name *"Elisabetta, "* ending the first half-line, is set so that the accented syllable, "-bet-," is on the downbeat, the primary accent, of the second measure. We found that the English name "Elizabeth" would fit, with respect to both syllable count and accent, into the second half-line, with the accented syllable, "-li-," on the third beat, the secondary accent, of the third measure.

Once the name was so placed, all the remaining English syllables, encompassing all the rest of the meaning of the line, had to be fit onto the notes left over, resulting in the English line given above. The exact musical setting for the Earl of Shrewsbury is shown in Figure 6.

Figure 6: "Elisabetta " into "Elizabeth": The Earl of Shrewsbury's Vocal Line

It is not always possible to find a place for an English name, either because the name itself will not fit or because it is too difficult, without warping English syntax, to fit English words with the required meaning onto the remaining notes of the musical phrase. In that case, we eliminated the name. For example, in Act II, Scene 2, Elizabeth tells Robert Dudley, "*. . . al tuo affetto prepara la tomba / quando spenta Stuarda sarà.* (P-V Score, II.2: 216) [Prepare a tomb for your affection / (for the time) when the Stuart woman shall be dead.] Our English line eliminates the name: "Take your affection and let it be buried, / buried forever with her in the grave."

Finally, it is possible to have an English name where the original Italian text had none. There are several reasons why this might be done: as compensation for a name omitted elsewhere in the English version despite its presence in the original Italian text; as a replacement in English for an Italian description of a person when the equivalent English description would not fit Donizetti's musical vocal line; and as necessary filler to compensate for the fact that Italian words usually have more syllables than do English words.

In Scene 3 of Act I, Elizabeth addresses Robert Dudley, Earl of Leicester, as "*Conte.*" The two-syllable Italian word literally means the one-syllable "Count" and is the equivalent in rank of the British "Earl," also one-syllable. In our English version, we substitute the two-syllable name, "Leicester" (pronounced "Lester").

Sometimes, the reasons for having a name in English where the Italian has none are more complex. For example, at the very beginning of the opera, before Elizabeth has even appeared onstage, the chorus praises her: *"La magnanima Regina"* (P-V Score, I.1: 3) [The magnanimous Queen]. Our singable English version is "Queen Elizabeth of England." Here, our English line resulted from two considerations. First, the three-syllable "*Regina*" had to be replaced with the one-syllable "Queen," hence the need for the name "Elizabeth" to supply filler syllables. Second, once "Queen" and "Elizabeth" were set, there was no way to have a natural-sounding English word meaning "magnanimous," so we continued with "of England" and put the praise word into a different line.

Our second method of minimizing semiotic clash involved the correction of minor historical inaccuracies. For example, early in Act I, Cecil incorrectly addresses Elizabeth directly by name in public. As mentioned above, royalty was not so addressed except during private intimate moments. Bardari's Italian line is *"Ti rammenta, Elisabetta, ch'è dannosa ogni pietà"* (P-V Score, I.2: 24-25) [Remember, Elizabeth, that all pity is dangerous]. We eliminate the un-historical direct address in our translation: "In this instance, any mercy has a fearful consequence." Note that our English line, while eliminating the direct address to "*Elisabetta* / Elizabeth" because it is un-historical, also eliminates the name altogether for the reason, discussed previously, that there is no good place in Donizetti's vocal line to set it, especially as it now has to be part of an indirect address.

Our third and most important attempt at minimizing semiotic clash and restoring historicity to the opera came in our treatment of Cecil's arguments. Cecil was the best character to employ for this endeavor, for he never discusses the love triangle that occupies so much of the rest of the opera. We did not so much change Bardari's libretto as point it more clearly, starting with Cecil's first warning to Elizabeth, given above, where Bardari's "Remember, Elizabeth, that all pity is dangerous" becomes, in our translation, "In this instance, any mercy has a fearful consequence."

In Act II, Cecil says to Elizabeth: *"E pensi? e tardi? e vive chi ti sprezzò? / chi contro te raduna Europa tutta ,/ e la tua sacra vita minacciò tante volte?* (P-V Score, II.1: 193) [Still considering? still delaying? and she who scorned you is still alive? / she who musters all of Europe against you? / and who threatened your sacred life so many times?]. To point these lines, instead of "scorned," we chose "defamed," which has political, rather than personal overtones. Instead of "musters all of Europe against you," we wrote "goads all Europe." "Musters" is clear, but "goads" is more forceful and derogatory. Instead of "threatened your sacred life" we wrote "whose assassins have stalked you." This is historically correct and more vivid. The whole translation of these lines reads: "You ponder. You waver. And Mary remains alive: / she who has so defamed you, who goads all Europe, / turning its kings against you, whose assassins have stalked you..."

Later, near the end of the opera, Cecil says to himself that *"fra noi la pace tornar vedrò.* (P-V Score, II.9: 315-16) [I shall see peace return to us]. Our version, "Peace will return to the realm today," changes the personal "us" to the impersonal "realm," emphasizing the political reasons for Mary's execution.

Cecil's last utterance in the opera is *"Or dell' Anglia la pace è secura, / la nemica del Regno già muor.* (P-V Score, II.10: 333-41) [Now the peace of England is secure, / the enemy of the realm at last dies]. This line requires no further pointing in the English translation. Our version is "Peace in England at long last is certain! / She will die and we are mightily thankful to God!" For reasons arising from concerns common to all opera translation, the non-literal phrase "we are mightily thankful to God" was required by the need to fit Cecil's line into the ensemble. However, the historic Cecil could certainly have said such a thing.

A Limited Reduction of Semiotic Clash

The measures discussed above could only slightly move the English translation of *Maria Stuarda* toward a historical drama recognizable as such to an English-speaking audience. The 19th-century music, inextricably entwined with the words, is always going to signal 19th-century Italy rather than 16th-century England. Nothing can, nor should, be done about that.

Ultimately, the success or failure of the translation must be determined by whether or not it works on stage. We hope there will be several tests, because the success or failure of a single production may be suggestive but cannot be conclusive.

Unfortunately, the translation has yet to receive a single production. This is not really surprising despite the fame of the composer, Donizetti, and the good reputation of the publisher, Ricordi. Worldwide, there are relatively few productions of any opera other than the 20 to 30 works in the standard repertory.

Moreover, even in English-speaking countries, only a tiny fraction of productions are performed in English translation.

Still, the prospects for productions of *Maria Stuarda* may be improving. The autograph of Donizetti's original score was found in Stockholm, Sweden, after being lost for over a hundred years, and the Ricordi edition, which includes our English translation, is the first published edition to be based on Donizetti's autograph (Dotto and Parker 1997: xlviii-xlix). Also, there have been a few productions in recent years, such as the one in the Netherlands in 1997. In addition, the Swedish film and stage director Ingmar Bergman drew attention to the work when he adapted and directed a production of Schiller's play. Bergman's production opened at the Royal Dramatic Theatre of Sweden in Stockholm on 16 December 2000, in a Swedish translation by Britt G. Hallqvist. There were many reviews, including one in *Göteborgs-Posten* on 18 December 2000 with the alliterative remark: *"Styrka, sinnlighet, skuld"* [Strength, sensuality, guilt]. Bergman's production will be followed by a production of the play in 2004 in the United States by the Pittsburgh Public Theater. Finally, and perhaps most important in an age when operatic performance is dominated by stars, there is the growing realization that *Maria Stuarda* is a marvelous showcase for two prima donnas who can act as well as sing.

Final Lurid Note

Unfortunately, placing two rival prima donna sopranos on the same stage can sometimes prove as fractious as placing two rival queens on the same island.

For the originally scheduled premiere of *Maria Stuarda* the two sopranos were Ronzi De Begnis and Anna Del Sere. Neither actually performed their characters because the opera's debut, according to Elizabeth Hudgston (1997), was canceled for reasons never fully explained (xli). It may have been banned, on the eve of its scheduled 1834 premiere at the *Teatro San Carlo* in Naples, because Queen Maria Cristina of Naples, a descendant of Mary Stuart, did not like sad subjects (xliii). In any event, the music was quickly adapted to an entirely different libretto and premiered under the title *Buondelmonte*. *Maria Stuarda* per se finally premiered in December 1835 at La Scala in Milan, but in an altered form (xli).

But actual performances were unnecessary for the two sopranos to display their mutual hatred. Again according to Hudson, "Tension between the two had apparently been building in rehearsal; finally, during the dress rehearsal of the Act One confrontation scene, they abandoned their regal impersonations to engage in an all-out fight. (1997: xlii).

Hudson then quotes the account published on 23 October 1834 in *Teatri, Arti e Letteratura,* an account describing the two sopranos as if they were personifications of the two historical queens:

> But not long after, at the dress rehearsal, Mary's unwillingness so enraged Elizabeth (the more naturally bad-tempered of the two) that, right in the middle of a finale, Elizabeth pounced on her rival, pulling her by the hair, slapping her, biting her, punching her in the face, and nearly breaking her legs in a flurry of kicks.
>
> Mary Stuart, at first stunned, summoned up her courage and defended herself against the Queen of England. But, alas, Elizabeth was the stronger . . . (1997: xlii-xliii)

And so, as usual, history was enacted twice, the first time as tragedy, the second as farce.

Notes

[1] All musical and verbal examples from Maria Stuarda in this article are taken from the critical edition of the piano-vocal score published by Ricordi in Milan in 1997. They are © Copyright 1997 by CASA RICORDI - BMG RICORDI S.p.A. for the piano reduction and the English translation, and are used here by permission.

[2] For a discussion of the standard problems encountered when translating opera for performance, see Apter, "The Impossible Takes a Little Longer" (1989) and "Questions of Quantity" (1989a); and Herman and Apter, "Opera Translation" (1991).

[3] Here and elsewhere, literal translations of lines from Schiller's play and Bardari's libretto are by Mark Herman and Ronnie Apter.

Bibliography

Apter, Ronnie. 1989. 'The Impossible Takes a Little Longer: Translating Opera into English' in *Translation Review* 30/31: 27-37.

——— 1989a. 'Questions of Quantity: Some Difficulties in Translating Opera for Performance in English' in *Ars Lyrica* 4: 19-28

Ashbrook, William. 1992. *Maria Stuarda* in *The NewGrove's Dictionary of Opera,* Volume III, Stanley Sadie (ed.). London: Macmillan Press Ltd.; and New York: Grove's Dictionaries of Music Inc.

Cowan, Ian B. 1971. *The Enigma of Mary Stuart.* New York: St. Martin's Press.

Donington, Robert. 1990. *Opera & Its Symbols: The Unity of Words, Music, & Staging*. New Haven and London: Yale University Press.

Donizetti, Gaetano. 1997 (opera first performed 1835). *Maria Stuarda* (1997). P-V Score (Critical edition piano-vocal score). Donizetti, Gaetano, composer; Bardari, Giuseppe, librettist; Wiklund, Anders, editor; Herman, Mark and Ronnie Apter, translators. Milano: Ricordi.

—— *Maria Stuarda*. 1976 (opera first performed 1835). Recording. Bonynge, Richard, conductor. London: Decca 425 410-2. Reissued as a set of CD=s by London Records in 1990.

Dotto, Gabriele and Roger Parker. 1997. Postscript [to the Historical Introduction to the critical piano-vocal score of Maria Stuarda]: A Critical Edition of Donizetti's *Maria Stuarda. xx-xxi (Italian version; xlviii-xlix (Engliosh version)*.

Fraser, Antonia. 1969. *Mary Queen of Scots*. New York: Dell Publishing Co., Inc.

Herman, Mark and Ronnie Apter. 1991. 'Opera Translation' in Mildred L. Larson (ed.) *Translation: Theory and Practice, Tension and Interdependence* (American Translators' Association Scholarly Monograph Series, Volume V). Binghamton: The State University of New York: 100-119.

Hudson, Elizabeth. 1997. Historical Introduction to the critical piano-vocal score of Maria Stuarda. xiii-xx (Italian version).

Plowden, Alison. 1999. *Two Queens in One Isle*. Phoenix Mill, Stroud, Gloucestershire: Sutton Publishing Ltd. [First published in 1984 by Harvester Press Ltd.]

Schiller, Friedrich von. 1965. *Maria Stuart* (play completed in 1800). Stuttgart: Philipp Reclam Jr. GmbH.

Wormald, Jenny. 1988 (revised 2001). *Mary Queen of Scots: Politics, Passion and a Kingdom Lost*. London and New York: Tauris Parke Paperbacks.

The Pentathlon Approach to Translating Songs[1]

Peter Low

When devising a singable song-translation, one has a very specific purpose: to produce a text which a singer can sing to an audience. Those who most stress the importance of thinking about the end-purpose — functionalists such as Hans Vermeer — use the term *skopos*. The making of singable translations is a very complex *skopos,* because the target text must fit the pre-existing music — its rhythms, note-values, phrasings and stresses — while still retaining the essence of the source text. This article discusses practical strategies for meeting these difficult requirements, and recommends what the author calls the "Pentathlon Principle," a deliberate balancing of five different criteria — singability, sense, naturalness, rhythm and rhyme. This balancing should be central to the overall strategy and also a guide to microlevel decision-making. Translators are warned against any *a priori* view that identifies a single feature of the source text as absolutely sacrosanct: the more margins of flexibility available, the greater chance of a successful result. Practical examples are taken from French popular *chanson*, German Lied, and Maori song, all translated into English.

Theoretical Remarks

The devising of singable texts is a particular challenge to a translator: one is subject to huge, multiple constraints imposed by the pre-existing music, which has many complex features — rhythms, note-values, phrasings and stresses — none of which one can simply ignore. One is constrained also by what one practitioner calls "the physical limitations of the vocal apparatus, the metrical rigors of a rigidly pre-set prosody, and the need to match verbal sense to musical color" (Apter 1989: 27). Besides, the ST (source text) is frequently rhymed, and rhyme is often desirable in this kind of song-translating — though not in others. Ideally, a clever illusion must be created: the TT (target text) must give the overall impression that the music has been devised to fit it, even though that music was actually composed to fit the ST. No wonder this task has at times been called impossible.

Given these requirements, a translator would be unwise to take an approach which concentrates on loyalty to the author and focuses narrowly on the characteristics of the ST. It is much more practical to adopt an approach which looks forward to the future function of the TT and stresses the importance of its end-purpose. For this, Hans J. Vermeer and other functionalists have chosen the word *skopos* (Greek for "aim, goal or target"). He uses this term *skopos* to designate the "goal or purpose, defined by the commission and if necessary adjusted by the translator" (2000: 230). He tries to use *skopos* thinking as a basis a general translation theory, and although he pays most attention to informative texts, he considers it applicable also to expressive texts, which naturally include song-lyrics. In functionalist thinking, the "commissioner" for a song-translation would be the specific or generic singer who will sing it.

According to Vermeer, translation methods and strategies should be determined by *skopos* (1978: 100). In his view, the *skopos* may even "help to determine whether the source text needs to be 'translated', 'paraphrased', or completely 're-edited'"(2000: 231). In the case of song, this means consideration and re-consideration of the prospective listeners to the translated song, of their situation in a different cultural polysystem and of their ability to comprehend and appreciate the song in the limited time (perhaps less than three minutes) during which they are hearing it. The result may be a choice to paraphrase rather than simply translate. Clearly, song is a case where mere loyalty to the source text will not produce good functional results — various other criteria have to be considered, criteria of a practical nature. Since the *skopos* of a singable translation is to be sung, with the pre-existing music, to an audience who knows the target language, the translator must pay careful attention to ensuring that the TT possesses those characteristics which will best help it to fulfil that function.

Now not all song-translating aims at a singable text, as I have shown elsewhere in a discussion of the various different *skopoi* which song-translators may have — and the different TTs which may derive from a single ST (Low, 2003). But the most difficult *skopos* is the singable TT, on account of its many constraints. In view of this difficulty, one should expect that a deliberate focus on function and purpose would help a translator to decide which are the features to prioritise in a given case and which are the features which may be sacrificed at less cost. (The same point applies also to other "special translating tasks" like dubbing films, or adapting cartoon strips — tasks in which unusual constraints must be met if functionality is to be achieved). Whether or not one wishes to apply *Skopostheorie* to all translational action (as Vermeer advocates), its emphasis on the end-purpose makes it a very practical approach to translating songs.

Another functionalist, Christiane Nord, has suggested that "the target text should be composed in such a way that it fulfils functions in the target situation that are compatible with the sender's intention" (1997: 92). Although "sender" there denotes the text's author, we might suggest in the case of songs that the composer is a secondary sender — as source of the music — and that the target situation in the concert-hall is created largely by the singer, who is the "user" of this verbal-musical message. The audience members constitute the "target-text receivers" as they listen to a live performance (or a recording on radio or CD).

Let us explore this matter a little further. Music can be viewed as an auditory code of communication, and specific pieces of music can be viewed as messages. Music is indeed a complex system of sounds, with dimensions of pitch and harmony, duration and rhythmic patterns, dynamics and timbre.Therefore songs, being a combination of words and music, partake of what Jakobson has called "two particularly elaborate systems of purely auditory and temporal signs" (1971: 701). It follows that the task of translating them should be viewed not as a narrowly linguistic operation. Indeed, because every song contains a non-verbal message — i.e., its music — it is possible for foreigners who do not know the language of its words to receive the message of the music nevertheless (particularly if they are familiar with its style) and even to claim to have "understood the song". This is not fully valid — they have lost the denotative and referential content — yet it may be partly true, because the music has been heard and the song's particular phonemes. And it will be more true for musico-centric songs — where the musical message is of chief importance — than for the less common logocentric songs (word-focused) which have greater difficulty in passing across language frontiers.

Usually one of these two codes precedes the other. It is common for the ST words to exist before the original music. In cases where the text of a song was written by one person and later set to music by another, we can speak of the composer's attempt to find a non-verbal message that is compatible with the verbal one. George Steiner put it thus (when discussing various musical settings of Goethe): "Each of these compositions is an act of interpretative restatement in which the verbal sign system is critically illuminated or, as the case may be, misconstrued by a non-verbal sign system with its own highly formal syntax"(1975: 419). In the finest song-settings, the composer has done a kind of translation or transmutation, using the verbal material as a source for a musical message which matches and enhances it.

It follows that song-translating is significantly different from most interlingual translating (e.g. poetry translation). This is particularly true of the devising of singable translations: here the TT — the verbal message in the new code — is intended specifically to be transmitted simultaneously with the very same non-verbal code that accompanied the ST.

For the nervous translator this fact provides a challenge: a pre-existing work of performance art — of a hybrid verbal-musical genre — must be reconstituted with a new set of words. At the same time it provides a consolation: the TT will not be a "stand-alone" text. Usually the composer has already "interpreted" the ST by non-verbal means, by musical devices intended to convey something of its beauty or emotional power. To take a fine example, in Claude Debussy's settings of Verlaine texts, the composer has already "translated the poems into music" when creating his melody and piano parts (Johnson and Stokes 2000: 96) (Claude Debussy 1862-1918, Paul Verlaine 1844-1896). Song-translators are therefore in a slightly different position from poetry-translators (who are sometimes accused of replacing good poems with a bad ones). Here — although the song is not sung in the original — the composer is present sharing with the translator the difficult task of communicating to the TL audience the subtlety and richness of the poet's text. Good performers help too, those performers who honour the words as well as the music — and their visual communication with face and hands can be seen as a third code, ideally serving the auditory codes of language and music. I think that song-translators can apply to their own efforts the remark that Alan J. Lerner once made about his own (original) texts: "My song-lyrics are scrawny creatures that should not be forced to parade naked on a printed page" (Lerner and Green 1987: 5).

Let me suggest also that even when a song uses the text of a genuine poem — perhaps by a poet as famous as Charles Baudelaire (1821-1867) — that text should be treated by the translator as an example not of the "poem" genre (largely a written genre) but of the related "song-lyric" genre (which is aimed at oral performance). One is not simply translating Baudelaire: one is translating Baudelaire as set by Henri Duparc (1848-1933), or as set differently by Emmanuel Chabrier (1841-1894) — in which case, according to one textbook of translation, a different TT is needed (Hervey & Higgins 2002: 63-64).

Song-translating is not, of course, an exact science. It is a practical craft exercised in the imperfect domain of words and meanings, where one is wrestling with the idiosyncrasies of the TL: its lexical gaps, its peculiar rhythms, its paucity of suitable rhymes etc. I turn now to consider some of its practitioners. Of the many people who have actually devised singable translations, relatively few have penned their thoughts about how it is done, and how it should be done.

The richest documentation I have found concerns the songs of Georges Brassens (1921-1981), a popular French creator of logocentric songs. His texts are so allusive, amusing and provocative that they might seem too daunting to tackle. Yet they are not, as is shown in the collection *Traduire et interpréter Georges Brassens* (1992-1993), where various authors discuss and demonstrate the making of singable translations into English, German, Swedish, Czech, Dutch, Italian etc. The best versions printed are excellent attempts to capture the style of Brassens.

Because of the constraints imposed by the pre-existing music, such song-translators resort to numerous methods in an attempt to overcome the difficulties they encounter. These include not only things like paraphrase, transposition and modulation — which are fairly standard methods — but also more robust and assertive devices. Here are some mentioned by various translators of Brassens: replacement metaphors, compensation in place, calque, omission, explicitation, cultural adaptation, superordinates, stylistic equivalence, the suppression of difficult verses, the use of added words to solve rhythmical problems and the replacement of rhyme with assonance. The best song-translators use a toolbox plus a "box of tricks"!

Among the translators of Brassens, Andrew Kelly offers the clearest piece of advice. In the course of a fine practical article, he gives the following list of injunctions:

> (1) Respect the rhythms;
> (2) Find and respect the meaning;
> (3) Respect the style;
> (4) Respect the rhymes;
> (5) Respect the sound;
> (6) Respect your choice of intended listeners; and
> (7) Respect the original. (1992-1993: 92)

All these things are undoubtedly desirable. This list shows Kelly's awareness of the communicative complexity of a real song performance — he can see that this complexity imposes on a translator a set of varied and competing duties. Now his list certainly seems daunting, yet his article makes it clear that would not call this *skopos* unattainable: on the contrary, he deems it possible to respect all of these features (on the whole). Not surprisingly, he interprets the word "respect" in a flexible rather than a rigid manner, saying, for example: "There is no need for slavish observation of original rhythms, simply respect with minimum departure within musical limits for reasons that are clear, such as better meaning, sound, naturalness of expression, accommodation of rhyme, etc." (1992-3: 95) The criteria listed here will all be discussed shortly.

A different source of advice comes from the classical music domain. Richard Dyer-Bennet, who devised an English version of Franz Schubert's (1797-1828) *Die schöne Müllerin,* attempted to state the general objectives of a singable translation. He says that the TT must be "singable, reasonably accurate, and modestly poetic" (reworded Emmons and Sonntag 1979: 292).

The four guidelines which he proposes are:

(1) The TT must be singable — otherwise any other virtues it has are meaningless;
(2) The TT must sound as it the music had been fitted to it, even though it was actually composed to fit the source text;
(3) The rhyme-scheme of the original poetry must be kept becaise it gives shape to the phjrases;
(4) Liberties must be taken with the original meaning when the first three requirement cannot otherwise be met.

The first guideline is pragmatic, and should seem self-evident, at least to anybody thinking about the *skopos.* The second guideline assumes rightly that (in a good song) there is a close relationship between text and music, a relationship so crucial that it must be preserved in any translated version. The fourth guideline implies that semantic accuracy is important but not paramount.

As for the third guideline, it merits further exploration. Though doubtless true for the Wilhelm Müller (1794-1827) poems used in Schubert's song-cycle, it is not equally true for (say) the German verse used in parts of Johann Sebastian Bach's (1685-1750) *Passions.* Although rhyme is a good way to retain the shape of the phrases, there may be other ways of doing so, verbal or musical. When poems are recited, rhyme is often a prominent sound-effect; but when they are sung, they take longer — so that rhyming words which are 5 seconds apart in recitation may be more than 10 seconds apart in a song. Besides, whereas in verse rhyme is usually the most prominent phonic effect, in songs it is submerged in the musical effects of tune and harmony. One could also ask Dyer-Bennet why he considers the giving "shape of the phrases" is sacrosanct (Emmons and Sonntag 1979:

292). What if, in a particular song, there are other desiderata that conflict with this one? I will return shortly to the question of rhyme.

These reasons and questions mean that I do not endorse the thinking behind this suggested guideline. It seems to imply a rigidity which I consider unnecessary and counterproductive. Fortunately he also insists (in guideline four) that "liberties" are permissible when justified by reference to the higher-ranked criteria.

Undoubtedly, the practical task of translating songs is impossible without the some taking of liberties. It follows, I believe, that a judicious approach to liberties can open the door to better versions. Consider for example the matter of a repeated phrase in the ST. A rigid or unthinking translator would render that line always in the same way, with the same TL phrase. That would be normal good practice. But a more flexible translator may at times choose a different option. If the line contains, for example, a particularly effective verb for which no single TL word is ideal, one might choose to render it in three different ways at different points in the song. The gain in semantic richness would arguably outweigh the loss of structural repetition. In songs, after all, verbal repetition is seldom so precious as to be non-negotiable — music usually provides plenty of repetition anyway.

The Pentathlon Principle

Building on the above reflections, this article expounds a practical *skopos*-based approach to the devising of singable translations. I call the devise the "Pentathlon Principle." Outlined once previously (Low 2003a), it assumes that a major difficulty of such translating is the need to balance several major criteria which often conflict. The Pentathlon Principle states that the evaluation of such translations should be done not in terms of one or two criteria but as an aggregate of all five. More fundamentally, it contends that this notion of balancing five different criteria can assist translators both in their overall strategic thinking and also in their microlevel decisions — in the practical task of choosing which of several possible words or phrases is the best option overall.

Now to speak of a pentathlon is merely a metaphor. But it is a more illuminating choice of metaphor than other metaphors, even that of "juggling" (though this better captures the sense of simultaneity). The pentathlon principle compares song-translators to Olympic pentathletes. They must compete in five dissimilar events, and must optimise their scoring overall, who must not omit to train for javelin and discus, and who must hold some energy in reserve for the 1500 metres. For this reason they sometimes choose to come second or third in one event, keeping their eyes on the whole day's challenge. They do not often achieve word-class results in a single event. But one quality they must develop to a high standard is flexibility.

Like the pentathlete in this metaphor, the translator of a song has five "events" to compete in — five criteria to satisfy — and must aim for the best total score. One criterion is *Singability*; one is *Sense*; one is *Naturalness*; others are *Rhythm* and *Rhyme*. These "events" are as dissimilar as the shotput and 100m sprint! Broadly speaking, the first four of these criteria correspond to the translator's duties — respectively — to the singer, to the author, to the audience, and to the composer. The fifth criterion (rhyme) is a special case.

Singability

Although this criterion is a pragmatic one, it must receive top ranking in this particular kind of translating. This is a logical result of thinking in terms of the TT's specific purpose, its *skopos*. It is entirely reasonable for the singer, as the commissioner of this translation, to ask for a usable product. One singer who has written well about these issues is Arthur Graham, who stresses the point that: "The singer needs words that may be sung with sincerity" (Graham 1989: 35). One composer who thought about them was Edvard Grieg (1843-1907), who once wrote: "Regardless of how beautiful the poetry and the music, if the declamation is found wanting, the songs will be put aside and ignored" (cited in Gorlée 2002: 180).

This emphasis on singability parallels a notion which is widely accepted in the translating of drama, that "effectiveness on stage" is a practical necessity and must receive priority (Gutt 1991: 389-391, Anderman 1999: 71-74). Just as drama-translation requires words that can be performed as part of an integrated whole (which also includes gestures, costumes, lighting etc.), so a singable song-translation requires "performability." It must function effectively as an oral text delivered at performance speed — whereas with a written text the reader has a chance to pause, reflect or even re-read.

Functioning effectively will mean different things for different songs, too — for example, some try to move the audience to tears while others seek to provoke laughter.

Although the singability of a text is something best judged by experienced singers, even a tone-deaf translator can learn something about it. In the case of English, anyone aware of the sounds of language can see that this language has many closed syllables, and frequent clusters of consonants at the beginning or end of words. Recitation can help to identify consonant clusters and other places where the singer will face problems with diction, particularly when the tempo is fast. If the English word or phrase which gives the best semantic solution may be hard to sing — the word "strict", for example, which has five consonants to one vowel — then it is better to incur some semantic loss and use "tight", with two consonants and a nice singable diphthong.

Also to be avoided is the placing of "under-sized vowels" on long, slurred or emphatic notes. Common English words like "it" and "the" can easily be sung to a short note, preferably a quaver, but can scarcely be held for a minim. Instead of placing "the" on a long note, the translator might turn to the demonstratives "these" or "those," which have good long vowels. Similarly, the word "little" might be rejected in favour of the more singable "tiny." Many singers insist that certain vowels cannot be sung on very high notes, and that very low notes similarly reduce the choice of singable vowels (Gorlée 2002: 167). Michael Irwin points out, however, that "a short vowel can be lengthened by a resonant succeeding consonant, or even, less obviously, by a preceding one. Thus 'can' and 'mat' are both more vocally promising than 'cat', but 'man' looks more inviting than all three" (1996: 97).

Another aspect of singability is the highlighting of particular words in the ST by musical means — they may be high-pitched, for example, or marked *fortissimo*. In these cases the composer is giving them special prominence. Such highlighted words should ideally be translated at the same location, because otherwise the sequential focus of the line will be altered and the musical highlighting will fall on a different word. As Apter has put it: the translator "must crest meaning where the melodic line crests" (Raffel 1988: 196).

This issue is more important in through-composed music than in texts which are set strophically. In a strophic song, each musical phrase is to some extent multi-purpose. But in through-composed songs each musical phrase is wedded to one group of words — it calls for not merely a phrase to match the metre (e.g. six notes ending in a long one) but a phrase to match those particular words (e.g. an unexpected noun on syllable two, a comma after syllable four).

A further aspect of singability is the pattern of stressed and unstressed syllables in any line of the TT. This matter is discussed below under the separate heading of rhythm.

Sense

How the Pentathlon Principle operates can also be seen in the problem of retaining the original meaning. In the normal translating of informative texts, for example, semantic accuracy is paramount; but the constraints of song-translating necessarily mean some stretching or manipulation of sense. The Pentathlon Principle calls for flexibility.

It is not that meaning ceases to be an important criterion, except in some exceptional cases like nonsense songs. However, our definition of acceptable accuracy can be wider here than in other translating. Thus a precise word may be replaced by a near-synonym, a narrow term by a superordinate term, a particular metaphor by a different one which functions similarly in the context. This stretching of sense may seem anathema to some orthodox translators; yet even they must admit that their work entails, quite naturally, the altering of syllable-counts — which is inconsequential in most circumstances. In a genre where syllable-count is important, the need to stretch sense arises just as naturally.

This matter of sense still deserves high ranking, however, simply because we are talking about translation — interlingual translating. I note in passing that some people ignore sense altogether: they take a foreign song-tune and devise for it a set of TL words which match the music very well but bear no semantic relation with the ST. While this may at times be good and appropriate, it is not translating, because none of the original verbal meaning is transmitted. Such practices have no place in discussions of translation.

194

All true song-translators acknowledge a duty towards the author of the ST. They must balance this against other duties which may conflict (to the singer, the composer, and the audience), but cannot abandon it altogether. This duty is greatest, I believe, when the ST deserves particular respect, because it has genuine poetic merit and/or because the value of the original song rests heavily on it.

Naturalness

The criterion requiring a translator to use the TL in a reasonably natural way involves various considerations such as register and word-order. It is associated particularly with the translator's duty to the audience — the receivers of the musico-verbal message. I believe that various writers on song-translation have assumed this, although few have actually emphasized the importance of naturalness in register and word-order. If I do so now, it is partly because many existing song-translations are very unnatural — so unnatural that they have led some people to the view that all song-translations are inevitably bizarre or ridiculous.

English classical singers have all encountered the oddly stilted versions of German Lieder which were in print decades ago (and sometimes still are). These manifest a kind of translationese which results from failure to assess the naturalness of both ST and TT, allied perhaps with insistence that semantic accuracy is the sole goal. Some seem to delight in archaisms (even when none are present in the ST) and in placing adjectives after nouns. A similar phenomenon occurs when arias are translated into German — Dinda L. Gorlée speaks of "bombastic clichés and hackneyed phraseology, inverted syntax, displaced accents, distorted rhythm and other infelicitous *ad hoc* solutions" (1997: 247). Some of these unusable versions were doubtless made by translators who knew both languages well. What doomed their efforts was poor strategy.

Of course there is a wide debate, at least in literary translation, about whether or not a translated text should conceal the fact that it has been translated; and few would argue that a difficult idiosyncratic poem can be adequately rendered by a version full of "reader-friendly" blandness. But the case of song-translating is untypical. A song-text must communicate effectively on first encounter. This places a premium on naturalness of language, because unnaturalness demands from the audience additional and superfluous processing effort. The TT is not worth making unless it can be understood while the song is sung.

I am not claiming that song-translations must avoid unnatural English at all costs: merely that naturalness is one of the five criteria which the translator must strive for. As Ernst-August Gutt says in more general terms (1991: 389):

> "Unnaturalness" in translated texts often seems to involve gratuitous processing effort on the receptor audience's part: perhaps due to interference from the original language or insufficient mastery of the receptor language, the expression used by the translator may turn out to require more than optimal processing cost on the audience's part.

In songs, of course, processing time cannot be lengthened at will, unlike written texts, which permit slow reading and even re-reading.

Rhythm

In a song, the music has its particular rhythm, clearly notated, which determines the rhythm in which the ST will be performed. The translator's duty to the composer requires a high degree of respect for this pre-existing rhythm.

Some authorities view this as a problem of syllable-count. They consider that a line of eight syllables — set to eight musical notes — must be translated into a line of eight syllables. Eugene Nida, for example, speaks of "precisely the right number of syllables" (1964: 177). And an expert on French song, Frits Noske, says that: "Musical prosody requires that the rhythm and number of syllables be identical with those of the original lines" (1970: 30).

Such an objective is indeed highly desirable. But their articulation of it seems to me too rigid. To take an example which Noske knew very well, nineteenth-century French composers who were setting poems strophically often made small changes to the rhythms from one verse to another. As Graham asks rhetorically: "Don't composers make such changes in setting strophic songs?" (1989: 34). Verse one may start with a single up-beat note, for example, while verse two — though equally octosyllabic — may start with two small upbeat notes and have a slur later in the line. Or two equal notes in one verse may be unequal in the next. Clearly composers did not all see the rhythmic details as sacrosanct.

According to the Pentathlon Principle, identical syllable-count is desirable; but in practice a translator who finds that an eight-syllable line is insolubly, unacceptably clumsy, may choose to add a syllable or subtract one. This should be done only in acceptable places, in a piece of recitative (say) rather than a lyrical phrase. And it should be done judiciously — the best place to add a syllable is on a melisma, and the best place to subtract a syllable is on a repeated note, because those methods alter rhythm without destroying melody.

Even changes to the melody are not completely out of the question either. May not a cautious translator sometimes choose deliberately to incur a loss in some small melodic detail rather than sacrifice (say) a verbal consideration such as meaning or natural word-order? I certainly do not mean this as a general licence to rewrite melodies, merely a suggestion that an occasional subtle piece of musical "tweaking" may be preferable to a glaring verbal gaffe. Which is more respectful to the song?

In some cases there may be a shortage of syllables in the TT, either because the ST had many short syllables or because the draft TT is very terse. The translator then has to choose between adding a new word or phrase, repeating a word or phrase, or dropping notes from the music. The best option is usually the first, I suggest, with this proviso: any words added must give the appearance of coming from the subtext of the source. For example, the TT may have a monosyllabic noun where three syllables are wanted, and one can easily precede this with a plausible, natural-sounding adjective that coheres with the overall feeling of the text without adding anything very striking to it. If, for example, a foreign language describes water with a pentasyllabic adjective meaning "rough," one may need in English to say "perilous and rough."

In languages like English (but unlike French) syllabic stress is actually more important than sheer syllabicity. Usually the translator will identify which notes in the song have been stressed by the composer (mostly down-beats) and will find a corresponding stressed syllable in English.

In any case, syllable-count is not an accurate measure of rhythm. Rhythm in songs is not the same as metre in traditional poetic scansion. An octosyllabic line of English or German verse can be analysed as (say) an iambic tetrameter, by virtue of its pattern of stressed syllables; but when a text is to be sung in English, one must consider not only the stresses but also the lengths of notes — which may vary between a quaver and a semi-breve. What one seeks is not a replication of the SL poem's metrical form, it is a match for the existing music. For these reasons, a song-translator must pay attention to the length of vowels — as indicated above in the section on "singability" — without ignoring the role of consonants either. In some cases one must also take account of rests. For example, a line which on paper was unbroken may in music contain a significant rest — the translator must avoid placing this gap in the middle of a word.

Rhyme

This issue has bedeviled song-translation, and has led to many unusable TTs. The reason, I believe, is faulty strategic thinking: consciously or unconsciously many translators have given rhyme a very high priority in every song they have attempted.

This issue arises in André Lefevere's article about English versions of Bertold Brecht (1898-1956). Lefevere criticises Hays and Bentley, translators of *Mother Courage,* for their renderings of the songs, saying: "The need to rhyme, moreover, leads to excessive padding" (2000: 240). Surprisingly, however, he does not ask how much rhyme is actually needed, nor does he criticise their apparent opinion that the English version needs to merely some rhyme, but exactly the same amount of rhyme as was found in the German edition — which is certainly disputable.

Actually, the Pentathlon Principle works particularly well in the question of rhyme, because it opposes rigidity of thinking. When rhyme is present in the ST, some translators simply do without it — and in cases where the rhyme can be lost without significant cost, they will be quite right. In other cases, however, to abandon all rhyme is to score a zero on a significant part of the scorecard. Some other translators will say: "Yes, I will retain rhyme,"and will then set their target at perfect rhymes as numerous as those in the ST and in the same locations. Sometimes they score very highly too! But it costs them heavily in other ways: the rhyme at the end of the line plays such a role in shaping that whole line that the tail indeed wags the dog.

Applying the Pentathlon Principle, by contrast, may mean saying: "Yes, I will have some rhyme. But I will seek some margin of flexibility... In this case the rhymes won't have to be as perfect or numerous as in the ST, and the original rhyme-scheme need not be observed. I will try to get a top score, but not at too great a cost to other considerations (such as meaning)." This is the kind of thinking I advocate.

For example, if the ST is a rhymed quatrain, I assume that the most important rhyme is the final one — but I might not care whether this line rhymes with line 1, 2, or 3. And I might not care whether the other two lines rhyme well, or at all. This is particularly true if the lines are short (if the ST rhymes after every 6 syllables rather than 10 or 12). It is a general rule that the tighter the rhyming, the more the rhyme will determine the whole line.

Besides, even where rhyme is the chosen option, this does not mean that every rhyme must be a perfect rhyme — i.e. identical phonemes at the end of the lines. There may well be places where imperfect rhyme is a better option because it incurs less semantic loss. The rigid insistence on perfect rhyme for "love", for example, has too often opened the window to the "turtledove" and the "stars above." Except at the end of a stanza, such imperfect rhymes as "move" or "enough" must be deemed acceptable.

A good account of these options, with snappy examples, is given by Apter, who speaks of "rhyme's cousins — off-rhyme (line-time), weak rhyme (major-squalor), half-rhyme (kitty-knitted) and consonant rhyme (slit-slat) — alone or in combination with other devices like assonance and alliteration" (1985: 309-310). Such devices multiply the options available to a translator seeking some kind of rhyme or chime, and therefore they significantly reduce the "enslavement to the rhyming dictionary" which has often produced forced or far-fetched TTs. One can even find near-rhymes for impossible English words like "orange" or "silver"!

Examples

A few translators have suggested to me that the strategies outlined above are not rigorous enough, and show too much willingness to sacrifice some verbal and even musical subtleties for the sake of a "user-friendly" TT. But on this point I am unrepentant: I contend that the pragmatic compromises involved in song-translating actually cohere with the intrinsic needs of the genre. A song-text is in essence an oral text, not a written one; and the TT is not worth making unless it meets a normal requirement of this *skopos*, namely that it can be understood during performance while the song is sung at the tempo largely predetermined by the composer.

Here follow some contrasting examples of songs translated into English: two French *chansons*, one German Lied, and a Maori *waiata*. Song is, of course, a very diverse art-form, with numerous sub-genres: a song may be (for example) a long narrative ballad, a sacred hymn, a complex aria from opera, a satirical jazz-song or a repetitive chant for dancing. But generally it is not the genre of a song that should determine the translator's approach. I would not assert, for example, that all the Beatles' songs should be treated similarly. Rather it is the specificity of each individual song which should guide the choice of strategy.

One question I consider important is: "Are the words of this song very important?" This question results in a polarity between logocentric and musico-centric songs, as explained above — with a "middle ground" for songs where words and music are of similar importance. The genre of jazz song, for example, contains songs which differ widely in this respect. These differences between individual songs point to differing "pentathlon strategies." Thus, when I judge a particular song to be musico-centric, I tend to choose options that score highly on singability even at the expense of sense. In logocentric songs I tend to favour sense over singability or rhythm, because the words (and their author) deserve to receive high priority. But such generalizations are probably less useful than is discussion of specific examples, which can show the application of "pentathlon thinking" to strategic decisions and to precise choices of wording.

My first example is a popular *chanson* by the Belgian singer-songwriter Jacques Brel (1929-1978). His works, intended for a wide French-speaking audience, were built on cabaret and music hall traditions which gave great importance to the words — words often written by the performers themselves. Brel's words, like those of Brassens, have often been translated — indeed he himself recorded Dutch translations of some of his songs. This is his best-known sentimental song:

NE ME QUITTE PAS (by Jacques Brel, commencement)

Ne me quitte pas
Il faut oublier
Tout peu s'oublier
Qui s'enfuit déjà
Oublier le temps
Des malentendus
Et le temps perdu
À savoir comment
Oublier ces heures
Qui tuaient parfois
A coups de pourquoi
Le coeur du bonheur

Ne me quitte pas, Ne me quitte pas, Ne me quitte pas,
Ne me quitte pas

Moi je t'offrirai
Des perles de pluie
Venues de pays
Où il ne pleut pas
Je creuserai la terre
Jusqu'après ma mort
Pour couvrir ton corps
D'or et de lumière
Je ferai un domaine
Où l'amour sera roi
Où l'amour sera loi
Où tu seras reine

Ne me quitte pas, Ne me quitte pas, Ne me quitte pas,
Ne me quitte pas […]

This classic tear-jerker, dating from 1959, is the very song that propelled Jacques Brel into the top echelon of singer-songwriters. It has become inseparable from the music he wrote for it, simultaneous with it. Brel's "heart-on-sleeve" performances, plus his very apt music, have perhaps distracted attention from the excellence of the words. The text is marked throughout by high emotion, a feeling of pitiful pleasing epitomized by the refrain. This emotion is developed through five stages, which correspond to the five verses of the complete song: a plea for forgetfulness (and implicitly forgiveness); a promise of impossible gifts; a promise of exorbitant language; a metaphorical argument about renewal; and a final verse of pathetic self-abasement. A translator should try to retain all these features.

The title-line requires particular attention, because it is the emotional core of the song — and occurs 23 times. Brel associates it with a distinctive five-note motif, and his performances exploit well the plosive consonants. One translator (Rod McKuen, better known as a singer-songwriter) used the phrase "If you go away" (McKuen 1996); but that is too weak and hypothetical. In Brel's text she is not just leaving, she is walking out on "poor little me"; and by the end of the song there are no ifs about it, she is already long gone — at least such is my interpretation (Low 1994).

My preferred option is "Don't abandon me." Though not perfect, it has the virtue of some good plosive consonants. A possible alternative is "Don't walk out on me." And for the last line of the refrain, I suggest that one sing — or rather murmur — the three syllables "Don't leave me." The inaccuracy of that rhythm is arguably compensated by the greater accuracy of meaning and emotion.

Careful attention must be given to rhythm. The lines of the ST are pentasyllabic with a stress on the end. In English (a more heavily stressed language than French), stresses will work best on the third and fifth syllables of the line, but in some parts of the melody it can be the second and fifth. Besides, it is not always essential to have exactly five syllables. Many lines start on two identical notes, which can be tied: it would therefore be acceptable for these to have occasionally four syllables (two iambs). Though less desirable, a line of six syllables is also possible, with one of the short notes repeated to produce the rhythm weak-weak-strong-weak-weak-strong (two anapaests).

Strategic decisions are needed also about rhyme. The ST uses rhyme almost throughout, or at least *rime faible*. The rhymes divide each twelve-line stanza into three clear quatrains, typically rhymed ABBA. Now given that rhyme is a normal feature of English sentimental songs, it would be strange to omit rhyme altogether. One possibility would be to reduce the number of rhymes to two lines per quatrain. In that case XAXA should be the main option, with AXXA as an alternative, and perhaps XXAA. It is particularly desirable that the last line of each quatrain be "clinched" with a rhyme. A different possibility is tried below: rhymes or near-rhymes on every line, with a great readiness to substitute ABAB for the ABBA scheme.

NE ME QUITTE PAS (start of version by Peter Low)

Don't abandon me   set aside the past
Let it vanish fast   from your memory
Let go every word   we misunderstood
Holding onto hurt   does more harm than good
And forget as well   all the whys and hows
that destroyed the spell   of our happy hours
Don't abandon me, Don't abandon me,
Don't abandon me, Don't leave me

I'll bring you a chain   of raindrop pearls
from lands where rain   no longer falls
I'll delve in the ground   till after I'm old
to weave you a gown   of luminous gold
I'll make a domain   where love is supreme
love's law will reign   and you will be queen
refrain […]

This song-translation, like most others, can easily be criticised on grounds of meaning (say) or rhythm. Almost as easily, alternative phrases can be proposed which score better on one or two criteria. Such suggestions can be infuriating to translators, who know very well that most lines in a TT can be "corrected" in at least one respect. What the Pentathlon Principle requires, however, is that for any proposed amendment to constitute a genuine improvement it must increase the overall aggregate calculated on all five criteria. Unless it does this, no proposed amendment has much value. With regard to the above version, I dare to claim that almost every attempt to "rectify" its undoubted imperfections would actually lead to a reduction in the total "pentathlon score" — and that is a key point of this whole argument.

Now here is a contrasting example from the same source: a light-hearted song which Brel wrote in 1962.

LES FILLES ET LES CHIENS (by Jacques Brel, commencement)

Les filles
C'est beau   comme un jeu
C'est beau   comme un feu
C'est beaucoup trop peu
Les filles
C'est beau   comme un fruit

Les filles
Ça vous pend au nez
Ça vous prend au thé
Ça vous prend les dés
Les filles
Ça vous pend au cou

C'est beau   comme la nuit
C'est beaucoup d'ennuis
Les filles
C'est beau comme un renard
C'est beau comme un retard
C'est beaucoup trop tard
Les filles
C'est beau tant que ça peut
C'est beau comme l'adieu
Et c'est beaucoup mieux

Ça vous pend au clou
Ça dépend de vous
Les filles
Ça vous pend au cœur
Ça se pend aux fleurs
Ça dépend des heures
Les filles
Ça dépend de tout
Ça dépend surtout
Ça dépend des sous

Mais les chiens
C'est beau comme des chiens
Et ça reste là
A nous voir pleurer
Les chiens
Ça ne nous dit rien
C'est peut-être pour ça
Qu'on croit les aimer […]

The form of this lyric makes it very tricky to tackle: it is dominated by rhyming tercets of pentasyllabic lines. These lines usually begin with the same words, and each tercet ends with a sort of witty punchline. The verbal form is clearly very important, and some might say that the difficulty of replicating it makes the song "untranslatable."As for the music, it uses the unusual metre of 7/8 time, and a brisk tempo with strong emphases. Brel's own performance bears some resemblance to the rappers of more recent decades.

But those features prove not that it is untranslatable; only that a successful version will require a creative translator with a good choice of strategies. My assessment is that although this song is logocentric, the form of the words actually counts more than the detailed meaning. My strategy therefore was to prioritise form and structure over sense; to insist on good rhythm and frequent punchy rhymes; and to render the overall meaning while permitting flexibility in the semantic detail. This may be called slippage or compromise, but I prefer to view it as compensation or re-creation. Often I use compensation in place — an idea or image appears in one part of the source but in a different location in the TT.

To insist on retaining the exact syllable-count would doom the enterprise. Brel has isolated phrases *"Les filles"* and *"Les chiens"* which can and must become monosyllables in English.

My strategic thinking, using the five criteria of my pentathlon, assumes that the pragmatic need for singability includes also the need to be amusing — the *skopos* requires the English version to have a similar effect on the audience as the original did. At the same time I note that naturalness of language is not a constant feature of Jacques Brel's text— in fact one salient feature is a playful approach to French. This invites or permits a translator to fool around with the target language, for the purpose of entertainment.

GIRLS AND DOGS (start of version by Peter Low)

Girls lovable as flames
lovable as games
love to call you names
Girls love to captivate
love to keep you late
love to make you wait
Girls lovely as the sky
lovely as goodbye
love to make you sigh
Girls lovable as fruit
lovable and cute
love to persecute

Girls need a gentle start
need a leading part
need to take your heart
Girls need to go to town
need a dancing-gown
knees up Mother Brown
Girls need to have a go
need to do-si-do
need to spend your dough
Girls need a bunch of flowers
need abnormal powers
needle you for hours

But dogs lovable as dogs
simply sit and stare
as you come and go
Yes dogs don't do dialogues
Maybe that explains
why we love them so […]

If this version comes close to the spirit of the ST, I give credit to the judicious exercise of flexibility. And let me reassure you that the end of the song is not anti-women!

The playful and ungrammatical allusion "knees up Mother Brown" may be a pointer to a general truth about comic songs. It think that because such songs welcome verbal play (often present in the ST), they permit the translator to use a wider "box of tricks" than can be used in serious songs. For example one can risk non-standard words — such as the monosyllabic dialect word "nowt" for the standard German pronoun "*nichts.*"

On one occasion, I solved a knotty problem by coining a word. Here is the refrain of "*Les Cigales,*" a light poem by Rosemonde Gérard (1866-1953) set to music by Chabrier in 1890:

Les cigales, ces bestioles
Ont plus d'âme que les violes.
Les cigales, les cigalons,
Chantent mieux que les violons.

The rhymes were not hard to solve, but the rhythm refused to fall into place until I invented a word never before seen in English (yet perfectly apt and comprehensible). Here is the result:

The cicadas, those tiny fellows,
out-vibrato the loudest cellos.
The cicadas' concerted din
out-performs any violin.

Such a coinage as "out-vibrato" would surely ruin the tone of a serious song.

Let me add in passing that the argument in favour of translating songs at all is particularly strong in the case of comic songs — with them, the need for the audience to understand the words in particularly great.

My next example is a serious *Kunstlied* (Art Song) from the nineteenth-century German repertoire. This particular tradition, developed notably by Franz Schubert (1797-1828), Robert Schumann (1886-1963) and Johannes Brahms (1833-1897), involves a close integration of music with poetry. The texts are often by famous poets, or at least recognized poets (as in the case chosen). This gives the translator a greater duty to respect their aesthetic quality. Besides, most songs are through-composed: even a poem in simple strophic form receives new or partly new music for each stanza (as in the case chosen). This means that the translator must recognize and try to replicate the attention which the composer has given to specific words and phrases.

German Art Songs were typically intended for an intimate drawing-room context and a cultivated middle-class audience. For such high-brow songs, singable translations are used much less than for popular songs — and much less today than fifty years ago. Rightly or wrongly, classical singers nowadays expect their audiences to want to hear the original German. Most recent translations, therefore, are non-singable versions devised specifically to assist non-German singers or their audiences (e.g. when printed in recital programmes or CD notes).

This example comes from the Lieder of Strauss (1885) (Richard Strauss 1864-1949). The words are by the Austrian Romantic poet Hermann von Gilm (1812-1864). It could perhaps be claimed that, given the melody and harmonic richness of Strauss's music, a fine performance in German can convey to non-German ears much of the Romantic fervour of the song.

Ja, du weißt es, teure Seele,
Daß ich fern von dir mich quäle,
Liebe macht die Herzen krank,
Habe Dank.

Einst hielt ich, der Freiheit Zecher,
Hoch den Amethysten-Becher,
Und du segnetest den Trank,
Habe Dank.

Und beschworst darin die Bösen,
Bis ich, was ich nie gewesen,
Heilig, heilig ans Herz dir sank,
Habe Dank.

The trisyllabic refrain required special attention from the outset. "Be thankful" is rhythmically impossible. "God be thanked" ends in two plosives, and would make the song too pious (the German is not "*Gott sei Dank!*"). My option of "Oh, give thanks" will work well if it is given a passionate performance (which this song needs anyway).

Since the rhymes *krank/trank/sank/dank* are so prominent, my strategy was to retain at least some rhyme — with the understanding that while perfect rhymes score best, imperfect rhymes would be acceptable. This flexibility made possible the choice of "pangs," "drank" and "sank," which are only one consonant away from rhyming perfectly with "thanks." The English word "sank" is particularly desirable, because *sank* is so prominent in the original — the melody line drops suddenly by no less than a seventh onto it.

As for the other lines, I eventually found three pairs of rhymes, of which two are good rhymes ("prophet/goblet" being little more than an assonance), and two involve little semantic loss — lines 9-10 score less well in this respect. If options as good as these had not been available, I would have dispensed with rhyme in the first half of each quatrain in my following singable translation of *Zueignung*:

Yes, you sense how much I languish,
how your absence feeds my anguish.
Love can bring the keenest pangs.
Oh, give thanks!

Once I posed as freedom's prophet,
holding high my silver goblet
and you blessed the toast I drank.
Oh, give thanks!

Yes, you saved my soul from capture
so that, raised to holy rapture,
fired with love in your arms I sank.
Oh, give thanks!

This singable version differs markedly from existing published translations intended only for reading, notably that of George Bird and Richard Stokes (Fischer-Dieskau 1977: 411). Their version scores more highly than mine both on sense and on naturalness (idiomaticity). By contrast, I expanded the meaning of line 3 because the option "Love makes hearts sick" is too short on syllables, and rejected the obvious "amethyst goblet" of line 6 in favour of something much more singable. But comparison is unfair: makers of a singable translations have more criteria to consider, and are never likely to achieve the semantic accuracy of translations in reference books or CD notes. That is why translations devised to be sung are unsuitable for other *skopoi*.

My final example is a non-European folksong: a *waiata* (song) in the traditional oral style of the Maori of Aotearoa New Zealand. Famous there chiefly for its attractive melody, this song has been made known internationally by the soprano Kiri Te Kanawa. The words were composed perhaps a century ago by Paraire Henare Tomoana (tribal affiliation Ngati Kahugnunu), who was working in a popular tradition. Although several versions are in circulation, this is probably the oldest:

POKAREKARE ANA

Pokarekare ana   nga wai o Waiapu
Whiti atu koe, e hine   marino ana e!
E hine e,   hoki mai ra!
Ka mate ahau i   te aroha e!

E kore te aroha,   e maroke i te ra,
Makuku tonu i   aku roimata e!

E hine e ...

Tuhituhi taku reta,   tuku atu taku ringi
Kia kite to iwi,   raruraru ana e!
E hine e ...

Whatiwhati taku pene,   kau pau aku pepa,
Ko taku aroha   mau tonu ana e!
E hine e ...

It is a simple strophic song, with four couplets each followed by the refrain. Here is my proposed version:

THE WATERS OF WAIAPU (version by Peter Low)

Though the waters of Waiapu   are perilous and stormy,
If you decide to cross them   they will be calm.
Oh darling girl   come back to me!
I'm overflowing   with love for you!

In the heat of the noonday   my love will never wither.
I will keep it watered   with the tears from my eyes.

I am sending you a letter   and a ring to fit your finger.
Of your family should see them   there'll be trouble for sure.

My only pen is broken   and I've run out of paper,
But the love inside me   will forever remain.

Let me try to assess this version by the five criteria of the Pentathlon strategy.

On rhyme, it doesn't compete at all. There is no real rhyming in the ST — indeed rhyme is not a standard feature of *waiata*. My strategic decision to disregard the possibility of rhyme (despite its presence in most English folksongs) enabled me to seek higher scores in sense, singability and naturalness.

On sense, it scores well. There are slippages, however. In the refrain *mate* means "sick and dying"; but the word "overflowing" is much more singable. The rendering of *iwi* (tribe) as "family" is also questionable.

It scores well also on naturalness of English. There are no awkward or inappropriately "poetic" effects, such as non-standard word-order. Line one is a case in point: the option "Though perilous and stormy are the waters of Waiapu", which would better match the rhythm and the ST word-order, was rejected in the name of naturalness. Nevertheless, this English version falls short of the elegant simplicity of the original.

As for the rhythm, it has been handled with great freedom. Examination of the ST shows that the syllable-counts there vary from one couplet to another — for example the first line of each couplet may have 14, 15, or 16 syllables. This fact invites the translator to be flexible. And I have an additional excuse: the tune often has two adjacent notes at the same pitch, which can easily be tied to make a longer one without altering the melodic shape. Perfect matching of syllables could have been achieved, of course, if priority had been placed on achieving it — but not without huge losses in other areas.

When it comes to singability, however, I reflect ruefully that this version will probably never be performed. With its many consonants, it fails to match the wonderfully singable ST, which was almost certainly sung before ever being written down, and which benefits from the consistently open syllables of this Polynesian language.

Conclusion

Let me now restate the Pentathlon Principle as a whole. When translating a song, keep your eyes fixed on the *skopos* — the function or purpose that your TT must fulfil. Do not consider *a priori* that any one feature of the ST is sacrosanct and must be perfectly retained. To consider anything sacrosanct *a priori* (whether rhyme, metaphor, syllabicity or whatever) is to accept a rigid constraint which may lead to great losses elsewhere. By tolerating some slippage — some small margins of flexibility in several areas — one can more easily avoid serious translation loss in any single area. A translator working by this principle attempts to score highly in the overall effect of the text, without insisting on unbeatable excellence on any single criterion.

Not surprisingly, the above approach is relevant also to opera translation. Not surprisingly, the above "hexathlon" approach is relevant also to opera translation. This is a *skopos* where attention must be paid to all my five criteria, plus dramatic effectiveness as well (because of this sixth "event," we might call it a "hexathlon"). My insistence on flexibility resembles at various points what Herman and Apter say in one of their articles about translating operas (1991). They do not rule out judicious changes in frequency or quality of rhyme, in the handling of phrases that were repeated in the ST, and in syllable-count — by slurring notes unslurred in the original or vice-versa. They obviously realise, from their experience as opera-translators, that rigid rules such as "replicate all rhymes" will tie their hands and bar the door to the best solutions. Similarly, the delicate problems of balancing different criteria when translating operas into German have been well stated by Kurt Honolka: "The opera-translator must always be tacking through between the Scylla of falsification and the Charybdis of an "*Opera-Deutsch*" that is wooden, unsingable, pallid or turgid" (1978: 31; tr. Peter Low).

Finally, I must admit that there is one respect in which song-translating differs greatly from an Olympic pentathlon: this task certainly does not require that the whole exacting programme be completed within one day. On the contrary, when translating a song one should take plenty of time so as to worry away at it and improve on the options one first thought of. Andrew Kelly has this to say: "Normally I made five to seven drafts and felt I had to return to the song with a fresh mind at least six times. Between times inspiration unexpectedly solved particular problems" (1992-1993: 111). That sounds like a typical experience of the kind of patient creativity needed for good results.

Notes

[1] All musical and verbal examples from Jacques Brel's songs in this article are © Copyright Editions Musicales Pouchenel, Brussels 1964 and © Warner Chappell Music France / Editions Musicales Pouchenel 1959, and are used here by permission.

Bibliography

Anderman, Gunilla. 1998. 'Drama Translation' in Baker, Mona (ed.) *Routledge Encyclopedia of Translation Studies*. London and New York: Routledge. 71-74.

Apter, Ronnie. 1985. 'A Peculiar Burden: Some Technical Problems of Translating Opera for Performance in English' in *Meta* 30 (4): 19-28.

Emmons, Shirley and Sonntag, Stanley. 1979. *The Art of the Song Recital*. New York: Schirmer.

Fischer-Dieskau, Dietrich. 1977. *The Fischer-Dieskau Book of Lieder*. New York: Knopf.

Gorlée, Dinda L. 1997. 'Intercode Translation: Words and Music in Opera' in *Target* 9 (2): 235-270.

—— 2002. 'Grieg's Swan Songs' in Semiotica 142 (1/4): 153-210.

Graham, Arthur. 1989. 'A New Look at Recital Song Translation' in *Translation Review* 29: 31-37.

Gutt, Ernst-August. 1991. 'Translation as Interlingual Interpretive Use' in Venuti, Lawrence (ed.) *The Translation Studies Reader*. London and New York: Routledge. 376-396.

Herman, Mark and Apter, Ronnie. 1991. 'Opera translation' in Larson, Mildred (ed.) *Translation, Theory and Practice, Tension and Interdependence*. Binghampton: State University of New York. 100-119.

Hervey, Sándor and Higgins, Ian. 2002. *Thinking French Translation*. London and New York: Routledge.

Honolka, Kurt. 1978. *Opernübersetzungen: Zur Geschichte der Verdeutschung musiktheatralischen Texte* (Taschenbucher zur Musikwissenschaft 20). Wilhelmshaven: Heinrichshofen's Verlag.

Irwin, Michael. 1996. 'Translating Opera' in Taylor, Jane *et al.* (eds) *Translation Here and There, Now and Then*. Exeter: Elm Bank. 95-102.

Jakobson, Roman. 1971. *Selected Writings II: Word and Language*. The Hague and Paris: Mouton.

Johnson, Graham and Stokes, Richard. 2000. *A French Song Companion*. Oxford: Oxford University Press.

Kelly, Andrew. 1992-1993. 'Translating French Song as a Language Learning Activity' in *Equivalences* 22 (1, 2) and 23 (1) [Special issue *Traduire et interpréter Georges Brassens*]. 91-112.

Lefevere, André. 2000. 'Mother Courage's Cucumbers' in Venuti, Lawrence (ed.) *The Translation Studies Reader*. London and New York: Routledge. 233-249.

Lerner, Alan and Green, Benny. 1987. *A Hymn to Him: The Lyrics of Alan Jay Lerner*. New York: Pavilion.

Low, Peter. 1994. 'Dramatic Monologue in the Songs of Brel' in *New Zealand Journal of French Studies* 15 (2): 24-33.

—— 2003. 'Translating Poetic Songs: An Attempt at a Functional Account of Strategies' in *Target* 15 (1): 95-115

—— 2003a. 'Singable Translations of Songs' in *Perspectives* 11 (2): 87-103.

McKuen, Rod. 1996. *Greatest Hits, volume 4*. CD from Delta. UPC 018111279628.

Nida, Eugene A. 1964. *Toward a Science of Translating: With Special Reference to Principles and Procedures Involved in Bible Translating*. Leiden: Brill.

Nord, Christiane. 1997. *Translating as a Purposeful Activity*. Manchester: St Jerome.

Noske, Frits. 1970. *French Song from Berlioz to Duparc* (tr. Rita Benson). New York: Dover.

Raffel, Burton. 1988. *The Art of Translating Poetry*. University Park and London: The Pennsylvania State University.

Steiner, George. 1975. *After Babel*. London: Oxford University Press.

Taylor, Jane *et al.* (eds) 1996. *Translation Here and There, Now and Then*. Exeter: Elm Bank.

Venuti, Lawrence (ed) 2000. *The Translation Studies Reader*. London and New York: Routledge.

Vermeer, Hans J. 1978. 'Ein Rahmen für eine allgemeine Translationstheorie.'in *Lebende Sprachen* 23 (3): 99-102.

—— 2000. 'Skopos and Commission in Translational Action' in Venuti, Lawrence (ed.) *The Translation Studies Reader*. London and New York: Routledge. 221-232.

The Saami Yoik: Translating Hum, Chant, or/and Song

Myrdene Anderson

Chanting stands out as a significant genre in the repertoire of vocal arts in many cultures. In much of the circumpolar arctic in particular, chanting constitutes the main if not the only vocal art form. As such, it may or may not be narrowly ritual in use, and may or may not include strings of verbal linguistic signs. Regardless of the status and roles of chanters, the contexts of chanting events, and the inclusion of linguistic elements, all chants can be said to be imbued with cultural meanings. Meanings will differentially condense around the active chanter, the setting, and the sometimes passive audience members. In the far northwest of Europe, the Saami (formerly Lapps) practice a chant form, the yoik (from *juoigos* in the Saami language, mediated by Scandinavian loan terms such as *joik*). The meanings inhering in yoik may challenge translation for a variety of reasons: words may be absent in the yoik, representation is denied by the yoikers, and the yoik may never be rendered the same twice. It's as though this arctic culture had anticipated Heraclitus's "One can't step into the same river twice." Nonetheless, meanings in terms of lesser shadings of opacity reward the translator's efforts.

Launching the Conundrum

Formerly called Lapps by outsiders, the Saami people reside in northernmost Europe, in regions stretching from Norway, across Sweden and Finland, to the Kola peninsula of Russia, mostly above the arctic circle. The most emblematic lifestyle, although practiced nowadays only by a minority, is nomadic reindeer pastoralism. The Saami language, along with Finnish, Estonian, and Hungarian, belongs to the Finno-Ugric family; some Saami, though, have their national language rather than Saami as a mother tongue. When their singular vocal art, yoik, does have lyrics, these will be in the Saami language, and a preponderance of performers come from the reindeer-breeding minority within this Fourth World indigenous ethnic minority.

This quintessential Saami *juoigos*, or yoik, is not song, but rather chant, or chant-unto-robust-hum. That is to say that the classic yoik is vocal without necessarily being verbal, but the vocal sounds are hardly random. The most common yoik form is that still found above the arctic circle, pentatonic and without half-tones, predominately quartet chains of vowels and dipthongs punctuated more by glottals than by consonants. The more contemporaneous in time, however, and the more southern the location in Lapland, the more likely that verbal elements of yoik will emerge from the chant, but without the result ever classifiable as song-like (Arnberg *et al.* 1969). The contrasting more verbal yoiks' perhaps linear narratives (called *luohti*) are subsumed to the nonlinear yoik chants which remain the substrate for the vocal art. Hence, this Saami marriage of language and music is not a democratic fusion as one might expect of song. However, Saami do recognize song (*lawla*) when this musical form enters Lapland from outside cultural influences, whether from religious practices or from commercial media.

An outsider might nonetheless consider the yoik *as* song, inasmuch as there are no other traditional vocal arts in Saami that occupy that western category. Even the early Saami author Johan Turi (1854-1936) admitted as much in his seminal insider's outline of the Saami culture (1910). In fact, to classify yoik as song does not purchase clarity, and defers if not precludes any appreciation of the special structures, functions, and contexts of yoik and its overarching Saami culture. In fact, the yoik's functions and contexts are not terminologically distinguished when to an outsider they would appear variously to be lullaby, hymn, self-musing, character-assassination, or cathartic outburst. Yoik is yoik regardless of the role of the yoiker, the intents of the yoiker, or the constituents of the setting.

In fact, the yoiker and setting are as much a part of the yoik as the yoik is a part of the yoiker and setting. The yoik, nonlinear and bereft of beginning, middle, or end, may appear to have a subject, but this, too, is illusory. Saami contend that the yoik (with or without words) is emphatically not *about* the subject; it *is* the subject (Somby 1995: 17). A yoik instantiates, rather than represents the subjects which often concern landscape, animals, or individual humans. Yoiking is a way of remembering (Turi 1910), of fusing disparate times, places, and actors, infused with feeling, with emotion. See the following joik chanting by Mari Boine (b. 1965):

Gumpet holvot

Ealán ealán beaivvis beaivái
ealán ealán beaivvis beaivát
oainnán oainnán maid dal buktibehtet
oainnán oainnán maid dal hutkabehet
ealán ealán beaivvis beaivát

Hálan hálan daid seamma ságaid
hálan hálan daid seamma ságaid
geardduhan ja geardduhan

geardduhan ja geardduhan

ja gumpet holvot
nu go álo leat dahkan
álo leat dahkan
álo leat dahkan
álo leat dahkan
álo leat dahket
álo leat dahket
álo leat dahkan

(…)

(Boine 1994)

English *readable, not singable, translation* by Myrdene Anderson:

The wolves howl

I live, live from day to day
I live, live from day to day
I wait to find out what you bring
I wait to see what you come up with
I live, live from day to day

I talk, talk the same words
I talk, talk the same words
repeating and repeating
over and over

And the wolves howl
as they always have done
through the ages
through the ages
through the ages
as they always have done
and always will do

Nowadays Saami insiders may be inspired to yoik for the benefit of outsiders, and outsiders may be inspired by yoik and may venture to engage in yoiking. In these instances, words may intrude, dominate, or constitute the chant. But even when words and narratives constitute the thread of the yoik, it may remain *juoigos* rather than be termed *luohti* despite the linguistic element, and will never be classed as song, *lavla*, even by bicultural individuals. For the most part, luohti labels just the lyric, which in turn is sometimes referred to as "poetry." In this essay, the fundamental musical form will be labeled *yoik* regardless of the intrusion of language or outside interpreters.

Issues of Translation

Translating a strictly vocal chant without words may appear oxymoronic, although meaning—indeed, meanings—are there, not in sound-symbolic terms but in the culture-bound evocation of the setting(s) and person(s) of/in/for the yoik. When the yoik is not just vocal but also verbal, similar reservations about translation obtain. This is because the words' pragmatic significance may wash out their semantic meanings. To hear yoik is a personal experience, and to yoik is beyond personal. And I realize I said "to hear" rather than "to listen to"; this is because "to listen to" connotes more motivated, analytic, and careful attention to some stimulus, natural or otherwise, which stimulus may be repeated or repeatable, inviting appreciative comparisons.

Instead, yoik is a perforce self-organizing improvisational performance. Yoiking is "in your face," more specifically "in both ears," and one does not listen to it, one hears it within a relationship which fuses the sound and setting with both sender and receiver. Of course, one might "listen for" yoik as one approaches a tent or dwelling, but once a yoik is heard, one is virtually plugged into the setting as the yoiker and yoik are recognized.

To a degree, yoik concerns nature — which is where it will most often be found. Saami do not identify themselves with a carpentered world; nature is their element. George Steiner (1983: 4) relates that in myth, music has had the power to build cities. Possibly, Saami yoik is a carpenter of nature, while evoking sacred *seidi* stones, the calving grounds, herding dog, individual draft reindeer. Nature contains folk, and yoik may also reference one's self or other humans. The yoik definitely contributes toward reputation, of persons and other animals, a fact of great importance in a culture privileging individuality and independence as much as the Saami do (Anderson 1978). An ecological chant would be the following Mari Boine's joik about "God's of nature (embody them)" with repeated refrain:

Álddagasat ipmilat

Din njeallječiegat ságat
din njellječiegat lanjat
din njellječiegat mojit
din njellječiegat lágat
váibadit hávkadit

> *Borši jogat, njurgu biekkat*
> *álddagat, ipmilat*
> *borši jogat, njurgu biekkat*
> *álddagat, ipmilat*
> *deavdet dáid*
> *deavdet dáid*
> *eatnama eatni vuoinnaiguin*

Din guovttesuorat ságat
din guovttesuorat lanjat
din guovttesuorat mojit
din guovttesuorat lágat
váibadit hávkadit

> *[refrain]*

English *readable, not singable, translation* for use of CD by Boine/Silset:

Gods of Nature (Embody Them)

Their hardened talk
their hardened state
their hardened smile
their hardened laws
drain me
suffocate me

> *Raging rivers*
> *howling winds*
> *lightning flashes*
> *God's nature –*

embody them
with Earth mother's spirit

Their double talk
their double state
their double smile
their double laws
drain me
suffocate me
drain me

[*refrain*]

(Boine 1998 nr. 5)

Yoiking has had a further association with shamanism, an institution discouraged for several centuries by the colonizing society which banned both the yoik and the drum sometimes accompanying yoik. While shamanism has been weakened or/and transformed, the drum has recently been revived, at least for recreation. The yoik never totally succumbed to the repression. What saved the yoik was its being an individual expressive outlet needing nothing more than inspiration. Individuals could yoik outdoors alone, indoors with others present, and for any reason.Yoiking remained a way to connect with nature and culture, in trance, and to defy outside influences, at least for some.

Music is mysterious, claims Yi-Fu Tuan (b. 1930); even the sounds of nature can invoke the other-worldly (Tuan 1998: 175-176). While the yoik may seem in some instances magical, there is no magical formula to enlighten the novice about what might be and what cannot be translated when it comes to the yoik. Music, language, the balance of culture, and the yoiker's experience make up the phenomenon. Therefore it seems prudent to explore the social history and a few characteristics about the singing form.

Back to Older Times and Forward to Ours

Scholars from a number of fields and cultural backgrounds have been fascinated by the yoik. Publications given to description date from before the 18th century, and by the mid-20th century, recordings augmented some of the textual documentation (Arnberg *et al.* 1969, Bodor 1971, Donner 1876, Launis 1908, Schefferus [1694] 1704, Somby 1995, Tirén 1942, Wiklund 1906, 1947). Even into contemporary times, books and dissertations delve into the yoik and its traditional styles and modern adaptations (Dana 2003, Edström 1978, Einejord 1975, Graff 1985, Jones-Bamman 2001, Kjellström *et al.* 1988, Lüderwaldt 1976). Saami are represented as both scholars and performers (e.g., Gaup 1979, Ruong [Arnberg, Ruong, and Unsgaard 1969], Jernsletten 1978, Turi 1910, Valkeapää [1988] 1997).

Saami have sometimes claimed that the yoik-*qua*-yoik was given to their people by the *uldo* spirits of the tundra (Lüderwalt 1976: 183). Nonetheless, particular yoiks today are sometimes created by known individuals, and even given from one person to another. They are not bought or sold, though, except when recorded, and that commercial "gift" to a wider hearing public breaks the charm of the genre, according to some Saami.

Some Saami traditionalists have questioned the authenticity of certain contemporary yoiks and yoikers. For instance, the yoiker may be perceived to have had *no* relationship with either Saami nature *or* Saami culture, and/or the yoiker may be suspected of having heard more yoiks on recordings than in their natural settings (Gaski 1987: 108). Nowadays, yoik compositions might even reflect upfront their commercial antecedents. The well-known late Finnish Saami artist, Nils-Aslak Valkeapää (1943-2001), has also remarked on the incongruity of the copyrighting of materials when they pertain to a cultural practice — this despite the fact that Saami culture privileges autonomy and individual ownership. See Valkeapää's poem "Trekways of the Wind" (1994), joiked under a different title by Mari Boine:

Eallin

Háldivččen addit šiela, eallin
geiget dan ráhkesvuhtii
ja cummá
oappáid ja vieljaid muodui'e
geat eai nagodan
geat jáhku masse
Riiki Riektái ja Vuoigatvuhtii
Olbmui
Ja vel idediige

ja vel, eallin

girdilit sávašin
eallima
álbmogiidda
mat eai šahten leat
ja mat fargga leat jávkame

ja vel, eallin
ve lattainšin
deidda
geat oidnetčuovgga ja čábbodaga
geat dovdet olbmo ja ráhkisvuoda
geat vurdet idida ja jáhkket dasa
dahkos ilu beasi ja čabbodat
devdos lihkku dan beasi
ja ráhkisvuohta

English *readable, not singable, translation* by Ralph Salisbury, Lars Nordström and Harald Gaski:

Life

I wanted to give you a gift, Life
hand it over to love
and kiss
the cheeks of brothers and sisters
those who did not have the strength
who lost faith
in the Kingdom, the Authority, and
Righteousness
in man
in tomorrow

and one more wish, Life
fly far
give life
to the people
who no longer are
and those who shall soon disappear

yes, and one single thing, Life
I wish

those
who see light and beauty
who know man and love
who await dawn and believe in it
that joy makes its nest and beauty
that happiness fills the nest
and love

(Boine 1998 nr. 1)

The extant older yoiks and those emerging today tend to be short personal pieces that can chain on themselves or even lend themselves to a multi-person rendition of competitive interlocking quasi-rounds. This feature of yoik derives from its scarcely having a beginning and its definitely having no end. Their themes may be about people, subsistence activities associated with reindeer herding, other animals, landscape, or nature generally, and these common yoiks are embued with profound personal power without being actually dangerous (Gaski 1987: 104; Kjellström *et al.* 1988: 21).

In earlier times there were *also* — one gathers *not instead* — long epic yoiks. Those yoiks were powerful unto dangerous, depending on the yoiker and the setting. The epics themselves may have had prehistories with various intents and purposes, but by the time they were noted at the beginning of the 1800s, these yoiks clearly folded in political statements objecting to the emerging conditions of colonialism. Other epic yoiks served the shamanistic rites for spiritual, therapeutic, and medicinal purposes, and also contributed to pedagogical themes such as reindeer management (Gaski 1987: 104).

Before a certain time in history-unto-prehistory, there were presumably both these epic yoiks and the still vibrant individual yoiks. Colonial pressure and censorship became particularly strong in the 19th century. Agents of the dominant society condemned both sorts of yoiks, for various reasons. One was their association with shamanism; it bears recalling that the shaman drum was utterly suppressed by Fennoscandian religionists and the dominant culture generally. Another reason was the yoik's emblematic ties to the Saami culture, making something little understood *still* more mysterious. Another reason behind the suppression of the yoik was the fact that it was associated with settings of alcohol consumption. These "settings" were hardly fixed places for the Saami, but rather the intersections of habitual coming and going on the tundra connected to the mobility of reindeer management.

In the dormitory schools where many Saami nomad children had to live during the past couple of centuries, there were long periods when the Saami language was discouraged, or downright forbidden, and the same went for yoiking into the recent 20th century (Gaski 1987: 8). These explicit restrictions intensified the less formal deculturation taking place where the Saami were outnumbered by colonizing members of the dominant national society. The 20th century proved to be a watershed. The German occupation during World War II and their scorched-earth policy during their retreat from north Norway was followed by a period of intense re-development, not only subsidized rebuilding of structures but also an extension of the German ground transportation routes suitable for vehicles other than reindeer-drawn sledges. Consequently, members of the dominant national society and tourists now have year-around equal access to Saami areas.

Today, the national media join with other forces marginalizing the Saami minority, but overall the tide has turned. In the 1960s, the Saami language could be heard on brief radio programs earmarked for practical weather reports and birthday greetings. Other than the scholarly recordings made by Swedish Radio on two expeditions in 1953 and 1954 (Arnberg *et al.* 1969), radio programs had limited material on the yoik. In the 21st century, the Saami presence is no longer just token on either radio or television. Yoiking documentaries and yoiking competitions are popular. The multi-media artist Nils-Aslak Valkeapää produced numerous programs reaching wide audiences throughout Fennoscandia and abroad. Saami programs, balanced between performance culture and political issues, familiarize and educate a wider public as well. On Saami television, there is even a sign-language interpreter for news programs.

Given the global Fourth World movement, and the increasing importance of Saami media throughout the far north, a number of persons and whole families have rediscovered their Saami roots, studied the language, and explored the yoik, even though their primary motivations may be sociopolitical pragmatics rather than expressive ethnic identity. Some rediscovering their roots have had families living not in Lapland but in North America for over a century, and in this case ethnic identity and/or romanticism explains the conversion (Anderson 2004).

The Social Life of the Yoik

The most common verbal constituents of yoik relate to the natural and social environment, the latter often focusing on a single individual. But nature is the larger player, or, one should say, the emotional associations with particular natural and interpersonal phenomena are the subject *and* object of the yoik, and these may be not just culture-bound, but idiosyncratic. Translation of anything always entails generative re-creation rather than bit-by-bit re-composition, and ordinarily the translator of a text should be a native-speaker of the *target* language (Anderson 2003). These guidelines will not assist in the translation of yoik, because of the cultural density and the personal tacit knowledge involved in yoiking, and the fact that often one is not dealing with "texts" (Gorlée 2004: 17ff), and as such will be opaque to any translation with fidelity. The verbal or just vocal constituents of a yoik do not sit still but are reinvented with each performance. Finally, if 30,000 of 100,000 Saami (both generous estimates) speak the language, very few will be competent in any other language besides the national language, and the number of non-Saami fluent in the Saami language might number in a finite number of dozens. So, potential willing and competent translators of yoik will never be able to meet the public interest in yoik. Fortunately, many outsiders are satisfied by Saami renditions of yoik, whether somewhat traditional or exploring other popular contemporary musical forms from jazz to throat-singing.

While I cannot claim expertise as a musician, a yoiker, or even a scholarly listener, I have lived in Norwegian Saami for a number of continuous and discontinuous years since 1972, and as a listener I am accustomed to hearing yoik in many settings (Anderson 1978). Yet, I cannot imagine a yoik performed in translation. Reading the occasional translation of verbal yoiks is not so helpful either. Times do change, however, and the yoik has crossed many cultural boundaries on its own terms, facilitated by popular performers. This aside, on encountering a volume and CD called *Joik for Kor* [Yoik for Choir] (Fjellheim 2002), I found it astonishing. The yoik is an individual performance even when several may be yoiking at the same time, and even if they yoik the same yoik! Yet, someone must be exploring yoik for choir, although surely not Saami themselves; this book is written in Norwegian.

Yoiking may inspire others to yoik, for many reasons. Sometimes, as when a yoik is used in a "lullaby" setting, the yoiker may be drowning out the noise of the other. I have often witnessed the yoik used to mask sounds, that is, noise, from the dominant culture. Even short yoiks may have many versions, and some yoikers have a large repertoire both of versions and of yoiks, that can be spontaneously rendered with authority, while proliferating at the same time even more variations. There's no attempt to yoik in time with another. In fact, to join in with the same or another yoik may serve to drown out the first performer. Any of these practices may induce trance.

As though these do not pose sufficient impediments to the translation of yoik, consider also that a yoik may be "owned." Here the data varies, but nothing will erase the mystical associations of owned yoiks. The owner need not be the originator, nor the usual performer. When such a yoik is yoiked, one yoiks the person directly, not the person's yoik. Similarly, one yoiks reindeer and landscape, not about them. The experience is quintessential firstness, and as such will be opaque to translation with fidelity.

Just as yoiks can be given to another, they can likewise be inherited. Gaski (1987:7) says that inheritance can be from father to son or mother to daughter, but this may vary from time to time and place to place, and in my experience neither gender nor inheritance are central to yoik.

Even babies may be given a yoik for their own and will be coached to yoik it. Sometimes children or adults will not just compose general yoiks, but create their own personal yoik(s), or create a yoik that can be given away as an owned yoik. An owned yoik may not be so typically yoiked by the owner, such as in the baby example above, for that could indicate being full of oneself. However, since few Saami lack in self-esteem, in my experience such yoiking-of-self may not trigger criticism. It is more typical that one yoiks the owned yoik of another person, in earshot or not. That would indicate a communion, a closeness, special knowledge. Or, with a few twists in intonation or words, the yoiking could chide or even inflict psychic harm.

In the past, I've called self-yoiks oral/aural signatures (Anderson 1984). As part and parcel of reputation, they carry particular weight in the culture. As in the case of the reindeer earmarks signifying ownership, yoiks can be "forged" to undermine or challenge reputation. They can be endorsed to enhance reputation. The valence of reputation, good or bad, means less than the acknowledgement of reputation.

Nicknames also figure prominently in the owned repertoire of a Saami, and nicknames may be incorporated into either owned self-yoiks or ordinary yoiks. Until very recently, the inventory of first names for either sex did not reach two dozen (Anderson 1984). Consequently, the only way to distinguish persons referentially by name has been: first, to give each individual a string of co-names or middle names following a first name; second, to insert ahead of that string another string designating male or female ancestors appropriate for disambiguation in a particular context; and third, to create nicknames. Any of these terms of reference may be situated in yoik. More brief terms of address may also be encountered in yoik.

As an aside, ownership is consonant with the other practices in this pastoral society. Each individual nomad regardless of age or sex has a reindeer-ownership mark for the ears of his or her own reindeer, and clothing will be decorated with something like stylized runic initials, which will also do as a "hide mark" for reindeer in weather too severe for ear-marking.

Certainly yoikers keep particular yoiks alive, but without reifying them as texts. Some non-owned individual yoiks live for centuries without any special care or feeding through ownership. Others of course taper off. The yoiks with the shortest lifetimes may well be those that have been fixed in vinyl, paradoxically enough. However, it's only through vinyl and some unusual early scholarship that we have any way to trace the inevitable development and evolution within the yoik *form* or *content*.

Yoikers and Yoiking

As emphasized, in keeping with the individualism foregrounded in Saami culture, yoiks are solo performances, even when others participate. These others may join in the same amorphous yoik, but not in unison — rather, as though a very loose round were intended. And/or those others may be yoiking something quite distinct, whether to drown out or contrapunctually to complement and enhance the original yoik.

Returning to the absent lullaby in Saami culture; yoik serves in this capacity, but with a twist. The caretaker of a baby may yoik casually for any reason, but when the baby is cranky, yoiking steps in to mask the disturbing unpleasant baby sounds as much as to comfort the baby. Saami prefer both babies and adults to be content — which may explain why the strictest teetotalers tolerate inebriated visitors, whether they be talking, yoiking, or sleeping.

A whimper from a baby calls for a soft yoik from the caretaker. If and when the baby persists or escalates its distress call, so does the yoiking. It is often not convenient to address the possible complaint of the infant. The adult caretaker has the stronger lung capacity, and will successfully drown out the sound from the baby. The baby meanwhile may become quiet from sheer exhaustion, and/or due to the trance-inducing quality of the yoik. And the baby may still have a complaint, let's say discomfort from wet diapers. However, the caretaker has taken the initiative in this "teachable moment," for in real life, life beyond the circle of loving caretakers and outside the comfort of tent or house, there will be unavoidable and inaddressable discomforts. Culture, an anticipatory system (Rosen 1985), hologrammically encrypts behavior backwards and forwards, to the amazement of the analytic observer — fallible or procrustean though the observer may be. And what better medium to feed forward and backwards than sound. Sound waves go around corners, linger, reverberate, and resonate, before entering into memory (Feld and Brenneis 2004).

Solo yoiks are regularly deployed to drown out any ambient noise: baby, motor, radio — or even silence. Solo yoiks, with or without words, also serve to insulate the yoiker or/and to induce a desirable dissociated state. In this manner, any yoik may function much as humming in the EuroAmerican tradition, posing its own challenges to translation. The same yoik may be rendered as digital chant, with or without verbal constituents, or as analogue hum.

Given the premium on independence and individuality in Saami culture, yoikers may fib or forget about the source of a yoik. They are not wont to explain a yoik. Share, yes; explain, no. Within the culture, the limits to meaning are already known: one meets the yoik more or less half-way to understand it.

In the now quaint early historical documentation of the Saami people and Saami culture, some claimed that the Saami had *no song*, thus distancing yoik from that western category of song. More quoted than this narrow and qualifiable observation, though, was an assertion that the Saami had *no dance*—and in fact that Saami were to be the only cultural group without dance. So, what is or was dance to those myopic observers?

If song is a vocal art distinguished from ordinary vocality associated with quotidian speaking, then dance might be a stylized use of the entire body, or some part of it, distingushed from ordinary quotidian motion. All the same, people in different cultural groups lie, sit, walk, and run as well as dance in a distinctive manner; some of that inflected use of the body might relate to climate, clothing, substrate, dominant activities, early childhood training. I cannot help but recall the written and filmic work of Alan Lomax (1915-2002), with respect to both song and dance (Lomax 1968-1969, 1976; Lomax and Berkowitz 1972). So, within the socioculture lurk endogenous layers of markedness, which may or may not align with the categories of the analyst. Some categories may be convincing as universals, which were those of primary interest to Lomax. Within a society and likewise between societies, what is conserved, and what dissipated, across genres of song, dance, and other behaviors?

When I first left for Saapmi or Saamiland or Lapland in 1971, I was of course extremely skeptical about the stereotyping of Saami as living in a dance-free environment. In fact, I was confronted with dance each time I heard yoik, and then I found dance elsewhere, or everywhere, as well. Yoik is executed with the whole outward body and the whole inward mind, and dance might merge with both sites of experience. One is compelled to reflect that dance also resists translation. Like the yoik, dance means what it *is* (Geertz 1976: 1485).

While yoiking, the yoiker swings back and forth, whether walking, riding, standing, or sitting; it's uncommon to yoik while recumbent, unless under the extreme influence of alcohol. Actually, a certain amount of town yoiking will be under the influence. Consider the difficulty of standing on two feet if inebriated either from trance or from substance. It is in fact impossible to stand securely on two feet; the solution is to establish a tripod, so that the two feet become three supports. As an aside, this analogy may pertain to other analytic projects of a semiotician!

Toddlers will often simulate this very dance when yoiking. To acquire what they imagine to be the suitable inebriated mind-state, they will with deliberation twirl around like dervishes (but, most often counter-clockwise rather than clockwise as dervishes). Once properly dizzy, the toddler will resume the yoik. The toddler will also take his or her knife, or any other handy object, or just a little fist (either left or right), and slam it down on an actual or imaginary surface. This is also part of the punctuation of the adult yoik-*cum*-dance. In this "dance," one cannot discount the importance of the "swing" of the traditional costume. The yoik performance falls somewhat flat in other clothing.

Back to translation, this merging of "song and dance," and internal and external experience, will certainly pose problems quite beyond the fact that there may be no original "texts," and too many contemporary ones! Once again, as in shamanic times, the phenomenon becomes "song and dance and accompaniment", although less likely token drums than instrumentation inspired from other cultural styles.

Squaring the Hypotenuse

Music and myth each invite and reflect the nonlinear, transcendental, and existential in culture (Barzun 1996), in part because they support the awe inherent in the experience of firstness (discussed by Gorlée in this book), emotion (Meyer 1956), and reverie (Bachelard [1960]1969), and by doing so defy the modernist faith in transparent progress and reductive rationality. Michel Poizat ([1986] 1992) quotes Claude Lévi-Strauss (b. 1908) who claimed that music "speaks" because of its "negative relationship" to language ([1971]1981: 647). Music is language without meaning. Does it matter which comes first, in either evolution or development? Perhaps not, but attention has of late xeroed in on just this question (e.g., Balter 2004, Feld and Fox 1993, Levman 1992, Lidov 2004, Pinker 1997, Wallin *et al.* 2000).

I would disagree with those who view music as derivative of language. But oh-oh, is yoik music or musical? Let's say yes, and yes. Poizat himself focused on opera, where the evolutionary trajectory might be from verbal expressions of emotion to wordless cry. I can imagine the yoik, in its fusion of sound and setting and experience, to have deeper chords than verbal language. Emotion resists verbalization in the first place, magnifying the challenge of translation (see Jourdain 1997, Meyer 1956, Gorlée 2004).

I conclude as I began, relucantly. Reluctantly I conclude that yoik most often will be opaque to translation. I'm not sure that translation will do for the yoik as much as what a sensitive novice might bring to the raw, inscrutable sound, belted out into the elements.

I will now try to focus on vinyl and other mediated modalities. What of "playing" a recorded yoik? Is yoik "more authentic" when married with visual images? Or will vision detract from the sound? Not only do I believe that vision assists in the case of yoik, but so do the noises that accompany yoiking — crunch of snow, barking of dogs, even motor of snowmobile — as long as the noise belongs to what's happening in the images rather than merely imported onto the disk. Still lacking though would be the smells and tastes and tactility of hearing yoik in a natural setting.

Ordinarily in translation one draws on a source language in one corner, and a target language in another corner, opposite in two-dimensional space as constrained by this model which will end up looking like a diamond inscribed within a square. The candidate for translation into another language will be also constructed within the idiom of culture, most likely the culture supporting the language. The translator seeks mediation among and between both languages and both cultures. To go directly from one language source to one target language would assume that the texts are not only language-independent but also culture-free and experience-neutral. Consequently the translator attempts to explore the comparable lived linguistic, cultural, and psychological experiences behind the source text and thrusts them forward into a fresh articulation (Gorlée 2004, Osimo 2002, Torop 2002). Right now I imagine as inevitable in the translation process, a periodic and persisting translating reverie (Bachelard [1960]1969 and discussed by Gorlée in this book), snaking off into space, escaping the diamond model. It could even swing back with malicious intent. That's what especially any translator of yoik has to take notice of, in addition to all the factors in ordinary song and quotidien language.

And this is what the target-language translator would be oblivious of. Could a Saami yoiker adequately translate any yoik, then? That would demand considerable competence not only in the target language but the target culture. Plus motivation. Yoik is so immediate and so personal and so very cultural that it's difficult to conjure up the motivation that might lead to translation. It's been done, and we non-Saami are the beneficiaries of those translations, but that's not to say they are more than rorschachs of the original yoik *and yoiking*. To pursue this line of thinking, regardless of the motivation and competence of the translator, can we imagine the nature of any effort of back-translation? To a Saami culture-bearer, any hypothetical back-translation would surely be ludicrous, a disjunct nonsensical tangle of overdetermined and underdetermined elements.

Briefly back to the hum, the hum can capture the inward and personal communion with self, tune, and environment that could align with some yoiking, although yoiking is usually rather emphatic in its rendering. Fernandez (1978) discusses the Asturian deepsong in such a way that it bears much resemblance to yoik. Geertz (1976) introduces a Moroccan poetry performance genre which straddles the style of ritual Quranic chant and secular speech. So there are analogues out there beyond the circumpolar chant form which has so often been discussed as a unique genre.

Ordinarily capturing brainwaves by any means surely insult experiential reality. But in this case — capturing yoik in contrasting modalities and in different settings—and of the yoiker and recipient — I'm sure brainwaves would tell us something fresh; something to look forward to; something to make the yoik even more inscrutable. And having mentioned this as a fanciful aside, it is the case that such research may yet unpack yoik on further levels, although I would resist the metaphor of "deeper" levels (consider Weinberger 2004, Peretz and Zatorre 2003). That would be the prerogative of experience-*qua*-experience, somehow mapping musement, charting enchantment, interrogating introspection, respecting emotion (see Juslin and Sloboda 2001). Aristotle (c. 330 BCE [1941]: 1312) may have had something to say: "There seems to be in us a sort of affinity to musical modes and rhythms, which makes some philosophers say that the soul is a tuning, others that it possesses tuning."

"Music is comparatively free of the superstition that reality is entirely what it appears to be, finite, bodily, visible, and therefore imitable" (Donoghue 1990: 82). Or, translatable? Yoik likewise asserts itself on its own terms, promising nothing through translation, but may bend to humble and respectful efforts.

Bibliography

Anderson, Myrdene. 1978. *Saami Ethnoecology: Resource Management in Norwegian Lapland.* Ph.D. dissertation, Yale University. Ann Arbor, Michigan: University Microfilms, 1979.

—— 1984. 'Proper Names, Naming, and Labeling in Saami' in *Anthropological Linguistics* 26.2: 186-201.

—— 2003. 'Ethnography as Translation' in Petrilli, Susan (ed.) *Translation Translation* (Approaches to Translation Studies 21). Amsterdam and New York: Rodopi. 389-397.

—— 2004. 'Reflections on the Saami at Loose Ends' in *Cultural Shaping of Violence: Victimization, Escalation, Response.* West Lafayette, IN: Purdue University Press. 285-291.

Aristotle. (c. 330 BCE) 1941. 'Politics, Book VIII, Chapter 5' in McKeon, R. (ed.) *The Basic Works of Aristotle.* Chicago: University of Chicago Press.

Arnberg, Matts, Israel Ruong, and Håkan Unsgaard. [1969]1997. *Joik. En Presentation av Samisk Folkmusik / Yoik. A Presentation of Saami Folk Music.* Stockholm: Sveriges Radio Förlag.

Bachelard, Gaston. [1960]1969. *The Poetics of Reverie* (tr. Daniel Russell). New York: Orion Press (French original: *La Poétique de la rêverie*. Paris: Presses Universitaires de France, 1960)

Balter, Michael. 2004. 'Seeking the Key to Music' in *Science* 306 (12 November): 1120-1122.

Barzun, Jacques. 1996. 'Is Music Unspeakable?' in *American Scholar* 65 (Spring): 193-202.

Bodor, Anikö. 1971. 'Analys och Beskrivning av Lapska Jojkar med Utnyttjande av "MONA": En "Case Study"' in *Trebetygsuppsats i Musikvetenskap*. Manuscript.

Dana, Kathleen Osgood. 2003. *Áilloháš: The Shaman-Poet and his Govadas-Image Drum: A Literary Ecology of Nils-Aslak Valkeapää*. Dissertation. Oulo: Oulu University Press.

Donner, Otto. 1876. *Lieder der Lappen*. Helsingfors: Suomalais-Ugrilainen Seura..

Donoghue, Denis. 1990. *Warrenpoint*. New York: Knopf.

Edström, Karl Olof. 1978. *Den Samiska Musikkulturen: En Källkritisk Översikt* (Skrifter från Musikvetinskaplige Institutionen 1). Göteborg: University of Götheborg.

Einejord, J.E. 1975. *Luotti-Juoigos-Dajahus. Innhald i Joiken*. Hovedoppgave in Saami. University of Oslo.

Feld, Steven, and Aaron A. Fox. 1994. 'Music and Language' in *Annual Review of Anthropology* 23: 25-53.

—— and Donald Brenneis. 2004. 'Doing Anthropology in Sound' in *American Anthropologist* 31 (4): 461-474.

Fernandez, James W. 1978. 'Syllogisms of Association: Some Modern Extensions of Asturian Deepsong' in Dorson, Richard M. (ed.) *Folklore in the Modern World* (World Anthropology Series). The Hague and Paris: Mouton. 183-206.

Fjellheim, Frode. 2002. *Joik for Kor: En Samling Joiker og Joikeinspirerte Komposisjoner Arrangert for Blandet Kor*. Trondheim: Vuelie Forlag.

Gaski, Harald. 1987. *Med Ord Skal Tyvene Fordrives: Om Samenes Episk Poetiske Dicting*. Skien: Davvi Girji, O.S.

Gaup, Ailo Andersen. 1979. 'Usikkerhet in Reindrifta; Fordommer mot Joik' in *Hverdag* 21/22 (May-June): 4-8.

Geertz, Clifford. 1976. 'Art as a Cultural System' in *Modern Language Notes* 81-6: 1473-1499.

Gorlée, Dinda L. 2004. *On Translating Signs: Exploring Text and Semio-Translation* (Approaches to Translation Studies 24). Amsterdam and New York: Rodopi.

Graff, Ola. 1985. *Joik som Musikalsk Språk*. Magistergrad thesis in Musicology. University of Oslo.

James, Jamie. 1993. *The Music of the Spheres: Music, Science, and the Natural Order of the Universe*. New York: Copernicus.

Jernsletten, Nils. 1978. 'Om Joik og Kommunikasjon' in Bjørkvik, Halvard (ed.) *Kultur på Karrig Jord* (Festschrift til Asbjørn Nesheim 70 År). Oslo: Norsk Folkemuseum.

Jones-Bamman, Richard. 2001. 'From "I'm a Lapp" to "I am Saami": Popular Music and Changing Images of Indegenous Ethnicity in Scandinavia' in *Journal of Intercultural Studies* 22.2: 189-210.

Jourdain, Robert. 1997. *Music, the Brain, and Ecstasy: How Music Captures Our Imagination*. New York: William Morrow.

Juslin, Patrik, and John Sloboda (eds) 2001. *Music and Emotion: Theory and Research*. Oxford: Oxford University Press.

Kjellström, Rolf, Gunnar Ternhag, and Håkan Rydving. 1988. *Om Jojk*. Hedemora: Gidlunds Bokforlag.

Langer, Susan 1949. *Philosophy in a New Key: A Study in the Symbolism of Reason, Rite and Art*. Cambridge: Harvard University Press.

Launis, Arnas. 1908. *Lappische Juoigos-Melodien*. Helsingfors: Suomalais-Ugrilaisen Seura.

Lévi-Strauss, Claude. [1971]1981. *The Naked Man: Mythologies, Vol. 4* (tr. John Weightman and Doreen Weightman). London: Jonathan Cape (French original: *Mythologiques IV : L'Homme Nu*. Paris : Plon, 1971)

Levman, Bryan G. 1992. 'The Genesis of Music and Language' in *Journal of Ethnomusicology* 36.2: 146-170.

Lidov, David. 2004. *Is Language a Music? Writings on Musical Form and Signification*. Bloomington: Indiana University Press.

Lomax, Alan. 1968-1969. *Folk Song Style and Culture*. Washington, D.C.: American Association for the Advancement of Science.

—————— and Norman Berkowitz. 1972. 'The Evolutionary Taxonomy of Culture' in *Science* 177 (21 July): 228-239.

—————— with Cantometrics Staff. 1976. *Cantometrics: A Method in Musical Anthropology*. Berkeley, CA: Extension Media Center, University of California.

Lüderwaldt, Andreas. 1976. *Joiken aus Norwegen: Studien zur Charakteristik und gesellschafftlichen Bedeutung des lappischen Gesanges* (Veröffentlichungen aus dem Übersee-Museum Bremen, Rehe D, Band 2). Bremen: Übersee-Museum.

Meyer, Leonard B. 1956. *Emotion and Meaning in Music*. Chicago: University of Chicago Press.

Osimo, Bruno. 2002. 'On Psychological Aspects of Translation' in *Sign Systems Studies* 30.2: 607-627.

Peretz, Isabelle, and Robert J. Zatorre (eds) 2003. *The Cognitive Neuroscience of Music*. Oxford: Oxford University Press.

Pinker, Steven. 1997. *How the Mind Works*. New York: Norton.

Poizat, Michel. 1992. *The Angel's Cry: Beyond the Pleasure Principle in Opera* (tr. Arthur Denner). Ithaca and London: Cornell University Press (French original is *L'opera, ou le cri de l'ange: Essai sur la jouissance de l' amateur d' opéra*. Paris: A. M. Metailie, 1986).

Rosen, Robert. 1985. *Anticipatory Systems: Philosophical, Mathematical and Methodological Foundations*. New York: Pergamon.

Schefferus, Johannes. [1674]1704. *The History of Lapland; Containing a Geographical Description, and a Natural History of that Country; with an Account of the Inhabitants, their Original (sic), Religion, Customs, Habits, Marriages, Conjurations, Employment, etc.* (tr. from the Latin) London: Golden-Ball in St. Paul's Church-yard for Tho. Newborough, and R. Parker under the Royal-Exchange.

Scott, Nathan A., Jr., and Ronald A. Sharp (eds) 1994. *Reading George Steiner*. Baltimore: Johns Hopkins University Press.

Somby, Ánde. 1995. 'Joik and the Theory of Knowledge' in Haavelsrud, Magnus (ed.) *Kunnskap og Utvikling*. Tromsø: Universitetsforlaget. 17.

Steiner, George. 1983. 'The City under Attack' in Boyers, Robert and Peggy Boyers (eds) *The Salmagundi Reader*. Bloomington: Indiana University Press.

—————— 1994. *Reading George Steiner*, Nathan A. Scott, Jr. and Ronald A. Sharp (eds). Baltimore: Johns Hopkins University Press.

Tirén, Karl. 1942. *Die Lappische Volksmusik: Aufzeichnungen von Juoikos-Melodien bei den schwedischen Lappen*. Mit einer Einleitung von Wilhelm Peterson-Berger; Rekonstruktion und Übersetzung der lappischen Originaltexte von Bjørn Collinder (Nordiska Museet: Acta Lapponica 3). Stockholm: Hugo Gebers Forlag.

Torop, Peeter. 2002. 'Translation as Translating Culture' in *Sign Systems Studies* 30 (2): 593-605.

Tuan, Yi-Fu. 1998. *Escapism*. Baltimore: Johns Hopkins University Press.

Turi, Johan. 1910. *Muittalus Samid Birra. En Bog om Lappernes Liv.* Copenhagen: Græbes Bogtrykkeri (tr. Emilie Demant) Foreword Hjalmar Lundholm. Illustr.

Valkeapää, Nils-Aslak. [1988]1997. 'The Sun, My Father' (tr. Raph Salisbury, Lars Nordström, Harald Gaski). Seattle: University of Washington Press.

Wallin, Nils L., Björn Merker, and Steven Brown (eds) 2000. *The Origins of Music.* Cambridge: MIT Press.

Weinberger, Norman M. 2004. 'Music and the Brain' in *Scientific American* 291-5 (November): 88-95.

Wiklund, Karl B. 1906. *Lapparnes Sång och Poesi.* Uppsala: Norrländska Studenters Folkbildningsförening.

Wiklund, Karl B. 1947. *Lapperne* (Nordisk Kulture 10, Nordisk Kultur Samlingsvaerk). Stockholm: Albert Bonniers Forlag.

Source texts:

Boine, Mari. 1994. *Leahkastin.* With Roger Ludvigsen, Helge A. Norbakken, *et al.* Sonet MBCD 94 523889-2.

———— 1998. *Bálvvoslatjna* (Room of Worship). With Gjermund Silset, Hege Rimestad *et al.* Sonet/Verve MCPS 5590232.

The Plurisemiotics of Pop Song Translation: Words, Music, Voice and Image

Klaus Kaindl

This contribution places popular music and its translation in a socio-semiotic framework and explores the triple emphasis in popular songs on language, music and image. In a first step the polysemiotic text is presented as a social fact.Toury's polysystemic approach and Jacono's concept of institutionalisation are used as a theoretical framework in order to explain the different interpretations of a song as a chain of interpretants. In a second step the term "text" is analysed in relation to music, and popular music in particular with the help of three concepts: *dialogics* (Bakhtin), *bricolage* (Lévi-Strauss) and mediation (Negus). In a last step the intertextual, *bricolage*-like and mediated caracter of popular song translation is demonstrated with the analysis of several interpretations of a French *chanson* and its German translations.

Introduction

Popular music is part of our daily lives, both in its aural dimension, e.g. in underground stations, shops, and restaurants, and in its visualized form, in TV and in concerts. It is a cross-cultural phenomenon, and as such it is a segment of high-volume translation. Popular songs are important mass media products through which cultures are articulated and hence communicated to people of different linguistic, historical and cultural backgrounds. Notwithstanding their presence, popular songs have largely been neglected in translation studies. And yet, the pervasive influence of popular songs is best reflected in the numerous translations available, translations which are – quite often – not identified as such. For example, the well-known Frank Sinatra hit "My way", which is attributed to Sinatra and considered as an original composition, goes back to a translation of a French song, *"Comme d'habitude"* by Claude François. The lyrics are altogether different, and so is part of the musical structure of the song, not to mention the voice of Frank Sinatra as opposed to that of Claude Francois. The German version, *"So leb' dein Leben"*, is based on the English text, whereas the Spanish translation, *"De acostumbro"*, goes back to the original French text.[1] Other songs are published simultaneously in different languages or exported to numerous countries so that it even becomes difficult to say what is the original and what the translation. The song "Itzy beenie teenie weenie yellow polkadot bikini," for instance, was a great hit in the fifties and came out almost simultaneously in English (sung by Brian Hyland), in French and Italian (sung by Dalida), and in German (sung, among others, by a group of male singers, the Diamond Singers).

It is fairly evident from these few examples why translation scholars have found it hard to treat this subject. "Who is (considered to be) the author of a song?" "What is the original and what is the translation?" "How can the substantial changes of the verbal as well as the musical text be explained?" Questions like these cannot be answered with the linguistic or literary tools which long dominated the scholarly approach to translations.

Studying the translation of popular songs is of interest not only from a simply language-oriented perspective. As popular songs can only be understood within wider patterns of social and semiotic relations, their study requires an interdisciplinary approach. At the same time, it is clear that studying the translation of popular songs also raises a number of fundamental difficulties. What is an adequate definition of translation, considering the substantial transformations on both the verbal and the nonverbal level of popular songs in translation? How do we deal with the nonverbal dimensions, i.e. with musical and visual elements, that are so central to popular songs and often considered more important than the verbal part? Are meanings transmitted as much through musical/visual signs as through verbal texts?

In this article I would like to address these questions. My starting point will be the current state of the art in the study of pop music translation. This is particularly important to me because the various approaches also illustrate the ways in which we understand and value popular songs, and the ways in which we define translations and understand cultures. I will then sketch out a socio-semiotic framework for the analysis of pop music translation. Finally, I will try to account for the various components of pop songs, such as lyrics, instrumentation and voice, and discuss some difficulties I had in applying traditional musical semiotics to popular music texts. The last section of this paper will be dedicated to the visualization of music in a cross-cultural context, the "look of sound", which seems to be the dominant mode of presentation in popular music today. What I can offer here is certainly not a definitive or comprehensive account of the subject. Rather, I would like this article to be treated as a starting point for an interdisciplinary approach in which translation scholars add, rather eclectically, some semiotic instruments to their conceptual and methodological toolbox.

Popular Music and Translation

Popular songs are often believed to be a trivial form of music and text. This is also reflected in the lack of interest in popular song on the part of translation scholars. Despite the high volume of song translation, the topic has received relatively little attention.[2] Problems of translation have been touched on, in an excursory manner, in articles published in the fields of literary studies, musicology, media studies and journalism, but few works have focused on song translation as a central theme. Haupt (1957) must be given credit for being one of the first to discuss the translation of popular music in her PhD thesis on stylistic and linguistic aspects of German popular songs. Haupt states that there are two types of translations: those which completely change the original text, and others which try to reproduce the source text and only make minimal changes necessitated by musical constraints (cf. 1957:228). However, she does not try to explain these different procedures and leaves the reader with the impression that changes of content are completely arbitrary.

Some explanations for the manipulations in pop song translations are given by Worbs (1963). In his study of the German *"Schlager,"* the predominant form of sung popular music between 1950 and 1970, he states, in a chapter on translation, that the lack of congruence between the textual and the musical message is a striking fact (cf. 1963: 36) which can be found in many translations of popular songs. In contrast to Haupt, he then gives two possible reasons for these manipulations. The first reason for massive changes lies in the image of the singer who has to fulfill certain expectations of his audience. Songs are shaped – in both style and content – by the rest of the repertoire of a singer. The second reason can be found in the "specific mentality of a nation" (1963: 46), which, in contemporary parlance, amounts to saying that the meanings of popular songs are contextually contingent and that their translation depends on the socio-cultural background. Without accounting for the way in which these factors (i.e. the target recipient, the cultural specificity) have a bearing on how we translate popular songs, Worbs tackles some important issues. Nevertheles, his general hypotheses have scarcely been heeded up to now.

One of the few exceptions is the empirical study by Stölting (1975), who, in one chapter of her book *Deutsche Schlager und englische Popmusik in Deutschland*, explores the transformations that English pop songs underwent in the process of translation in the years between 1960 and 1970. Similar to

Haupt, she distinguishes two groups of translated song texts (cf. 1975: 125): In the first group the subject is completely changed, and only the melody of the song is kept. In the second group the original theme is more or less preserved. Stölting is interested only in the changes in this second group, and explains these partly with reference to musico-structural constraints. But the main source for shifts in content and style, according to Holtz, is the fact that the contents of popular songs are determined by culture-specific expectations of the audience. With the emphasis on the ideological background of the social and cultural situation, Stölting broadens the spectrum of research in popular song translation, although her study is focused on the linguistic level and excludes those texts which completely change the subject of the original song. She also ignores the role of the non-verbal elements and of the performer in shaping the broader meaning of popular songs.

The few works exclusively devoted to the translation of songs focus on linguistically demanding songs, first and foremost by French *"auteurs-compositeurs-interprètes"* such as Georges Brassens and Jacques Brel. These – mostly linguistically inspired – approaches tend to concentrate on aspects of language in the narrow sense, such as metaphors and puns (e.g. Steinwender 1992), and analyse translations from a normative, i.e. equivalence-oriented, point of view (e.g. Blaikner 1992/93). There are only a few studies which take broader cultural and non-verbal aspects into consideration. Pamies Betrán (1992/93), for example, views popular song translation not as a linguistic but as a cultural transfer, and analyses various strategies for translating culture-specific linguistic elements. Steinacher (1997), in turn, regards the verbal part of a song as a "flexible, multi-functional component of the artistic message" (1997: 186) that can only be analysed and translated in close interrelation with the non-verbal dimensions of the song text.

Despite some remarks on the role of non-verbal elements and the cultural dimension of translation, the emphasis on language in most of the studies on pop song translation forecloses a broader engagement with the socio-semiotic context in which popular songs are situated. Quite often, the relationship between text and music is not even acknowledged, and the focus is only on linguistic aspects such as metaphor, changes in style, and content. But even when the non-verbal dimension is mentioned (e.g. Rabadán 1991, Steinacher 1997), it is normally reduced to the structural constraints of the music on the verbal text. Of course it is true that the music predetermines certain syntactical and prosodic decisions of the translator, but the role of the non-verbal constituents of the text goes far beyond formal and structural aspects.

Most of these approaches take for granted that the meanings of a song text (and its translation) are only functions of linguistic forms, and that the broader social and cultural context is of little interest in song translation. However, if we want to explain the changes and manipulations in translations of song texts we have to start with the analysis of the socio-semiotic setting of the production and translation of popular songs.

A Socio-Semiotic Framework for the Translation of Popular Music

In translation studies, a socio-semiotic framework has been developed by Itamar Even-Zohar (1997, 1990), Gideon Toury (1995) and Theo Hermans (1999), among others. The basic idea is that translations can be thought of as a set of interdependent texts embedded in various subsystems which form a complex polysystem. The notion of literature (including translation) as a system has its origin in Russian Formalism and in Prague-School Structuralism. The representatives of the systemic view reject the traditional positivistic and prescriptive analysis and criticism of translations established in linguistics and literary studies. According to the systems-oriented approach, not only literary texts but also translations present characteristics which are the result of their interrelations with other texts in the system. Therefore, translations, whether they are viewed from the perspective of the process, product or function, can only be studied in a relational manner. The individual and distinctive features of a translation in a given period, genre, etc. can therefore only be determined in the context of such relations. The semiotic dimensions of such an approach are clear: it underlines the importance of the chain of interpretants in Peirce's definition of a sign. It is only in the context of a given society that a work, be it literary or musical, makes sense and has a certain value. And it stresses the intertextual relationships of translations which, as I intend to show, are a predominant feature of popular song translations.

A system in the definition of Even-Zohar (1990: 85) can be thought of as a "network of relations which can be hypothesized for an aggregate of factors assumed to be involved with a sociocultural activity." Such a system is structured around a canonized powerful centre with the most prestigious literary works, genres, etc.; its periphery, which is less organized than the centre, is where all forms of 'low' literature tend to be situated. The centre/periphery structure leads to another binary opposition which determines the dynamics of a system, i.e. the opposition between canonized and non-canonized products.[3] Canonicity is not an inherent feature of texts, but is attributed by individuals, groups or institutions; it is therefore a social category (cf. Even-Zohar 1990: 15-17). A third opposition concerns the function of texts, i.e. whether a literary work has an innovative or a conservative function within the system, or, in the words of Even-Zohar, whether it has a "primary" or "secondary" function (cf. 1990: 20-22).

If literature as a cultural artifact constitutes a system with a systemic evolution, it is reasonable to think of other cultural products as systems as well. If we consider musical production within a system, many forms of popular music, considering their prestige, certainly belong to the periphery and are considered as part of mass production. But there are some additional characteristics of mass communication that cannot be captured with the oppositional structure of Even-Zohar's systemic approach. That is why Lambert goes beyond systems and pleads for the design of maps of mass communication (cf. Lambert 1989 and Lambert/Delabastita 1996). His groundbreaking conception of mass media translation with special regard to audiovisual translation is also valid for popular music: The production and distribution of popular songs are determined by its international nature and have to be understood as a complex, disjunctive order, which cannot be reduced to center-periphery models; a strong concentration of a few globally acting major companies can reach a worldwide audience; popular music makes extensive use of various forms of multimedia technology; and – as mentioned at the outset – it has become an integral, even invasive, part of our daily lives.

The most important aspect, however, which is not discussed by Lambert in the context of mass media production, concerns storage: Popular songs cannot be treated as *scored* or *notated* objects; they primarily exist as *mediated* objects. It is therefore the process of mediation that has to be at the centre of any translational analysis. The concept of mediation in this context goes far beyond its technical function, as has been argued by Hennion (1993), who, together with Negus (1996), was one of the first to define mediation and its importance for popular music. According to Negus, we can identify three levels of mediation: (cf. 1996: 66-69):

1. Mediation as "intermediary action" concerns the processes and interactions taking place between the production and consumption of popular music and encompasses all the interventions of institutions and persons (i.e. record companies, video directors, disc

jockeys, etc.) that are responsible for the production, distribution and consumption of popular music. The various interventions cannot be understood as neutral but function as gatekeeping, which plays an important role particularly in international contexts (cf. Negus 1996: 67).

2. Mediation as "transmission" takes into account the impact of technology on musical production, distribution and consumption. Negus explicitly refers to the impact of music videos and the role of musical instruments as transmission mediators (cf. 1996: 68). Both technologies, with regard to both the visual and acoustic dimensions, have a direct influence on the creation and reception of the musical text.

3. Mediation of "social relationships": Although the social dimensions of mediation are implicitly present already in the first two meanings of mediation, Negus views questions of power structures and ideology and their impact on the production and consumption of popular music as a category in its own right, and stresses the importance of judging popular songs "critically in terms of how they may communicate a limited range of specific meanings which might ideologically privilege particular interests." (1996: 69)

The focus on mediation does not necessarily lead to the extinction of the text as an analytical tool. The view that only mediation is "real" appears to be taken by Hennion (1993: 248), who argues that popular music does not exist outside mediations (1997: 432). Without denying the primordial role of mediation in the constitution of the popular music text, I would rather consider popular songs as multiple texts that are intextricably linked to the institutions and social settings of musical production and reception. The various channels of dissemination; the practices of musicians and consumers; the visual styles associated with different musical genres and presented in the form of video clips, CD booklets, and record covers; the specifics of sound; and the general discourses about popular music transported by the various media – all of these do not shape and influence songs and their translation from the outside, but are an integral part of a complex whole.

If we accept the idea of popular music as a mediated multiple text, we need a definition of "text" that reflects the complex reality of popular music translation. In this context, I find the concept of *"bricolage"* particularly useful. To my knowledge, this concept, which was initially developed by anthropologist Claude Levi-Strauss (1966: 19-21), was first used in the field of popular music by Dick Hebdige in his book *Subculture* (1979), where he assimilates post-structuralist aspects of semiology as introduced by Julia Kristeva and Roland Barthes. The mediated mode of existence of popular songs, as described above, renders obsolete the idea of a notated, originary text as the starting point for translation. Translation is not primarily based on a written text, but has recourse simultaneously to a range of technologies, media, institutions and public discourses. In this sense, the term *"bricolage"* can be applied in relation to verbal, vocal and musical appropriation. In the process of translation a number of elements, including music, language, vocal style, instrumentation, but also values, ideology, culture, etc., are appropriated from the source culture and mixed with elements from the target culture. The translator in this sense becomes a *"bricoleur"* who chooses various components of the multiple text which he combines and connects in order to form a new unified, signifying system. His translational action is not arbitrary but takes place in the process of mediation of which the translator and his product are a part. Thus, the translation always reflects aspects of a given group in the target culture.

Consequently, translation in the field of popular music cannot be viewed as an operation replacing material of the source text by (equivalent) target-text material, but should be seen as *"dialogics"* in the sense of Bakthin (1984). According to Bakthin, meaning is always situated in specific social and historical contexts, and this primacy of context makes every sign heteroglot, i.e. no text, discourse, genre, etc. exists alone but is part of a textual, discursive and generic network and stands in a dialogic relationship with previous or future utterances. Translation always depends in one way or another upon what has previously been said or written. Any translation works through dialogue at various levels: dialogues with previous texts, genres, styles of the source culture and the target culture, dialogues between (musical, verbal and visual) discourses, dialogues between producers and addressees (real or imagined), dialogues between various interpretations of an individual song. These various echoes, traces, contrasts lead to a multiple-voice signifying stream and to a concept of translation that is intertextual, in process and never complete.

To sum up this socio-semiotic foundation for the translation of popular music:

- Translation is not primarily the result of a transfer of textual structures; translation is connected with the social world in which it is located as a human activity, inextricably interwoven with people's social and cultural lives.

- Popular music can be structured as a system. Translation, like any text production, takes place in these polysystemic structures where the notion of a stable text does not exist. Translation in the field of popular music often occurs in dispersed and fragmented form, in other cases translations are not based on entire texts but use a combination of partial translation and original text production (e.g. cover-versions, song families or sampling). Instead of texts as structured entities, the notion of a multiple text which is the result of mediation processes becomes the centre and starting point for translation research in this area.

- Popular song translations are often produced via numerous intermediate stages and make no clear distinction between translation and operations like adaptation, editing, imitation and so on. The concepts of "*bricolage*" and "*dialogics*" seem to be useful tools for understanding the nature of song translation and doing justice to the hybrid nature of popular music.

Musical Semiotics and Popular Music

Having sketched out a framework to explain the socio-semiotic mechanisms influencing the production and reception of popular music and its translation, we still need more specific information about the role the music plays in the process of cross-cultural transfer. If we assume that music can relate to certain associative and affective concepts, we have to ask if these associations and references are shared in the same way by adressees in the source and target cultures. How does the musical message interact with the respective society and culture? These questions are presumably dealt with by semiotics, but given the characteristics of popular music that differentiate it from other musical forms, traditional tools of musical semiotics are of little use (cf. Tagg 2000: 77-79).

There have been various attempts to capture these characteristics in a definition. Often it is the term 'popular' and the commercial dimension that serve as key criteria. In this vein, popular music is characterized as devoid of any orginality or complexity, as serving only to meet existing emotional and physical needs. This leaves no room for the (romantic) notions of artistic individuality and autonomy which are thought to give a work of art its universal, unique quality. Instead, popular music is seen as responding to technical and commercial constraints in reproducing existing patterns in a trivial and popularizing fashion, the implication being that it is targeted upon an undemanding mass-market audience.

What is problematic about this point of view is, among other things, the belief that the essence of popular music resides in the textual material rather than constituting the result of a culturally and socialy determined practice. Foregrounding the latter, Green (1999: 6) rightly asserts that "there is no such thing as popular music existing independently of the social world." Thus, it is the cultural environment, inherently changeable rather than static, that determines the meaning and relative value of cultural products (cf. also Hall 1981: 228). The popular is not something which can be extracted from the text; it is a socio-cultural construct.

This cultural-constructivist perspective is eminently significant for translation: Values – in this case, "popular" status – are assigned not on the basis of text surface features, but as a result of a particular cultural practice which also determines the transcultural transfer. The massive interventions, alterations and manipulations frequently observed in translations of popular music do not occur arbitrarily, seemingly without care for a supposedly trivial or worthless musical work, but are shaped by the values and meanings of the socio-cultural environment into which popular music is being transferred.

Rather than opt for one or another inherently evaluative definition, I would like to follow Tagg (2000) in proposing a number of phenomenological features of popular music which are also relevant to a culture-oriented, sociologically sensitive and semiotics-based view of text and translation (cf. Tagg 2000: 75-77):

- Popular music, in its various forms, is inseparably linked with the industrialization of society and its technological means of (increasingly specialized) production and distribution.
- Popular music is produced with a view to mass distribution, sold on mass markets, and mediated through mass media.
- The text in popular music is usually not fixed as a written score but in the form of sound recordings (CD, record, cassette tape) and video recordings.

Consequently, the analysis of popular music and its translations cannot be based solely on esthetic standards which are generally derived, also in musical semiotics, from classical music. The written score, which usually serves as the point of departure for studies in musical semiotics, is of little relevance for popular music, which is often not written down but stored and disseminated in the form of audio and video recordings. Having focused its attention on music laid down in a written score, musical semiotics has failed to develop appropriate analytical tools for a number of tonal and acoustic parameters which are important in popular music.[4]

Nevertheless, the plurisemiotic nature of the song text makes it highly amenable to semiotic studies as they bridge the conceptual gap between the verbal and nonverbal and they deal with all structures of signs, including those deemed extra-linguistic. Semiotics has great potential also for contributing to translation studies, but here, too, it has remained under-used, according to Dinda L. Gorlée (1994). The rather limited use made of semiotic theories in translation studies in general and in the translation of pop songs in particular, may be due to the fact that "a great deal of linguistic formalism has crept into the semiology of music, the extra-generic question of relationships between musical signifier and signified and between the musical object under analysis and society being either regarded with intradisciplinary scepticism as intellectually suspect, or as subordinate to congeneric relations inside the musical object itself" (Tagg 2000: 78).[5] Another reason why popular music seems to be a difficult subject for musical semiotics may be that most semiotic studies in the field of music focus on the written text and treat music as a scored object. In the words of Eero Tarasti: "Musical performance is one of the most fascinating and at the same time neglected areas of musical research" (1995: 435).

One of the few scholars to deal with semiotic aspects of popular music is Philip Tagg, who suggests a "hermeneutic-semiological method" (2000: 82) which takes into consideration a multitude of musical factors of performed popular music. His approach can also serve as a starting point for a translation-relevant analysis:

- aspects of time (e.g. tempo, metre, rhythm);
- aspects of melody (e.g. timbre);
- orchestration (e.g. instrumentation, voice type);
- aspects of tonality and texture (e.g. harmony, relationships between voices and instruments);
- dynamic aspects (e.g. audibility, accentuation);
- acoustical aspects (e.g. distance between sound source and listener, simultaneous 'extraneous' sounds);

- electromusical and mechanical aspects (filtering, compressing, phasing, distortion, mixing)

I would like to demonstrate the impact of performance on popular music with various versions of "*Les Enfants du Pirée*", a famous song written for the film *Jamais le Dimanche*. I will concentrate on aspects of time, arrangement (orchestration) and voice as identified by Tagg and, of course, on the verbal text. The original was written in Greek by Manos Hadjidakis, who is – together with L. Larue – also responsible for the French version. Both versions were sung by Melina Mercouri, who also sung the first German version entitled "*Ein Schiff wird kommen*". The German lyrics were written by Fini Bausch on the basis of the French version, as can be gleaned from the record cover. Almost simultaneously, Dalida presented her interpretation of the song – in French and in German. For both singers, the song was a big hit in France but did not have the same commercial success in Germany. Only a few months later, two more German versions were published, sung by Lys Assia and Caterina Valente, this time with bigger success. But "the" version of the song, published in the same year, was the one performed by Lale Anderson, which became the most popular interpretation of this song in Germany. The process of semiosis shows a clear tendency towards, as Lawrence Venuti (1995) would call it, "domestication", i.e. the text – verbal, vocal and musical – was gradually adapted to German conventions for popular songs, and the "foreignizing" musical, vocal and verbal elements were gradually eliminated.

French version
Verse 1:
Noyé de bleu souls le ciel grec,
Un bateau, deux bateaux, trois bateaux
s'en vont chantant.
Griffant le ciel à coups de bec,
Un oiseau, deux oiseaux, trois oiseaux
font du beau temps.
Dans les ruelles d'un coup sec,
Un volet, deux volets, trois volets
claquent au vent.
En faisant une ronde avec
Un enfant, deux enfants, trois enfants
dansent gaiement.

Chorus:
Mon Dieu que j'aime ce port
du bout du monde
Que le soleil inonde de ses reflets dorés.

Mon Dieu que j'aime sous leurs
bonnets oranges
Tout les visages d'anges des enfants
du Pirée.

Verse 2:
Je rêve aussi d'avoir un jour
Un enfant, deux enfants, trois enfants
jouant comme eux.
Le long du quai flânent toujours
Un marin, deux marins, trois marins
aventureux.
De notre amour on se fera
Un amour, dix amours, mille amours
noyées de bleus
Et nos enfants feront des gars
Que les filles un beau jour, à leur tour,
 rendront heureux.

Chorus

German version I
Verse 1:
Ich bin ein Mädchen von Piräus
und liebe den Hafen, die Schiffe
und das Meer.
Ich lieb' das Lachen der Matrosen
und Küsse, die schmecken nach See,
nach Salz und Teer.
Es lockt der Zauber von Piräus,
d'rum stehe ich Abend für
Abend am Kai.
Und warte auf die fremden Schiffe
aus Hongkong,
aus Java aus Chile und Shanghai.

Chorus:
Ein Schiff wird kommen, und das
bringt mir den einen, den ich so lieb'
wie keinen und der mich glücklich macht.
Ein Schiff wird kommen und meinen
Traum erfüllen
Und meine Sehnsucht stillen,
die Sehnsucht mancher Nacht.

Verse 2:
Ich bin ein Mädchen von Piräus,
und wenn eines Tages mein Herz

ich mal verlier',
dann muss es einer sein vom Hafen,
nur so einen Burschen wünsch' ich
für's Leben mir.
Und später stehen meine Kinder
Dann Abend für Abend
genau wie ich am Kai
Und warten auf die fremden
Schiffe aus Hongkong,
aus Java, aus Chile und Shanghai.

Chorus

Let us first look at the verbal text. In the film, the singer is a prostitute who describes the Greek harbour of Pireus, with fisher boats, sun, and people. The singer is in love with this scenery, and the song is a kind of love song to the country. She sings about having children without mentioning a special man; instead she sings of "one love, "ten loves", thousand loves. In German, the story underwent several changes. Pireus and Greece are not the thematic focus of the song. The German song is about "the one and only", the man who will make her happy for the rest of her life. Whereas in French she is in love with the life she lives as a prostitute in the harbour of Pireus, she is now full of desire for one man, who has not yet arrived. Thus, the German text becomes much more moralistic than the original, which is a typical characteristic of German popular song texts of this period. Interestingly, the vocal presentation of Mercouri completely undermines the moralistic verbal text. Her voice is deep; she sounds like a woman who drank too much; a strong accent characterizes her as a foreigner; and the very lascivious intonation, especially in the first part of the second verse, which is not sung but spoken, enhances the realistic depiction of the character. The instrumentation of the original version, that is, bouzoukis and accordions, was retained, and so was the structure of the song, i.e. instrumental introduction, verse, chorus, instrumental bridge, verse, chorus, and instrumental coda, as well as its length (3 minutes and 20 seconds).

The second version, by Dalida, is almost one minute shorter, i.e. 2 min. 35. The instrumental bridge was eliminated and the instrumental coda replaced by a shorter version accompanied by Dalida singing "*la-la-la*". But the main reason for the shorter duration lies in the tempo, which is much quicker now. What is also interesting is the instrumentation of this version. The folkloric dimension is still present; there are bouzoukis, but also other instruments like xylophone, double bass and rhythm guitar, which were more common in

Germany at the time. Also, the vocal presentation differs from Mercouri's version. The text is still presented with an accent and even with some "oriental" vocal ornamental elements. While these do not correspond to the Greek character of the song but to the Egyptian origins of Dalida, they serve to identify her as a foreign woman. In contrast to Mercouri, Dalida's voice is "softer", not as lascivious. Although her voice is deep, hers is a "cleaner" version, sung, and not spoken, with a more traditional intonation. In the chorus, Dalida stresses especially the words "the one" whom she loves like "nobody else", foregrounding the more decent and proper dimension of the character. The multiple voices put together in this version – German and Greek instrumental elements, oriental vocal elements, German language – are a typical example of *bricolage*-translation that stands in a dialogic relationship with the co-present texts of Mercouri, the film and its visual presentation of the character singing the main theme as well as the cultural background and image of the singer.

The process of domesticating *bricolage*-translation continues with Lys Assia and Caterina Valente. The verbal text in these versions is sung without a foreign accent (especially in the case of Valente, who presents the character as a German woman), and with a clear voice and the typical intonation of "*Schlager*", the dominant genre in Germany from the 1950s to the 1970s. Valente aimed at being more than a singer of Schlager and tried to build up a more jazzy image. This is probably why her version of this song starts with the sound of snapping fingers. Instead of bouzoukis, Valente uses mandolin banjos, double bass and accordion. These are not used to create a folkloric impression of Greece but rather serve to create a more "modern" sound corresponding to the image of the singer.

> German version II
> Verse 1:
> *Ich bin ein Mädchen aus Piräus*
> *und liebe den Hafen, die Schiffe*
> *und das Meer.*
> *Ich lieb' das lachen der Matrosen,*
> *ich lieb' jeden Kuss, der nach Salz*
> *schmeckt und nach Teer.*
> *Wie alle Mädchen in Piräus*
> *so stehe ich Abend für*
> *Abend hier am Kai,*
> *und warte auf die fremden Schiffe*
> *aus Hongkong,*
> *aus Java, aus Chile und Shanghai.*

Chorus:
Ein Schiff wird kommen, und das
bringt mir den einen, den ich so lieb
wie keinen, und der mich glücklich macht.
Ein Schiff wird kommen und meinen
Traum erfüllen
und meine Sehnsucht stillen,
die Sehnsucht mancher Nacht.

Spoken:
Und jetzt bist du da, und
ich halt' dich in meinem Arm.
Gib mir noch einen Zug
aus deiner Zigarette. Schau, unter
unserem Fenster der Hafen
mit den bunten Lichtern.
Da drüben in der Bar, aus der
die Musik herüberkommt,
hab' ich in den letzten Monaten
jede Nacht gesessen,
mit fremden Matrosen getanzt
und hab' doch nur das eine gedacht:

Chorus

The last version, by Lale Anderson, changes the structure of the song and, once again, its content (German version II). The song lasts 2 min. 52. It starts with an instrumental introduction followed by the 1st verse and the chorus. Instead of the second verse, Anderson introduces a spoken passage. Whereas in the first German version the main motif is the desire of the one and only man in the woman's life, this desire is now fulfilled. Anderson tells us that her beloved man is here, she smokes a cigarette with him (the only sign of lasciviousness accorded to the character), tells him that when he was not here, she danced with other men but was only thinking of him all the time. The voice is now without the strong foreign accent of Mercouri and Dalida; we are listening to a German woman, the text is sung straightforward without any of the lascivious vocal characteristics of Mercouri. As regards the instrumentation, a new rhythmic instrument, typical of the German *Schlager* genre, is now dominant: the jazz brushes and, of course, strings and double bass.[6]

Changes in the verbal text, changes in the vocal presentation, changes in the musical structure and changes in the instrumentation – all these manipulations serve one goal: domesticating the character presented in the song and domesticating the foreign genre by giving the verbal text a new content, by letting the character sing in the typical style of German popular singers of the time and by introducing instruments familiar to German traditions of popular music.

Video Clips and Translation

Mediated popular music contains not only aural codes but also visual codes, which are often inseparably linked to the acoustic event. The most influential form of visuality nowadays is the music video. Whereas there are a number of semiotically motivated studies of video clips, there are, to my knowledge no translation-relevant analyses of this phenomenon. Although there is a large number of works in the field of audiovisual translation, the importance and relevance of music television seems to be completely ignored by translation scholars. The globalisation of musical production stimulates translation in two ways: On the one hand, it enhances those practices "which adapt homogenized global musical forms into heterogeneous dialogues of national sovereignty" (Mitchell 1996: 264); on the other hand, the dominating (US-American) music industry, in search of new musical styles and sounds originating outside the Anglo-American music production, takes over foreign sounds and combines them with English texts creating a new genre, the so-called 'world music'.

Music videos constitute complex audiovisual forms in which sound, language and image are closely interrelated in a functional relationship. The transfer from an aural code into a visual code can be understood as an intersemiotic translation in the sense of Jakobson (1959). The key to understanding the mechanisms of such an intersemiotic transfer lies in the analysis of reciprocal dependencies and potential relations between the various elements. Such an approach was developed by Goodwin (1993), who views pop songs in terms of their narratives. Employing the concept of synaesthesia, Goodwin states that the images of music videos are frequently connected to the music in various ways: an iconographic relationship may exist in the form of "personal imagery", "images associated purely with the music itself", "visual signifiers deriving from national-popular iconography" and "popular cultural signs associated with music" (cf. Goodwin 1993: 56). According to Goodwin, the concept of synaesthesia permits an understanding of video clips in terms of musical elements. Goodwin discusses five aspects of music (tempo, rhythm, arrangement, harmonic development and acoustic space) that have a direct bearing on the visual dimension of the clip (cf. 1993: 49-71.).

Goodwin focuses on the relationship between image and music and neglects the verbal component of music videos. In fact, the visual aspect is interlinked not only with the musical but also with the verbal code. Each of the three codes uses iconic, indexical and symbolic signs which are functionally interrelated with one another. Goodwin introduces three concepts to indicate how the relations between sound and image are mediated and combined in very specific ways: illustration, amplification and disjuncture (cf. 1993: 86-88). These relational categories can be applied to the verbal dimension as follows:

Illustration comprises relationships in which the narrative proceeds in parallel in various semiotic codes. Thus, the visual component may express the moods, stories, etc. articulated in the lyrics or in the music. Amplification refers to relationships in which the narrative is complemented by the other semiotic codes. The visual presentation, for instance, may add something new to the verbal or musical levels, extending and complementing rather than contradicting the meaning of the other sign systems. Disjuncture, finally, refers to those instances in which a contrast or contradiction is created, e.g. between the visual level and the words or music, as in the case of rapid cuts or racing camera movement during a slow piece of music.

As an example of the multiple relationships between images, lyrics and music I will analyse music videos of a Turkish song and its English translations. The song is called "Simarik" and was a great hit in Turkey, where it was sung by one of the country's most famous pop singers, Tarkan. Originally, a video was produced only for the Turkish audience. Its huge success encouraged the producers to distribute the song also for an international market. For this release of "Simarik", a new video was produced, which was shown on MTV. Three years after the success of "Simarik", the American singer Stella Soleil released a cover-version of the song, sung in English. Her version was covered again by an Australian singer, Holly Valance. Both female singers also produced a video of the song.

SIMARIK (by Tarkan)

Turkish version	Literal Translation

Verse 1:

Takmis koluna elin adamini
Beni orta verimden çatlatiyor
Ağzinda sakizi şişirip şişirip
Arsiz arsiz patlatiyor

Verse 1:

Taking some other man by the arm
She's tearing me in two
Blowing bubbles with her gum
She bursts them impudently

Verse 2:

Belki de bu yüzden vuruldum
Sahibin olamadim ya
Siğar mi erkekliğe seni simarik
Değişti mi bu dünya

Verse 2:

Maybe that's why I've been ensnared by her
Because I don't have her
Can my masculinity accept you spoilt thing?
Has the world turned upside down?

Verse 3:

Çekmiş kaşina gözüne sürme
Dudaklar kipkirmizi kiritiyor
Bi de karşima geğmiş utanmasi yok
Inadima inadima siritiyor

Verse 3:

She's lined her eyes with mascara
Her lips coquettishly bright red
Flaunting in front of me audaciously
Grinning, merely to spite me

Verse 4:

Biz böyle mi gördük babamizdan
Ele güne rezil olduk
Yeni adet gelmiş eski köye vah
Dostlar mahvolduk

Verse 4:

We weren't raised that way
She's making us look like a fool
New customs have come to town
Boys, we're lost

Chorus (repeat twice):
Seni gidi findikkiran
Yilani deliğinden ğikaran
Kaderim püsküllü belam
Yakalarsam (mwah)

Chorus:
You vamp you
You lure the snake from its place
My fate's crazy venture
If I get a hold of you (mwah)

Ocağina düştüm yavru
Kucağina düştüm yavru
Sicağina düştüm yavru
El aman

I've fallen in your furnace, baby
I've fallen in your lap, baby
I've fallen for your warmth, baby
That's the way it is[7]

Repeat:
Verse 1+4
Chorus

"*Simarik*" – in its Turkish version – tells the story of girl who is breaking the conventions of Turkish society. She blows bubbles with her chewing gum, makes them snap brutally, has make-up on her face, and is not shy at all with men; in short, she does not correspond to the traditional image of a Turkish woman. Her behaviour drives men who do not know how to react crazy, and yet, as the iconic sound of a kiss shows, the male narrator loves this new, modern woman. The text is an ironic statement about the gender roles of women in Turkey. The changes of the behavioural codes and conventions of women are not seen as negative; on the contrary, they are seen as very positive. The iconic sound of the kiss as well as the upbeat sound of the music are clear indicators for this positive evaluation of the emancipation of women.

At first sight, the musical signs in this song serve to indicate its location: Tarkan's music has a distinctive and easily recognizable sound. He draws elements from traditional Turkish music styles and mixes them with Western pop idioms. The way he sings is a kind of arabesque style, typical of Turkish popular music and also folk music. But the mixture of two distinct pop styles – the Turkish and the Western style – can be seen in the verbal narratives also to reflect the mixture of gender roles in Turkish society.

The monochrome of the clip and the stark shadows are used to suggest a *film-noir* atmosphere. At the beginning of the song, Tarkan is in a voyeuristic position, observing an elegant, sophisticated woman. Gradually the position of male voyeur and female object of desire changes. First Tarkan sits in the dark and observes the woman, then he sits on a stage and finally he dances more and more ecstatically on the same stage, whereas the woman is enclosed in the virtual world of television from where she watches Tarkan dancing. This reversal of the situation, which turns the person on TV into an observer of what happens on the "real" stage, once again symbolizes the reversal of gender roles. At one time he takes up the movements of the woman, imitating her way of putting gel on her hair. Tarkan's body language is sometimes quite confusing; he moves his body in unconventional ways (for a Turkish man, at least). At times he girates like a belly dancer, but his dancing cannot be considered as effeminate. Instead, Tarkan presents a multi-sexual persona and, by exposing his body, an object of desire. The fast cuts, the frequent use of flashes and especially the dancing movements of Tarkan are the iconographic visual expression of the musical aspects of tempo and also rhythm.

The relationships between visualization and music can partly be described as illustration: the depiction of a spoilt girl, on the one hand, and her emancipation, on the other, symbolized by the relation between observed object and observing subject. But there is also amplification: in one scene of the video, he prepares gifts for the girl and asks a young boy to bring them to her, none of which is mentioned in the lyrics. The focus on the gender role of the man, too, is a clear amplification of the verbal text. In the video he is no longer the one who observes and possesses the woman; rather, he himself becomes an object of voyeurism and desire. This is symbolized by the dancing man, who integrates in his movements also feminine gestures and bodily expressions. What is visualized is not so much the identity of the woman described in the lyrics as the subversion of the dominant gender roles constructed around heterosexual male-female oppositions.[8]

For the second version, this time produced for an international market, the verbal text has been reduced, only verses 1 and 4 and the chorus are sung, verses 2 and 3 have been deleted. The video starts with dissolving figures who fade away like fata morganas. The setting of the story is now a Mediterranean town. Tarkan is walking down the street, when he realizes that he is being pursued by at first two and finally by many women, one of them dressed up for marriage. Here again the presentation of the woman could partly be interpreted as illustrating the text: self-confident, dressed in a Western style, and taking the initiative rather than waiting for the man to make the first move. The iconic sound of kisses can be heard throughout the song. This time the kisses originate not with the singer but with the women, who do not kiss a man but merely produce a kissing sound while laughing and looking into the camera. This symbolizes satisfaction with their emancipation and thus illustrates the verbal text. Other symbolic signs also illustrate the emancipation of Turkish women: in a short sequence Tarkan hides from the women who pursue him and leans against a wall. When he turns his head to the left, the camera captures a graffiti with the year 1881, the year in which Kemal Atatürk, the father of the liberation of Turkish women, was born. Besides the illustrative relationship with the verbal text, the visuals also amplify the song text, again in a gendered way. Towards the end of the video the director, Emmanuel Saada, uses the technique of superimposing images so that the viewer sees various figures at the same time. This creates the impression of blurred images which are not easily distinguishable. Watching the video in slow motion, one realizes that some of these figures are not women but transvestites or transsexuals. Together with the blurred figures who fade into a landscape in simmering heat, the symbolic force of the visual narratives becomes evident: the visual text does not deal only with women, but also with men and with the fact that there are no clear-cut gender boundaries, not only between (heterosexual) men and women but also between hetero-, homo- and transsexual beings.

KISS, KISS (by Stella Soleil)

English version I

Verse 1:
MWAH! When you look at me, tell me what you see,
This is what you get, it's the way I am.
When I look at you, I wanna be, I wanna be,
Somewhere close to heaven with Neanderthal man.
Don't go, I know you wanna touch me here, there and everywhere,
Sparks fly when we are together, you can't deny the facts of life.

Chorus:
You don't have to act like a star, trying moves in the back of your car,
But you know that we can go far, coz tonight you're gonna get my (mwah, mwah)
Don't play the games that you play, coz you know that I won't run away,
Why aren't you asking me to stay, coz tonight I'm gonna give you my (mwah, mwah).

Verse 2:
You could be mine, baby, what's your star sign?
Won't you take a step into the lion's den.
I can hear my conscience calling you, calling you.
Say I'm gonna be a bad girl again, why don't you come on over,
We can't leave this all undone, got a devil on my shoulder,
There's no place for you to run.

Chorus
Bridge (repeat twice – simultaneously with Turkish text):
If you forget, I'll remind you, if you're paranoid, I'm behind you.
If you lose your head, I'll find you, sending you my kiss.
Ocağina düştüm yavru, kucağina düştüm yavru.
Sicağina düştüm yavru, el aman.

Chorus (repeated twice)

Owing to the huge success of this song – it reached Top Ten positions in various European countries – an English version was produced, performed by Stella Soleil. For this new production the text was completely changed. The iconic sign of a kiss in the original is now translated into the symbolic verbal sign "Kiss", which serves as the title and the main theme for the song. Whereas the kiss in the original symbolized approval of the new gender roles of women and men, the narrative in the lyrics now turns it into an unmistakably sexual symbol. The song is about a girl inviting a man to have sex with her, which is presented as "a fact of life". The verbal text deals no longer with the social dimension of gender but with the sexual emancipation of women, who now take over the initiative in the game. The original instrumentation is retained, and the ethnic dimension is also stressed by the integration of Tarkan's voice, which can be heard at the beginning with the iconic sign of the kiss and later when his voice is heard simultaneously with Stella Soleil's. This piece of music is an example of so-called world music. The foreign sounds in combination with the English language create a "*bricolage* effect", a bringing together of different musical sounds and languages with explicit intertextual references to the original. In this sense, this version represents a typical example of hybridisation.

The setting of the video reflect this hybridity: The clip starts with a view of an island, which the camera is approaching at high speed. The singer is shown dancing on the beach, time and again with a focus on her bright red lips. Interspersed are images of a Mexican playing the guitar and a horseman galloping along the beach. In the second part of the clip, men and women of prehistoric costumes and hairstyle are seen performing a kind of tribal dance, in contrast to the image of Stella Soleil, who is shown standing on a cliff amid crashing waves. The foreign, oriental quality of the music is visually re-interpreted as something primitive and wild. While it is true that the Stone Age people can be viewed as an illustration of the "Neanderthal man" in the lyrics, the relationship between the visual and the verbal domains is largely one of disjuncture.

KISS, KISS (by Holly Valance)

English version II

Verse 1:
MWAH, MWAH! When you look at me, tell me what you see,
This is what you get, it's the way I am.
When I look at you, I wanna be, I wanna be,
Somewhere close to heaven with Neanderthal man.
Don't go, I know you wanna touch me here, there and everywhere,
Sparks fly when we are together, you can't deny the facts of life.

Chorus:
You don't have to act like a star, trying moves in the back of your car,
But you know that we can go far, coz tonight you're gonna get my (mwah, mwah)
Don't play the games that you play, coz you know that I won't run away,
Why aren't you asking me to stay, coz tonight I'm gonna give you my (mwah, mwah).

Verse 2:
You could be mine, baby, what's your star sign?
Won't you take a step into the lion's den.
I can hear my conscience calling you, calling you.
Say I'm gonna be a bad girl again, why don't you come on over,
We can't leave this all undone, got a devil on my shoulder,
There's no place for you to run.

Chorus
Bridge: If you forget, I'll remind you, if you're paranoid, I'm behind you.
If you lose your head, I'll find you, sending you my kiss.
Don't, don't, (mwah, mwah), I, I, don't, don't, ki-ki, I, I.
Don't, don't, (mwah), don't, don't, don't, oh yeah.
Don't have to act like a, trying moves in the back of your,
But you know that we can go, coz tonight you're gonna get my.
Ahh, ahh, mwah.

Chorus (repeated twice)

For the latest English version by Holly Valance, not only the language but also the instrumentation are profoundly changed. Now the electronic pop sound prevails, the voice and the instruments are synthesized and distorted by computers. Towards the end, the singer only produces fragments of the refrain which is interspersed with the sounds of kisses. The staccato effect thus created, enhanced by flashes which are rhythmically synchronised with the music, symbolizes the sexual culmination. This highly artificial sound is illustrated by the visual presentation. Holly Valance is placed with a couple of male dancers in a completely virtual environment where flashes and neon lights render tempo and rhythm of the music. The visuals are highly "sexed up"; when the singer produces the sound of kisses (which she does very often), the camera regularly focuses on the genital regions of the singer and her dancers. Moreover, the DJ's scratching, visualized in the video, becomes a symbol of sexual stimulation as the camera captures the DJ's finger and positions the singer in such a way that the finger points straight to her vagina. The musico-verbal narratives in this video are in a dominantly illustrative relationship with the visuals; the musically produced artificiality of sound is rendered in a highly technological setting and the verbally expressed sexual allusions are stressed by cuttings and camera movements.

Whereas in the first example – *"Les Enfants du Pirée"* – we observed a process of domestication of a foreign song, we now have a translational process that goes from ethnicity to globalization. The original version is more and more transformed into a typical product of the globally predominant

Western dance pop music. The folkloric elements only serve as "decoration" and no longer represent an element that serves to localize the song in a given socio-cultural context. Whereas the videos of the Turkish versions are constructed around a narrative, the English versions focus on the rhythmic dimension of the song, centered on dances with sexual connotations. The discursive element of the foreign song is visually eliminated and reduced to its mere motor-sensual aspects.

Conclusion

Adopting a view of translation as a socio-semiotically determined practice, I have argued here that the characteristics of popular culture and mass communication of popular music have a decisive impact on the shape of the translation. This claim certainly requires substantiation by further studies. Nevertheless, the concepts of mediation, bricolage and dialogics, outlined here in very brief terms, have proved useful for the analysis of changes and manipulations of popular songs under translation. These changes involve all elements of the mediated song text. Popular music is in a dialogic relationship with various types of verbal, musical, visual as well as social and cultural elements. While it is true that translation studies, having taken a 'cultural turn', is no longer focused on language as such, there is still a lack of translation-relevant methods for the analysis of nonverbal elements. Semiotics would permit a holistic analysis of the interaction and interdependence of the various elements of popular songs and could permit a deeper understanding of their role and influence in translation. Placed at the intersection of media studies, cultural studies, musicology, literary studies, semiotics and translation studies, popular songs are certainly a challenge for any scholarly approach. What should have emerged from this article is that popular songs are a worthy subject of investigation that calls for interdisciplinary cooperation.

Notes

[1] For a comparison of the French original with the English and German translations cf. Kaindl (2003).

[2] Neither the Routledge Encyclopedia of Translation Studies (Baker 1998) nor the *Handbuch Translation* (Snell-Hornby et al. 1998) list popular songs as a relevant subject of translation studies.

[3] This centre/periphery opposition goes back to Tynjanov (1978) who first applied the notion of system to literature.

[4] Tagg lists a number of such parameters, such as sound, timbre, electromusical treatment etc. cf. (2000: 77).

[5] Of course there are also a number of publications which combine semiotic approaches with sociological, psychological and hermeneutic insights (to mention just a few: Karbusicky 1986 Jacono 1996, Tarasti 2002). However, in none of these publications are the analytical models applied to popular music.

[6] What is interesting in this context is the visual mediation of the song at the time of its release. On the record cover of Mercouri's version we see the singer in a rather provocative pose, with one hand on her hip and the other holding a cigarette, dressed in a tank top with a low neckline. On the cover of Anderson's version, the singer is dressed in turtle-neck sweater, her smiling face dominating the picture.

[7] For the English translation cf. http://tarkanplace2001.tripod.com/olurum_sana_english.htm.

[8] The image of Tarkan as a singer also plays an important role in this gendered interpretation. Due to his use of make-up in his stage performances and videos, his body language, the fact that he was the first public figure in Turkey to wear an earring (on his left ear), his sometimes unusual clothing, briefly: his camp attitude in combination with a certain macho behaviour, he is considered in Turkey as a unique, even revolutionary artist.

Bibliography

Source texts:

Andersen, Lale. 1996. *Das Beste von Lale Andersen*, EMI (CD 7243 8 38127 2 1).
Dalida. 1993. *Am Tag als der Regen kam*, Bear Family Records (BCD 15 756 AH).
http://tarkanplace2001.tripod.com/olurum_sana_english.htm.
http://www.mp3wma.net.mpg (Video: Holly Valance – Kiss, Kiss).
http://zpgvidz.cjb.net (Video: Stella Soleil – Kiss, Kiss).
Mercouri, Mercouri.. 1994. *Melina Mercouri Master Serie*, Podis (CD 523131-2).
Mercouri, Mercouri. . 1960. *Ein Schiff wird kommen*, Polydor (M45 24353).
Valente, Caterina.. 1990. *Die großen Hits*, Teldec (CD 2292-46412-2)
http://www.tarkan.com (Videos: Tarkan – Simarik).

Secondary literature:

Baker, Mona (ed.). 1998. *Routledge Encyclopedia of Translation Studies*. London and New York: Routledge.
Bakhtin, Michail M. 1984. *Problems of Dostoevsky's Poetics*. (tr. and ed. C. Emerson). Minneapolis: University of Minnesota Press.
Blaikner, Peter. 1992-1993. 'Brassens en allemand' in *Equivalences* 22/1-2: 171-181.
Even-Zohar, Itamar. 1990. 'Polysystem Studies' in *Poetics Today* 11/1 (Special issue).

———— 1997 'Factors and Dependencies in Culture: A Revised Outline for Polysystem Culture Research' in *Canadian Review of Comparative Literature* 24/1: 15-34.
Goodwin, Andrew. 1993. *Dancing in the Distraction Factory: Music Television and Popular Culture*. London and New York: Routledge.

Gorlée, Dinda L. 1994. *Semiotics and the Problem of Translation: With Special Reference to the Semiotics of Charles S. Peirce* (Approches to Translation Studies 12). Amsterdam and Atlanta, GA: Rodopi.

Green, Lucy. 1999. 'Ideology' in Horner, Bruce and Thomas Swiss (eds) *Key Terms in Popular Music and Culture*. Oxford: Blackwell. 5-17.

Hall, Stuart. 1981. 'Notes on Deconstructing the Popular' in Samuel, Raphael (ed.) *Peoples, History and Socialist Theory*. London: Routledge and Kegan Paul. 227-240.

Haupt, Else. 1957. *Stil- und sprachkundliche Untersuchungen zum deutschen Schlager*. Unpubl. PhD thesis. University of München.

Hebdige, Dick. 1979. *Subculture. The Meaning of Style*. London and New York: Routledge.

Hennion, Antoine. 1997. 'Baroque and Rock: Music, Mediators and Musical Taste' in *Poetics* 24: 415-435.

———— 1993. *La passion musicale: Une sociologie de la médiation*. Paris: Métailié.

Hermans, Theo. 1999. *Translation in Systems. Descriptive and System-oriented Approaches Explained* (Translation Theories Explained 7). Manchester: St. Jerome.

Holtz, Christina. 1980. *Comics: Ihre Entwicklung und Bedeutung*. München: K.G. Saur.

Jakobson, Roman. 1959. 'On Linguistic Aspects of Translation" in Brower, Reuben A. (ed.) *On Translation* (Harvard Studies in Comparative Literature 23). Cambridge, MA: Harvard University Press: 232-239.

Jacono, Jean-Marie. 1996. 'Quelles perspectives sociologiques pour une sémiotique de la musique' in Tarasti, Eero (ed.) *Musical Semiotics in Growth*. Imatra: International Semiotics Institute and Bloomington, IN: Indiana University Press: 263-275.

Kaindl, Klaus. 2003. "Ein Schiff wird kommen... ': Kultur-, Adressaten- und Textspezifik bei der Übersetzung von Popularmusik' in Nord, Britta and Peter A. Schmitt (eds) *Traducta Navis. Festschrift zum 60. Geburtstag von Christiane Nord*. Tübingen: Stauffenburg: 83-101.

Karbusicky, Vladimir. 1986. *Grundriß der musikalischen Semantik* (Texte zur Forschung 56). Darmstadt: Wissenschaftliche Buchgesellschaft.

Lambert, José. 1989. 'La Traduction, les langues et la communication de masse. Les ambiguités du discours international' in *Target* 1/1: 215-237.

———— and Delabastita, Dirk. 1996. 'La traduction de textes audiovisuels: modes et enjeux culturels' in Gambier, Yves (ed.) *Les transferts linguistiques dans les médias audiovisuels*. Villeneuve d'Ascq: Presses Universitaires du Septentrion: 33-58.

Lévi-Strauss, Claude. 1966. *The Savage Mind* (tr. anonymous). Chicago: University of Chicago Press [French original: *La pensée sauvage*. Paris: Plon, 1962]

Mitchell, Tony. 1996. *Popular Music and Local Identity: Rock, Pop and Rap in Europe and Oceania*. London: Leicester University Press.

Negus, Keith. 1996. *Popular Music Theory. An Introduction*. Cambridge, UK: Blackwell.

Pamies Bertrán, Antonio. 1992-1993. 'De l'intraduisibilité à l'intertextuel dans l'oeuvre de Georges Brassens' in *Equivalences* 22/1-2: 49-71.

Rabadán, Rosa. 1991. *Equivalencia y traducción: problemática de la equivalencia translémica inglés-español*. Léon: Universidad de Léon.

Snell-Hornby, Mary *et al.* (eds). 1998. *Handbuch Translation*. Tübingen: Stauffenburg.

Steinacher, Susanne. 1997. 'Vom Rock'n Roll zum Wiener Schmäh. Translation als Mittel der Akkulturation' in Nadja Grbic and Michaela Wolf (eds) *Text, Kultur, Kommunikation. Translation als Forschungsaufgabe*. Tübingen: Stauffenburg: 183-201.

Steinwender, Bettina. 1992. *Übersetzung und Chanson*. Unpubl. PhD thesis. University of Vienna.

Stölting, Elke. 1975. *Deutsche Schlager und englische Popmusik in Deutschland. Ideologiekritische Untersuchung zweier Textstile während der Jahre 1960-1970*. Bonn: Bouvier.

Tagg, Philip. 2000. 'Analysing Popular Music: Theory, Method and Practice' in Middleton, Richard (ed.) *Reading Pop. Approaches to Textual Analysis in Popular Music*. Oxford: Oxford University Press: 71-103.

Tarasti, Eero. 2002. *Signs of Music: A Guide to Musical Semiotics*. Berlin: Mouton de Gruyter.

———— 1995. 'Après un rêve': A semiotic analysis of the song by Gabriel Fauré' in Tarasti, Eero (ed.) *Musical Signification. Essays in the Semiotic Theory and Analysis of Music*. Berlin and New York: Mouton de Gruyter: 435-469.

Toury, Gideon. 1995. *Descriptive Translation Studies – and Beyond*. Amsterdam and Philadelphia: John Benjamins.

Tynjanov, Juri. 1978. 'On Literary Evolution' in Matejka, Ladislav and Krystyna Pomorska (eds) *Readings in Russian Poetics. Formalist and Structuralist Views*. Ann Arbor: University of Michigan Press: 66-78.

Venuti, Lawrence. 1995. *The Translator's Invisibility. A History of Translation*. London and New York: Routledge.

Worbs, Hans-Christoph. 1963. *Der Schlager. Bestandsaufnahme – Analyse – Dokumentation. Ein Leitfaden*. Bremen: Carl Schünemann.

Musical Comedy Translation: Fidelity and Format in the Scandinavian *My Fair Lady*

Johan Franzon

Song translation blurs the border between translation proper and adaptation. This article suggests a definition of song lyric translation as a text that is similar to its source text in aspects relevant to its target culture presentation as a staged narrative to music. This is based on the *skopos* view that a functional translation must be translated according to the purpose of the transfer. According to a theatrical communication model, the presentation of a musical comedy song can be seen as involving levels of context: a staged performance, a narrative co-text, and the verbally empty rhetorical shape of the music, all of them cohering in a multimedial message. The translator's work can be seen pragmatically as adaptation to the aspects of the original context which are present for the new receptors. Some of the functional units available for the song translator to preserve or adapt are deictic reference, plot information, cultural reference, and musical and intermedial coherence. An analysis of the three Scandinavian translations of the musical *My Fair Lady* shows that even when translating for a purpose and context similar to that of the source text, many differences in choices of factual detail and context-related explication arise. If the song translation is to be functional on stage, some fidelity can be expected, but the similarity will be on the contextual-functional rather than the textual-semantic levels. Functions related to the multimedial presentation as such seem to be more elusive than those related to staging and co-text.

Changing Things

In song translation, the sense and facts of the source texts are often changed. This is as evident in popular song translation as in musical theatre translation, where greater fidelity to the source text generally would be expected. The kind of liberties taken can be briefly shown by looking at the refrain of Pirate Jenny's song in the play written by Bertolt Brecht (1898-1956). As drama translation scholar Lefevere (1982) once asked what happened to Mutter Courage's cucumbers in another play by Brecht, one might ask how many cannons there were on board Pirate Jenny's ship.

German source text:
Und ein Schiff mit <u>acht</u> Segeln
Und mit <u>fünfzig</u> Kanonen
Wird liegen am Kai.
  (Bertolt Brecht 1928)

English target text:
And a ship, a Black Freighter
With a skull on its masthead
Will be coming in.
  (tr. Marc Blitzstein 1954)

Swedish target text:
Och ett skepp med <u>sju</u> segel
och med <u>femti</u> kanoner
ses lägga till här.
  (tr. Ebbe Linde 1957)

French target text:
Un navire de haut bord

<u>Cent</u> canons aux sabords
Entrera dans le port.
  (tr. A. Mauprey 1962)

Finnish target text:
Ja se suuri purjelaiva

– <u>sata</u> tykkiä siinä –
juuri saapunut on.
  (tr. Elvi Sinervo 1969)

New English target text:
And the ship, <u>eight</u> sails
shining,
<u>Fifty-five</u> cannons wide, sir,
Waits there at the quay.
  (tr. Frank McGuinness 1991)

Most recent English target text:
There's a ship in the harbour
With <u>four dozen</u> cannon
And they're pointing at you.
  (tr. Jeremy Sams 1994)

Ex. 1. "Die Seeräuber-Jenny" from *Die Dreigroschenoper* (Brecht & Weill 1928, my emphasis)[1]

As the multilinguist will note, the cannons double to a hundred in French and Finnish (*cent, sata,* where the direct translation would be *cinquante canons* or *viisikymmentä tykkiä*). Neither sails nor cannons were mentioned in the first English version of the song, but Lotte Lenya, the original Jenny, who sang the song to great effect in the 1954 Off-Broadway production, did not seem to mind. In a recent version, used in London in 1994 and 2003, the cannons numbered 48 (named four dozen), which makes a closer approximation than the 55 cannons suggested in an earlier translation. The Swedish target text keeps the number of cannons but change the sails from eight to seven, thereby adding alliteration (*skepp – sju,* both prononced with a /sh/ sound). The fact that the monosyllabic *acht* is the bisyllabic *åtta* in Swedish hints at an explanation. The most obvious reason for changes such as these is the need to fit the music of Kurt Weill (1900-1950). Would the target texts above be considered translations at all without the premise of being set to music?

The task of translating songs fits badly into a traditional, linguistic definition of translation as "the replacement of textual material in one language (SL) by equivalent material in another language (SL)" (Catford 1965: 20). Rather, the task is one of "creative transposition," to use the term Roman Jakobson (1959: 238) chose for the translation of poetry. Another suitable designation would be an **adaptation**, since the target lyrics must be adapted to the musical line. That word, however, implies that "translation proper" is an alternative method and that a distinction between them can be drawn. In song translation, adaptation may well be the only possible choice. Toury states that a "translation is any target language utterance which is presented and regarded as such" (1980: 20), which the six target texts quoted above certainly were. A target text not presented as a translation may differ even more. In 1965-1966, two of Jacques Brel's *chansons, "Ne me quitte pas"* and *"Le moribund,"* were offered to the American music market as "If You Go Away" and "Seasons in the Sun." The pop song versions, designed for presentation on records and radio, had English lyrics by Rod McKuen that owed little more than the musical shape and a few textual passages to the source texts. They appear as simplifications compared to the Brel translations made by Mort Shuman and Eric Blau for the 1968 stage review *Jacques Brel Is Alive and Well and Living in Paris*. The theatrical format, with the author's name in the title, brought greater fidelity to his wit and satire, but the theatre song versions certainly were not literal translations either. In an earlier article (Franzon 2001), I have imagined a gradual cline between the often arbitrary source text relations of the commercial music market and the relative respect for the author in theatrical contexts. The literary integrity of the songs of Brecht and Brel places them at one end of the field of popular musical theatre. With commercial pop songs at the other end, the genre of musical comedy might be placed somewhere in the middle.

An examination of the three Scandinavian translations of the famous Broadway musical comedy *My Fair Lady* (1956) will show that much variation is possible even when song translators work under similar conditions and for a presentation aiming at close reproduction of the original. As a musical, *My Fair Lady*, created by Frederick Loewe (music), Alan Jay Lerner (libretto), and Moss Hart (director), may be rather unique in its solid dramatic construction and devotion to a literary source. The story of how the flower seller Eliza Doolittle transforms herself into a lady (or Lady) under the supervision of Professor Henry Higgins is taken *verbatim*, only shortened, from George Bernard Shaw's play *Pygmalion* (1914). But *My Fair Lady* also represents the relatively unified genre of Broadway musicals (circa 1940-1975), whose creators put much effort and money into experimenting with the multifaceted use of song for theatrical communication. As an example of the varied use of song in popular style for dramatic purposes, *My Fair Lady* is representative, even something of an ideal type. My purpose in this essay is to take a close look at which communicative clues may be considered relevant for the theatrical functionality of singing and which options song translators may have in the compromise between fidelity and formatting strategies. I admit the case of musicals is particular and not necessarily representative for song translation in general, but as far as the singing is theatrical or presentational, the analysis and theoretical framework may be partly relevant also to other kinds of "vernacular song" – a term used by musicologist Banfield (1996: 137-160) to discuss similarities in the construction of showtunes and popular music, nursery rhyme, folk song, and otherwise.

Fidelity and Format

What do musical comedy translators do when they translate? One of the very few musical comedy translators who have commented on their practice, Grandmont (1978: 98) metaphorically compares the practice to the minute labors of a Benedictine monk. Of the few translation theorists who comment on song translation, Nida (1964: 177) discusses the "severe restrictions," while Hervey and Higgins (1992: 138) call libretto translation an "extremely demanding task," on account of having to mind musical and dramatic constraints as well as audience preconceptions as to what a song of a certain type should be like. To answer the question thoroughly, a pragmatic, functional view of translation is useful. As there is a source text relation but also constraints on the target presentation, I find the concepts of **fidelity** and **format** helpful. Fidelity (of some kind) is what distinguishes a translated song from all-new lyrics to old music. Formatting is what may transform a useless (literal) lyric translation into a singable and performable one. The generality of the term fidelity covers the fact that the recreation of source text qualities – of rhymes, vowel sounds, semantic, stylistic, or narrative content, or a little bit of each – is necessarily a selective task. In my view, formatting would stand for the functional design of a text for a presentational situation that involves non-verbal elements. In formatting, the shape and style of the message vehicle exerts strong influence on the arrangement, but also the choice of verbal material. All texts must be somehow formatted to be presented, but in the area of audio- or multimedial translation such concerns are primary.

In translation theory, an interpretation of optimal fidelity is Gutt's (2000: 135) definition of "direct translation" as something presented as equivalent to a direct quotation. By preserving "all the communicative clues of the original, such translation would make it possible for the receptors to arrive at the intended interpretation of the original, provided they used the contextual assumptions envisaged by the original author." In practice, translators often find that this goal is unattainable. For more selective fidelity, Gutt (2000: 107) introduces the concept of "indirect translation," which is a translation that simply resembles the original "closely enough", where the translator decides "in what respects the translation should resemble the original – only in those respects that can be expected to make it adequately relevant to the receptor language audience". Indirect translators do not "insist on identity of the messages in every detail; they are content with a high degree of approximation" (Gutt 2000: 97). The strategy often involves the explication of contextual assumptions which are implicit in the source text. Communicative clues are seen in relation to the **context**, the cognitive environment available for the receptor when receiving the text (Gutt 2000: 26-27). Theatrical song translation could be similarly defined as the production of a target text that resembles its source text in respects relevant to its presentation as a staged narrative to music.

The formatting of song lyrics is most similar to the kind of translation Nord (1991; 1997a) describes as an instrumental rather than a documentary translation. The purpose of such a target text is to be "an instrument in a new TC [target culture] communicative action, ... for which the ST [source text] serves as a kind of model" (1991: 72) rather than a complete document of the content of the original. Focussing on what function the properties of the source text may serve in the new communicative situation, Nord (1997b) encourages translators and researchers to look for functional units in texts rather than to start with predefined linguistic or structural features.[2] As in *skopos* theory, the adequacy of the target text for the new purpose (intratextual coherence) is given priority over its optimal likeness to the source text (intertextual coherence). Nord's functional units, like Gutt's communicative clues, raise the attention from the textual surface to the level of the intentions of the original author and of the context where it performs a function.

The rewriting of the songs of Brecht's *Mutter Courage* in Broadway musical comedy style is seen by Lefevere (1998) as a case of acculturation. Studying translations made for the stage (of spoken plays), Aaltonen (1996) finds that acculturation, adaptation to target culture tastes and conventions, is practically inevitable to some degree. The different cultural context is prone to exert influence, but in song translation, as in play translation, there is also a dramatic and theatrical context to consider. Much as the translation of musical theatre may share the strategies of the popular song market, where the respect for the original source lyric is secondary to the purpose of producing a successful song, a musical comedy song also brings with it much of the context "envisaged by the original author." The play as a whole forms an extensive dramatic co-text. The music is often played according to the score provided by the theatrical licensing agency. The staging and the cultural context is inevitably new, but the dramatic co-text will influence how they are interpreted. Though the translation of songs in musical theatre thus can be expected to preserve the communicative clues, the translation must also be indirect and selective. What will be investigated is which functional units may be recognized in relation to the constrained format and how reasonably professional song translators use them for instrumental adaptation and creative reinterpretation. I sidestep the problem of drawing the line between translation, adaptation, and the complete rewording, rewriting, or "re-lyricking" that is common practice in the popular song market by limiting my study to one musical comedy, whose commissioner very much asked for "translation proper."

Theatre as the Presentation of a Representation

The formatting of a song translation basically involve relations to music and to a performance situation. Both can be seen as three-tiered by using the theatrical communication model of Ivo Osolsobě (1992a) as a framework. Songs in musicals make nuanced use of this three-tiered situation and the translated text may be adjusted to it in ways similar to or different from the source text. The model builds on the classic communication model of Jakobson (1960) and pictures theatre as "a form of human communication representing human communication by means of human communication" (Osolsobě 1992b: 241):

(situation three:)   CONTEXT$_3$

       ADDRESSER$_3$ _______________MESSAGE$_3$_________ADDRESSEE$_3$

                                CONTACT$_3$

                                CODE$_3$

(situation two:)   CONTEXT$_2$

       ADDRESSER$_2$_______________MESSAGE$_2$_________ADDRESSEE$_2$

                                CONTACT$_2$

                                CODE$_2$

(situation one:)
       ADDRESSER$_1$ ___________________________________ADDRESSEE$_1$

                                CONTACT$_1$

                                CODE$_1$

Figure 1. Three-tiered diagram of theatrical communication (Osolsobě 1992a: 212).

The diagram describes theatrical communication as consisting of communicative exchanges on three levels, which *seriatim* will be called **narrative, staging,** and **presentational**. The narrative level (situation three) refers to the fictional exchanges between the characters within the dramatic world. The staging level (situation two) refers to the make-believe interaction between actors in a staged environment, which represents the exchange of situation three. The presentational level (situation one) refers to the delivery of the message to audiences, where it gains value in connection to the preconceptions and associations of the listeners

In Osolsobě's conception (1992a), the two upper communicative exchanges (situation two and three) serve as the "message" and "context" of the theatrical communication (situation one). Drawing on Jakobson's distinction between referential, emotive, conative, poetic, phatic, and metalingual functions in communicative acts, all of which are vital but may be balanced differently, the three levels can be functionally distinguished. The narrative level, with its major base in the dramatic text, supplies most of the material for a referential function, while the staging makes its most vital contribution to the poetic, emotive and conative functions, as these are strengthened, even

269

created by the interpersonal address of the actors. The verbal codes$_3$, of some recognizable dialect or register, and the actors' behavioural codes$_2$, more or less taken from life, merge in the theatrical message where they are supplemented by the theatrical codes$_1$ used for communicating with the local audience. The latter codes are what allows or entices the theatrical body language to be deliberately visible and "telling" and the dramatic lines to be more coherent than real speech, even literary. The theatrical codes$_1$ can be either culturally inherited or negotiated metalingually with audiences, for example through elements of self-reference in the text.

In a musical, the staged narrative is presented in the form of a series of distinct songs. The mere fact that a theatrical situation is presented in the song form implies a special dramatic significance. Osolsobě, who has directed and translated musicals, as well as studied musical theatre (most concisely in a book in Czech language [1974] and articles in German and English languages [1971, 1984]), claims:

> *Musical theatre possesses a powerful heuristic instrument* ... This instrument is the song, or more exactly, *the song-shaped musical scene.* ... What does musical theatre do? It takes songs and song-like cyclic forms (sequences of songs, rondo-like forms with repetitions, refrains and choruses) and applies them to situations to which they seem to fit. *A situation thus becomes labelled, denoted, represented or, if you wish, modelled by the song*, and at the same time, *articulated, dissected, and classified* by its respective parts. The song functions therefore as a picture, diagram, or model of the situation. It displays certain properties ... and enables us to transfer them from the model to the represented situation. (Osolsobě 1984: 1743, his emphasis)

The artificiality of (sung) presentation is not disguised in a perfect blend of the three levels (of figure 1), as in naturalistic theatre and often in opera. The presentational quality of singing is used to highlight the particular situation. Commenting on Osolsobě, musical theatre scholar Banfield notes that the interchange between story and song number almost inevitably adds an element of self-reflection or commentary on communication in general:

> *In opera, traditionally, the music commands an exclusive viewpoint of the drama, like the authorial film camera ... In the musical, however, music – we might do better to call it song, so as to include the lyrics – has traditionally behaved much more self-consciously and presentationally, that is, as one mode of representation rather than its governing medium; ... it can often not just move in and out of the drama but in and out of itself, and is more dramatically agile, perhaps therefore even more epistemologically aware (thus serving as a model of human self-knowledge), than in most opera. (Banfield 1993: 6f)*

Banfield recognizes the dramatic agility of singing in musicals in a distinction between diegetic and non-diegetic song, two presentational modes which in fact are three, as the song-shaped musical scene may present the inner monologues of the characters as well as "characters who think they are talking and characters who know they are singing" (1993: 187). The last kind, song acknowledged as song within the fiction of a play, is called diegetic, "sung by a character who knows that she is singing, and it implies that the other characters onstage know it too" (Banfield 1993: 184f). Combining entertainment and dramatic art, applying songs to situations, the singing in musicals may always include a grain of presentational self-consciousness. Musicals easily can and often do borrow features from "theatrical forms based on pure presentation: music-hall, circus, [and the revue, which] does not want to represent anything and communicate anything and, as a 'showcase for everything,' it simply wants to exhibit the beauty of its precious materials, be it splendid settings and lavish costumes or flawless naked bodies" (Osolsobě 1992b: 243f).

Concentrating on the lyric, the translator's working material, I have distinguished five presentational modes of singing in musical theatre, based on the following questions: Who sings to whom? How many people sing? Are they aware of singing? Which level is dominant: narrative content, interaction between actors, or performance-as-performance? The varied use of song and its theatrical consequences can be shown in an extension of Osolsobě's diagram, and exemplified by the score of *My Fair Lady*:

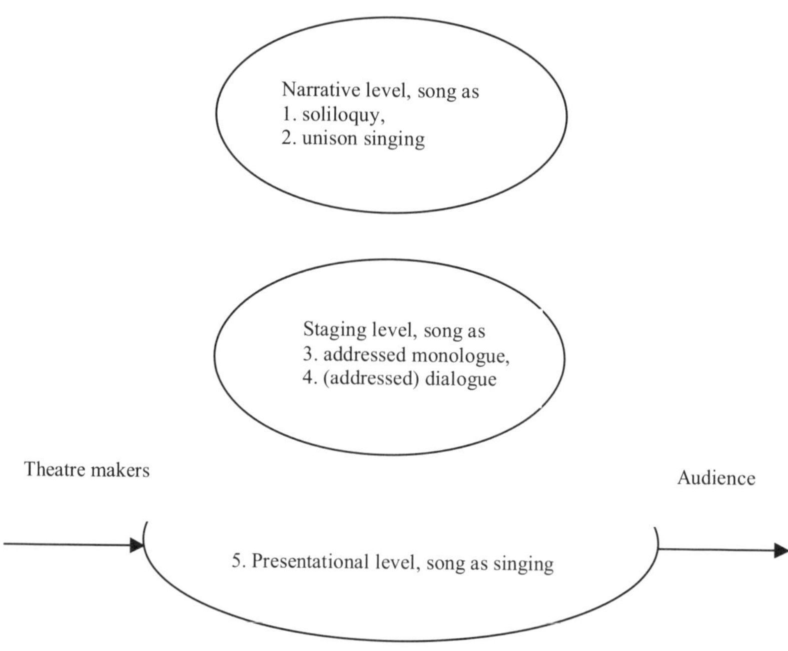

Figure 2. Five presentational modes of singing in musicals. An application of the three-tiered diagram of Osolsobě (1992a).

A song functioning mainly on the narrative level is similar to the soliloquy in spoken drama (an interior meditation by which "one character, alone on stage, uses his thoughts aloud ... to convey directly to the audience information about a character's motives, intentions, and state of mind" (Abrams 1981: 180). In *My Fair Lady*, the ideal example is "I've Grown Accustomed to her Face," the monologue sung by (the protagonist) Higgins. Unison singing generally implies a display of shared convictions, as in "Ascot Gavotte," the collective monologue of the British upper classes. Even though such songs may be staged to great effect, the impression is one of a moment frozen in time, in which dramatic information gets the centre of attention. The staging level makes a more significant contribution when singing functions as addressed monologue or dialogue. When Higgins addresses the crowd with the question "Why Can't the English?," or when solos, duos, choral singing and spoken comments intertwine in the song number "You Did It," the interaction between actors or between actors and their environment shares the social, spatiotemporal context of the spoken dialogue. Such numbers more or less depend on physical acting to make an impact, as actors represent "characters who think they are talking." Finally, when the presentational level is dominant, singing is actually presented as singing. Diegetic singing is scarce in *My Fair Lady*, perhaps there are only the cockneys humming and whistling a reprise of "Wouldn't It Be Loverly" in the second act, where the point is made that Eliza (the female protagonist) listens to them. A different but more clear-cut example is the Embassy Ballroom scene, placed by Shaw (1957: 66) in optional parentheses, but built up in the musical to provide visual splendour, diegetic music, and social dancing.

Besides interacting with a performance situation, the words must interact with music, the message vehicle that exerts the major constraints on the text. As Kaindl (1995) points out in regards to opera, words, music, and staging form a *Gestalt*, a meaningful whole, to which every element and fragment contributes. The format of the verbal text may however place weight on different aspects of the music. Drawing from the diagram above and referring back to the intratextual coherence of the functional target text, I distinguish between the prosodic form, to which the lyric must be adjusted to be comprehensible; the structural form, to which the lyric may be adjusted through poetic design; and the semantic implication of the music, which the words may explicate. If the first aspect supports the referential function of the lyric, the second performs a poetic, and the third a metalingual function, as it explains what the music means. Prosodic coherence, the matching of syllables to notes, verbal stress to musical accent, etc., is a major challenge in opera translation, where the challenges of vocalization and the risk of unintelligibility are greater (as demonstrated in Apter 1985, Apter and Herman 1995). The implied meaning music carries has been studied in relation to translation, for example, in the dramatic value of operatic parts/ranges (Kaindl 1995: 116-144), a composer's "word painting" in setting a libretto (Tråvén 1999: 299-370), and the euphonic and cultural resonances of art songs (Gorlée 2002). No less important – and at least in popular music more noticeable – is the fact that music not only fixes the intonation and adds to the meaning, but offers an aural structure which may be perceived as rhetorically potent but verbally empty. The movement of the melody through harmonic progression, song sections, repeated/different strains, or predictable/surprising turns may support the arrangement of the narrative and be supported by repetition, rhyme, parallelism, focus, and all the techniques of verse design (creating a poetic function through patterned similarities, as described by Jakobson [1960]; cf Gorlée 2002: 166-169). Osolsobě states that

> *... the analogies between language and music are not to be seen between the acoustic forms of music and language, but, first of all, between the logical structure of both. ... The melody, the musical vault, has in a song the same function with respect to the strophic discourse, as in language the sentence melody with respect to the sentence. It enables safe orientation in the discourse, distribution of logical accents, the topic-comment organization, the right placing of points. (Osolsobě 1974: 238)*

Osolsobě's "safe orientation" is played even safer in popular music theatre as it relies on conventional song forms – repeated and alternate song sections in formats AABA, ABAC or other combinations. The repetition of a title or "hook" phrase and the more speech-like prosody of the music help the lyrics to be easily digested. The lyricist-translator can, hypothetically, choose the lengths to which he will go to make the text coherent with the musical information, either semantically – being persuasive and affecting in presentation, structurally – being artful in declamation, or prosodically – being a stylized speaking voice.

In a roughly parallel way, the lyricist-translator may choose how explicit the links to the narrative, staging-related, or presentational contexts will be. As dramatic dialogue by inference paints a picture of an often fairly coherent "universe of discourse" (Elam 1980: 148-153), song lyrics that are short in length can do the same in relation to a narrative context. Drawing from the three-layered communication situation described above (figure 1 and 2), functional units, or communicative clues, may be found in the properties of playwriting: character, conflict (interpersonal address), plot, milieu (context), and language (code). The actors' contribution is not encoded as such in dramatic texts, as quite a few translation scholars have pointed out (Bassnett 1998, Espasa 2000, Aaltonen 2000), but theatre semioticians and other translation scholars have nevertheless worked to find links between the written text and a prospective performance (Elam 1980: 32-87, Pavis 1992: 136-158, Snell-Hornby 1997, Totzeva 1999). Theorists cannot draw definite parameters, but the performance situation will entice actors to do, speak, or show things that are inspired or even dictated by the verbal text. Functional units may be found in pronouns, verbal modes, utterances implying emotion or attitude (interpersonal address), deictic or spatiotemporal references, mention of props (context), and implied staged activity, including gestures or verbal behaviour (contact, code). In relation to music, the prosodic lines, the structure of similarity and contrast, and the perceived impact of the music may serve as functional units. Rather than direct translation, equivalent to the quoting of verbal content, the song translator's task would be to perform a creative transposition, approximating the source text as much as possible or as little as necessary, and perhaps negotiating between the formats determined by the functional units.

Adapting to a Theatrical Format in Musical Comedy Translation

My Fair Lady in Swedish, Danish and Norwegian offers an opportunity to compare strategies of song translators on relatively equal premises, save for the creative input of the translators themselves. The three languages are relatively similar in structure and vocabulary – so similar that linguists treat them as an extended speech community.[3] The national differences in pronunciation, speech habits and culture are small by global standards, and should be somewhat equalized in song and in translations from the same source text. The languages and theatrical scenes were alike enough to allow Lars Schmidt (Swedish), to work in all Nordic countries from the 1940s and further, introducing American plays and musicals through his publishing company *Nordiska Teaterförlaget*. Impressed by the original Broadway production of *My Fair Lady*, Schmidt decided to produce Scandinavian versions that were "just as good," which to begin with meant identical design of sets and costumes.[4] Schmidt commissioned target texts from translators with ample experience in drama and/or musical comedy translation, and in writing verse, popular song lyrics and/or revue material: Gösta Rybrant into Swedish, Holger Bech and Arvid Müller into Danish, and André Bjerke into Norwegian. The outcome was successful long runs, in Stockholm from February 1959 and Copenhagen and Oslo from January 1960. The first two productions were directed by the Danish Svend Åge Larsen, who followed the London edition of *My Fair Lady* as closely as he could. All three translations were published in book form (Lerner 1959a, 1959b, 1959c) and are still used in productions of this musical.[5] The instructions and wishes of the commissioner are central to the *skopos* theory of translation (Nord 1997a: 27-31). As far as background data goes, the four translators studied here worked towards similar goals and were reviewed and approved by a commissioner with an unusual – and, at the time, even criticized – mindset towards fidelity.

The three translations are, each in its own way, different from the source text. They are not direct translations, but differ in very evident ways in the wording and phrasing of the target lyrics. They do, however, share a tendency to prioritize intratextual coherence on the narrative and staging level of the presented song number. This is done through creative re-interpretation of the functional units. A link to a functional context is created by using other words than those of the closest possible semantic approximation of the source text. Sometimes the translators change the balance between the four contextual formats: narrative, staging, presentational, musical. Sometimes they differ between themselves as to which format to adhere to. The evidence of choices taken can be seen as a validation of these formats as distinct possibilities in the song translator's strategies.

Facts of plot and dramatic milieu are often referred to, sometimes more explicitly than in the source text. When, in "A Hymn to Him," Lerner describes men as being "Ready to help you through any mishaps" (1956: 109), the Swedish translator paraphrases this as "prepared as the scout is when fire is loose" (my back-translation, Lerner 1959a: 135). The added reference suits the context that the audience is confronted with: the overgrown schoolboys Higgins and Pickering and Edwardian England, where Robert Baden-Powell founded the Boy Scout movement in 1907. Specific plot reference is also sometimes added, as in the first strophe of the ensemble piece "You Did It":

	English source text	**Swedish target text**	**Norwegian target text**
	Pickering:	*Pickering:*	*Pickering:*
A1	Tonight, old man, you did it!	*Förbaske mig, du gjorde't,*	*Iaften har du vunnet!*
	You did it! You did it!	*du gjorde't, du gjorde't.*	*Du vinner! Du vinner!*
	You said that you would do it,	*Du lovade att göra't* *Och du vann ditt vad.*	*Du sa du skulle vinne,* *og ved Gud du vant!*
	And indeed you did.		
A2	I thought that you would rue it;	*Fantastiskt, det är ordet,*	*Jeg sa du ingensinne*
	I doubted you'd do it.	*du kunde't, du gjorde't.*	*kan skape en kvinne.*
	But now I must admit it	*Jag trodde faktiskt inte*	*Nu ser jag du har kunnet:*
	That succeed you did.	*på en sån bravad.*	*Det er faktisk sant!*

Ex. 2. Extract from "You Did It" (Lerner 1956: 85f; Lerner 1959a: 105f; Lerner 1959c: 85).

The song occurs at a major turning point of the drama and highlights the central plot point that Higgins managed to pass Eliza off as a lady. All three translations make this point explicit: "You promised to do it and you won your bet," "You win! You win!" and the Pygmalion-like passage "I said you never ever could create a woman" (my back-translation). In Danish, the equivalent phrase *"Og De vandt Deres væddemål!"* crops up later in the song. By explicating narrative fact, the balance of the three layers (of figure 1) is presumably changed. What is gained in dramatic relevance is lost in presentational effect. Lerner, honouring Broadway traditions, admired lyrics that "not only characterized and dramatized but did what all good music and lyrics should do: they gave a universality to each situation" (1985: 196). A quality of the source text is that its first strophe (quoted above) sounds like a generic song of victory and congratulation. To make the song stand out as a self-sufficient song, Lerner kept references general and used poetic devices (alliteration and half rhymes like "did it–indeed," "doubted–do it"). This authorial intention is lost in the target lyrics – the alliteration of "*vann ditt vad*" is a weaker compensation. Making the narrative level dominate is defensible, given the narrative focus of the song. A concrete dramatic situation may also lend itself to staging; a production in Swedish (Helsinki 2003) had Pickering hand over a banknote to Higgins at this moment, a gesture not as easily suggested by the English lyric.

With co-text surrounding the song, formatting the text for a dramatic purpose seems not to be a major problem. But an opposite strategy is also quite possible. The lyricist-translator may choose either to integrate the song actively into the specific fictional world or to neutralise it into a more general sphere of reference. Source songs may unite both functions. Eliza's first song, "Wouldn't It Be Loverly?," presents material comfort as the main theme of her dream. But true to the style of a popular song, it also contains a dream of romance. The double function is seen in the last (A4) section of the AABA song, which speaks of love, but climaxes on the material "good care": "Someone's head restin' on my knee, / Warm and tender as he can be, / Who takes good care of me… / Oh, wouldn't it be loverly?" (Lerner 1956: 23f). All Scandinavian target lyrics opt for a clear-cut romantic resolution through strategic alterations of the third A4 line: "someone I can love," "and then a bit of love," and "and tender just to me" (additions underlined). The song is basically a soliloquy, but even though the song as a whole motivates the character's later actions, it adds little in the way of specific plot information. In the theatrical presentation (Figure 2), the translations can be said to tip the balance over towards song-as-song, which might showcase the singer's personal charms or please cultural preconceptions, as opposed to song-as-narrative, which models character and plot. A target culture presentation that sees the musical play as a light and romantic entertainment would have no problem with this manipulation. The notion that a young girl's dream of homemaking must end in romance is as conventional in New York and London as in Scandinavia, perhaps even more so. Therefore, I would rather call it functional re-interpretation, or manipulation, than acculturation.

The translators are aware of the fact that the song will be physically staged. In the angry song which Eliza addresses to her suitor, the title phrase "Show Me" is closely translated as *"vis det"* ("show it") in Danish but becomes the more physical *"fang meg"* ("catch me") in Norwegian, even though *"vis det"* is a current phrase in Norwegian too. The re-interpretation creates an explicit link to both the narrative and staging level of the text: At that point in the story, Freddy Eynsford-Hill intends, but fails, to "catch" Eliza. In the same song, Eliza exclaims: "Say one more word and I'll scream." The last word is suitably placed on a high, long note. This is closely rendered in Danish as *"Sig ét ord til og jeg skri'er"* – contracting *"skriger"* ("scream") into *"skri'er,"* which is possible in Danish, but not in Norwegian. The Norwegian translator instead writes *"Ett ord til nu, og jeg slår!"* – 'One word more now and I will strike [hit you].' The translator keeps a strong monosyllabic predicate verb on the musically focussed last note, but also exchanges the musico-semantic link, the vocal stage direction, for a gestural one.

There may sometimes be a choice between serving the narrative and serving the stage. The song section where Higgins tells the story of how a rival linguist almost exposed Eliza has a strong narrative focus, but there is also staged interpersonal address. The song is an addressed monologue, told to an audience of servants, and some visible acting may therefore be expected as the actor portrays the self-conscious telling.

English source text	**Danish target text**	**Norwegian target text**
Higgins:	*Higgins:*	*Higgins:*
Oozing charm from ev'ry pore,	*Som en slimet ål, der snor*	*Fet av charme og glatt som laks*
He oiled his way around the floor.	*sig – som en sporhund på sit spor –*	*i olje gled han rundt for straks,*
Ev'ry trick that he could play, He used to strip her mask away.	*prøved han konstant, ved Gud, at regne pigens herkomst ud!*	*efter bruk av alle knep, å fjerne masken <u>med et grep</u>*

Ex. 3. Extract from "You Did It" (Lerner 1956: 88; Lerner 1959b: 89; Lerner 1959c: 87, my emphasis).

The temptation to show how the rival tried "to strip her mask away" would seem irresistible in the Norwegian account of "tricks to remove the mask with one grip," but nonexistent in the Danish explication of dramatic fact: "he attempted constantly, by God, to figure out the girl's background." Both translators leave out the specific "floor" of the Embassy Ballroom, but the Norwegian translator preserves the action of "gliding around" while the Danes add the less deictic metaphors of a squirming eel and sniffing dog. It is not mandatory for every Norwegian actor playing Higgins to demonstrate the grip, nor impossible for a Danish actor to make an impression in some other visual way, but translators can be more or less aware, helpful, or explicit in presenting one level of theatrical communication as relevant.

Staged activity can be inferred from the presentational situation and sometimes also from the co-text. These two target lyrics have moved "carry me to the church" and "shake my hand" from Lerner's stage directions to the song itself. It results in what on comparison would seem like a more physical interpretation of the words "boot" and "salute":

English source text	**Danish target text**	**Norwegian target text**
Doolittle: (Solemnly shakes hands with all. [...]	*Doolittle: (giver højtideligt hånd til alle*[...]	*Doolittle: (trykker alle i hånden,* [...]
A4 I'm gettin' married in the morning'	*Jeg ska' ha bryllup nu til morgen!*	*Jæ ska' bli gift på morrakvisten.*
Ding dong! The bells are gonna chime…	*Ta' dog og hjælp en gammel ven!*	*Ding, dong! ska kjerkeklokka slå.*
Hail and salute me	*Vis, I er stærke –*	*Syng hosianna,*
Then haul off and boot me...	*bær mig til kærke.*	*men ta mæ-i handa,*
And get me to the church,	*Vis, at I er mænd,*	*og få mæ-i kjerka straks,*
Get me to the church...	*der snildt ka' klare dén.*	*få mæ-i kjerka straks,*
For Gawd's sake, get me to the church on time!	*Ja, ta' og bær' mig hele vej'n derhen!*	*for Guds skyld: få mæ-i kjerka straks jæ må!*
(DOOLITTLE is lifted high in the air and carried off to the grim inevitable.)	*(DOOLITTLE blivet løftet op og båret ud – mod den uundgåelige og frygtelige skæbne.)*	*(Doolittle blir løftet høyt opp, og båret bort til sin uunngåelige, mørke skjebne.)*

Ex. 4. Extract from "Get Me to the Church on Time" (Lerner 1956: 104; Lerner 1959b: 107; Lerner 1959c: 105, my emphasis).

The translators have used the potential coherence with staging to gain manoeuvring space for their musical versification. Doing so, they may of course also influence the staging. Being an addressed monologue, the song depends on staged interaction to become theatrical. It would be slightly incongruous if Doolittle did not shake hands or get lifted up in the air as he sings of it.

Deictic words, finally, are units specifically intended to connect a speaker to his context. Their relevance to dramatic discourse is emphasized by the theatre semiotician Elam (1980: 137-144). Their relation to body language is obvious (Elam 1980: 72ff). This addressed monologue by Higgins shows a similarity to dialogue in its repeated reference to place and co-characters. The translators use deictic reference in a roughly equal way when Eliza is referred to and Pickering addressed (though they may for example change a possessive pronoun "her place" to a demonstrative "this swamp"). When Lerner states his refrain on a more general level; "Why can't the English teach their children how to speak?," the translators become even more general: All drop the reference to "children" – saving syllables, but also making the drama relevant reference to Eliza as a child of the street more implicit. Two of them also drop "the English."

English source text	**Swedish target text**
Higgins:	*Higgins:*
<u>This</u> is what the British population	*Shakespeares arv, förvanskat till förvildning*
Calls an element'ry education. [---]	*<u>Det</u> är brittisk bottenskolebildning. [---]*
It's 'Aooow' and 'Garn' that keep <u>her</u> in <u>her place</u>.	*<u>Sånt</u> håller <u>henne</u> kvar i <u>denna sump</u>.*
Not <u>her</u> wretched clothes and dirty face.	*Inte <u>hennes</u> lort och <u>hennes</u> lump.*
A1 Why can't the English teach their children how to speak?	*Varför kan inte engelsmännen tala rent?*
<u>This</u> verbal class distinction by now should be antique.	*<u>Hon</u> borde lärts i skolan, men nu är det för sent.*
If <u>you</u> spoke as <u>she</u> does, <u>sir</u>,	*Om <u>ni</u> förde samma språk,*
Instead of the way <u>you</u> do,	*ja vad skulle ske?*
Why, <u>you</u> might be selling flowers, too.	*Då stod <u>ni</u> i socialgrupp 3.*

Danish target text	**Norwegian target text**
Higgins:	*Higgins:*
<u>Det</u> er i den samlede befolkning	*<u>Her i landet</u> kalles <u>denne</u> talen*
godkendt folkeskole-sprogfortolkning. [---]	*for den nye læreboknormalen. [---]*
Det er hverken <u>hendes</u> ansigt eller klæ'r,	*<u>Hun</u> dømmes til et liv i en kloakk,*
det er sprogets skyld, <u>hun</u> virker så vulgær. –	*ikke av <u>sin</u> skitt, men av <u>sitt</u> snakk!*
A1 *Hvorfor kan folk dog ikke tale sproget rent?*	*Kan ikke folk bli lært sitt sprog <u>i dette land</u>?*
Hvorfor skal det forvrænges så hæsligt og gement?	*Et sproglig klasseskille er gammel uforstand.*
Hvis <u>De</u> talte sådan, <u>sir</u>,	*Ja, snakket <u>De</u> slik som <u>hun</u>,*

<table>
<tr><td>var <u>De</u> en proletar,</td><td>Istedefor slik <u>De</u> gjør,</td></tr>
<tr><td>en tarvelig, associal barbar!</td><td>fikk <u>De</u> også selge blomster, <u>sir</u>.</td></tr>
</table>

Ex. 5. Extract from "Why Can't the English?" (Lerner 1956: 20; Lerner 1959a: 25; Lerner 1959b: 16; Lerner 1959c: 17, my emphasis).

In this example, deictic units are vital tools for the formatting of the creative transposition, and the Scandinavian translators use them in different ways. The Norwegian refrain says: "Cannot people be taught their language <u>in this country</u>?," and the demonstrative pronoun easily includes Norway as well as the Great Britain pictured on stage. In Danish, the effect is softer, but similarly felt in the general reference and the definite article: "Why cannot <u>people</u> then speak <u>the</u> language properly? / Why must it be distorted in an ugly and common way?" A few lines earlier, the two had neutralised "the British population" into "the whole population" and "<u>here</u> in the land," respectively. Sly, topical references will make the song active on the presentational level, much like a revue number. (The Norwegian even adds a reference to "*læreboknormalen*," the schoolbook spelling standard which was much debated in Norway in 1959.[6]) Here, this is in perfect translational order, since the source song also draws on cultural preconceptions of revue songs, most specifically Noel Coward's famous satire "Mad Dogs and Englishmen (go out in the midday sun)." The opposite choice is taken by the Swedish target text. It makes the dramatic, rather than the presentational relevance explicit as it preserves the "<u>British</u> elementary education" and adds "Shakespeare's heritage" – a reference to a literary classic which is not in the original lyric at all (but in the spoken dialogue). "<u>This</u> verbal class distinction" becomes "<u>She</u> should have been taught in school," thus pointing explicitly at the character within the fiction. All three solutions can be subsumed under the concept of acculturation, but the effect is different, most clearly on the presentational level. In Danish and Norwegian, the satiric song seems to satirize local urban dialect as well. The Swedish audience is placed on the outside, looking in. (One might argue that this also is the position of Lerner, the American, and Shaw, the Irishman.) Domestic allusions may break the narrative frame, but here, the topicality is soon overruled when the plot proceeds and other matters become objects of Higgins's discontent. The most functional aspect from the point of view of the stagers is that deictic units are there at all, so that the actor can give an impression of being part of the fictional stage world.

Elements Lost or Compensated

Being indirect, the translations quoted above certainly do not reproduce all the communicative clues of the originals. As perhaps evidenced from the scattered examples, communicative clues connected to narrative and staging functions are quite often preserved, or strengthened through rephrasing. Original textual properties that function mainly on the presentational level seem to be more easily lost. For example, translators often make large or small adaptations of culture-specific items. As the transposition of song lyrics seems to give free reign to such adaptation, importance should be placed on how the changes are suited to the narrative and presentational contexts.

English source text	**Swedish target text**
Higgins:	*Higgins:*
B3 You want to talk of <u>Keats or Milton</u>;	*Du talar varmt om <u>Shakespeares</u> dramer.*
She only wants to talk of love.	*Hon talar helst om ditt och datt.*
You go to see a play or ballet,	*Och vad är <u>Louvrens</u> vackra damer*
And spend it searching for her glove.	*mot hennes nya, dyra hatt?*

Danish target text	**Norwegian target text**
Higgins:	*Higgins:*
B3 *Man går i Operaen til "<u>Carmen</u>",*	*Snakk du om <u>Shakespeare</u>, og hun prater*
tre timers skøn musik i træk,	*om Bibben som er glad i Bob,*
Men ak, det hele mister charmen,	*og har du tenkt deg i teater,*
da hendes handsker de blir væk.	*så finn først hennes øredobb!*

Ex. 6. Extract from "I'm an Ordinary Man" (Lerner 1956: 38; Lerner 1959a: 49; Lerner 1959b: 35; Lerner 1959c: 38, my emphasis).

Here, Higgins uses cultural celebrities to present himself as higher-minded than a hypothetical wife. In translation, Keats and Milton are replaced with Shakespeare, the opera *Carmen*, and the Louvre. The fidelity is on a functional rather than a semantic level. The translators evidently decided the most relevant purpose was to present "high culture" and chose items from a simpler or more universal code to achieve the purpose. Two of the references are not even British, but none is incoherent with the context of London in 1912. Most importantly, a fluent verse format is preserved. The rhyme scheme is even overmarked – ABAB instead of ABCB. (The verse is least fluent, or singable, in Norwegian, where consonant-rich words, "*Snakk du*" and "*finn først*," are placed on non-stressed syllables.)

An obvious case of acculturation is the insertion of a target culture literary allusion. In the song above (Ex. 6), the Swedish Higgins goes on to sing, not "let a woman in your life," but instead "let no devil cross the bridge," quoting a famous 19th century Fenno-Swedish poet, Johan Ludvig Runeberg's (1804-1877). The quote is from the poem *"Sven Dufra"* in Runeberg's poem cycle *The Tales of Ensign Stå*l (1848), dealing with the Russo-Swedish War (1808-1809) and the stubborn resistance of the brave Finnish soldiers, adopted as a national epic in Finland. The phrase is well known as a famous paraphrase in both Sweden and Finland. In their target lyrics, however, the Norwegian and Danish translators choose a literal translation: "let a woman in your life." But even such patriotic allusions cohere with the presentational context, as an example from the Danish and Norwegian translators shows:

	English source text	**Danish target text**	**Norwegian target text**
	Eliza:	*Eliza:*	*Eliza:*
A1	There'll be spring ev'ry year without you.	*Det blir forår hvert år – uden Dem!*	*Det blir vår alle år uten deg.*
	England still will be here without you.	*Gamle England består – uden Dem!*	*Gamle England består uten deg.*

Ex. 7. Extract from "Without You" (Lerner 1956:116; Lerner 1959b:122; Lerner 1959c:118, my emphasis).

The direct translation of "year" as *"år"* may have invoked *"består"* as a rhyme. The verb contains an allusion to the Danish national anthem, whose last stanza states *"Vort gamle Danmark skal bestå"* ("Our old Denmark will last," Adam Oehlenschläger 1819). In the performance situation, the self-confident Eliza is supposed to impress Higgins with her new-found sophistication. (Lerner has her half-quoting Shakespeare: "And without much ado / we can all muddle through.") Having her refer to "England" instead of "Denmark" makes the phrase coherent in the narrative context. The coded connotation carried by the words *gamle* and *bestå* is potentially disrupting, but as it does not explicitly clash with the co-text, what might remain is the impression of a well-set phrase, the implication of a slight parody or a learned/lyrical register, somehow familiar but quickly passed over. Studying acculturation in naturalistic, spoken plays, Aaltonen notes that theatre texts seem "to tolerate substantial inconsistency in detail, as the audience does not have the time or need to reflect on details" (1996: 204).

What is most evidently lacking in the translations is sensitivity to the occasional metalingual reference to the song number as such. The well-known song number "Get Me to the Church on Time" puts special emphasis on presentational values. The narrative value of the song is limited; Doolittle repeatedly implores his friends to help him celebrate the last night before his wedding. The staging potential is greater; it includes an extended dance number which functions as a theatrical representation of the celebration. In an Anglo-American cultural context, the song is easily understood as a pastiche of British music-hall songs, describing human woes in humorous ways while inviting listeners to sing along in the choruses:

English source text

Doolittle:

A1 I'm getting married in the morning.
Ding! Dong! the bells are gonna chime.
Pull out the stopper!
Let's have a whopper!
But get me to the church on time!

A2 I gotta be there in the mornin'
Spruced up and lookin' in me prime.
Girls, come and kiss me;
show how you'll miss me.
But get me to the church on time!

B3 If I am dancin',
Roll up the floor.
If I am whistlin'
Whewt me out the door!

Swedish target text

Doolittle:

Klockan ska klämta när det dagas.
Ding dång, den ringer ut min frid.

Hattar ska rulla.
<u>*Ni får bli fulla,*</u>
men för mig till min brud i tid.
Dit ska jag jagas, när det dagas,
<u>*rakad och nykter*</u> *och timid.*
<u>*Blir jag i mössan* –</u>
osäkra bössan,
men för mig till min brud i tid.
Och <u>*om jag öppnar*</u>
<u>*min breda trut*</u>
Så får ni <u>*vissla* –</u>
<u>*pssst! – på närmsta snut.*</u>

Danish target text

Doolittle:

A1 *Jeg skal ha' bryllup nu til morgen!*
Snart ringer klokkerne for mig!
Kom, kære venner,
<u>*fold jeres hænder*</u>
Og ta' og <u>*føl mig lidt på vej!*</u>

A2 *For jeg skal giftes nu til morgen!*
<u>*Fremtiden ligger sort som beg*</u>.
<u>*Pi'er, kom og trøst mig,*</u>
kys, kram og kryst mig
Og ta' og føl' mig lidt på vej!

B3 *Og sku' jeg nægte*
at følle med,
Så <u>*sving den højre*</u> – – *uiit!* –
og slå mig ned!

Norwegian target text

Doolittle:

<u>*Jæ ska' bli gift på morrakvisten!*</u>
Ding, dong! Ska' kjerkeklokka slå.
<u>*Ta høl på kagga,*</u>
<u>*heis alle flagga,*</u>
men få <u>*mæ-i*</u> *kjerka straks jæ må!*
Jæ ska' te pers på morrakvisten,
pønta og fjong fra topp te tå.
Kom, jenter, favn mæ,
elsk mæ og savn mæ
men få mæ-i kjerka straks jæ må!
Og har jæ schlitt mæ,
så hent et tjor,
og <u>*blås i fløyta:*</u>
fhuit! mæ hjem te mor!

Ex. 8. Extract from "Get Me to the Church on Time" (Lerner 1956: 102; Lerner 1959a: 126f; Lerner 1959b: 105; Lerner 1959c: 102f, my emphasis).

In the source text, imperative verb forms serve the interaction between the singer and his audience ("come and kiss me," "Roll up the floor"). This function is preserved, but reinterpreted by other verbs or forms of address: "follow me a bit on the way," "you may get drunk." There are also intermedial links, an onomatopoetic "Ding! Dong!," which is preserved in two translations, and a "Whewt," which is to be whistled by either Doolittle or some members of the chorus (as evidenced on the original cast recording). The whistling is preserved, but reinterpreted as a police whistle, the swing of a striking fist, and a toot on a flute, respectively. What is lost in all translations is the self-reference achieved by the parallel wordings in the song's B sections: "If I am dancin'" (quoted above), "If I am flyin'," "If I am wooin'." Even more metapresentational are the phrases "Pull out the stopper / Let's have a whopper" (A1 above) and "Kick up a rumpus." They make the song half-diegetic, since Doolittle appears almost to acknowledge the on-going performance. To the audience, such phrases add a metalingual dimension, since they explain what the upcoming dance and merriment would depict. But even though Lerner makes the point clear in the stage direction "The crowd pulls out the stopper and has a whopper; a final street dance of farewell" (1956: 103), none of the phrases above, nor the stage direction, is translated closely. The metapresentational quality is largely lost in paraphrases with either less physically immediate metaphors ('make a hole in the keg / raise all flags,' Norwegian A1) or other actions ('fold your hands,' Danish A1; 'If I open my wide mouth,' Swedish B3).

The translators chose other means than semantic reproduction to produce a theatrically effective, entertaining song. Besides the explication of staged action (Ex. 4 above), all translators adapted their target lyrics to the dramatic co-text and to domestic song formats, each in his own way. In Swedish, several references to drinking have been added ('you may get drunk,' 'shaved and sober,' 'should I get tipsy'). They suit the character of Doolittle and the Swedish tradition of drinking songs. The Norwegian lyrics are coated more thickly in the local urban dialect (evidenced in the dialectal spelling of pronouns *jeg* and *meg* as *jæ* and *mæ* and grammatical forms such as *kagga* and *flagga* instead of *kaggen* and *flaggene*). Dialectal forms were used in both the dialogue of the musical and for comic effect in revue songs at the time. The Danish version emphasizes the sadness of Doolittle's fate ("The future is black as tar," "Girls, come and console me") and has him begging pitifully: "follow me a bit on the way." The obvious reason is that the role was slated for Osvald Helmuth (1894-1966), a revue artist famous in Denmark for his psychological portrayals in sung monologues, which were often tailored for him by the *My Fair Lady* song translator Arvid Müller.

Instead of a music hall cheerleader or master of the revels, Doolittle is presented as a drunken wedding orator, a rustic comic, or a semi-tragic lamenter. New textual clues seem to serve the added authorial intentions, but the original self-reference, specifically designed for the musical's traditional song-and-dance number, is overlooked.

In the performance situation, the lyric interacts with the context provided by music and the staged narrative. If one expects that the intermedial links that are vital for this interaction would be preserved (to "resemble the original – only in those respects that can … make it adequately relevant to the receptor language audience", Gutt 2000: 107), the choices of translators may also be criticized:

English source text

Eliza:

A4 Then they'll <u>march</u> you, 'enry 'iggins, to the wall;
And the King will tell me: 'Liza, sound the call.'

Swedish target text

Eliza:

Henry Higgins skall ställas mot en mur.

Jag får själv bestämma var och när och hur.

Danish target text

Eliza:

A4 *Og der står du, Henry Higgins, vigtigper!*
Kongen siger: "Værsgo', Liza, kommandér!"

Norwegian target text

Eliza:

Dem vi' schtille ræ mot mur'n, din viktigper!

Og så sier kongen: "Liza, kommander!"

Ex. 9. Extract from "Just You Wait" (Lerner 1956: 50; Lerner 1959a: 65; Lerner 1959b: 49; Lerner 1959c: 51, my emphasis).

When this vengeful song is performed in context, it is apparent that the music turns martial just when Eliza starts imagining Higgins's execution. Lerner places the accent on the word "march," and on the first accented note of Loewe's march. The word helps to showcase both the change in musical expression and whatever action the actress may want to apply. Since music naturally invites to movement and the purpose of the song number is to display an angry mood, some action, by hand or foot, in time with the orchestra, very easily can be imagined to illustrate the entrance of an execution squad. In all three translations, however, the phrase "march you … to the wall" is paraphrased as "be put against the wall" and "there you stand," which surely makes the lyric less optimally coherent with the the staging and the musical context. Again, the translators seem less sensitive to textual elements that help define the song's character as a sung presentation.

Balancing Factors to Music

Of course, a singable song translation must be coherent with the music. The prosodic comprehensibility, structural patterning, and semantic reflection may show varying degrees of fidelity in target lyrics, but a sharp distinction can hardly be drawn, since all three converge in a well-made lyric. A basic strategic choice seems to be between trying to keep as much as possible of the original sense, which may impede the musical fit, or keeping as little as necessary, to allow greater musical coherence. The verse and refrain of a simply structured, but contextually multifaceted song demonstrate which choices can be made by the three aspects of the musical formatting.

	English source text	**Swedish target text**
	Eliza:	*Eliza:*
verse	Bed! Bed! I couldn't go to bed,	*Sömn? Sömn? Vad ska jag sova för?*
	My head's too light to try to set it down.	*Nej, inte för allt guld som finns att få.*
	Sleep! Sleep! I couldn't sleep tonight,	*Sömn…! Sömn…! När allt är som en dröm*
	Not for all the jewels in the crown.	*och jag går bland skyar i det blå.*
A1	I could have danced all night!	*Jag kunde dansa så,*
	I could have danced all night!	*jag kunde sväva så*
	And still have begged for more.	*den ljusa natten lång.*
A2	I could have spread my wings	*Jag dansar fram bland moln*
	And done a thousand things	*upp mot den blå kupoln*
	I've never done before.	*och livet är en sång.*
B3	I'll never know	*Kan någon säga*
	What made it so exciting;	*vad det är som hänt mig?*
	Why all at once	*Så har jag aldrig förut känt.*
	My heart took flight.	
A4	I only know when he	*När han bjöd upp till dans*
	Began to dance with me,	*jag miste vett och sans.*
	I could have danced, danced, danced all night.	*Det var en dans, en dans, en dans.*

	Danish target text	**Norwegian target text**
	Eliza:	*Eliza:*
verse	*Seng! Seng! Åh, hvem kan gå i seng,*	*Seng! Seng! Hva kan få meg i seng?*
	når hjernen kører som en grammofon?	*Mitt hode er for lett til å bli lagt!*
	Søvn! Søvn! En ren umulighed	*Søvn! Søvn! Hva kan få meg i søvn?*
	– selv om jeg så fik en million!	*Ikke hele kronens perleprakt!*
A1	*Jeg kunne danse nu!*	*Jeg kunne, fylt av sang,*

	(Danish, cont.)	(Norwegian, cont.)
	Jeg kunne svæve nu *til Paradisets port!*	*ha danset natten lang,* *og latt meg hvirvle bort.*
A2	*Blot danse rundt i ring* *og gøre tusind ting,* *jeg aldrig før har gjort!*	*Jeg kunne svevd omkring,* *og gjort ti tusen ting* *jeg aldri før har gjort.*
B3	*Jeg aner knapt* *hvad der har skapt den stemning –* *hvorfor mit hjerte ta'r på vej.*	*Hva kan med ett* *ha gjort meg så lykksalig* *at hjertet tok et himmelsprang?*
A4	*I en fortryllet dans* *slog det i takt med hans* *og råbte "Dans – dans – dans – med mig!"*	*Han la sin arm om meg,* *og siden kunne jeg* *ha bare danset natten lang!*

	English source text	**Swedish target text**
	Eliza:	*Eliza:*
verse	Bed! Bed! I couldn't go to bed, My head's too light to try to set it down. Sleep! Sleep! I couldn't sleep tonight, Not for all the jewels in the crown.	*Sömn? Sömn? Vad ska jag sova för?* *Nej, inte för allt guld som finns att få.* *Sömn…! Sömn…! När allt är som en dröm* *och jag går bland skyar i det blå.*
A1	I could have danced all night! I could have danced all night! And still have begged for more.	*Jag kunde dansa så,* *jag kunde sväva så* *den ljusa natten lång.*
A2	I could have spread my wings And done a thousand things I've never done before.	*Jag dansar fram bland moln* *upp mot den blå kupoln* *och livet är en sång.*
B3	I'll never know What made it so exciting; Why all at once My heart took flight.	*Kan någon säga* *vad det är som hänt mig?* *Så har jag aldrig förut känt.*
A4	I only know when he Began to dance with me, I could have danced, danced, danced all night.	*När han bjöd upp till dans* *jag miste vett och sans.* *Det var en dans, en dans, en dans.*

	Danish target text	**Norwegian target text**
	Eliza:	*Eliza:*
verse	*Seng! Seng! Åh, hvem kan gå i seng,* *når hjernen kører som en grammofon?* *Søvn! Søvn! En ren umulighed* *– selv om jeg så fik en million!*	*Seng! Seng! Hva kan få meg i seng?* *Mitt hode er for lett til å bli lagt!* *Søvn! Søvn! Hva kan få meg i søvn?* *Ikke hele kronens perleprakt!*
A1	*Jeg kunne danse nu!* *Jeg kunne svæve nu* *til Paradisets port!*	*Jeg kunne, fylt av sang,* *ha danset natten lang,* *og latt meg hvirvle bort.*
A2	*Blot danse rundt i ring* *og gøre tusind ting,* *jeg aldrig før har gjort!*	*Jeg kunne svevd omkring,* *og gjort ti tusen ting* *jeg aldri før har gjort.*
B3	*Jeg aner knapt* *hvad der har skapt den stemning –*	*Hva kan med ett* *ha gjort meg så lykksalig*

<table>
<tr><td></td><td>hvorfor mit hjerte ta'r på vej.</td><td>at hjertet tok et himmelsprang?</td></tr>
<tr><td>A4</td><td>I en fortryllet dans</td><td>Han la sin arm om meg,</td></tr>
<tr><td></td><td>slog det i takt med hans</td><td>og siden kunne jeg</td></tr>
<tr><td></td><td>og råbte " Dans – dans – dans – med
mig!"</td><td>ha bare danset natten lang!</td></tr>
</table>

Ex. 10. Extract from "I Could Have Danced All Night" (Lerner 1956: 58f; Lerner 1959a: 76; Lerner 1959b: 59; Lerner 1959c: 61f).

The original lyric presents itself as a soliloquy, most clearly when the simple construction of the refrain stanza (AABA) uses five syntactic sentences for the four musical sections, each starting with "I..." The musical hook is the strain that carries the title phrase: three short notes followed by a long one on the downbeat – metrically a paeonic foot ("I could have danced"), followed by a iambic foot ("all night"). The musical gesture repeats itself in different harmonic constellations throughout the song, starting and concluding in the key of C major. The lyric creates unity by supporting the key word *danced* with the half rhyme *once* and through syntactic parallelism – "I could have spread…," "I'll never know…" Musico-semantically, the repeated four-note gesture may signify tripping dance steps, an exploding emotion, or the stubborn single-mindedness of Eliza at that moment of the drama. As the refrain starts and ends with repeated mentions of *danced/dance* (twice in A1, four times in A4) in a hypothetical verb tense, the dancing appears as a metaphor for the joy the singer expresses. The notion is supported by metaphors of flight: "spread my wings", "my heart took flight." In the contrasting B3 section Loewe creates harmonic suspense by touching E major, and then G major, for a bar or two, before an emphatic return to C major upon entering the final A section. The contrast between the uncertainty and certainty expressed by the key changes is reflected in Lerner's phrases "I'll never know…" – "I only know…" The source lyrics thus display an expert coherence between music and lyrics in prosodic, structural, and semantic aspects.

Judging by the narrative level, the Norwegian translator has done "better" than his colleagues. The Norwegian translator alone keeps the "jewels in the crown" ("*kronens perleprakt*") which form a link to the British milieu. By closely rendering the A2 line "I could have … done a thousand things / I've never done before", he preserves the subtle reference to the fact that Eliza triumphantly managed to say "the rain in Spain" instead of "rine in Spine" a moment ago. Also, the hypothetical verb tense ("I could have danced" – "*Jeg kunne … ha danset*"), a marker of Eliza's new-found verbal sophistication, is kept. But this close approximation has been achieved at the expense of the musical fit. A most blatant prosodic modification is the run-on line that starts the Norwegian refrain with a not very speech-like participle appositive: "I could, filled with song / have danced the night long." There is a basic prosodic coherence, as the words "*fyllt*" and "*danset*" are naturally stressed. Such an enjambment is also quite natural in recited poetry, but, when sung, it does not 'say' the two repeated phrases of the melody. The predominance of short vowels (*perleprakt, sang, omkring, ett, himmelsprang, natten lang*) does not make the lyric unsingable, but they are not optimally suited to the long, high and line-ending notes they are placed on.

A prosodically coherent text format can probably be expected from the hands of experienced songwriters. But the looser approximation seems to be in the better position to achieve a musical fit. In the verse of the song, the Danish and Swedish translations add words, "*grammofon*" and "*i det blå*", that sets long vowels on the last note of the verse (where "*perleprakt*" has a short syllable and unvoiced consonants). The Danish lyrics choose open-ended diphthongs ("*ta'r på vej*" – "*med mig*") for the notes that end the B3 and A4 sections. These extended notes arguably are the structurally most important ones.[7] The Swedish approximation is looser still, rendering the A2 section as "I dance along on clouds up towards the blue cupola…" This added line sings well on repeated, long vowels (*så, på moln, blå*), but the subtle plot reference is lost. It continues with a poetic cliché: "and life is a song." The addition can be called a metapresentational comment, since it purports to explain why the character is singing. For this presentational value, the narrative specificity is sacrificed or disregarded.

As for structural coherence, the translators have gone to different lengths in providing compensation. The preservation of the euphonic, patterned stylisation of the source text – *begged, spread, never, never, know, so, know* – would indeed be a monk's work to pursue (referring to Grandmont 1978). In compensation, there are repeated /å/ sounds in Swedish and /ng/ sounds in Norwegian, as well as assonance in "*danset natten lang*." Again, the Danish version presents the most worked-through attempt at musical coherence. It will be noted, though, that its alliteration, inner rhyme, and assonance – "*rundt i ring – tusind ting*", "*knapt – skapt*", "*-tryllet dans – takt med hans*", "*Paradisets port*" – occur mostly on added words. (The last-mentioned addition, 'The Gate of Paradise', may be called an acculturation. In a state church Lutheran culture, such a metaphor is probably closer at hand than it would be on non-confessional Broadway.)

What differs most significantly in Swedish and Danish is the way the song situation presents itself: the impression of personal meditation is less clear when the sentences do not start with the first personal pronoun ('I') as in the original. The simple message "I Could Have Danced All Night" is still there, more or less, but the Danish translation exchanges the specific temporal reference 'night' for the deictic 'I could dance now, I could float now.' The Swedish lyric goes for poetic embellishment: 'I could dance so, I could float so, the bright night long.' Through the omission of the repetition and the change of verb form to the present tense, the title phrase comes through less as a metaphor for joy and more as a description of actual dancing. Both the Swedish and Danish texts do seem to have picked up on the here-and-now of the stage moment ('dance <u>now</u>'). Both add verb particles which suggest spatial action ("*dansar <u>fram</u>*," 'dance forward/along,' "*danse <u>rundt</u>*," 'dance around'). Although the actress would not necessarily be dancing, at least not very intensely, being physically committed to sustaining notes, any movement she would choose to do would very easily be understood in relation to the dancing described in these lyrics.

Musico-semantic aspects seem more elusive than prosody and rhetorical structure. The musical uncertainty of "I'll never know" (B3 section) is probably preserved in the Danish paraphrase "I hardly sense" ("*Jag aner knapt*") and possibly also in the Swedish open question: "Can anyone say…" The Norwegian version is more faithful to the semantic content, but as the song is structured, the B3 section appears to raise a rhetorical question: "What can suddenly have made me this exhilarated?", to which the A4 section has a ready answer: "He put his arm around me, and then…" As the uncertainty is lost, the semantic link to the music seems weaker. In the A4 section, Loewe's melody segments the concluding phrase as three short, three long syllables, and then two more on chords that close the song on a strong, authentic cadence (G major to C major) – "I could have / danced, danced, danced / all night." The Norwegian version is the only translation to preserve the structural closure achieved by returning to the title phrase, "*danset natten lang*." However, the literal translation sabotages the breath the singer could use to sing the two last, long notes (between "*nat-*" and "*-ten*").[8] The freer Swedish translation preserves the repetition: "*en dans, en dans, en dans*," but it also makes the verse line sound like three equal iambs and does not reflect the harmonic closure of the last two notes of Loewe's score. The Danish translators have minded singability as well as "the right placing of points" (Osolsobě 1974: 238). They keep "danced, danced, danced" on the three long chords by changing the verb form from the perfect to the imperative: "[My heart shouted:] Dance! Dance! Dance! [with me]." As a compromise between fidelity and format, the Danish solution appear as the one most optimally balanced. Only the reference in the verse to a spinning gramophone (and possibly the rhyme word as well, the great sum of "a million") comes through as an anachronism in the historic age when "phonograph" was the normal word in all Scandinavian languages.

Conclusions in an Open Field

The key concepts of this essay have been **fidelity** and functional design, which I refer to as **format**. The three Scandinavian translations of *My Fair Lady* studied above display a highly selective fidelity. The verse form, partly determined by the structure of the music, is generally preserved, but the semantic content of the source lyric is handled very freely. If the target lyrics quoted above are to be regarded as translation at all, it must be because they have been made instrumentally functional to a production of the musical *My Fair Lady*. They seem to ensure that the lyrics function as parts of a dramatic text and as a scenario for a staged performance. As vocal translations, the target texts cannot be as fully coherent with the music as the original lyric, but at least in prosodic and structural respects the target texts may prove themselves coherent enough. The method of conjuncting with a context independently of the imaginary close approximation of the source text sense, or choosing to emphasize one functional aspect over another, for example dramatic integration over deictic potential, can be referred to as **functional re-interpretation**. There is also occasional evidence that the translators minded domestic cultural preconceptions of what characterizes certain songs in popular style. What seems to be more easily affected in the process of creative transposition is the more subtle effects of how the song presents itself, the character or the situation, or reveals how the authors may have wanted the number to be staged or the music to be perceived. The case is particular, but I do not expect it to be very different from song translation in general, at least in popular or theatrical contexts. What may once have been a perfect union can in translation only be a functionally balanced compromise.

Concludingly, to make an "extremely demanding task" manageable at all, song translators raise the level of fidelity from the textual-semantic to the contextual-functional. The strategies involved are necessarily combines functional units of various kinds and weight which cannot easily be separated. The theatre semiotic model of Osolsobĕ (1992a, 1992b) allows the fictional, physical, and audience-directed aspects of the song number to be observed, and the *skopos* model of Nord (1991, 1997a) allows goals for particular translation assignments to be flexible. The multifaceted concerns can most concisely be formulated as six questions:

> On the coherence of the text with the theatrical presentation:
> 1. How does the situation or person present itself in the song? (Is it similar enough to the ST?)
> 2. Does the song invite, suggest or demand staged interaction?
> 3. What dramatic information is referred to, telling what story?
>
> On the coherence of the text with the musical information:
> 4. Does the text make the music meaningful (in terms of musical expression, arrangement, connotation)?
> 5. Does the text rhetorically suit the music (in terms of harmonic progression, strophic structure, focus on certain words and phrases)?
> 6. Do the phrases prosodically fit the music (in terms of intonation, stress, vowel quality)?

How many cannons were there on Pirate Jenny's ship (Ex. 1)? The counter-question would be: In what context would it matter? From a source text point of view, the simple poetry of concrete objects and figures in Brecht's verse is largely lost in most translations. Judged from a factual, nautical point of view, a hundred cannons might be too heavy for a normal-sized frigate. But arguably, the words of the song stand there not only for themselves, but as part of a song in performance. It is usually performed either as a diegetic song by Polly Peachum or as a soliloquy by Jenny Diver of the brothel. As they are mentioned nowhere but in this self-sufficient song, the number of sails and cannons matters less. The narrative key point is that the ship presents a menace to the community that holds Jenny captive. The "skull on its masthead" of the first English lyric takes its piratical cue from the song's title and makes it explicit. This lyric, arguably the freest of the six, is the only one with a perfect prosodic fit to the syllables of Weill's music. Musico-semantically, the ship makes an impact as the *Sprechgesang*-like verses give way to the melodious refrain. Some translations make this relation more lyrical by adding description: "eight sails <u>shining</u>," "*navire <u>de haut bord</u>*" ('ship of high freeboard') and "*<u>suuri</u> purjelaiva*" ('big sailboat'), by also providing more singable vowels on the big notes than Brecht did. Quite a few translations add deictic reference: "Waits <u>there</u> at the quay," "*<u>juuri</u> saapunut on*" ('has just arrived'), "*ses lägga till <u>här</u>*" ('is seen to anchor here'). Is this a coincidence or is it characteristic for the situational consciousness of the song translator? The most recent English lyric seems especially wise to place a second person pronoun on the refrain's focussed last note – "pointing at you" – thereby enabling the actress to convey the threat or emotion while addressing her audience, either the actual one or her co-actors. Either way, the song translator easily becomes not only a melodic versifier, but also a dramatist and a stager, creating his own text world for the performer to tell and enact.

Notes

[1] The snippets of text are quoted after books Brecht (1967: 38; 1969: 44), Lindström (1966: 286) and recordings The Threepenny Opera (TER 1101), Juliette Gréco: Master Series (Polygram 830955-2), 20th Century Blues (RCA Victor 74321-38656-2), The Threepenny Opera (CDJAY 1244).

[2] Nord states that "I start from the hypothesis that text function is not something inherent in the text, but a pragmatic quality assigned to a text by the recipient in a particular situation after intuitively or cognitively analysing both the function signals offered by the situational factors … and the linguistic, stylistic, semantic or non-verbal textual markers indicating the sender's intention(s)" (1997b: 43), adding: "One particular function can be marked on various levels, and all those markers pointing to a particular function or subfunction form a 'functional unit'" (1997b: 45, cf 1997a: 68-73).

[3] English surveys of the linguistic and sociolinguistic interrelations within the Nordic language community (=the three middle Scandinavian, the island Scandinavian; Icelandic and Faeroese, and the Non-Nordic languages; Finnish, Sami, and Inuit) are given in Haugen (1976) and Vikør (2001). Discussing sociolect and slang, Haugen (1976: 58) makes a note on the similar resources the My Fair Lady translations drew on.

[4] The dictum that sets and staging must be copied in every new production became standard procedure for highly commercial musicals some years after My Fair Lady, and is now referred to as a replica production. In his account of the Scandinavian productions, Schmidt (1995: 108-145) claims free will and respect for the original was the impetus. In his memoirs, briefly and, of course too, in retrospect, Lerner (1978: 135) writes that he was the one to insist on the copying.

[5] Public performances of the musical in Scandinavia (grand rights) are still sublicensed by Nordiska Strakosch Teaterförlaget in Copenhagen. The songs as independent items are copyrighted through Warner/Chappell Music (small rights). Further reproduction infringes copyright.

[6] In Norway, the national language standard was under heated debate at the time, while in Denmark, national pronunciation has gone through rather rapid changes in the 20th century, with "low" Copenhagen speech habits as a radical ingredient. Stockholm "cockneys" have had less influence over national spelling and pronunciation.

[7] On the same end notes, the Swedish lyrics have short syllables, ending with consonants (känt, dans). In both Swedish and Norwegian, a phrase like "ta en dans, dans, dans med mig/meg" would be possible.

[8] This is hard to avoid for linguistic reasons: Scandinavian words and phrases tend to be trochaic (natten) where English ones are monosyllabic or iambic (the night). The other Scandinavian translators preserves the *Luftpause* by rephrasing.

Bibliography

Primary Sources:

Brecht, Bertolt. 1967. *Stücke III. Dreigroschenoper. Mahagonny. Badener Lehrstück.* Berlin and Weimar: Aufbau.

—— 1969. *Kolmen pennin ooppera.* (tr. Max Rand, Turo Unho, Elvi Sinervo). Helsinki: Otava.

Lerner, Alan Jay. 1956. *My Fair Lady.* London and New York: Penguin Books.

—— 1959a. *My Fair Lady* (tr. Gösta Rybrant). Stockholm: Bonniers.

—— 1959b. *My Fair Lady* (tr. Holger Bech, Arvid Müller). Copenhagen: Gyldendal.

—— 1959c. *My Fair Lady* (tr. André Bjerke). Oslo: Aschehoug.

Lindström, Göran. 1966. *Dramatik.* Stockholm: Uniskol.

Loewe, Frederick and Alan Jay Lerner. 1956. *My Fair Lady* (Vocal Score). Essex, England: Warner Chappell Music. International Music Publications.

Shaw, Bernard. [1914]1957. *Pygmalion. A Romance in Five Acts.* London: Longmans, Green and Co.

Secondary Sources:

Aaltonen, Sirkku. 1996. *Acculturation of the Other. Irish Milieux in Finnish Drama Translation.* Joensuu: Joensuu University Press.

Abrams, M.H. 1981. *A Glossary of Literary Terms.* 4th ed. New York *et al.*: Holt, Rinehart and Winston.

—— 2000. *Time-Sharing on Stage. Drama Translation in Theatre and Society.* Clevedon *et al.*: Multilingual Matters.

Apter, Ronnie. 1985. 'A Peculiar Burden: Some Technical Problems of Translating Opera for Performance in English' in *Meta* 30/4: 309–319.

—— and Mark Herman. 1995. 'The Worst Translations: Almost Any Opera into English' in *Translation Review* 48-49: 26-32.

Banfield, Stephen. 1993. *Sondheim's Broadway Musicals.* Ann Arbor: The University of Michigan Press.

—— 1996. 'Sondheim and The Art That Has No Name' in Lawson-Peebles, Robert (ed.) *Approaches to the American Musical.* Exeter: University of Exeter Press. 137-160.

Bassnett, Susan. 1998. 'Still Trapped in The Labyrinth: Further Reflections on Translation and Theatre' in Susan Bassnett and Lefevere, André (eds) *Constructing Cultures. Essays on Literary Translation* (Topics in Translation 11). Clevedon *et al.:* Multilingual Matters. 90-108.

Catford, J. C. 1965. *A Linguistic Theory of Translation. An Essay in Applied Linguistics.* London: Oxford University Press.

Elam, Keir. 1980. *The Semiotics of Theatre and Drama.* London and New York: Routledge.

Espasa, Eva. 2000. 'Performability in Translation: Speakability? Playability? Or Just Saleability?' in Upton, Carole-Anne (ed.) *Moving Target. Theatre Translation and Cultural Relocation.* Manchester, UK and Northampton, MA: St. Jerome. 49-62.

Franzon, Johan. 2001. 'The Pseudotranslation of Popular Songs?' in Kukkonen, Pirjo and Hartama-Heinonen, Ritva (eds) *Mission, Vision, Strategies, and Values. A Celebration of Translator Training and Translation Studies in Kouvola.* Helsingfors: Helsinki University Press. 33-44.

Gorlée, Dinda L. 2002. 'Grieg's Swan Songs' in *Semiotica* 142-1/4: 153-210.

Grandmont, Suzanne de. 1978. 'Problèmes de traduction dans le domaine de la poésie chantée' in *Meta* 32/1: 97–107.

Haugen, Einar. 1976. *The Scandinavian Languages. An Introduction to their History*. London: Faber and Faber.

Hervey, Sándor and Higgins, Ian. 1992. *Thinking Translation. A Course in Translation Method: French to English*. London and New York: Routledge.

Jakobson, Roman. 1959. 'On Linguistic Aspects of Translation' in Brower, Reuben A. (ed.) *On Translation*. New York: Oxford University Press. 232-239.

—— 1960. 'Closing statement: Linguistics and Poetics' in Sebeok, Thomas A. (ed.) *Style in Language*. Cambridge, MA: MIT Press. 350-377.

Kaindl, Klaus. 1995. *Die Oper als Textgestalt. Perspektiven einer interdisziplinären Übersetzungswissenschaft* (Studien zur Translation 2) Tübingen: Stauffenburg.

Lefevere, André. [1982]2000. 'Mother Courage's Cucumbers: Text, System and Refraction in a Theory of Literature' in Venuti, Lawrence (ed.) *The Translation Studies Reader*. London and New York: Routledge. 233-249.

—— 1998. 'Acculturating Bertolt Brecht' in Bassnett, Susan and Lefevere, André (eds) *Constructing Cultures. Essays on Literary Translation* (Topics in Translation 11). Clevedon *et al.*: Multilingual Matters. 109-122.

Lerner, Alan Jay. [1978]1994. *The Street Where I Live*. New York: Da Capo Press.

—— 1985. *The Musical Theatre. A Celebration*. New York, *et al*: McGraw-Hill.

Nida, Eugene A. 1964. *Toward a Science of Translating, With Special Reference to Principles and Procedures Involved in Bible Translating*. Leiden: E. J. Brill.

Nord, Christiane. 1991. *Text Analysis in Translation. Theory, Methodology, and Didactic Application of a Model for Translation-Oriented Text Analysis* (tr. Christiane Nord and Penelope Sparrow). Amsterdam and Atlanta: Rodopi.

—— 1997a. *Translating as a Purposeful Activity. Functionalist Approaches Explained* (Translation Theories Explained) Manchester: St. Jerome.

—— 1997b. 'Functional Units in Translation' in Mauranen, Anna and Puurtinen, Tiina (eds) *Translation – Acquisition – Use* (AFinLa Yearbook 1997). Jyväskylä: University Press. 41-50.

Osolsobě, Ivo. 1971. 'Der vierte Strom des Theaters als Gegenstand der Wissenschaft, oder Prospekt einer strukturalen Operettenwissenschaft' in Zavodsky, Arthur (ed.) *Otazky divadla a filmu. Theatralia et cinematographica II*. Brno: UJE. 11-41.

—— 1974. *Divadlo které mluví, zpívá a tancí. Teorie jedné* kommunikacní formy. Prague: Supraphon.

—— 1984. 'Vienna's Popular Musical Stage as a Semiotic Institution' in Borbé, Tasso (ed.) *Semiotics Unfolding. Proceedings of the Second Congress of the International Association for Semiotic Studies, Vienna July 1979* (Approaches to Semiotics 68). Berlin *et al.*: Mouton. Vol 3: 1739–1751.

—— 1992a. *Mnoho povyky pro sémiotiku. Ne zcela úspěšný pokus o encyklopedické heslo sémiotika divadla*. Brno: Agency G.

—— 1992b. 'On the Three Frontiers of Theatrical Freedom: The Liberated Theatre of Voskovec & Werich in Prague, 1927-38' in Schmid, Herta and Striedter, Jurij (eds) *Dramatische und theatralische Kommunikation. Beiträge zur Geschichte und Theorie des Dramas und Theaters im 20. Jahrhundert*. Tübingen: Gunter Narr. 238-252

Pavis, Patrice. 1992. *Theatre at the Crossroads of Culture* (tr. Loren Kruger). London and New York: Routledge.

Schmidt, Lars. 1995. *Mitt livs teater*. Höganäs: Bra Böcker.

Snell-Hornby, Mary. 1997. '"Is This a Dagger Which I See Before Me?" The Non-verbal Language of Drama' in Poyatos, Fernando (ed.) *Nonverbal Communication and Translation: New Perspectives and Challenges in Literature, Interpretation and the Media*. Amsterdam and Philadelphia: John Benjamins. 187-201.

Totzeva, Sophia. 1999. 'Realizing Theatrical Potential: The Dramatic Text in Performance and Translation' in Boase-Beier, Jean and Holman, Michael (eds) *The Practices of Literary Translation: Constraints and Creativity*. Manchester: St. Jerome. 81-90.

Toury, Gideon. 1980. *In Search of a Theory of Translation*. Tel Aviv: Porter Institute.

Tråvén, Marianne. 1999. *Don Giovanni – Don Juan. Om översättning av musikaliskt bunden text. En studie av Mozarts Da Ponte-opera Don Giovanni i sex svenska översättningar* (Studier i musikvetenskap 8) Stockholm: University of Stockholm.

Vikør, Lars S. 2001. *The Nordic Languages. Their Status and Interrelations*. Oslo: Novus Press.

Multimedia Sources:

Juliette Gréco: Master Series (Polygram 830955-2)

My Fair Lady (Columbia records, CD reissue: B000067AS1).

20th Century Blues (RCA Victor 74321-38656-2)

The Threepenny Opera (TER 1101)

The Threepenny Opera (CDJAY 1244).

Notes on Contributors

Myrdene ANDERSON (myanders@purdue.edu) — anthropologist, linguist, and semiotician — received her PhD from Yale University in 1978 and teaches on the faculty at Purdue University, West Lafayette, Indiana. Since 1971, Anderson has spent nearly eight years among the Saami reindeer breeders in Norwegian Lapland, where her research has explored ethnoecology focusing on the dynamic processes linking language, culture, and nature. The Saami semiosphere includes a unique musical form called the yoik, a chant which itself links performers, cultural setting, and natural environment. As nomadic emblems, yoiks invite a semiotic analysis of text, tradition, and cultural memory. In addition, Anderson has explored issues of deception, tools and toys, real and metaphorical trash, commodities and consumption, and so-called artificial life. Her recent edited and coedited publications include *On Semiotic Modeling* (1991), *Refiguring Debris-Becoming Unbecoming, Unbecoming Becoming* (1994), *Educational Perspectives on Mathematics as Semiosis: From Thinking to Interpreting to Knowing* (2003), and *Cultural Shaping of Violence: Victimization, Escalation, Response* (2004).

Ronnie APTER (ronnie.apter@cmich.edu) is Professor of English at Central Michigan University (Mount Pleasant, MI), and has also taught at the Rijksuniversiteit Groningen in The Netherlands and in Vienna, Austria. Her specialties are 20th-century British and American Poetry, Science Fiction, the Inter-relation of Words and Music, and Translation. A published poet and translator of poetry, she is the author of several articles on translation and two books: *Digging for the Treasure: Translation After Pound*, about Ezra Pound's contribution to the translation of poetic forms into English; and the Bilingual Edition of the *Love Songs of Bernart de Ventadorn* in Occitan and English: *Sugar and Salt*, including literal, poetic, and singable translations of Bernart's lyrics. In collaboration with Mark Herman, she has translated 20 operas into performable English. She is a recipient of New York University's Thomas Wolfe Poetry Award and Central Michigan University's President's Award for Outstanding Research and Creative Activity.

Johan FRANZON (johan.franzon@helsinki.fi) teaches Swedish language and translation at the Department of Translation Studies, University of Helsinki. Franzon has translated *The Wizard of Oz* (1989), *Grease* (1994), *Cabaret* (1995) and other musicals into Swedish, and now works on a Ph.D. on the translation of the songs of musical comedy. Title *Making Words Sing: Functional Design of Musical Comedy Translation* (dirs. Pirjo Kukkonen and Dinda L. Gorlée). His research interests are vocal translation, drama translation, translation into Scandinavian languages. Recent publication is the article "The pseudotranslation of popular songs?" (2001).

Harai GOLOMB (golomb@post.tau.ac.il) holds a PhD in literary theory, Master's Degrees in Comparative Literature and Music Theory, and a B.A. in Hebrew Linguistics. Professor at the Faculty of Arts, Tel-Aviv University, teaching in three of its Departments: Theatre Studies, Musicology, and the Interart Programme (Multi-Disciplinary Studies in the Arts). A music critic for the Israeli printed and electronic press. Topics of his research and university courses include: The Poetics of Chekhov's plays; Readings in Modern Poetry in the Original and in Translation (Hebrew and English); Music and Drama in Mozart's operas; Analysis of Recorded Musical Performance; Glenn Gould: Performer, Interpreter, Communicator; *Amadeus*: Film, Theatre, Music, Myth and Fictionality; Verse Drama (mainly Shakespeare's); Comparative-Contrastive Poetics of Temporal Arts (Music vs. Literature/Drama). He has published academic studies on drama, prose fiction, poetry and music, and on their interrelations and interactions, as well as hundreds of concert press-reviews in the general Israeli press; he has publicly lectured worldwide, and actively participated in numerous conferences in all his fields, in Israel and around the globe. He has produced tens of music-linked Hebrew translations of solo and choral songs from various European languages and published MLTs of libretti (mainly Mozart's) in bi-lingual books. His MLTs were used in Israel for live performances of operas in young persons' concerts, for 'surtitles' synchronised with New Israeli Opera and Israel Festival operatic productions, and for subtitles in television broadcasts. Golomb is now writing a book on Chekhov's plays.

Dinda L. GORLÉE (gorlee@xs4all.nl) received her PhD within translation studies and semiotics from University of Amsterdam in 1993. Gorlée now directs a multilingual legal translation office in The Hague, is Research Associate of Wittgenstein Archives, University of Bergen, and Director of doctoral dissertations in Department of Translation Studies, University of Helsinki. Gorlée taught at the Universities of Groningen, Bergen, Innsbruck, Ouagadougou, and Helsinki; Research Fellow at the Research Center for Language and Semiotic Studies of Indiana University in Bloomington, Peirce Edition Project in Indianapolis, and the Grieg Collection in Bergen. Gorlée is jury member to assign the *Mouton D'Or* prize for the best articles in *Semiotica*. Gorlée wrote the books *Semiotics and the Problem of Translation:*

With Special Reference to the Semiotics of Charles S. Peirce (1994) and *On Translating Signs: Exploring Text and Semio-Translation* (2004), which is dedicated to Thomas A. Sebeok (1920-2001). After publishing on the translation of the libretti of Wagner and Grieg, Gorlée is now writing on the translation of Wittgenstein's works and the translation of lyrics in Grieg's songs.

Mark HERMAN (hermanapter@earthlink.net) is a literary translator, technical translator, chemical engineer, playwright, lyricist, musician, and actor (Shepherd, MI). In collaboration with Ronnie Apter, he has translated 20 operas into English. Many of the Herman-Apter translations have been performed throughout the United States, Canada, and England, and seven have been or soon will be published by Ricordi in Milan, Italy. Among the Herman-Apter editions are the first ever Czech-English piano-vocal scores of Bedřich Smetana's *Dvě vdovy* / Two Widows and *Prodaná nevěsta* / The Bartered Bride, the first ever Italian-English piano-vocal score of Giuseppe Verdi's *Un giorno di regno*, and the first ever performing edition of Alessandro Scarlatti's *Eraclea*.

Klaus KAINDL (klaus.kaindl@univie.ac.at) is associate professor at the Centre for Translation Studies of the University of Vienna. He also teaches translation studies at the University of Innsbruck. Kaindl is a theater and opera lover and a concertgoer. His research interests are the translation of opera, popular music, comics as well as translation history and theory. Kaindl has published numerous articles in these new areas of translation studies. He is the author of the books *Die Oper als Textgestalt* (1995) and *Übersetzungswissenschaft im interdisziplinären Dialog* (2004) and has co-edited among others *Translation Studies — An Interdiscipline* (1994) and *Translation as Intercultural Communication* (1997).

Peter LOW (peter.low@canterbury.ac.nz) directs the French program at the University of Canterbury, New Zealand. Various of his published articles concern French poetry, popular and classical song, and translation theory. He has often prepared songs either for singing or for recital programmes — over 100 of his song translations can be be viewed on the http://www.lieder.net website — and he has prepared surtitles for operas by Rossini, Verdi, Gounod, Bizet, Offenbach and Delibes. He is also a pianist, harpsichordist and song-writer.

Marianne TRÅVÉN (mariannet@home.se) studied cultural sciences, social anthropology, art and musicology at the University of Stockholm, Sweden and music and vocal science at the University of Mozarteum in Salzburg, Austria. She holds a Ph. D. in Musicology and a Magister in Music. Her dissertation *Don Giovanni — Don Juan: Om översättning av musikaliskt bunden text* (University of Stockholm, 1999) deals with the interrelationship between text and music in Mozart's Da Ponte opera *Don Giovanni,* and the specific problems that this intimate relationship poses for the translator of the libretto. Tråvén is a regular guest at conferences in the fields of translation studies, vocal science and musicology. Since 2002 she is also active as a Curator for *Sveriges Teatermuseum* in Stockholm.

Name Index[1]

A

Aaltonen, Sirkku 267, 274, 283
Abrams, M.H. 272
Adorno, Theodor W. 90
Albrecht, Christoph 30, 66
Allanbrook, Wye J. 159
Allan, David 36
Anderman, Gunilla 192
Anders, Charles R. 30
Anderson, Lale 246, 250, 260
Anderson, Myrdene 5, 14, 213, 215, 216,
    222-225, 299
Andrew, J. S. 90
Apel, Willi 22
Apter, Ronnie 5, 7, 13, 163, 183, 193, 199,
    211, 273, 299, 301
Aristeas 89
Aristotle 230
Arnberg, Matts 213, 219, 222
Ashbrook, William 172f.
Assia, Lys 246
Atatürk, Kemal 255
Augustine, Saint 89

B

Bach, Johann Sebastian 23, 69, 190
Bachelard, Gaston 228f.
Baden-Powell, Robert 276
Baker, Mona 259
Bakhtin, Michail 235
Balter, Michael 228
Banfield, Stephen 266f., 270, 271
Bardari, Giuseppe 164f., 168, 170-172, 177,
    178, 180, 183
Barnstone, Willis 89, 91
Barr, Andrew 22
Barthes, Roland 242
Barzun, Jacques 228
Bassnett, Susan 278
Bateson, Gregory 92
Baudelaire, Charles 188

Baughen, Michael 91
Bausch, Fini 246
Beardsley, Monroe C. 156
Bech, Holger 275
Beethoven, Ludwig von 7, 23, 168
Bell, John L. 22, 30, 47, 65, 79
Bentley, Eric 2198
Beneviste, Émile 10f.
Bergman, Ingmar 183
Berkowitz, Norman 227
Berlioz, Hector 23
Bird, George 208
Bizet, Georges 301
Bjerke, André 275
Blackwood, Adam 167
Blaikner, Peter 238
Blake, William 22, 38
Blau, Eric 265
Blew, W. J. 91
Bluhm, Heinz 68
Bodor, Anikö 219
Boine, Mari 214-219, 221
Boleyn, Anne 178
Bolinger, Dwight 157
Bond, Mark Evan 119
Born, Gunthard 105
Borthwick, Jane Laurie 86
Bosch, Hieronymus 69
Bourgeois, Louis 78
Brady, Nicholas 77
Brahms, Johannes 206
Braley, Bernard 29
Brassens, Georges 189, 200, 238
Brecht, Bertold 198, 263-265, 267, 293
Brecht, Martin 67ff., 70f.
Brel, Jacques 200-205, 211, 238, 265
Brenneis, Donald 226
Britten, Benjamin 156
Brooke, Stopford Augustus 83ff.
Browne, Marmaduke E. 153, 158
Buddha 23
Buelow, George J. 104
Buñuel, Luis 38
Burnmeister, Joachim 103
Byrne, Mary 36
Byron, George 90

C

Campbell, R. 91
Carlyle, Thomas 67, 71, 73, 75

Praetorius, Michael 104
Procter, Francis 28
Purcell, Henry 157
Pushkin, Alexander 156

R

Rabadán, Rosa 238
Raffel, Burton 193
Rauch, Irmengard 45
Rengsdorf, K.H. 18
Robinson, Douglas 14, 90f.
Rosen, Robert 228
Rossini, Gioacchino 301
Runeberg, Johan Ludvig 283
Ruong, Israel 219
Ruwet, Nicolas 9
Rybrant, Gösta 275

S

Saada, Emmanuel 255
Salisbury, Ralph 220
Sams, Jeremy 143, 144, 154, 160, 264
Santen, Felix 79
Sapir, Edward 37
Sarna, Nahum F. 21
Sarti, Laura 145, 155, 159
Saussure, Ferdinand de 9, 44ff., 49, 90
Savan, David 59
Scarlatti, Alessandro 301
Scheffcyzyk, A. 48
Schefferus, Johannes 219
Schikaneder, Emanuel 157
Schiller, Friedrich von 163, 167-171, 177,
    182f.
Schlegel, Katharina von 86
Schmidt, Lars 67, 87
Schmidt, Hans 275
Schmidt, Lars 294
Schubert, Franz 190, 206
Schumann, Robert 206
Scott, Sir Walter 90
Sebeok, Thomas A. 45
Sechrist, Alice Spiers 70
Shakespeare, William 121, 123, 151, 156,
    281ff., 300
Shapiro, Michael 92
Shaw, George Bernard 265, 273
Short, T. L 91f.
Shuman, Mort 265

Sibelius, Jean 85
Silset, Gjermund 217
Sinatra, Frank 235
Sinervo, Elvi 264
Singer, Milton 90
Sloboda, John 230
Smalley, William A. 91
Smetana, Bedřich 301
Smith, Robert E. 92
Snell-Hornby, Mary 259, 274
Sola, Wäinö 86
Soleil, Stella 252, 256
Somby, Ande 214, 219
Sonntag, Stanley 190
Soukup, Paul A., S.J. 91
Speelman, Willem Marie 90
Spitta, Friedrich 67, 71
Spitzer, Michael 10, 90
Spohr, Louis 77
Spottiswoode, John 167
Stavans, Ilan 76, 87
Steinachter, Susanne 238
Steiner, George 93, 191, 216
Steinwender, Bettina 238
Stokes, Richard 188, 208
Stölting, Elke 237f.
Strand Harboe, Heidi 79
Strauss, Richard 207f.
Stuart, Henry, Lord Darnley 165, 169, 177
Stuart, Mary, Queen of Scots 163-183
Sulzer, Johann Georg 103, 118
Svartvik, Jan 21
Swinburne, Algernon Charles 168

T

Tagg, Philip 243-246, 260
Talbot, George, Earl of
    Shrewsbury 163, 172
Tarasti, Eero 8, 245, 260
Tarkan *see* Özel, Tarkan
Tate, Nahum 77
Taylor, Jane
Te Kanawa, Kiri 208
Thring, Godfrey 67, 73, 76
Thuswalder, Werner 81f.
Tirén, Karl 219
Todorov, Tzvetan 44
Tomoana, Paraire Henare 208
Torop, Peeter 229
Totzeva, Sophia 274

Subject Index[1]

A

Acculturation, national and cultural : 267, 281ff. (see: Translation)
Accuracies and inaccuracies (see Fidelity)
Adaptation : 264f. (see: Translation)
Art song (Lied, *Kunstlied*) : 13, 189, 210ff.

B

Bible translation : 18ff., 33
Bricolage : 235, 241ff., 249, 257, 259

C

Christmas carol : 80-85
Categories, Peirce's (firstness, secondness, thirdness) : 47-66, 70, 87f., 224
Chanson (see Popular music) : 13f., 235, 238, 265
Chant (see Yoik)
Clashes, semiotic, in different religious viewpoints, fiction versus myth, history versus historical fiction, setting versus music : 13, 163-183
Constraints and liberties of vocal translation : *passim* (see Virtues and vices in vocal translation)

D

Dance and song : 226ff., 254, 258f., 284ff, 289
Diflection of text and tune, Peirce's : 58-66
Deixis : 264, 280, 291ff.
Dialogics, Bakthin's : 242f., 259
Dialogue, monologue, soliloquy and unison singing : 272f.
Diegetic and non-diegetic song : 273
Domestication and foreignizing : 246, 249ff.
Drama play : 115, 121, 126, 268-275 (part. figures 269 and 272), 293f.

[1] References in the Subject Index do not include Bibliography.

Dyadism and triadism (semiotic) : 42-46

E

Emotion : 27, 41, 61, 65, 74, 103f., 223 (see Icons, Musement, Peirce's firstness)
Equivalence, literal and dynamical : 33, 65, 67, 87, 91
Etherial things, Dewey's : 55f., 92

F

Feeling (see Emotion)
Fidelity (see Translation); — and anachronisms, (in)accuracies : 122, 143ff., 164, 179ff., 198ff., 223, 282-287; — and format : 266ff.
Firstness (see Categories, Peirce's)
Folksong : 13f., 175, 208ff., 213-230

G

Gestalt : 273
Glossolalia : 18
Gradatio figure (in opera) : 108, 134

H

Habit (habituality), Peirce's : 34ff., 52, 87
Hum (see Yoik)
Hymn (spiritual song, church song) : 13, 17-101, 214

I

Icons (symbolic icons, Peirce's firstness) : 66-88, 74, 105
Illustration, amplification and disjuncture, Goodwin's : 252
Imitation and otherness : 26-33
Improvisation : 216

L

Lamento figure (in opera) : 104, 111-115, 134, 147
Libretto (see Song lyrics)
Logocentrism and musicocentrism : 8ff., 104f., 126ff., 187
Lullaby : 214, 223ff.

M

Mass culture : 69, 76, 235, 240, 244, 259
Meaning (sense) in music and text : 10, 61,
    92, 103f., 194f., 213, 216, 228, 242
Mediation : 229, 242f., 259
Mind, matter, God : 46-53
MLT (Music-Linked Translation) (in opera)
    : 121-161
MLV (Music-Linked Verbal Text) (in
    opera) : 122-137, 156, 158
Monologue and dialogue : 275
Musement (meditation, reverie, trance) : 27,
    53-58, 92 , 218, 224, 228f. (see Icons,
    Peirce's firstness)
Musical comedy (musical) : 14, 267-298

N

Narrative, staging and presentational
    formats (in musical comedies): 273f.
    (part. figure 276), 280
Naturalness of song-text : 195f.
Nature : 216ff.

O

Opera : 13, 103-120, 121-161, historical
    background of — : 163-183;
    cronology of — musical genre : 125f.

P

Paralinguistic and extralinguistic features in
    text and music : 107-111
Paraphrase and vocal translation : 21, 26ff.
Pentathlon Principle : 13f., 185, 191- 211
    (see Singability, Sense, Naturalness,
    Rhythm and Rhymes)
Performance, artistic (see Libretto and Song
    lyrics)
Poetry : 31, 33, 39ff., 131, 187, 216, 264
Polysystem : 235, 239, 243
Popular music (pop music) : 235-260
Proper names and nicknames : 178ff., 224f.
Prayer : 17, 23ff., 59
Psalms, hymns and spiritual songs : 21ff.

R

Referential, poetic, and metalingual
    functions of text and tune : 277
Rewording, translation proper, transmutation
    (see Translation, intralingual, interlingual
    and intersemiotic)
Reverie (see Musement)
Rhetoric, musical : 103-115
Rhymes of song-text : 144, 156f., 196f., 202
Rhythm of song-text : 196ff., 202

S

Sapir-Whorf hypothesis : 37
Schlager (popular hit): 30, 235ff., 239, 246,
    250, 252
Segmental (suprasegmental) phonemes (in
    vocal translation) : 127f., 130, 132, 157
Semiotics : *passim*
Semio-translation : 86
Sense of song-text (see Meaning)
Shamanism : 218, 221, 228
Singability : 192ff.
Singer-oriented, translator-oriented and
    listener-oriented approaches to vocal
    translation : 132ff., 158
Singers in foreign languages : 139f.
Skopos : 185f., 190ff., 205, 210f., 214f.,
    267, 271, 279, 297
Socio(cultural) semiotics : 235, 239-243
Song, indicative, declarative and hortatory
    — : 27, 52
Song lyrics (libretto) and artistic
    performance : 13, 103-119 (part. figure
    106), 138, 141, 156, 187-191, 213-216,
    223ff. (see Libretto)
Sprechgesang : 293
Stress and accentuation : 122, 127f.
Subtitles and surtitles, supratitles and
    supertitles : 138ff.
Symbolic icons (see Icons)
Synaesthesia, Goodwin's : 251

T

Tirata figure (in opera) : 104.
Tmesis figure (in opera) : 115, 119
Togetherness, Peirce's (communal belief) :
    20, 39, 49, 52
Trance (see Musement)

Song and significance